WORLDCOMP'13
July 22-25, 2013
Las Vegas Nevada, USA
www.world-academy-of-science.org

PROCEEDINGS OF THE 2013 INTERNATIONAL CONFERENCE ON FOUNDATIONS OF COMPUTER SCIENCE

FCS 2013

Editors

Hamid R. Arabnia
George A. Gravvanis
George Jandieri
Ashu M. G. Solo
Fernando G. Tinetti

FIREWALL MEDIA
(An Imprint of Laxmi Publications Pvt. Ltd.)
An ISO 9001:2008 Company
BENGALURU • CHENNAI • COCHIN • GUWAHATI • HYDERABAD
JALANDHAR • KOLKATA • LUCKNOW • MUMBAI • RANCHI • NEW DELHI
BOSTON (USA) • ACCRA (GHANA) • NAIROBI (KENYA)

This volume contains papers presented at The 2013 International Conference on Foundations of Computer Science (FCS'13). Their inclusion in this publication does not necessarily constitute endorsements by editors or by the publisher.

Branches

Bengaluru	080-26 75 69 30	
Chennai	044-24 34 47 26,	24 35 95 07
Cochin	0484-237 70 04,	405 13 03
Guwahati	0361-254 36 69,	251 38 81
Hyderabad	040-27 55 53 83,	27 55 53 93
Jalandhar	0181-222 12 72	
Kolkata	033-22 27 43 84	
Lucknow	0522-220 99 16	
Mumbai	022-24 91 54 15,	24 92 78 69
Ranchi	0651-220 44 64	

PUBLISHED IN INDIA BY

FIREWALL MEDIA
(An Imprint of Laxmi Publications Pvt. Ltd.)

An ISO 9001:2008 Company
113, GOLDEN HOUSE, DARYAGANJ,
NEW DELHI - 110002, INDIA
Telephone : 91-11-4353 2500, 4353 2501
Fax : 91-11-2325 2572, 4353 2528
www.laxmipublications.com info@laxmipublications.com

C—
Printed at:

Foreword

It gives us great pleasure to introduce this collection of papers to be presented at the 2013 International Conference on Foundations of Computer Science (FCS'13), July 22 through 25, 2013, at The New Tropicana Hotel, Las Vegas, USA.

An important mission of the World Congress in Computer Science, Computer Engineering, and Applied Computing (a federated congress to which this conference is affiliated with) includes *"Providing a unique platform for a diverse community of constituents composed of scholars, researchers, developers, educators, and practitioners. The Congress makes concerted effort to reach out to participants affiliated with diverse entities (such as: universities, institutions, corporations, government agencies, and research centers/labs) from all over the world. The congress also attempts to connect participants from institutions that have* ***teaching*** *as their main mission with those who are affiliated with institutions that have* ***research*** *as their main mission. The congress uses a quota system to achieve its institution and geography diversity objectives "* By any definition of diversity, this congress is among the most diverse scientific meeting in USA. We are proud to report that this federated congress has authors and participants from 82 different nations representing variety of personal and scientific experiences that arise from differences in culture and values. As can be seen (see below), the program committee of this conference as well as the program committee of all other tracks of the federated congress are as diverse as its authors and participants.

The program committee would like to thank all those who submitted papers for consideration. About 65% of the submissions were from outside the United States. Each submitted paper was peer-reviewed by two experts in the field for originality, significance, clarity, impact, and soundness. In cases of contradictory recommendations, a member of the conference program committee was charged to make the final decision; often, this involved seeking help from additional referees. In addition, papers whose authors included a member of the conference program committee were evaluated using the double-blinded review process. One exception to the above evaluation process was for papers that were submitted directly to chairs/organizers of pre-approved sessions/workshops; in these cases, the chairs/organizers were responsible for the evaluation of such submissions. The overall paper acceptance rate for regular papers was 25%; 7% of the remaining papers were accepted as poster papers (at the time of this writing, we had not yet received the acceptance rate for a few individual tracks.)

We are very grateful to the many colleagues who offered their services in organizing the conference. In particular, we would like to thank the members of the Program Committee of FCS'13, members of the congress Steering Committee, and members of the committees of federated congress tracks that have topics within the scope of FCS. Many individuals listed below, will be requested after the conference to provide their expertise and services for selecting papers for publication (extended versions) in journal special issues as well as for publication in a set of research books (to be prepared for publishers including: Springer, Elsevier, BMC, and others).

- *Dr. Alireza Abbasi; School of Engineering and Information Technology, University of New South Wales (UNSW), Canberra, Australia*
- *Prof. Afrand Agah; West Chester University of Pennsylvania, Pennsylvania, USA*
- *Dr. Selim Aissi (World Congress Steering Committee); formerly, Chief Strategist - Security, Intel Corp., USA; Senior Business Leader & Head of Global Enterprise Security Architecture, Visa Corporation, USA*
- *Prof. Babak Akhgar (World Congress Steering Committee); Fellow of the British Computer Society, CITP; Professor of Informatics; Co-Director of CENTRIC (Centre of Excellence in Terrorism, Resilience, Intelligence & organised Crime research), Sheffield Hallam University, Sheffield, UK*
- *Prof. Nizar Al-Holou (World Congress Steering Committee); Professor and Chair, ECE Department; Vice Chair, IEEE/SEM-Computer Chapter; University of Detroit Mercy, Detroit, Michigan, USA*
- *Prof. Hamid R. Arabnia (World Congress Steering Committee); Professor, Computer Science; Editor-in-Chief, The Journal of Supercomputing (Springer); Elected Fellow, Int'l Society of Intelligent Biological Medicine (ISIBM); The University of Georgia, Department of Computer Science, USA*
- *Peyman Arebi; Assistant Professor, Department of Computer Engineering, Technical and Vocational University, Bushehr, Iran*

- *Prof. Ezendu Ariwa (Publicity Vice-Chair); Chair, IEEE Consumer Electronics Chapter, UK&RI; Visiting Professor, Gulf Univ., Bahrain; Visiting Professor, Univ. of Lagos and Kano State Polytechnic, Nigeria*
- *Prof. Juan Jose Martinez Castillo; Director of The Acantelys Research Group and Coordinator of the Computer Engineering Department, Universidad Gran Mariscal de Ayacucho, Venezuela*
- *Prof. Juan Cuadrado-Gallego; Universidad de Alcala, Edificio Politecnico, Madrid, Spain; Ecole de technologie superieure, University of Quebec, Canada*
- *Prof. Kevin Daimi (World Congress Steering Committee); Director, Computer Science and Software Engineering Programs; Department of Mathematics, Computer Science and Software Engineering; University of Detroit Mercy, Detroit, Michigan, USA*
- *Somdip Dey; St. Xavier's College (Autonomous), Kolkata, India*
- *Prof. George A. Gravvanis (Vice-Chair of FCS; Democritus University of Thrace, Greece*
- *Prof. Houcine Hassan; Universitat Politecnica de Valencia, Spain*
- *Dr. K. S. S. Iyer; Symbiosis Institute of Telecom Management, Pune, India*
- *Prof. George Jandieri (World Congress Steering Committee); Georgian Technical University, Tbilisi, Georgia; Chief Scientist, The Institute of Cybernetics, Georgian Academy of Science, Georgia; Georgia*
- *Prof. Seifedine Kadry (PDPTA); School of Engineering, American University of the Middle East, Kuwait*
- *Prof. Dong Hwa Kim (FCS); Department of Electronic and Control Engineering, Hanbat National University, Korea; Visiting Professor, Budapest University of Technology and Economic, Hungary; International Einstein awardee for Scientific achievement (2010)*
- *Prof. Dattatraya V. Kodavade (World Congress Steering Committee); Head of Computer Science and Engineering, D.K.T.E Society's Textile & Engineering Institute, Ichalkaranji, Maharashtra State, India*
- *Dr. Vitus S.W. Lam; Chartered Member of The British Computer Society; Senior IT Manager, Information Technology Services, The University of Hong Kong, Hong Kong*
- *Prof. Kun Chang Lee (World Congress Steering Committee); Professor of MIS and WCU Professor of Creativity Science, Business School and Department of Interaction Science, Sungkyunkwan University, Korea*
- *Muhammad Naufal Bin Mansor; Intelligent Signal Processing Group (ISP), University Malaysia Perlis, Kangar, Perlis, Malaysia*
- *Prof. George Markowsky (World Congress Steering Committee); Professor and Associate Director, School of Computing and Information Science; Chair International Advisory Board of IEEE IDAACS; Director 2013 Northeast Collegiate Cyber Defense Competition; Cooperating Professor Math. and Statistics Department UMaine and School of Policy & International Affairs UMaine; University of Maine, Orono, Maine, USA*
- *Dr. Sara Moein; Editorial Board, International Journal of Science and Technology; Faculty of Engineering, MultiMedia University, Malaysia*
- *Dr. Ehab Morsy; Suez Canal University, Egypt and Siegen University, Germany*
- *Dr. Ali Mostafaeipour; Industrial Engineering Department, Yazd University, Iran*
- *Dr. Saurabh Mukherjee; Banasthali University, Banasthali, Rajasthan, India*
- *Prof. Prashant R. Nair (EEE + FECS + ICOMP); Vice-Chairman, ITA Faculty, AMRITA-TIFAC Centre of Excellence in Cyber Security; Amrita University, India*
- *Dr. Asoke Nath; Department of Computer Science, St. Xavier's College, India*
- *Prof. G. N. Pandey (World Congress Steering Committee); Vice-Chancellor, Arunachal University of Studies, Arunachal Pradesh, India; Adjunct Professor, Indian Institute of Information Technology, Allahabad, India*
- *Prof. James J. (Jong Hyuk) Park (World Congress Steering Committee); Professor of Computer Science and Engineering, Seoul National University of Science and Technology (SeoulTech), Korea; President, KITCS; President, FTRA; Editor-in-Chiefs: HCIS, JoC and IJITCC Journals*
- *Dr. Liang Shi; Senior Researcher, McAfee, USA*
- *Ashu M. G. Solo, (Publicity Chair); Fellow of British Computer Society, Principal/R&D Engineer, Maverick Technologies America Inc., USA*
- *Prof. K. Subramani; West Virginia University, USA*
- *Prof. Fernando G. Tinetti (World Congress Steering Committee); School of Computer Science, Universidad Nacional de La Plata, La Plata, Argentina; Co-editor, Journal of CS and Technology (JCS&T)*
- *Dr. Predrag Tosic (World Congress Steering Committee); Microsoft, Washington, USA*
- *Prof. Vladimir Volkov (World Congress Steering Committee); The Bonch-Bruevich State University of Telecommunications, Saint-Petersburg, Russia*
- *Prof. Patrick Wang (IPCV + MSV + CGVR); Fellow of IAPR, ISIBM, WASE; Zijiang Chair Professor, ECNU, Shanghai and NTUST, Taipei, Taiwan; Founding President and CEO, Wang Teknowlogy Lab.; MIT Research Consultant; Harvard University, Adj. Faculty, USA; Northeastern University, Boston, MA, USA*

As Sponsors-at-large, partners, and/or organizers each of the followings (separated by semicolons) provided help for at least one track of the World Congress: Aldebaran Robotics Inc., USA (http://www.aldebaran-robotics.com); Altera Corporation, USA (http://www.altera.com/); Computer Science Research, Education, and Applications Press (CSREA); Impulse Accelerated Technologies, Inc., USA (http://www.impulseaccelerated.com/); NVIDIA Corporation, USA (http://www.nvidia.com/object/about-nvidia.html); Parallella Community, Supercomputing for Everyone, USA (http://forums.parallella.org/); Pico Computing, Inc., USA (http://picocomputing.com/); SemiWiki.com, The Semiconductor Wiki Project, USA (http://www.semiwiki.com/); Solarflare Communications, Inc., USA (http://www.solarflare.com/); Stream Computing, Performance Engineers, The Netherlands (http://streamcomputing.eu/); Taylor & Francis, UK (http://www.taylorandfrancis.com/); US Chapter of World Academy of Science (http://www.world-academy-of-science.org/) ; and WEBestSOL & Webest Solutions Ltd, UK (http://webestsol.com/). In addition, a number of university faculty members and their staff (names appear on the cover of the set of proceedings), several publishers of computer science and computer engineering books and journals, chapters and/or task forces of computer science associations/organizations from 5 countries, and developers of high-performance machines and systems provided significant help in organizing the conference as well as providing some resources. We are grateful to them all.

We express our gratitude to keynote, invited, and individual conference/tracks and tutorial speakers - the list of speakers appears on the conference web site. We would also like to thank the followings: UCMSS (Universal Conference Management Systems & Support, California, USA) for managing all aspects of the conference; Dr. Tim Field of APC for managing the printing of the proceedings; and the staff of the New Tropicana Hotel in Las Vegas for the professional service they provided. Last but not least, we would like to thank the Co-Editors of FCS'13: Prof. Hamid R. Arabnia, Prof. George A. Gravvanis, Prof. George Jandieri, Ashu M. G. Solo, and Prof. Fernando G. Tinetti.

We present the proceedings of FCS'13.

Steering Committee, 2013
http://www.world-academy-of-science.org/

Contents

SESSION: HPC + LOAD-BALANCING + APPROXIMATION ALGORITHMS + N-P HARD PROBLEMS

SESSION: GRAPH BASED METHODS + RELATED ISSUES

SESSION: FORMAL VERIFICATION + AUTOMATA

SESSION: ENCRYPTION + CALCULUS + TESTING METHODS AND NEW METHODOLOGIES

SESSION: QUANTUM COMPUTING

SESSION: GRAMMAR RULES AND TEXT COMPRESSION METHODS

SESSION

HPC + LOAD-BALANCING + APPROXIMATION ALGORITHMS + N-P HARD PROBLEMS

Chair(s)

TBA

Stencil and Lattice Structures for Field Equation Model Simulations on GPUs

D.P. Playne & K.A. Hawick
Computer Science, Massey University, North Shore 102-904, Auckland, New Zealand
email: k.a.hawick@massey.ac.nz
Tel: +64 9 414 0800 Fax: +64 9 441 8181

April 2013

ABSTRACT
Field equations can be numerically simulated by approximating a continuous space field by a discrete lattice. There are a number of different lattice geometries that can be used to approximate continuous space which may cause structural artefacts in the simulation. These different lattice structures require the use of different stencil operators to approximate the spatial terms of the field equations. We show how different lattice geometries and associated stencil operators can be implemented in a stencil library which is used in conjunction with a code generator to produce code for field equations simulations that can run on a CPU or GPU.

KEY WORDS
lattice geometry, stencil operators, field equation simulations; GPU.

1 Introduction

Field equations are a family of computational models which describe the behaviour of a field of interacting matter or entities. These equations model a system represented by a field in continuous space but can be simulated numerically by approximating the field as a lattice of discrete cells and the spatial terms of the equations with stencil operators. Such equations can be used to describe - heat distribution, quenching binary alloys [2, 10], interacting species populations [14, 19] and superconductivity [6].

Rectilinear lattices are commonly used to approximate a continuous field due to their simple geometry, easy mapping to computer memory and simple stencil operators. Some previous work on hexagonal stencils can be found in [15, 20] but this work does not consider how stencils and lattices can be automatically generated and manipulated.

In this work we develop a stencil library that generates the stencil operators required by a field equation simulation based on the lattice geometry used. This stencil library is used in conjunction with a code generator presented in [9]. A parallel code generation approach is now possible due to the advent of portable parallel languages such as OpenCL and the general revitalisation of data-parallel computing that has been stimulated by cheap GPUs and other accelerators. Generally exposure to the original mathematics of a PDE along with knowledge of the numerical discretisation scheme desired, gives a software generation tool more power to identify the parallelisation potential of the problem and specifically target a high performance implementation. The roles and emphasis of performance and portability are then reversed in this approach and portability may be achieved through implementations of the OpenCL target code.

Figure 1: Three-dimensional Ginzburg-Landau simulation.

In fact using our approach we believe it is possible to construct a number of inherent templates that will support generation of several target languages including CUDA, OpenMP or OpenCL. There appears to be considerable scope for automatic generation of stencil source code that makes use of heuristics and other practical experience to

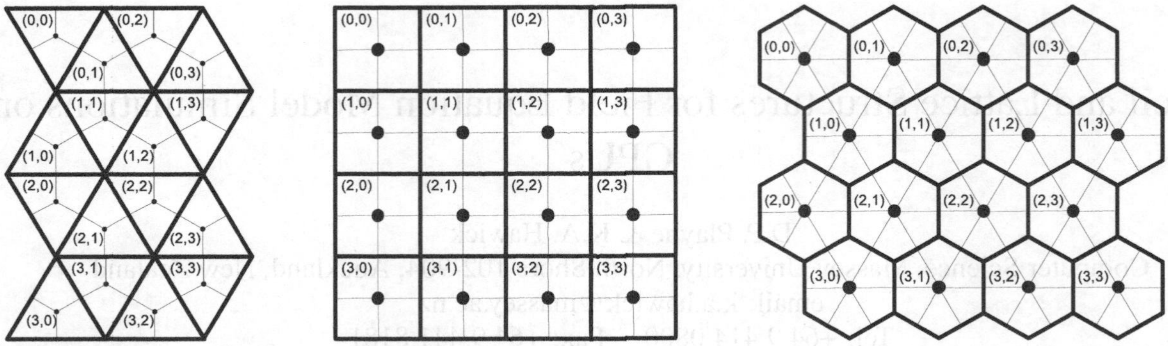

Figure 2: Two dimensional lattice geometries - triangular, rectangular and hexagonal.

achieve optimised implementations on present and emerging multicore processing devices [5].

Stencil operators have been in use for parallel program optimisation for some years [11, 18]. In the case of image operators where a particular stencil might be well-known with specific name it is straightforward to develop an optimised software library of optimised operator routines. For solving PDEs it is however harder to develop a general purpose library and automated code generation for a particular PDE with particular initial/boundary conditions and solver algorithm is more attractive [12]. Datta and collaborators discuss stencil generation using Lisp-parsing of Fortran-like expressions for the mathematics of the equation under consideration and a system that generates the stencil in C or Fortran code [3]. It is then possible to apply the standard apparatus and systems of parallel programming such as message passing, parallel compiler macros or supercomputer vendor proprietary optimisation tools to obtain a working parallel implementation that can target modern multicore devices amongst other platforms [4].

In Section 2 we discuss some different lattice structures and the different stencil operators that can be used with them in Section 3. Section 4 discusses some of the implementation issues of mapping non-rectilinear lattices onto computer memory and presents some source which does so. Some simulation and performance results are presented in Section 5 and we draw some conclusions from this work in Section 6.

2 Lattice Structures

To simulate a field equation numerically, the continuous field representing the system must be approximated by a lattice of discrete cells so it can be stored in computer memory as an array. Each value in the array approximates the average state of the field within that discrete macroscopic cell. The spatial interactions of the field equations are defined in terms of spatial calculus operators which must be approximated by discrete stencils that can be applied to the lattice approximating the field. The most common lattice geometry used to approximate continuous space is the rectilinear lattice which divides space into rectangular shapes. This lattice geometry is commonly used as it is simple to comprehend, can be easily extended to divide n-dimensional space and can be mapped directly into an array in computer memory.

However, there are a number of different lattice structures which can also be used to approximate a continuous field. These more unusual lattice structures are often only applicable to fields with a certain number of dimensions. There is only one regular way to divide a one-dimensional field whereas in two-dimensions a continuous field can be divided into a number of different regular lattices. Figure 2 shows three possible structures for a two-dimensional lattice - triangular, rectilinear and hexagonal. Each cell in a triangular lattice has three neighbours while the rectilinear has four and the hexagonal has six.

The rectilinear and hexagonal lattices discussed in this research are both Bravais lattices [1, 13] because they fulfil the condition that an infinite lattice appears exactly the same from any lattice point. The triangular lattice does not fulfil this condition because neighbouring triangles must be inverted for them to fit together. Irregular lattices can also be used to approximate continuous space but these require stencils to be generated on a per-cell basis and are not considered in this work.

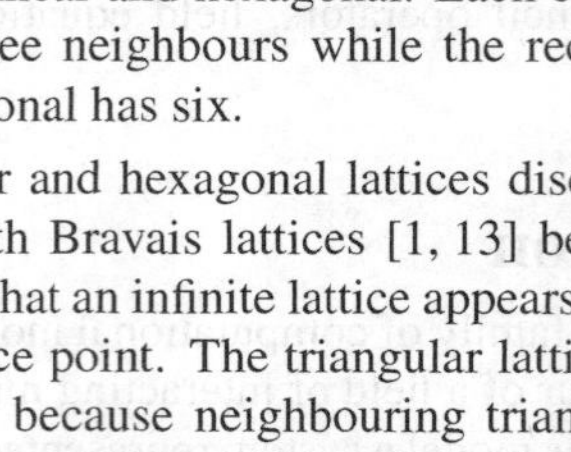

Figure 3: Two hexagons with distance $h = 1$ between the centres and side length t.

The hexagonal lattices used in this work fix the distance between each hexagon at 1. This gives a side length of $t = \frac{h}{tan(\frac{\pi}{3})} = 0.577$ which means each hexagon cell in

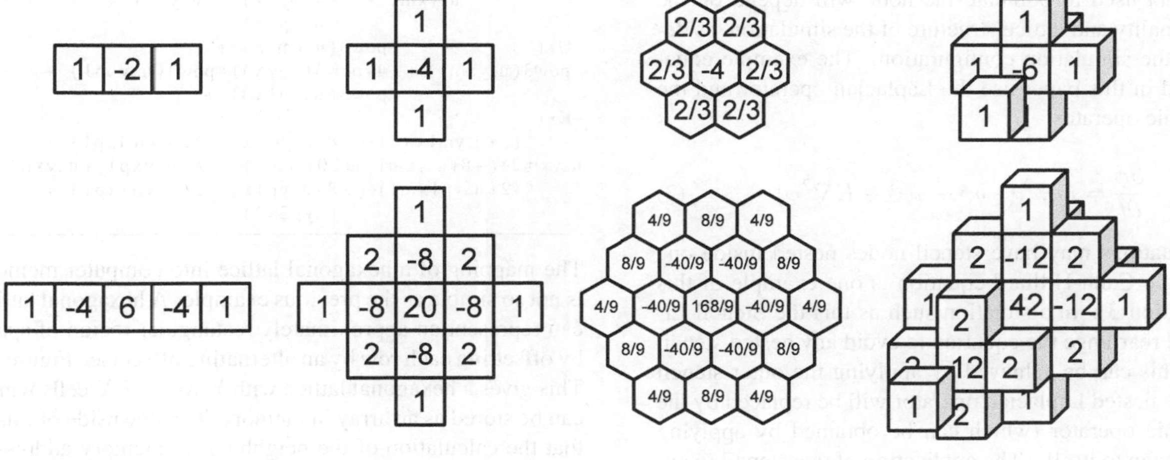

Figure 4: The Laplacian stencil (top) and the Biharmonic stencil (bottom) shown in one-, two- and three-dimensions.

the lattice represents an area of $A = \frac{3\sqrt{3}}{2}t^2 = 0.866$. This means that a hexagonal lattice with more lattice points will be required to simulate the same field area as a rectilinear lattice with $h = 1$. Conceptually dividing a field into a hexagonal lattice is simple but it will have implications on both the stencils used to approximate the spatial terms of the equation and the way the lattice must be stored in computer memory.

3 Stencils & Library

The example field equation models in this research (the Heat, Lotka-Volterra, Ginzburg-Landau and Cahn-Hilliard equations) all use the Laplace operator for the spatial term (the Cahn-Hilliard equation also uses the biharmonic operator). The Laplace operator or Laplacian is given by the divergence or the gradient of a function in Euclidean space. In Cartesian space this is given by the sum of second partial derivatives in each dimension. Equation 1 gives the formula for the continuous laplacian operator in n-dimensions.

$$\nabla^2 = \sum_{i=1}^{n} \frac{\partial^2}{\partial x_i^2} \tag{1}$$

When a continuous field is approximated by a lattice of discrete cells this continuous Laplacian must be replaced by a discrete approximation. The continuous Laplace operator can be adapted to the discrete form shown in Equation 2 which is suitable for generating difference equations [20]:

$$\nabla^2 = \frac{\delta^2}{\delta x_i^2} - \frac{\triangle x_i^2}{12}\frac{\delta^4}{\delta x_i^4} + \frac{\triangle x_i^4}{90}\frac{\delta^6}{\delta x_i^6}\cdots \tag{2}$$

This series is truncated at the $\delta^2/\delta x_i^2$ term which gives a second derivative operator accurate on the order $\triangle x_i^2$. This leads to the discrete stencils shown in Figure 4 for rectilinear lattices in one-, two- and three-dimensions as well as the two-dimensional hexagonal lattice. Also shown in Figure 4 are the stencils for rectilinear and hexagonal lattices representing the $\delta^4/\delta x_i^4$ term or the biharmonic operator (∇^4). These stencils can be obtained by applying the laplacian stencil to itself ($\nabla^4 = \nabla^2 \cdot \nabla^2$).

The Stencil Library is capable of providing and manipulating the stencils approximating the spatial calculus operators for rectilinear and hexagonal lattices. This Stencil Library is used in conjunction with a source code generator described in [9]. The Stencil Library allows the definition of a field equation to be kept separate from the specifics of the dimensionality and lattice geometry used for a particular simulation. Some PDE problems that arise in areas of physics can be simulated in higher dimensions and it is useful to be able to separate the dimension from other problem details and thus generate software for any number of dimensions. Hyper-dimensionality library support apparatus is discussed in [7] which the Stencil Library uses to produce spatial stencils.

The library must have the capability to provide stencils of the correct dimensionality and lattice structure as requested by the code generator. Currently the Stencil Library has functions to generate rectilinear stencils any number of dimensions, hexagonal stencils in two-dimensions and arbitrary data-types.

When simulation source code is generated, the Stencil Library is given a simulation tree by the code generator. This tree contains all the information about the field equation and the configuration of the simulation. The Stencil Library will examine this tree to identify nodes representing spatial operators and inject the appropriate stencil data. The specific stencil data used to populate the node will depend on the dimensionality and lattice structure of the simulation, as defined by the simulation configuration. The example equations used in this paper use the Laplacian operator and the Biharmonic operator.

$$\frac{\partial \phi}{\partial t} = m\nabla^2 \left(-b\phi + u\phi^3 - K\nabla^2\phi\right) \quad (3)$$

Some equations may have stencil nodes nested inside one another, the Cahn-Hilliard equation is one example of this (see equation 3). In a situation such as this the Stencil Library will rearrange the equation to avoid any nested stencil nodes. This can be achieved by applying the outer stencil to the The nested Laplacian operator will be replaced by the Biharmonic operator (which can be obtained by applying the Laplacian to itself). The application of one stencil to another can be computed by applying a stencil to every point on the other stencil. The rearranged Cahn-Hilliard equation can be seen in equation 4.

$$\frac{\partial \phi}{\partial t} = m\left(-b\nabla^2\phi + u\nabla^2\phi^3 - K\nabla^4\phi\right) \quad (4)$$

4 Implementation

Computationally simulating a field equation using a rectilinear lattice involves a straightforward mapping of the lattice onto computer memory. The lattice structure can be easily represented in computer memory and so calculating the memory addresses of the neighbouring lattice points required for stencil operators is also straightforward. The only complication involved in calculating neighbouring memory addresses is on the boundaries, in this research periodic boundary conditions are used to avoid artefacts from boundaries. The code listing showing the calculation of neighbouring values and computation of the Cahn-Hilliard model is shown in Listing 1.

Listing 1: Neighbouring memory address calculation and model calculation code for a two-dimensional Cahn-Hilliard equation on a rectilinear lattice point (x,y). The variables in the calculation of the model with the form u_yx are the values fetched from the lattice u at position (x,y).

```
int ym2 = (y <= 1)    ? (y-2)+Y : y-2;
int ym1 = (y == 0)    ?  Y-1    : y-1;
int yp1 = (y == Y-1) ? 0       : y+1;
int yp2 = (y >= Y-2) ? (y+2)-Y : y+2;

int xm2 = (x <= 1)    ? (x-2)+X : x-2;
int xm1 = (x == 0)    ? X-1     : x-1;
int xp1 = (x == X-1) ? 0       : x+1;
int xp2 = (x >= X-2) ? (x+2)-X : x+2;

...

M*(
-B*(         u_ym1x   +
             u_yxm1 + (-4*u_yx) + u_yxp1 +
             u_yp1x) +
U*(          pow3(u_ym1x) +
pow3(u_yxm1)+(-4*pow3(u_yx))+pow3(u_yxp1) +
             pow3(u_yp1x)) +
-K*(         u_ym2x   +
     (2*u_ym1xm1)+(-8*u_ym1x)+(2*u_ym1xp1) +
u_yxm2+(-8*u_yxm1)+(20*u_yx)+(-8*u_yxp1)+u_yxp2 +
     (2*u_yp1xm1)+(-8*u_yp1x)+(2*u_yp1xp1) +
             u_yp2x))
```

The mapping of a hexagonal lattice into computer memory is not so simple as the previous example. A hexagonal lattice can represent an approximately rectangular region of space by offsetting each row by an alternating offset (see Figure 2). This gives a hexagonal lattice with Y rows of X cells which can be stored as an array in memory. The downside of this is that the calculation of the neighbouring memory addresses in a simulation using a hexagonal lattice depends on the row number. Effectively it gives rise to selecting one of the two stencils shown in Figure 5.

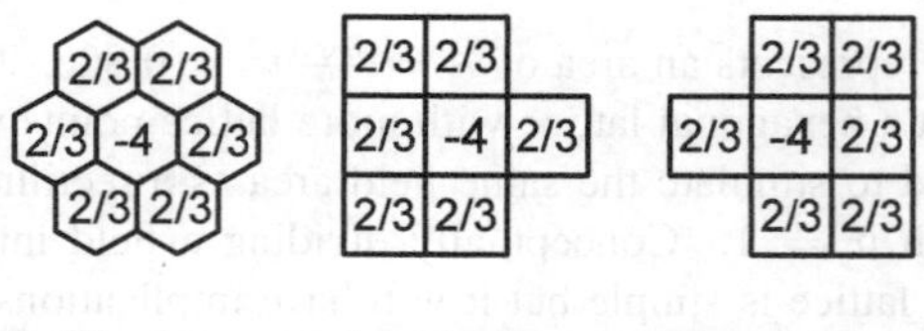

Figure 5: The hexagonal laplacian stencil and the two row-dependent rectilinear stencils.

These two stencils can be implemented by changing the calculation of the neighbouring lattice point memory addresses based on whether the lattice point is on an odd or even row. The code to perform these address calculations and the computation of the Cahn-Hilliard simulation on a hexagonal lattice is shown in Listing 2. Note that not only has the number of neighbouring addresses increased but the model calculation has also become more complex using additional neighbouring values as compared to the code example in Listing 1.

Listing 2: The code to calculate the memory addresses of the neighbouring cells and compute the Cahn-Hilliard equation on a hexagonal lattice point (x,y).

```
int ym2 = (y <= 1)    ? (y-2)+Y : y-2;
int ym1 = (y == 0)    ?  Y-1    : y-1;
int yp1 = (y == Y-1) ? 0       : y+1;
int yp2 = (y >= Y-2) ? (y+2)-Y : y+2;

int xm2 = (x <= 1)    ? (x-2)+X : x-2;
int xm1 = (x == 0)    ?  X-1    : x-1;
int xp1 = (x == X-1) ? 0       : x+1;
int xp2 = (x >= X-2) ? (x+2)-X : x+2;

int xm15 = (y%2 == 0) ? xm2 : xm1;
int xm05 = (y%2 == 0) ? xm1 : x;
int xp05 = (y%2 == 0) ? x   : xp1;
int xp15 = (y%2 == 0) ? xp1 : xp2;

...
```

```
 M*(
-B*(2.0/3.0)*( u_ym1xm5 + u_ym1xp5      +
           u_yxm1 + (-4*u_yx) + u_yxp1 +
               u_yp1xm5 + u_yp1xp5)    +
 U*(2.0/3.0)*(
        pow3(u_ym1xm5) + pow3(u_ym1xp5)     +
  pow3(u_yxm1)+(-4*pow3(u_yx))+pow3(u_yxp1) +
        pow3(u_yp1xm5) + pow3(u_yp1xp5))    +
-K*(4.0/9.0)*(
        u_ym2xm1 + (2*u_ym2x) + u_ym2xp1         +
(2*uym1xm15)-(10*uym1xm05)-(10*uym1xp05)+(2*uym1xp15)+
 u_yxm2-(10*u_yxm1)+(42*u_yx)-(10*u_yxp1)+u_yxp2 +
(2*uyp1xm15)-(10*uyp1xm05)-(10*uyp1xp05)+(2*uyp1xp15)+
        u_yp2xm1 + (2*u_yp2x) + u_yp2xp1))
```

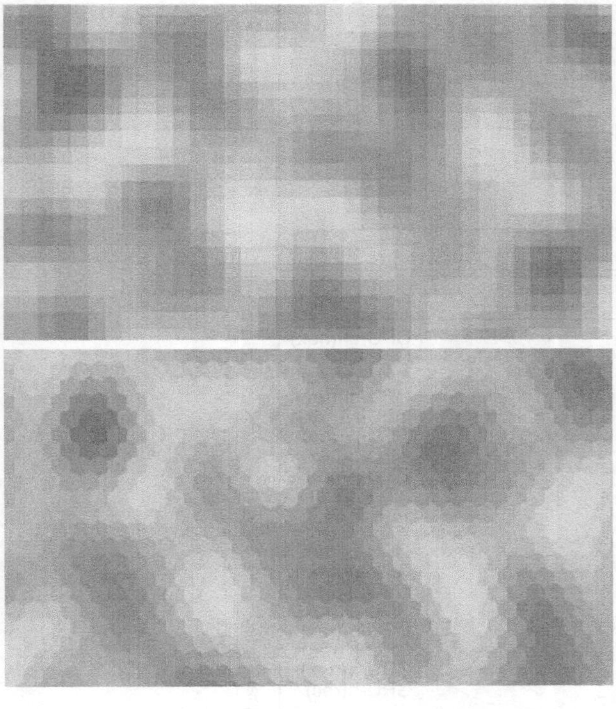

Figure 6: Two snapshots of Cahn-Hilliard simulations - computing on the rectilinear (top) and hexagonal (bottom) lattices from Figure 2.

The simulation of a field equation requires this calculation to be performed for each cell in the lattice and integrated over time using an appropriate integration method. This can be done by a CPU processor by iterating over every cell, computing the new value and writing it to another lattice or in parallel by a device such as a GPU in which each cell will be updated by a different thread executing on many processors. This work is concerned mainly with the lattices and spatial stencils but the further details of the simulation generation and structure can be found in [9].

5 Results

The first result of this research is that the simulation generator is able to produce code for field equation simulations using both rectilinear and hexagonal lattices. This involves generating stencils for both lattice types as required by the models, applying them to each other when required by the equation and mapping both the lattice and the stencil memory address calculation onto memory. This has been achieved successfully for the rectilinear lattice in one-, two- and three-dimensions as well as the less simple hexagonal lattice in two dimensions. Screen captures of the two-dimensional Cahn-Hilliard equation computed using a rectilinear and a hexagonal lattice are shown in Figure 6.

One of the major requirements for the generator system is that it should produce fast and efficient simulation code. The performance of the code produced by the our system's C++ and CUDA generators is indistinguishable from existing hand-written code. These hand-written comparison codes have been developed and optimised over a number of years, details of their optimisations can be found in [8, 16, 17]. The performance of the four equations Heat, Cahn-Hilliard, Ginzburg-Landau and Lotka-Volterra equations are presented for a number of simulation configurations. These simulations have been computed on both rectilinear lattices and hexagonal lattices. Figure 7 shows the timing results of these simulations in two-dimensions for N={1024, 2048, 3072, 4096, 5120, 6144, 7168, 8192}. These simulations have been computed on a Intel i7-970 and an NVIDIA GeForce GTX580.

From these performance plots it can be seen the the different field equations have different performance based on their individual computation and memory requirements. In all cases the simulations on hexagonal lattices are slower than the rectilinear lattice simulations. The extra memory transactions and computation required to compute the hexagonal stencils will always have a negative performance impact. This penalty is especially visible for the Cahn-Hilliard equation which uses the biharmonic operator. The simulation of this model on a hexagonal lattice requires 19 neighbouring lattice points instead of the 13 required by the two-dimensional rectilinear biharmonic operator.

6 Discussion and Conclusions

In summary, we have discussed how continuous space can be approximated by discrete lattices with different geometries and how spatial calculus terms can be formulated as stencil operators on these different lattices. The formulation and application of these stencils can be performed automatically by a stencil library which can reorder equations to avoid nested stencils. This sometimes requires the library to apply one stencil to another. The stencil library also provides a mapping from the lattice structure onto computer

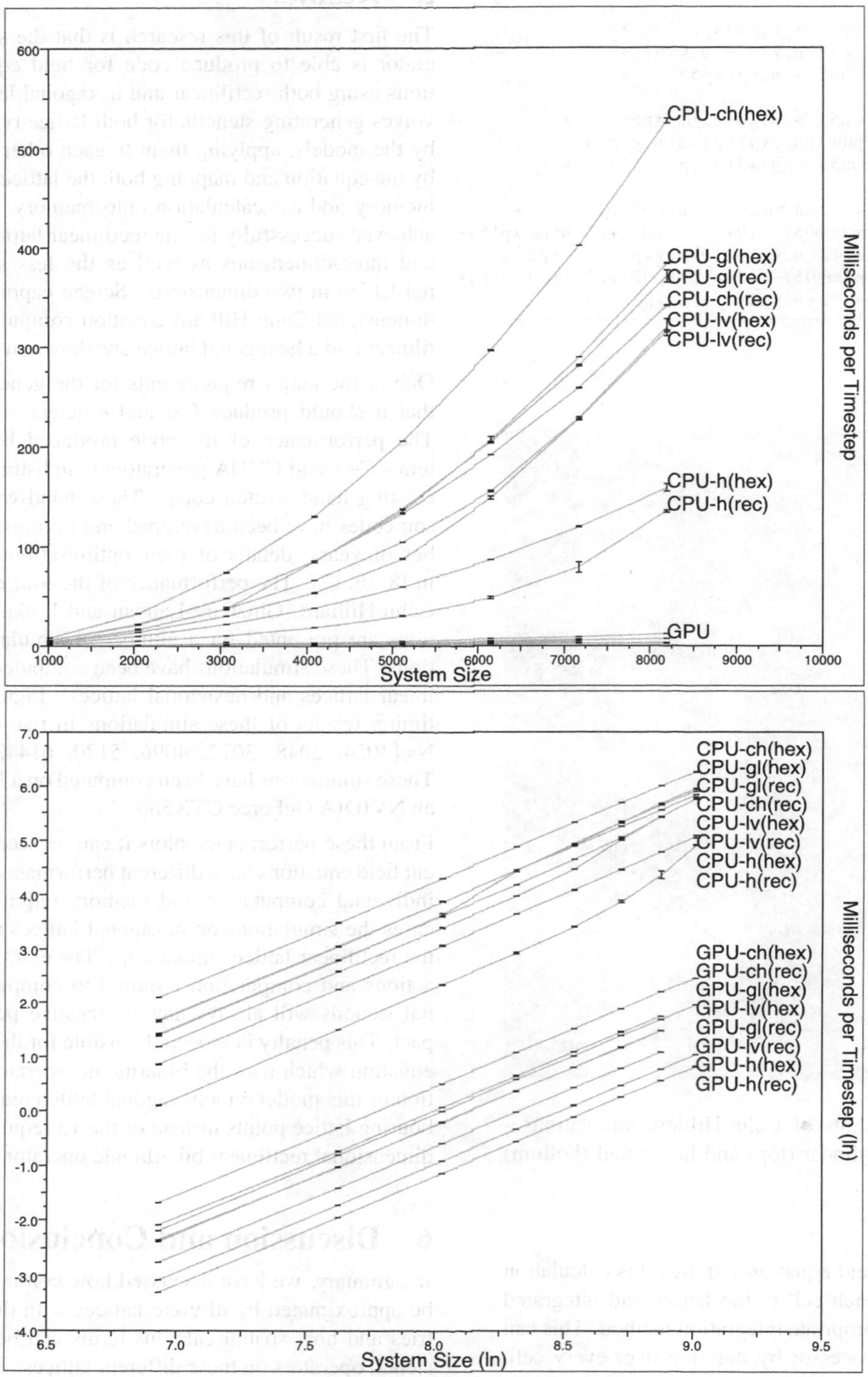

Figure 7: A performance comparison of the Cahn-Hilliard (ch), Ginzburg-Landau (gl), Lotka-Volterra (lv) and Heat (h) equation simulations using rectilinear lattices (rec) and hexagonal lattices (hex) in C++ (CPU) and CUDA (GPU). Results are shown in normal scale (top) and ln-ln scale (bottom).

memory so that the lattice can be stored in an array.

The data provided by the stencil library can be used by a code generation system which produces source code to numerically simulate field equations. A number of field equations have been tested with this code generation system using both rectilinear and hexagonal lattices to approximate the continuous field. The system has generated simulation code in C for use on a CPU processor as well as CUDA for use on a parallel graphical processing unit.

The functionality of separating a model definition from the lattice geometries allows models to be tested on different lattices with ease. This makes it easy to test models with a range of lattices to ensure any structural patterns formed by the model are representative of the model and not an artefact of the particular lattice geometry used.

There is scope fro future work to implement other lattice structures in three-dimensional space such as face-centred cubic, body-centred cubic and hexagonal close-packed. Some of the field equation models in our class can be generalised to higher dimensions and in particular some physics-oriented problems involve four and higher dimensional field equations. Our stencils library and approach also generalise to higher dimensional problems.

The computational performance we attained with our stencils library and the code generated for running on accelerators such as a GPU is extremely encouraging. However the real value of this approach is being able to experiment with different calculus operators, different lattices, and other algorithmic details relatively easily – for the same equation under study. In addition, this approach lowers considerably the development and testing effort involved in studying another (new) equation.

References

[1] Bravais, A.: Memoire sur les systemes formes par les points distribues regulierement sur un plan ou dans l'espace. J. Ecole Polytech 19, 1–128 (1850)

[2] Cahn, J.W., Hilliard, J.E.: Free Energy of a Nonuniform System. I. Interfacial Free Energy. The Journal of Chemical Physics 28(2), 258–267 (1958)

[3] Datta, K., Kamil, S., Williams, S., Oliker, L., Shalf, J., Yelick, K.: Optimization and performance modeling of stencil computations on modern microprocessors. SIAM Review 51(1), 129–159 (2009)

[4] Datta, K., Murphy, M., amd S. Williams, V.V., Carter, J., Oliker, L., Patterson, D., Shalf, J., Yelick, K.: Stencil computation optimization and auto-tuning on state-of-the-art multicore architectures. In: Proc. ACM/IEEE Conf. on Supercomputing (SC'08') (2008)

[5] Ganapathi, A., Datta, K., Fox, A., Patterson, D.: A case for machine learning to optimize multicore performance. In: First USENIX Workshop on Hot Topics in Parallelism (HotPar'09). Berkeley, CA, USA. (March 2009)

[6] Ginzburg, V.L., Landau, L.D.: (Published in English in Collected papers of L.D.Landau, Oxford Press, 1965, pp138-167). Zh. Eksp. Teor. Fiz. 20, 1064 (1950), edited I.D. ter Haar

[7] Hawick, K.A., Playne, D.P.: Hypercubic Storage Layout and Transforms in Arbitrary Dimensions using GPUs and CUDA. Concurrency and Computation: Practice and Experience 23(10), 1027–1050 (July 2011)

[8] Hawick, K.A., Playne, D.P.: Numerical Simulation of the Complex Ginzburg-Landau Equation on GPUs with CUDA. In: Proc. IASTED International Conference on Parallel and Distributed Computing and Networks (PDCN). pp. 39–45. No. CSTN-070, IASTED, Innsbruck, Austria (15-17 February 2011)

[9] Hawick, K.A., Playne, D.P.: Simulation software generation using a domain-specific language for partial differential field equations. In: 11th International Conference on Software Engineering Research and Practice (SERP'13). p. SER3829. No. CSTN-187, WorldComp, Las Vegas, USA (22-25 July 2013)

[10] Hawick, K.A.: Domain Growth in Alloys. Ph.D. thesis, Edinburgh University (1991)

[11] James, H.A., Patten, C.J., Hawick, K.A.: Stencil methods on distributed high performance computers. Tech. Rep. DHPC-010, Advanced Computational Systems CRC, Department of Computer Science, University of Adelaide (June 1997)

[12] Kamil, S., Chan, C., Williams, S., Oliker, L., Shalf, J., Howison, M., Bethel, E.W., Prabhat: A generalized framework for auto-tuning stencil computations. In: Proc. Cray User Group (CUG) Atlanta, Georgia,. pp. 1–11 (May 2009), http://escholarship.org/uc/item/23p6g5nj

[13] Kittel, C.: Introduction to Solid State Physics. Wiley (2004), iSBN 978-0-471-41526-8

[14] Lotka, A.J.: Elements of Physical Biology. Williams & Williams, Baltimore (1925)

[15] Morii, F.: Distortion analysis on discrete laplacian operators by introducing random images. In: Proceedings of the Third International Conference on Image and Graphcis (ICIG'04) (2004)

[16] Playne, D.P., Hawick, K.A.: Visualising vector field model simulations. In: Proc. International Conference on Modeling, Simulation and Visualization Methods (MSV'09). pp. 3–9. WorldComp, Las Vegas, USA (13-16 July 2009)

[17] Playne, D., Hawick, K.: Data Parallel Three-Dimensional Cahn-Hilliard Field Equation Simulation on GPUs with CUDA. In: Proc. 2009 International Conference on Parallel and Distributed Processing Techniques and Applications (PDPTA'09). pp. 104–110. WorldComp, Las vegas, USA (13-16 July 2009)

[18] Reed, D.A., Adams, L.M., Patrick, M.L.: Stencils and problem partitionings: Their influence on the performance of multiple processor systems. IEEE Transactions on Computers C 36(7), 845–858 (jul 1987)

[19] Volterra, V.: Variazioni e fluttuazioni del numero d'individui in specie animali conviventi. Mem. R. Accad. Naz. dei Lincei, Ser VI 2 (1926)

[20] Woodward, M., Muir, F.: Hexagonal finite difference operators and 3-d wave equation migration. Stanford Exploration Project 38, 195–206 (198)

The Complexity and Algorithm for k-Duplicates Combinatorial Auctions with Submodular and Subadditive Bidders

Wenbin Chen[1,2,3], Lingxi Peng[1], Jianxiong Wang[1], Dongqing Xie[1], Fufang Li[1] and Maobin Tang[1]
[1]School of Computer Science, Guangzhou University, P.R. China
[2]Shanghai Key Laboratory of Intelligent Information Processing, Fudan University, P.R. China
[3]State Key Laboratory for Novel Software Technology, Nanjing University, P.R. China

Abstract—*In this paper, we study the problem of maximizing welfare in combinatorial auctions with $k(> 1)$-duplicates of each item, where k is a fixed constant (i.e. k is not the part of the input) and bidders are submodular or subadditive. We exhibit some upper and lower approximation bounds for k-duplicates combinatorial auctions. First, we show that it is NP-hard to approximate the maximum welfare for k-duplicates combinatorial auctions with subadditive bidders within a factor of $2-\epsilon$ where $\epsilon > 0$ unless $P = NP$. Secondly, we propose a 2-approximation algorithm for k-duplicates combinatorial auctions with submodular bidders.*

Keywords: Approximation Algorithm; Combinatorial Auctions; NP-hard

1. Introduction

We consider the allocation problem in combinatorial auctions with $k(> 1)$-duplicates of each item where k is a fixed constant. In the past years, there has been much interest in combinatorial auctions. In a combinatorial auction, there are a set M of m items and n bidders. These items are being sold to bidders. Every bidder i has a valuation function (it is also called utility function in some cases) $v_i : 2^M \rightarrow R^+$. We suppose that the valuation function is monotone, which means for every two bundles $S, T, S \subseteq T \subseteq M$ it holds $v(S) \leq v(T)$, and normalized $v(\emptyset) = 0$. The goal is to find a partition $(S_1, \ldots, S_n)$ of the m items that maximizes the total utility or *social welfare*, i.e., $\Sigma_i v_i(S_i)$ is maximized. We call such an allocation an optimal allocation.

The k-duplicates combinatorial auction is the allocation problem in combinatorial auctions with k-duplicates of each item where k is a fixed constant. Every bidder is still interested in at most one unit of each item and every valuation is still defined on the subsets of M. It is the generalization of a combinatorial auction (where $k = 1$).

Since the size of the input is exponential, we suppose that we have oracles for accessing it. There are two common types of query methods. One common type of queries is the *"value queries"*. Given a bundle of S, a value query answers $v(S)$ for a valuation v. From a "computer science" perspective, this kind of query is very natural.

Another kind of query is the *"demand queries"*. Given a vector $p = (p_1, \ldots, p_m)$ of item prices, a demand query replies a set that maximizes the profit, i.e. maximizes $v_i(S) - \Sigma_{j \in S} p_j$. Demand queries are very natural from an economic point of view. It is known that demand queries can simulate values queries in polynomial time [4].

In this paper we study the important cases where all bidders are known to have subadditive and submodular valuations; a valuation is called *subadditive* if $v(S \cup T) \leq v(S) + v(T)$ for all $S, T \subseteq M$; a valuation is called *submodular* if $v(S \cup T) + v(S \cap T) \leq v(S) + v(T)$ for all $S, T \subseteq M$. It is known that every submodular valuation is subadditive [17].

For general utility functions, the combinatorial auction problem is NP-hard. In [4], it has been shown that there are no polynomial time algorithms with a factor better than $O(\frac{\log m}{m})$ if value queries are used. In [18] and [21], it has also been shown that there are no polynomial time algorithms with a factor better than $O(\frac{1}{m^{1/2-\epsilon}})$ even for single minded bidders. If demand queries are used, achieving any approximation factors better than $O(\frac{1}{m^{1/2-\epsilon}})$ requires exponential communication [20]. More results on the combinatorial auction problems with general utilities can be found in [7].

The allocation problem with subadditive utility functions is still NP-hard. Using demand queries, a $O(\log m)$ approximation algorithm for combinatorial auctions with subadditive utility function is given in [8]. In the same paper, an incentive compatible $O(\sqrt{m})$ approximation algorithm is also presented if value queries is used. Recently, Feige give an approximation algorithm that obtains the approximation ratio of 2 ([12], [13]). As for complexity results, it is shown that an exponential amount of communication is required for achieving an approximation ratio better than 2 in [8]. In [12] and [13], it is proved that there are no polynomial time algorithms approximating the maximum welfare within a factor $2-\epsilon$ unless $P = NP$, when bidders are subadditive. Thus the approximation ratio 2 is the best possible for the combinatorial auctions with subadditive utility functions.

In [17], a strict hierarchy of subclasses within the class of subadditive valuations is presented: $OXS \subset GS \subset SM \subset XOS \subset CF$. The CF is the class of subadditive (complement-free) valuations; SM is the set of submodular valuations; The XOS is the set of those valuations that can be defined by XOR-of-ORs of singleton valuations.

For the combinatorial auctions with XOS utility functions, a greedy algorithm achieving an approximation ratio of 2 is given in [8], [9]. An improved ratio of $\frac{e}{e-1}$ is obtained in [10] and [12]. It is shown that it is NP-hard to approximate the optimal allocation with XOS valuations to within any factor of $\frac{e}{e-1} - \epsilon$ [8], [9]. It is also proved that exponential communication is required for achieving any approximation ratio better that $\frac{e}{e-1}$ when all bidders are XOS.

In the past years, combinatorial auctions with submodular bidders have also received much attention. A greedy 2-approximation algorithm is given in [17] and the approximation ratio is improved to $(2-\frac{1}{n})$ in [10] when value queries is used. In [22], Jan Vondrák design a randomized continuous greedy $\frac{e}{e-1}$-approximation algorithm for the submodular welfare problem in the value oracle model. In [1], Ittai Abraham and Moshe Babaioff et al. develop polynomial-time approximation algorithms and truthful mechanisms for welfare maximization with bidders with hypergraph valuations. When demand queries is used, there is a random polynomial time approximation algorithm that obtains an approximation ratio of $\rho < \frac{e}{e-1}$ [14]. In [8], it is shown that it is NP-hard to approximate the optimal allocation for combinatorial auctions with submodular bidders to within a factor better than 51/50, unless $P = NP$. Khot et al. improve this result, prove that there are no polynomial time algorithms that can obtain an approximation ratio better than $\frac{e}{e-1}$ using value queries only, unless $P = NP$ [16]. The case of additive valuations with a budget limit is a subcase of submodular valuations. It is NP-hard to find the optimal allocation in a combinatorial auction with valuations that are additive with budget limit [17]. In [2], a randomized algorithm with an approximation ratio of $\frac{e}{e-1}$ is presented, which can be derandomized. Some other subcases of submodular valuations have also been studied (e.g. identical bidders [8], [9], online settings [19].)

In [5], an incentive compatible mechanism for multi-unit combinatorial auctions is given. In particular, this includes the case where each good has exactly k units, i.e. k-duplicates combinatorial auctions. In [11], Dobzinski and Schapira exhibit a polynomial time $\min\{\frac{n}{k}, O(m^{\frac{1}{k+1}})\}$ approximation algorithm for k-duplicates combinatorial auctions using demand queries only and show that exponential communication is required for achieving an approximation ratio better than $\min\{\frac{n}{k}, O(m^{\frac{1}{k+1}-\epsilon})\}$, where $\epsilon > 0$. In the same paper, they also give an algorithm that achieves an approximation ratio of $O(\frac{m}{\sqrt{\log m}})$ using only a polynomial number of value queries and prove that it is impossible to approximate a combinatorial auction with k-duplicates to a factor of $O(\frac{m}{\log m})$ using a polynomial number of value queries. They studied the case where all valuations are general utility functions. In [6], a $O(\sqrt{m})$ approximation algorithm for k-duplicates combinatorial auctions with subadditive valuations using value queries and a $O(\log m)$ approximation algorithm for k-duplicates combinatorial auctions with subadditive valuations using demand queries are given.

In this paper, we study the computational complexity of k-duplicates combinatorial auctions with subadditive bidders and approximation algorithms for k-duplicates combinatorial auctions with submodular bidders.

Our Results

In this paper, first, we prove some lower bounds for subadditive bidders. We show that it is NP-hard to approximate the maximum welfare for k-duplicates combinatorial auctions with subadditive bidders within a factor of $2-\epsilon$ where $\epsilon > 0$ unless $P = NP$. Secondly, we provide some approximation algorithm. We give a 2-approximation algorithm for k-duplicates combinatorial auctions with submodular bidders.

Structure of the Paper

In section 2, we study the computational complexity for k-duplicates combinatorial auctions with subadditive valuations. In section 3 we present a 2-approximation algorithm for k-duplicates combinatorial auctions in which all valuations are submodular. Finally, in section 4 we present some conclusions and some open problems.

2. The complexity for k-duplicates combinatorial auctions with subadditive valuations

In this section we study the computational complexity for k-duplicates combinatorial auctions with subadditive valuations. In the following, we show that it is NP-hard to approximate the optimal allocation within a factor of $2-\epsilon$ for k-duplicates combinatorial auctions with subadditive valuations, where $\epsilon > 0$.

In order to get the computational complexity, we will give a polynomial time reduction from the maximum independent set problem for hypergraphs to k-duplicates combinatorial auctions with subadditive valuations. First, we give two definitions as follows.

Definition 1 *A k-uniform hypergraph $H_k(V, E)$ consists of a set of vertices V and a collection E of k-element subsets of V that are called hyperedges. An independent set of H_k is a set of vertices such that no subset of these vertices form a hyperedge in H_k.*

Definition 2 *The Maximum Independent Set (MIS) problem for Hepergraphs is the following problem: Given a hypergraph H_k, find a maximum independent set.*

In [3], it is shown that for every $\epsilon > 0$, there is an $\alpha > 0$ such that it is NP-hard to distinguish between "yes cases" in which a graph has an independent set of size αn and "no cases" in which every independent set is of size at most $\epsilon\alpha n$. A gap-preserving reduction from the MIS problem for graphs to the MIS for k-uniform hypergraphs is given in [5] and [15]. Thus the following conclusion holds.

Lemma 1 ([5] and [15]) *Let $k \geq 2$ be a fixed integer, for every $\epsilon > 0$, there is an $\alpha > 0$ such that it is NP-hard to distinguish between "yes cases" in which a k-uniform hypergraph has an independent set of size αn and "no cases" in which every independent is of size at most $\epsilon\alpha n$.*

In the following, we give a reduction from the MIS problem for k+1-hypergraph to the k-duplicates combinatorial auctions with subadditive valuations. The reduction is the extension of Feige' reduction and is similar to that in [5], where it is shown that it is NP-hard to approximate k-duplicates combinatorial auctions to within a factor of $O(m^{\frac{1-\epsilon}{k+1}})$ unless $NP = ZPP$, for every fixed $k \geq 1$ and $\epsilon > 0$.

Theorem 1 *For every $\epsilon > 0$, it is NP-hard to approximate the optimal allocation within a factor of $2 - \epsilon$ for k-duplicates combinatorial auctions with subadditive valuations.*

Proof: By lemma 1, it is NP-hard to distinguish between "yes cases" in which a $k + 1$-uniform hypergraph has an independent set of size αn and "no cases" in which every independent set is of size at most $\epsilon\alpha n$. Given an instance of $k + 1$-uniform hypergraph $H_{k+1} = (V, E)$, we define an instance of k-duplicates combinatorial auctions with subadditive valuations as follows: Let the hyperedges of the hypergraph H_{k+1} be the items with k duplicates of each item and let the number of bidders be αn. Every bidder has the same subadditive valuation. The subadditive valuation is defined as follows. Suppose S is a subset of items. If there is some vertex such that S contains all items whose corresponding hyperedges are incident with it, the utility $v(S) = 2$. Otherwise, $v(S) = 1$. We show that the utility function is subadditive. Let S and T be any two subset of items. By definition of v, $v(S)+v(T) \geq 1+1 = 2$ and $v(S \cup T) \leq 2$. So $v(S \cup T) \leq v(S)+v(T)$. Thus the utility function v is a subadditive valuation. On yes cases, by giving each bidder the items corresponding to hyperedges incident with some vertex of a maximum independent set, the maximum welfare is $2\alpha n$. On no cases, the maximum welfare is at most $(1 + \epsilon)\alpha n$. The reason is as follows. Since the maximum independent set is of size at most $\epsilon\alpha n$ on no cases, the number of its corresponding bidders is $\epsilon\alpha n$. We assign each such bidder the items corresponding to hyperedges incident with that vertex. Thus there are $2\epsilon\alpha n$ walfare for these $\epsilon\alpha n$ bidders; For other $(1 - \epsilon)\alpha n$ bidders, if one such bidder are assigned to all items whose corresponding hyperedges are incident with it, then the vertex corresponding to that bidder and the maximum independent set contain a hyperedge. Thus the item corresponding to the hyperedge is assigned to $k+1$ different bidders, this contradict the fact that the duplicate of each item is k. Thus for other $(1 - \epsilon)\alpha n$ bidders, there are no bidder that are assigned to all items whose corresponding hyperedges are incident with it. Thus their welfare are at most $(1 - \epsilon)\alpha n$. So on no cases, the welfare are at most $2\epsilon\alpha n + (1 - \epsilon)\alpha n = (1 + \epsilon)\alpha n$. Thus the hardness factor is $\frac{2\alpha n}{(1+\epsilon)\alpha n} = 2 - \epsilon$.

3. A 2-approximation algorithm for submodular valuations

In this section we present a 2-approximation algorithm for k-duplicates combinatorial auctions in which all valuations are submodular, which extends the algorithm of [17]. In [17], an equivalent definition of submodular valuations is as follows: for all $S \subseteq T$ and $x \notin T$, $v(S \cup x) - v(S) \geq v(T \cup x) - v(T)$. That is, the *marginal value* of each item decreases as the set of items already acquired increases. The approximation algorithm is as follows.

Input: $v_1, \ldots, v_n$-submodular valuations, given as black boxes.

Output: An allocation $S_1, \ldots, S_n$ which is 2-approximation to the optimal allocation.

The Algorithm:

1) Initialize $S_1 = S_2 = \ldots = S_n = \emptyset$.
2) For $x = 1, \ldots, m$ do:
   a) Let $j_1, \ldots, j_k$ be the bidders whose value of $v_j(x|S_j)$ is the highest, the second high, ..., the k-th high, where $v_j(x|S_j) = v_j(S_j \cup x) - v_j(S_j)$.
   b) Allocate x to $j_1, \ldots, j_k$, i.e. $S_{j_1} \leftarrow S_{j_1} \cup \{x\}, \ldots, S_{j_k} \leftarrow S_{j_k} \cup \{x\}$.

Obviously, the above algorithm requires only a polynomial number of operations.

Theorem 3 *The above algorithm provides a 2-approximation to the optimal allocation for k-duplicates combinatorial auctions in which all valuations are submodular.*

Proof: We denote by Q the original problem and define a new problem Q' on the $m - 1$ remaining items with k-duplicates of each item after item 1 is removed: i.e., item 1 is unavailable and $v_{j_1}, \ldots, v_{j_k}$ are replaced by $v'_{j_1}, \ldots, v'_{j_k}$ with $v'_{j_1}(S) = v_{j_1}(S|\{1\}) = v_{j_1}(S \cup \{1\}) - v_{j_1}(\{1\}), \ldots, v'_{j_k}(S) = v_{j_k}(S|\{1\}) = v_{j_k}(S \cup \{1\}) - v_{j_k}(\{1\})$, where $j_1, \ldots, j_k$ are those bidders to whom item

1 was allocated. All other valuations $v_i, i \neq j_1, \ldots, j_k$ are unchanged. Notice that the above algorithm can be viewed as first item 1 is allocated to $j_1, \ldots, j_k$ and other items are assigned using a recursive call on Q'.

Let $ALG(Q)$ denote the value of the allocation produced by above algorithm and $OPT(Q)$ denote the value of optimal allocation. Let $p_1 = v_{j_1}(\{1\}), \ldots, p_k = v_{j_k}(\{1\})$. By the definition of Q', we have $v'_{j_1}(S) + v_{j_1}(\{1\}) = v_{j_1}(S \cup \{1\}), \ldots, v'_{j_k}(S) + v_{j_k}(\{1\}) = v_{j_k}(S \cup \{1\})$. So we get $ALG(Q) = ALG(Q') + p_1 + \cdots + p_k$. We will show that $OPT(Q) \leq OPT(Q') + 2(p_1 + \cdots + p_k)$. Let $S_1, \ldots, S_n$ be the optimal allocation S for Q, and assume that $1 \in S_{l_1}, \ldots, 1 \in S_{l_k}$ and $v_{l_1}(\{1\}) \geq v_{l_2}(\{1\}) \geq \ldots \geq v_{l_k}(\{1\})$. Let S' be the allocation of item $2, \ldots, m$ that is the remaining allocation when k-duplicates of item 1 are removed in the allocation S. This is a possible solution to Q'. Let us compare $OPT(Q')$ to $OPT(Q)$. All bidders except $l_1, \ldots, l_k$ get the same allocation and all bidders except $j_1, \ldots, j_k$ have the same valuation. Without loss of generality, assume that $l_1 \neq j_1, \ldots, l_k \neq j_k$. Since $v_{l_i}(S \cup \{1\}) - v_{l_i}(S) \leq v_{l_i}(\{1\})(i = 1, \ldots, k)$, the bidders $l_1, \ldots, l_k$ lose at most $v_{l_1}(\{1\}) + \cdots v_{l_k}(\{1\})$. But $v_{l_i}(\{1\}) \leq v_{j_i}(\{1\}) = p_i$ for all $i(i = 1, \ldots, k)$. Thus the bidders $l_1, \ldots, l_k$ lose at most $p_1 + \ldots + p_k$. By the monotonicity of $v_{j_i}(i = 1, \ldots, k)$, $v'_{j_i}(S_{j_i}) = v_{j_i}(S_{j_i} \cup \{1\}) - v_{j_i}(\{1\}) \geq v_{j_i}(S_{j_i}) - p_i$ (for all $i = 1, \ldots, k$). Therefore $OPT(Q') \geq OPT(Q) - 2(p_1 + \ldots + p_k)$.

By lemma 1 of [17], Q' also consists of submodular valuations. Thus the proof is concluded by induction on Q': $OPT(Q) \leq OPT(Q') + 2(p_1 + \ldots p_k) \leq 2ALG(Q') + 2(p_1 + \ldots p_k) \leq 2ALG(Q)$.

4. Conclusions

In this paper, we have studied the computational complexity for k-duplicates combinatorial auctions with subadditive valuations. What are the computational complexity for k-duplicates combinatorial auctions with submodular or XOS valuations ? The problem should be further studied. About approximation algorithms, how to improve the approximation ratio 2 for submodular valuations. What is the upper bound for k-duplicates combinatorial auctions with subadditive or XOS valuations ?

Acknowledgment

We would like to thank the anonymous referees for their careful readings of the manuscripts and many useful suggestions.

Wenbin Chen's research has been supported by the National Natural Science Foundation of China (NSFC) under Grant No.11271097, the research project of Guangzhou education bureau under Grant No. 2012A074., the project IIPL-2011-001 from Shanghai Key Laboratory of Intelligent Information Processing, and the project KFKT2012B01 from State Key Laboratory for Novel Software TechnologyčňNanjing University. Lingxi Peng's research has been partly supported by the National Natural Science Foundation of China (NSFC) under Grant No.61100150. and the research project of Guangzhou education bureau under Grant No. 2012A077. Jianxiong Wang's research was partially supported under Guangzhou City Council's Science and Technology Projects funding scheme (project number 12C42011622), under Guangdong provincial education department's Yumiao early career researchers development funding scheme (2012WYM0105 and 2012LYM0105) and the research project of Guangzhou education bureau under Grant No. 2012A143. Dongqing Xie's research has been partially supported by Yangcheng Scholars Project under Grant No. 10A033D and Key Science and Technology Innovation Projects of Guangdong Province's Universities under Grant No. CXZD1144. Fufang Li's research has been supported by Natural Science Foundation of Guangdong Province of China under Grant No. S2011040003843. Maobin Tang's research has been supported under Guangdong Province's Science and Technology Projects under Grant No. 2011B020313023 and 2012A020602065 and the research project of Guangzhou education bureau under Grant No. 2012A075.

References

[1] I. Abraham, M. Babaioff, S. Dughmi, T. Roughgarden, "Combinatorial auctions with restricted complements," in *2012 ACM Conference on Electronic Commerce*, 2012, pp. 3–16.

[2] N. Andelman and Y. Mansour, " Auctions with budget constraints," in *SWAT04*, 2004, pp.26–38.

[3] S. Arora, and S. Safra, "Probabilistic checking of proofs: a new characterization of NP," *Journal of ACM*, 45(1), pp. 70–122, 1998.

[4] L. Blumrosen and N. Nisan, "On the computational power of iterative auctions I: Demand queries," in *2005 ACM Conference on Electronic Commerce*, 2005, pp. 29–43.

[5] Y. Bartal, R. Gonen, and N. Nisan, " Incentive compatible multi unit combinatorial auctions," in *TARK 03*, 2003, pp. 72–87.

[6] Wenbin Chen, Jiangtao Meng, "Approximation Algorithms for k Duplicates Combinatorial Auctions with Subadditive Bidders," in *COCOA 2007*, LNCS 4616, pp.163–170.

[7] P. Cramton, Y. Shoham, and R. Steinberg (editors). *Combinatorial Auctions*, MIT Press, 2005.

[8] S. Dobzinski, N. Nisan, and M. Schapira, "Approximation algorithm for combinatorial auctions with complement-free bidders," *Proceedings of 37th Annual ACM Symposium on Theory of Computing,* 2005, pp. 610–618.

[9] S. Dobzinski, N. Nisan, and M. Schapira, "Approximation algorithm for combinatorial auctions with complement-free bidders," *Math. Oper. Res.* 35(1), pp. 1–13, 2010.

[10] S. Dobzinski, M. Schapira, " An improved approximation algorithm for combinatorial auctions with submodular bidders," *Proceedings of the Seventeenth Annual ACM-SIAM Symposium on Discrete Algorithms*, 2006, pp. 1064–1073.

[11] S. Dobzinski, M. Schapira, "Optimal upper and lower approximation bound for k-duplicates combinatorial auctions," 2005, Working paper.

[12] U. Feige, " On maximizing welfare when utility functions are subadditive," *Proceedings of the 38th Annual ACM Symposium on Theory of Computing,* 2006, 41–50.

[13] U. Feige, "On maximizing welfare when utility functions are subadditive," *SIAM J. Comput.* 39(1), pp. 122–142, 2009.

[14] U. Feige, J. Vondrák, " Approximation algorithms for allocation problems: Improving the factor of $1-\frac{1}{e}$," *FOCS'06*, 2006, pp. 267–276.

[15] T. Hofmeister, H. Lefmann, "Approximating maximum independent sets in uniform hypergraphs," *Proceedings of the Twenty-Third Mathematical Foundations of Computer Science*, 1998, pp. 562–570.

[16] S. Khot, R. Lipton, E. Markakis and A. Mehta, "Inapproximability results for combinatorial auctions with submodular utility functions," *WINE 2005*, 2005, pp. 92–101.

[17] B. Lehmann, D. Lehmann, and N. Nisan, "Combinatorial auctions with decreasing marginal utilities," In *2001 ACM conference on electronic commerce*, 2001, pp. 18–28.

[18] D. Lehmanm, L. O'Callaghan, and Y. Shoham, " Truth revelation in approximately efficient combinatorial auctions," In *1999 ACM Conference On Electronic Commerce*, 1999, pp.96–102.

[19] A. Mehta, A. Saberi, U. Vazirani and V. Vazirani, "Adwords and generalized online matching," *46th Annual IEEE Symposium on Foundations of Computer Science* , 2005, pp. 264-273.

[20] N. Nisan and I. Segal, " The communication requirements of efficient allocations and supporting prices," *Journal of Economic Theory*, 129(1), pp. 192–224, 2006.

[21] T. Sandholm, "An algorithm for optimal winner determination in combinatorial auctions," In *IJCAI'99*, 1999, pp. 542–547.

[22] Jan Vondrák, "Optimal approximation for the submodular welfare problem in the value oracle model," *Proceedings of the 40th Annual ACM Symposium on Theory of Computing*, 2008, pp. 67-74.

Optimising Computations for Evaluating Ising and Potts Model Partition Functions by Exact Enumeration

K.A. Hawick and D.P. Playne
Computer Science, Massey University, North Shore 102-904, Auckland, New Zealand
email: {k.a.hawick, d.p.playne }@massey.ac.nz
Tel: +64 9 414 0800 Fax: +64 9 441 8181

April 2013

ABSTRACT

The Ising and Potts discrete lattice are useful baselines of comparison for many systems and theoretical calculations in statistical physics. While these models are traditionally studied using Monte Carlo sampling techniques it is also useful to exactly enumerate their partition functions using brute-force coding techniques. Recent advances in bitwise manipulation and parallel processing technology have made these techniques computationally feasible for the Q=3,4 state Potts model as well as the 2 state Ising spin model. We report on bit-packing and graphical processing unit implementations to improve the number of model states that can be exactly enumerated per second and discuss implications for uses of this approach with various observables.

KEY WORDS
partition function; enumeration; brute force; summation; multicore, GPU.

1 Introduction

The Ising model [17] is a well studied statistical mechanics model of a magnetic system exhibiting a phase transition [33]. The Ising model has been very widely used as a baseline of comparison for many real systems, theoretical [21,34] and simulation models [16] in statistical and solid state physics [31], and in other areas such as neural models of the brain and complex networks such as polymer systems [22]. The Potts model [30] extends the Ising system by allowing more than just two simple spin states. The Ising and Potts models are both formulated as a discrete and regular lattice of individual spins that can take on a number of different values but which will align (ferromagnetic model) or anti-align (anti ferromagnetic model) with their nearest neighbouring sites. The degree of alignment changes drastically at a critical temperature - known as the Curie temperature for real systems [38]. Above T_c the spins are still random with no large spatial structure, whereas below T_c large droplets and regions of aligned spins spontaneously form.

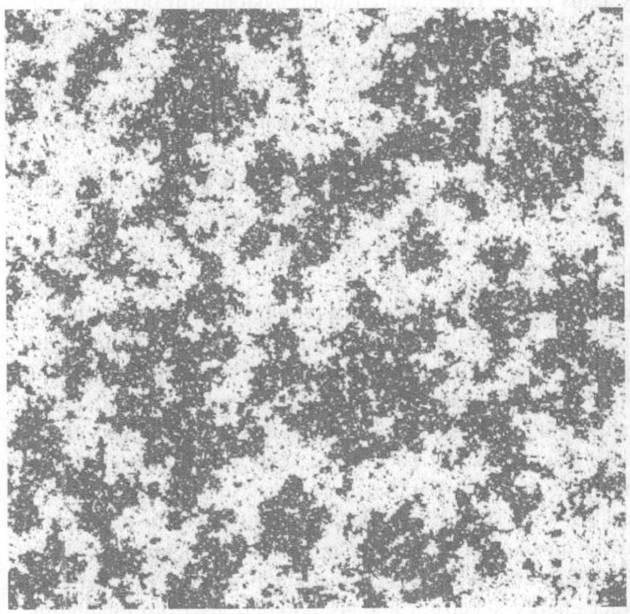

Figure 1: Long range clusters in a Critical 512^2 Ising model.

Figure 1 shows a sample Ising model system around its critical temperature. These models are usually studied using Monte Carlo sampling techniques [6, 7, 15, 25]. A model system is initialised at a high temperature with uniformly random spins and then quenched to a particular temperature T of interest and an algorithm like those of Metropolis or Glauber is used to allow the system to relax or equilibrate at that temperature. Measurements can be made on the simulated system and if the transition probabilities for the changes are chosen correctly according to a Boltzmann energy factor the procedure samples the various discrete starts according to their importance or probability of occurrence.

It is useful however to attempt to evaluate the partition function [11,20,32] – or sum over the individual states – of these models directly. The number of states M_2 of the 2 state Ising model grows as $m = 2^N$ where $N = L^d$ is the number of spin sites. M grows very fast indeed and the system shown in Figure 1 has $N = 512^2$ spin sites and so has 2^262144 different discrete states in its configuration space. The number of states in a Q-state Potts model system grows even faster – as Q^N. It is not feasible to enumerate the states explicitly for such a large system, but nevertheless it is valuable to explore changes to the partition function by studying small systems.

A great deal of work was done in the 20th Century in attempting to evaluate Ising model partition functions [13] for small systems [19] and has covered various model sizes [5] and special cases to try to understand for example finite size effects [2]. The Ising model has been solved analytically for the 2 dimensional case although it is still instructive to compare its known properties with those that result from enumerating its partition function on small square lattice Ising systems [23]. The 3 dimensional system still poses a challenge and its properties have only been approximately evaluated using simulation techniques. It is therefore of great and continued interest to understand the properties of a 3 dimensional Ising system using even a partial enumeration of its partition function [3, 4, 29].

There is also continued interest in exactly enumerating other systems such as the Potts model either directly [10, 24] or using symmetries or other approaches to restrict the state space traversed [9, 36].

Recently however advances in parallel processing technologies have allowed us to enumerate the states in small Potts systems. Our focus in this present paper is to investigate the computational feasibility of exact enumerations of 2 and 3 dimensional Ising and Potts systems using ordinary programming techniques; bit packing to keep the data structures in memory; and data parallel techniques using graphical processing units (GPUs). A decade of advances in processing power means that what were month long calculations in the 1990s are now feasible in a matter of hours. We obtain the exact energy spectrum and its populations from evaluating the partition function [1] but these new techniques open up scope for tracking more elaborate observables than just the energy as part of the traversal of the model's state space.

We focus on the zero field Ising [37] and Potts system but finite field versions of the models also offer scope for further work. Other related problems such as the inverse Ising model [27] involving deduction of the temperature from observed state samples, may also benefit from improved partition enumeration information. We believe that enumerations of the individual component size histograms may give insights into droplet formation and noise and fluctuations [12] in the model.

Our article is structured as follows: In Section 2 we briefly summarise the Ising and Potts models before giving a description of the statistical mechanical partition functions in Section 3. We describe our implementation methods using bit packing to keep data structures in memory cache and graphical processing unit data parallelism in Section 4. We present some timing and performance results and some preliminary partition function spectra for the Potts system in Section 5. We discuss the computational scope for this technique in Section 6 and offer some tentative conclusions and ideas for further study in Section 7.

2 Ising & Potts Models

The Ising model is formulated as a set of spin variables $\sigma_i = \pm 1$ arranged on a lattice - usually on a d-dimensional grid of size $N = L^d$ where length L is as large as can practically be simulated.

The energy functional or Hamiltonian of the Ising model is:

$$\mathcal{H} = -\mathcal{J} \sum_{\langle i,j \rangle} \sigma_i \sigma_j \qquad (1)$$

This has no explicit time dependence or dynamical scheme associated with it, and so one must be imposed artificially. We do not give details of the normal Monte Carlo dynamical sampling approach here as it is well described in the literature [7, 8].

The main point to emphasise for the work reported in this present paper is that each spin is independent and in the case of the Ising model can take on $Q = 2$ states. A small Ising system of for example $N = 4^2, 5^2$ still has a considerable amount of symmetry present in it. There are a finite number of possible energy levels and they have a large degree of degeneracy - that is a great many of the possible arrangements of the spin variables in the system leads to the same energy level.

The Potts model extends the Ising model by allowing the "spins" to take on a discrete range of integer values. The consequence is that for a Q state system the number of possible arrangements of spin values goes as a power of Q which obviously grows even faster for high Q.

3 Partition Function

The thermodynamic partition function or sum over the states of the system is usually denoted as Z and is given by:

$$Z_N(T) = \sum_{\sigma_1} \sum_{\sigma_2} \cdots \sum_{\sigma_N} \exp\left(-\mathcal{H}(\{\sigma_i\})/k_B T\right) \qquad (2)$$

where each degree of freedom σ_i takes the 2 values 0,1 for the Ising model or the Q values for the Q-state Potts extension of the Ising model. There are in fact a great deal of configurations that have identical energies due to symmetries and so the partition function can be expressed as:

$$Z_N(T) = \sum_l g_l \exp\left(-E_l/k_B T\right) \qquad (3)$$

Where the sum is over all the energy levels labelled by l, and each level has degeneracy g_l.

The exact pattern of degeneracies varies somewhat for the small systems we are able to enumerate depending upon whether they are even or odd in their lengths.

Since our system is discrete we can evaluate them by building up an exact histogram of how many states fall into each energy level. This exact histogram can then be used to evaluate other statistical and theoretical properties of the model. Once the partition function [14] or an approximation to it is obtained there are other techniques such as locating its zeros [18] that can be applied to make further deductions on the model properties. In this present paper we only evaluate the energy level degeneracies and use this as a means of scoping the computational effort and attainable performance to make further studies.

This is a powerful technique but its use is limited by the rapid growth of the number of states $M_S = Q^{N=L^d}$ in the model. In practice we have been limited by computer clock speeds and memory performance to only very small systems sizes. We can however explore various computational optimization techniques to speed up this calculation so that new Q values and higher system sizes might be explored.

4 Enumeration of States

The easiest method of enumerating through all the possible combination of spin variables σ_i is to create an array of integer values to represent the system. The possible system states can be generated by iterating through every combination of values in this array. For an Ising model each site can be {0,1} while for a Potts model each site can have the values {0..Q-1}.

Listing 1: Array enumeration algorithm uses an array `spin` to store all of the system states and a series of `for` loops to iterate through the possible states. The array n stores the indexes of each site's neighbours and NORTH and WEST are used as indexes into this array.

```
int spin[N];
for(spin[0]=0; spin[0]<Q; spin[0]++)
...
for(spin[N-1]=0; spin[N-1]<Q; spin[N-1]++) {
  long long E = 0;
  for(int i = 0; i < N; i++) {
    E+=(spin[i]==spin[n[i][NORTH]])?-1:1;
    E+=(spin[i]==spin[n[i][WEST] ])?-1:1;
  }
  histogram[E+offset]++;
}
```

The energy of a system can be calculated from the number of like-like bonds in the system. To determine the number of like-like bonds in a system, all the sites in the array must be iterated through and compared to the neighbouring values. This is slow for practical reasons however and if we can get all the neighbours and spin state information in cache it will be considerably faster to traverse than if main memory accesses are needed. An example of the code to iterate through every possible state for a system stored in an array and calculate the energy of each system can be seen in Listing 1.

4.1 Bit Enumeration

An Ising system is a series of spins that are either up or down, and so each site can be represented by a single bit. For an Ising system that is small enough to be enumerated, these bits can be stored in a single 64-bit integer. A 64-bit integer can represent an Ising system up to a maximum size of 8x8 or 4x4x4. The process of generating the different Ising configurations is then simplified to iterating through the possible integer values $\{0..N-1\}$ where N is the system size.

When an Ising system is represented by a single integer, the process of calculating the total energy of the system can be reduced to a series of bit-logic expressions. To do this expressions must be formulated to create integer values that represent the neighbours of each cell. The number of neighbours that must be calculated will be the same as the number of dimensions of the system. This is because the energy must be calculated for each bond in the system. The left bond of one atom is the same as the right bond of the other atom and thus only needs to be calculated once.

Logic expressions are also formulated to determine how many like-like bonds each atom has. In two dimensions only the cases where the atom and two like-like bonds or no like-like bonds because the only other option is to have one of each in which case the energy is 0. This process results in two integers, the first which has a 1 for every atom that has two like-like bonds and the second has a 1 for every atom with zero like-like bonds. The number of 1s in each of these integers can then be counted and multiplied by 2 and -2 respectively to give the total energy of the system. A code listing in C showing this process for a two-dimensional Ising enumeration is shown in Listing 2.

Listing 2: Bit enumeration algorithm stores the system state as an `long long` and iterates through this integer value. A series of bit masks and logic operations are used to compute the energy of the system. `__builtin_popcountl()` is a built in CPU function to count set bits in an int.

```
long long n1, n2, e1, e2, s1, s2;
for(long long i = 0; i < N; i++) {
  //Calculate neighbours
  n1 = ((i&n1_mask1) >> X) |
       ((i&n1_mask2) << ((Y-1)*X));
  n2 = ((i&n2_mask1) >> 1) |
       ((i&n2_mask2) << (X-1));
  //Calculate Energy
  s1 = (  (i^n1)  &  (i^n2));
  s2 = ((~(i^n1)) & (~(i^n2)));
  e1 = __builtin_popcountl(s1&e1_mask);
  e2 = __builtin_popcountl(s2&e2_mask);
  E = ((e1*2) - (e2*2));
}
```

In this code listing, `n1` and `n2` represent the neighbours in the X and Y dimensions respectively. Each one can be calculated by extracting values using masks and shift operations. Then the values `s1` and `s2` are calculated which represent the number of atoms with two like-like bonds and no like-like bonds. These are calculated using XOR, AND and NOT operations. Finally built in CPU functions are used to count the number of bits in each integer and multiplies them by 2 and -2 to give the total energy. This process is shown for a 3x3 Ising system in Figure 2.

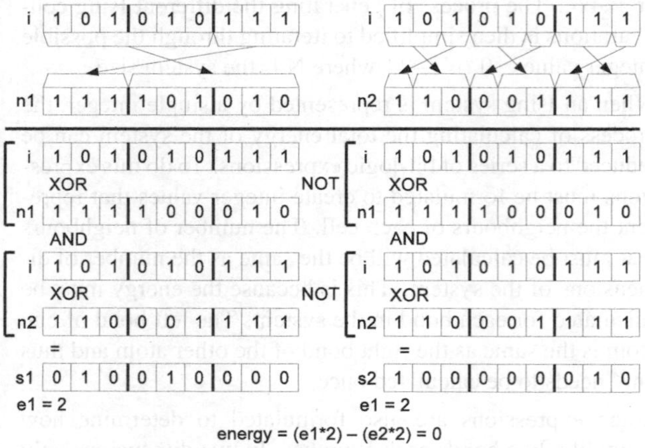

Figure 2: The process of calculating the energy of a 3x3 system state **i** in bit representation.

4.2 CUDA Implementation

The enumeration of the Ising model is a perfect candidate for parallelisation as the energy calculation for each state can be performed completely independently of the other states. The most simple approach for enumerating the Ising model on a GPU is to launch a single thread for each possible system state. Each thread's unique thread id then represents the Ising system state it is measuring in bit format. Each thread can then perform the same bit logic expressions as the CPU bit-enumeration implementation to calculate the energy of the system.

CUDA devices with compute capability 3.0 and above support a maximum of 1024 threads per block and a maximum grid size of $(2^{31}-1)$ in the X dimension and 65535 in the Y and Z dimensions [28]. This easily allows for enough threads to enumerate systems of a size that can be computed in a realistic time frame. Because the masks used in the neighbouring value calculations are exactly the same for every thread, they are stored in constant memory to minimise global memory transactions.

Once the energy of a system state has been calculated they must be collected together into the energy histogram. Due to the parallel nature of the computation this must done carefully using atomic instructions to ensure the correct values are saved in the histogram. One option that was explored was for each block to collect a local energy histogram in shared memory and then upload it to the global energy histogram once all threads in the block had finished their computation. However, in practice this was found to decrease the performance of the enumeration.

Listing 3: Bit enumeration CUDA kernel to compute the energy histogram of an Ising system. The bit masks are stored in constant memory and atomicAdd is used to update the energy histogram stored in global memory. The function `__popcll()` is a built-in GPU function to count the number of set bits in an integer..

```
__global__ void kernel(
        unsigned long long *histogram) {
  long long i = (((long long)blockIdx.x *
                  (long long)blockDim.x) +
                  (long long)threadIdx.x)*
                   STATES_PER_THREAD;
  for(int j=0; j<STATES_PER_THREAD; j++){
    long long n1,n2,s1,s2,e1,e2,E;
    n1 = ((i&n1_mask1[0])>>1LL)  |
         ((i&n1_mask2[0])<<(X-1LL));
    n2 = ((i&n2_mask1[0])>>X)    |
         ((i&n2_mask2[0])<<((Y-1LL)*X));

    //Calculate Energy
    e1 = ((i^n1) & (i^n2));
    e2 = ((~(i^n1)) & (~(i^n2)));
    s1 = __popcll(e1&c_e1_mask[0]);
    s2 = __popcll(e2&c_e2_mask[0]);
    E = ((s1*2) - (s2*2));
    atomicAdd(&histogram[E+offset],1ULL);
    i++;
  }
}
```

The final method of tuning the CUDA implementation of the enumeration is to vary the number of states each thread is responsible for computing. Rather than launching one thread for each system state, it is more efficient for each thread to compute the energies of multiple system states (especially for larger system sizes such as 6x6) as it avoids the overhead of managing and launching extra threads. For this system size it was found that computing 256 system states per thread was the most efficient and provided a performance gain of approximately 7% over computing one state per thread.

5 Performance Results

The performance results of the different enumeration implementations from Section 4 have been gathered using an 3.50GHz Intel i7-2700K using GNU gcc 4.5 with optimisations and an NVIDIA GeForce GTX680 using CUDA 5.0. The results of testing these three implementations are presented in Table 1.

From this table it can be seen that naive array implementation provides the worst performance, for the largest Ising

Q	system size	Array Enumeration time (sec)	Bit Enumeration time (sec)	CUDA Enumeration time (sec)
2	4x4	0.005129	0.002707	0.000103
	5x5	1.39604	0.571924	0.024464
	6x6	4249.92	1220.14	42.7585
	3x3x3			0.146955
	4x3x3			93.0353
	4x4x3			515215
3	3x3	0.000684		
	4x4	1.42689		
4	3x3	0.009277		
	4x4	140 629		

Table 1: Performance comparison of the 3 implementations.

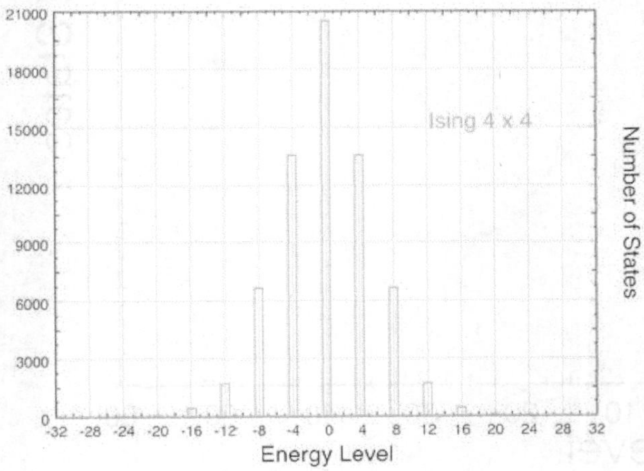

Figure 3: Energy Spectra with exact population numbers of states for 4x4 periodic Ising model

system size tested (6x6) it took this implementation 70 minutes to complete which means it can measure approximately 16 million states per second. Compressing the system state into a single integer and using bit logic expressions reduced this time to 20 minutes which means the bit enumeration method can measure approximately 56 million states per second. Computing the bit logic expressions on a GPU using CUDA reduced the compute time to under 45 seconds and gave and average of 1.6 billion measurements per second. These results mean that enumerating the Ising model on a GPU can provide a speedup of approximately $\approx$ 100x over the array enumeration and $\approx$ 30x over the bit enumeration.

Figure 3 shows the energy histogram of all the possible states of a 4x4 Ising model. It can be seen from this figure that not all energy states are possible in an Ising system and that for a size such as this with even lengths in each dimension the histogram is symmetric. For system sizes with odd lengths the histogram will not be symmetric as it is always possible for all the states in a system to be the same but for an Ising system there is not always a configuration where every spin is different to all of its neighbours.

The number of states that fill each energy level grow very rapidly but it is also important to note the combinatorially large range of scales between the most probable energy level and that of less probable but non-empty one. For this reason it is useful to plot the populations on a logarithmic scale.

Figure 4 shows the periodic Ising models of size $N = 4^2, 5^2$ plotted on a logarithmic scale. We see the characteristic parabolic shape which agrees with other work such as that of Beale [1]. Our small system show distortions from the parabolic shape - these are due to finite size effects and manifest themselves as pinches in the shape at th side wings. It is also interesting to note that the 5^2 system is not symmetric., This is due to checkerboard pattern high energy configurations - where like like spins manage to avoid one another. Such checkerboard patterns require an even number of spins in each dimension so they are present in the spectrum for 4^2 but not 5^2.

Figure 4 also shows data for the Potts system with $Q = 3$. We see that the parabola shifts so its peak is now around energy of 10 instead of around zero. Also there is an asymmetry for both the 4^2 and 5^2 Potts systems that are linked to the odd $Q = 3$ number of states.

6 Discussion

Computational capabilities have moved on in recent years and even using a very simple brute force enumeration of states without exploiting any symmetries we can tackle Potts systems with $Q = 3, 4, ...$ that would not have been computationally feasible a decade ago. We obtained some significant performance enhancements just by packing the data structures into bit patterns instead of decomposing as conventional integers or long integers. This indicates how sensitive calculations on modern processors are to the cache and memory management system. Modern computer systems have somewhat faster clock speeds, and somewhat faster memory management systems than they did a decade ago, but neither of these two factors has improved as much as might have been hoped, extrapolating from Moore's law [26] and the previous three decades. The availability of an order of magnitude more processing cores allows a direct factor of ten in speedup as state enumeration does parallelise almost perfectly by splitting the task into independent jobs.

A key result is that we have managed to obtain nearly two orders of magnitude of performance increase using a GPU accelerator. There would appear to be significant potential in a cluster of CPUs, with multiple CPU cores and/or multiple GPUs to tackle this sort of enumeration problem.

While many researchers have invented special tricks and symmetries that can be exploited in the exact enumeration of the energy states, it is important that we not be wholly reliant on such symmetries that may not apply to other observables such as component cluster, monomers, and other

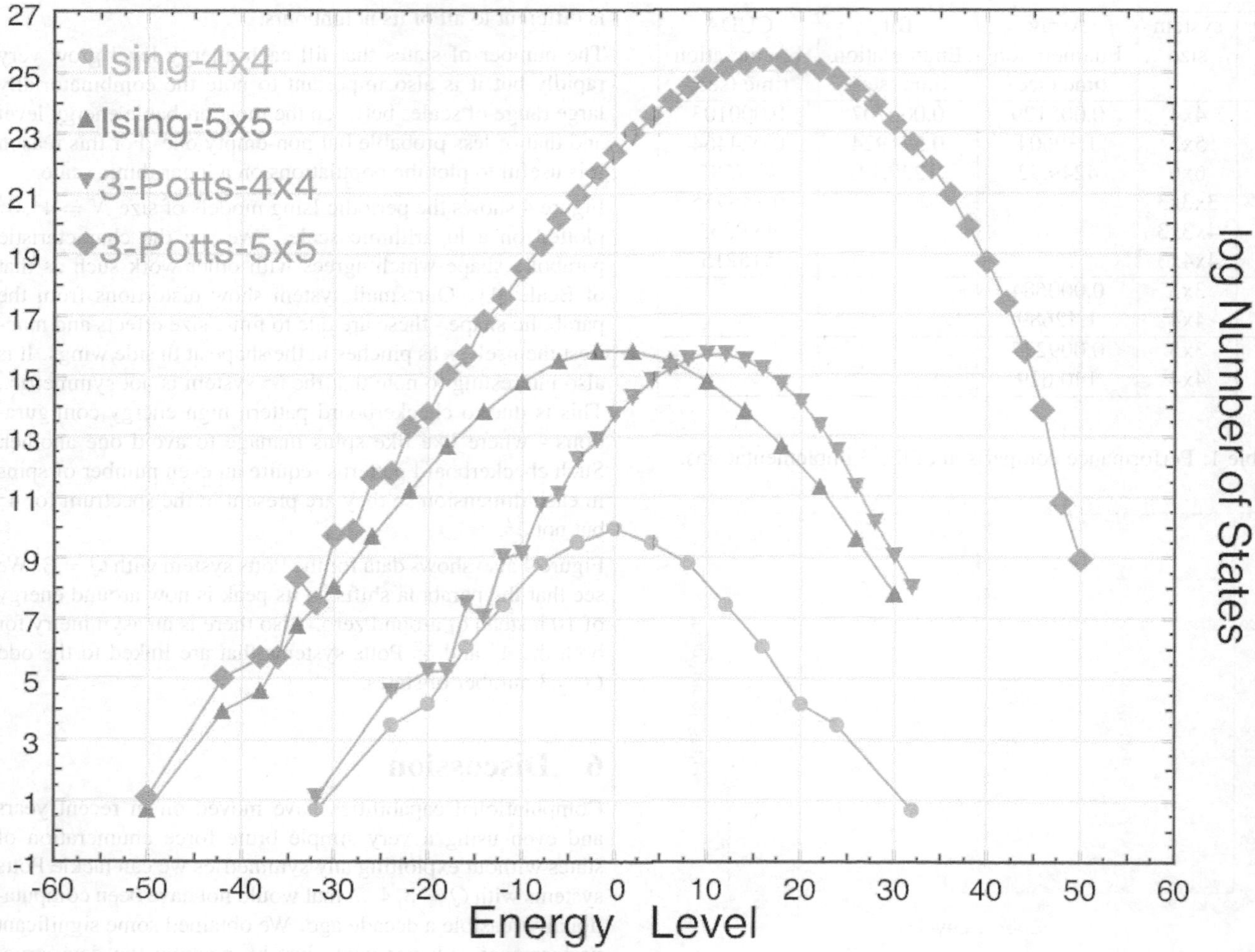

Figure 4: Energy Spectra for 2-Dimensional periodic Potts and Ising models on 4x4 and 5x5 lattices, plotted on log scale.

lattice pattern operators.

It is likely to be useful to identify histograms of component clusters as they are used in Monte Carlo renormalisation calculations on the Ising and related model. Components also play a significant part in cluster update algorithms such as those of Wolff [39] and of Swendsen and Wang [35]. It is likely to be instructive to determine what the relationship is between cluster size, family and scaling and so forth, and these update processes.

7 Conclusion

In summary we have explored three different methods for enumerating the Ising model on a CPU and a GPU. The bit enumeration method of provided the best performance results by reducing the amount of memory required to represent a system state and by performing the energy calculation as a series of bit-logic expressions. This enumeration method improved the performance on the CPU from 15 million states per second to 56 million states per second. The GPU provided the best overall performance and was able to measure 1.6 billion states per second, 100x faster than the CPU array enumeration method.

We have managed to obtain some preliminary results for small Potts model systems and identified interesting asymmetries and other features in the Potts exact partition function energy spectrum that are worthy of further exploration. We hope to be able to experiment with three dimensional Potts systems for $Q = 3, 4$ by parallel job decomposition of the enumeration task. We also hope to be able to incorporate fast code for identifying other oberservables such as the number of monomers and component clusters in small Ising and Potts systems.

There is also scope for future work in formulating the bit-logic expressions for computing the Potts model using the bit-enumeration method on both the CPU and the GPU as well as extending the bit-enumeration method to explore the Ising and Potts model in three-dimensions. The analysis of the model could also be extended to calculate more than just the energy of a system but also the count the number of monomers, dimers, number of clusters or their sizes.

References

[1] Beale, P.D.: Exact distribution of energies in the two-dimensional ising model. Phys. Rev. Lett. 76, 78–81 (1996)

[2] Bhanot, G., Duke, D., Salvador, R.: Finite-size scaling and the three-dimensional ising model. Phys. Rev. B 33(11), 7841–7844 (Jun 1986)

[3] Bhanot, G.: A numerical method to compute exactly the partition function with application toz(n) theories in two dimensions. J. Stat. Phys. 60, 55–75 (1990)

[4] Bhanot, G., Salvador, R., Black, S., Carter, P., Toral, R.: Accurate estimate of nu for the three-dimensional ising model from a numerical measurement of its partition function. Phys. Rev. Lett. 59, 803–806 (1987)

[5] Bhanot, G., Sastry, S.: Solving the Ising model Exactly on a 5x5x4 Lattice using the Connection Machine. J. Stat. Phys. 60(3/4), 333–346 (Nov 1990), thinking machines Preprint CS89-10

[6] Binder, K., Heermann, D.W.: Monte Carlo Simulation in Statistical Physics. Springer-Verlag (1997)

[7] Binder, K. (ed.): Monte Carlo Methods in Statistical Physics. Topics in Current Physics, Springer-Verlag, 2 edn. (1986), number 7

[8] Binder, K. (ed.): Applications of the Monte Carlo Method in Statistical Physics. Topics in Current Physics, Springer-Verlag (1987)

[9] Chang, S.C., Shrock, R.: Exact partition function for the potts model with next-nearest neighbour couplings on arbitrary-length ladders. Int. J. Mod. Phys. 15, 443–478 (2001)

[10] Chang, S.C., Shrock, R.: Some exact results on the potts model partition function in a magnetic field. Tech. rep., National Cheng Kung University, Taiwan (2009)

[11] van Dijk, W., Lobo, C., MacDonald, A., Bhaduri, R.K.: Zeros of the partition function and phase transition. arXiv 1303.4770, McMaster University, Canada (2013)

[12] Droz, M.: Noise and fluctuations in equilibrium and non-equilibrium statistical mechanics. Tech. rep., University of Geneva (2001)

[13] Fronczak, A., Fronczak, P.: Exact expression for the number of states in lattice models. Tech. rep., Warsaw University of Technology, Poland (2013)

[14] Galluccio, A., Loebl, M., Vondrak, J.: New algorithm for the ising problem: Partition function for finite lattice graphs. Phys. Rev. Lett. 84, 5924–5927 (2000)

[15] Hastings, W.K.: Monte carlo sampling methods using mrkov chains and their applications. Biometrika 57, 97–109 (1970)

[16] Hawick, K.A.: Domain Growth in Alloys. Ph.D. thesis, Edinburgh University (1991)

[17] Ising, E.: Beitrag zur Theorie des Ferromagnetismus. Zeitschrift fuer Physik 31, 253–258 (1925)

[18] Janke, W., Kenna, R.: Analysis of the Density of Partition Function Zeroes - A Measure for Phase Transition Strength, pp. 97–101. Springer (2002), computer Simulation Studies in Condensed-Matter Physics XIV

[19] Kaufman, B.: Crystal statistics ii. partition function evaluated by spinor analysis. Phys. Rev. 76, 1232–1243 (1949)

[20] Kim, S.Y.: Exact partition functions of the ising model on l x l square lattices with free boundary conditions up to l = 22. J. Korean Physical Society 62, 214–219 (2013)

[21] Kirkpatrick, S., Gelatt, C.D., Vecchi, M.P.: Optimization by simulated annealing. Science 220(4598), 671–680 (May 1983)

[22] Lee, J.H., Kim, S.Y., Lee, J.: Exact partition function zeros of a polymer on a simple-cubic lattice. Phys. Rev. E 86, 011802–1–7 (2012)

[23] Malarz, K., Magdon-Maksymowicz, M.S., Maksymowicz, A.Z., Kawecka-Magiera, B., Kulakowski, K.: New algorithm for the computation of the partition function for the ising model on a square lattice. Int. J. Mod. Phys. C 14(5), 689–694 (2003)

[24] McDonald, L.M., Moffatt, I.: On the potts model partition function in an external field. J. Stat. Phys. 146, 1288–1302 (2012)

[25] Metropolis, N., Rosenbluth, A.W., Rosenbluth, M.N., Teller, A.H., Teller, E.: Equation of state calculations by fast computing machines. J. Chem. Phys. 21(6), 1087–1092 (Jun 1953)

[26] Moore, G.E.: Cramming more components onto integrated circuits. Electronics Magazine April, 4 (1965)

[27] Nguyen, H.C., Berg, J.: Mean-field theory for the inverse ising problem at low temperatures. Phys. Rev. Lett. 109, 050602–1–5 (2012)

[28] NVIDIA: CUDA C Programming Guide, 5.0 edn. (October 2012)

[29] Pearson, R.B.: Partition function of the ising model on the periodic 4x4x4 lattice. Phys. Rev. B 26, 6285–6290 (1982)

[30] Potts, R.B.: Some generalised order-disorder transformations. Proc. Roy. Soc pp. 106–109 (1951), received July

[31] Raychaudhuri, S.: Kinetic Monte Carlo Simulation in Biophysics and Systems Biology (2013)

[32] Sangaranarayanan, M.V.: Two-dimensional ising model in a finite magnetic field for the square lattice of infinite sites-partition function and magnetization. arXiv 1302.1084, Indian Institute of Technology, Madras (Jan 2013)

[33] Stanley, H.E.: Introduction to phase transitions and critical phenomena. Oxford Science Publications (1987)

[34] Strasberg, P., Schaller, G., Brandes, T., Esposito, M.: Thermodynamics of a physical model implementing a maxwell daemon. Phys. Rev. Lett. 110, 040601–1–5 (January 2013)

[35] Swendsen, R.H., Wang, J.S.: Nonuniversal critical dynamics in Monte-Carlo simulations. Phys. Rev. Lett. 58(2), 86–88 (Jan 1987)

[36] Vernier, E., Jacobsen, J.L.: Corner free energies and boundary effects for ising, potts and fully-packed loop models on the square and triangular lattices. arXiv 1110.2158, Ecole Normale Superieure, France (2011)

[37] Vinothkumar, M., Nandhini, G., Sangaranarayanan, M.V.: Partition function of the two-dimensional nearest neighbour ising models for finite lattices in a non-zero magnetic field. J. Chem. Sci. 124, 105–113 (2012)

[38] Wohlfarth, E.P.: Theory and experiment in metallic magnetism. J. Magn. and. Magn. Mat. 45, 1–8 (1984)

[39] Wolff, U.: Collective Monte Carlo Updating for Spin Systems. Phys. Lett. 228, 379 (1989)

A Functional Approach to Finding Answer Sets

Bryant Nelson, Josh Archer, and Nelson Rushton
Texas Tech Dept. of Computer Science
(bryant.nelson | josh.archer | nelson.rushton) @ ttu.edu

Texas Tech University
Department of Computer Science
Box 43104
Lubbock, TX 79409-3104

Submitted to FCS 2013

Keywords: Functional Programming, Answer Set Prolog, Logic Programming

Abstract: A naive answer set solver was implemented in the functional programming language SequenceL, and its performance compared to mainstream solvers on a set of standard benchmark problems. Implementation was very rapid (25 person hours) and the resulting program only 400 lines of code. Nonetheless, the algorithm was tractable and obtained parallel speedups. Performance, though not pathologically poor, was considerably slower (around 20x) than that of mainstream solvers (CLASP, Smodels, and DLV) on all but one benchmark problem.

1. Introduction

In his 1990 paper "Why Functional Programming Matters", John Hughes argues that functional programming allows for an improvement in productivity due to improved modularity. Through the encoding of the solutions to many non-trivial problems we have been convinced of Hughes' hypothesis. We set out to further test this hypothesis by encoding an Answer Set Solver in SequenceL. We hypothesize that a functional language would allow the programmer to implement an Answer Set Solver more quickly than a procedural language, and that the resulting program would be more readable and understandable.

Finding answer sets is an NP-Complete problem, and over the last few decades a few solvers have been developed that tackle this problem. The current juggernauts in this area are the DLV, CLASP, and SMODELS solvers, all of which are very efficient. The problem would seem to benefit from a parallelized solver, yet CLASP only has a branch (CLASPar) dedicated to this, and DLV has been "experimenting" with parallelization in their grounder [DLVPar]. Moreover, all of the competitive solvers are written in C/C++ and span over hundreds of large files.

SequenceL is a high-abstraction, auto-parallelizing, functional language. It is auto-parallelizing in the sense that programs, written in a high-level, declarative language without concern for command execution, are then compiled into optimized multicore C++. This abstraction frees the programmer from the burden of manually implementing a parallel solution and allows them to focus on solving the problem at hand.

SequenceL also appears to be very easy to read, even to those who have never programmed in SequenceL. By *easy to read* we mean that given a sufficient level of understanding of the language's syntax, the relationship between the syntax and semantics of statements is *obvious enough*. The designers of SequenceL had simplicity in mind when developing the groundwork for the language. They aimed to accomplish this by the "ruthless pursuit of utmost simplicity" with respect to the language's complexity.

SequenceL was chosen as the implementation language in order to, in addition to the above, explore the effect of auto-parallelizations on a naturally parallelizable problem.

We hypothesized that a naïve functional ASP Solver could be developed more quickly, and be more readable than a procedural implementation of the same. We also hypothesized that automatic parallelizations would allow the solver to perform within an acceptable range of time requirements for some problems.

2. Motivation

The problem of finding answer sets of non-disjunctive Answer Set Programs is an area that has had substantial research over the past few decades. The declarative programming paradigm had, based on preliminary research, never been applied to this problem. Upon initial observations it was obvious that a simple answer set solving algorithm could be easily expressed declaratively. It was also apparent that this declarative implementation would also be considerably easier to read than a procedural implementation.

The methods of programming declaratively effectively involve envisioning what a solution to a problem looks like, formally specifying this solution, and directly implementing it. Therefore, if a solution to a problem (especially one that is computationally substantial) is already stated precisely, then encoding the declarative attempt at said solution appears to be easier than doing so procedurally. It appeared that this was the case with the algorithm chosen for finding answer sets: the algorithm [Gelfond 2013] was proven, stated at least partially as definitions rather than algorithms, and modular enough to suit a vision for a functionally written program.

Even before work began to write this solver, around the time we had looked at enough existing procedural solutions to intelligently speak about them, we had the hypothesis that a declarative solver would be easier to read when compared to the existing ones. From the use of SequenceL to solve other common problems, and by observing the massive size of the CLASP code, it was apparent that SequenceL implementation would exemplify the readability of a declarative approach.

Our literature survey revealed not a lot of work has been done on parallelization of Answer Set Program solving. The only parallel solver found was CLASPAR, created by the same people behind CLASP.

This solver used a master-slave based approach where the master would determine which sub-processes the slaves would handle in a very procedural way. It was apparent that a great deal more thought went into the parallelization of the algorithm than the solution itself.

All of these points led to experimenting with implementing an Answer Set Program solving algorithm in SequenceL, an auto-parallelizing high-level declarative programming language.

3. Methods

Algorithm Selection

The choice of algorithm was based on the criteria of simplicity, verifiability, and availability. An initial attempt was made to look at the algorithm that the current non-parallel version of CLASP encoded; this was done in an effort to create the best "apples-to-apples" comparison with a top solver. However, after a moderate amount of effort the actual algorithm could not be found and it was impossible to easily decipher what it was from just looking at the available source code. This was due to two major issues; the first was the sheer size of the program [insert actual size of the one we got], and the second was the fact that, in general, it is difficult to discern the algorithm from procedurally written code.

Initially, the idea of going with the DLV route of solving answer sets was considered, but it was decided against because that would involve creating a grounder and integrating it with the solver. It was decided that the grounding would be done by GRINGO. Once again, this was chosen to create an "apples-to-apples" comparison with the *solver*. Future work is planned for exploring a system which intelligently grounds atoms as needed, as opposed to grounding everything as most solvers currently do.

After exploring the other two options, it was decided to use the simplest algorithm possible, short of brute force guessing and checking, which was the algorithm found in [Gelfond 2013]. This algorithm is completely naive -- that is, it does nothing but find the answer set of a grounded Answer Set Programs with zero heuristics and with nothing more than the direct definition of Answer Set Programs. This algorithm had a proof of correctness, and was readily available for encoding.

Algorithm Implementation

The algorithm chosen is both sound and complete with respect to the domain, but parts of it were presented in different ways. Moreover, there were two major methods with which the pieces were described: *effective definitions* and *sequential algorithms*.

A *sequential algorithm* is one that lists a sequence of instructions that need to be executed in order to compute the desired result; this is the description of most commercial implementations. An *effective definition* is a mathematical definition that implicitly embodies an algorithm for computing the function it defines. For example; if we define $gcd(m, n)$ as the largest integer which is a divisor of *m* and a divisor of *n*, then this definition is not effective. On the other hand if $gcd(m, n)$ is defined as the largest integer in the closed interval [1,*m*] which is a divisor of *m* and a divisor of *n*, then the definition is effective because the search has been limited to a finite space

A SequenceL program is essentially a set of effective definitions. In the following example are two function specifications; the first (*Least*) is defined algorithmically, whereas the second (*IsAnswerSet*) is specified mostly by definitions.

```
function Least
  input: A definite program Π
  output: the answer set of Π
var X, X0 : set of atoms;
begin
  X := ∅;
  repeat
    X0 := X;
    X := TΠ(X);
  until X = X0;
  return X
end
```

```
function IsAnswerSet
  input: interpretation I and program Π
  output: true if I is an answer set of Π; false otherwise
begin
  Compute the reduct, Π^I of Π with respect to I;
  Compute an answer set, A, of Π^I;
  Check whether A = atoms(I) and return the result;
end;
```

Again, *Least* was specified algorithmically, and as such there was a bit of translation needed in order to encode this correctly in SequenceL. The effort needed in showing correctness of the encoded *Least* lies not in checking whether the translated description entails the SequenceL code (because this is *obvious*), but rather ensuring that the translation of the algorithmic description into a definition is correct.

```
function Least
  input: A definite program Π
  output: the answer set of Π
var X, X0 : set of atoms;
begin
  X := ∅;
  repeat
    X0 := X;
    X := TΠ(X);
  until X = X0;
  return X
end
```

$$Least(P,X_0) = \begin{cases} X \text{ when } X_0 = X \\ Least(P,X) \text{ otherwise} \end{cases}$$

$$\text{where } X = X_0 \cup T_{\Pi}(P,X_0)$$

```
Least(P(1), X0(1)) :=
    let
        X := remdups(X0 ++ TP(P, X0));
    in
        X when eq_bag(X, X0)
    else
        Least(P, X);
```

The ease with which the function *IsAnswerSet* was written was indispensable in the creation of this solver. As mentioned above, the actual translation from the specification into a definition is the bulk of the work; here that is already done and therefore the SequenceL encoding this is *obviously* correct.

```
function IsAnswerSet
  input: interpretation I and program Π
  output: true if I is an answer set of Π; false otherwise
begin
  Compute the reduct, Π^I of Π with respect to I;
  Compute an answer set, A, of Π^I;
  Check whether A = atoms(I) and return the result;
end;
```

```
IsAnswerSet(P(1), I(0)) :=
    let
        reduct := Reduct(P, I);
        A := AnswerSet(reduct);
    in
        eq_bag(A, I.PositiveLiterals);
```

If the specification can be mathematically proven to be correct, then the SequenceL code is as well by default.

Effective Definition vs. Algorithm

The following is an illustration of the difference between the definitional and algorithmic styles mentioned above; the *Reduct* is a well-known and integral concept for finding answer sets of programs, and it is defined with what appears to be a very procedural mindset.

Definition 2.2.4 (*Answer Sets, Part II*)

Let Π be an arbitrary program and S be a set of ground literals.

By Π^S we denote the program obtained from Π by:

1) *removing all rules containing not l such that $l \in S$;*

2) *removing all other premises containing not.*

It is easy to see that this *Reduct* is computed by performing these steps as specified, and in sequential order. This does not affect the nature of the result yielded; but it is stated procedurally. Compare this with the following equivalent specification:

Definition 2.2.4.2 (*Answer Sets, Part II*)

Let Π be an arbitrary program and S be a set of ground literals.

By Π^S we denote the program from Π consisting of:

1) *the positive part of all rules whose negative part $\cap S = \{\}$;*

Here, the *Reduct* clearly ***is*** something, namely the items satisfying *(1)*. This specification is declarative, it states what something consists of instead of the computation required to yield the desired result.

State of the Art

In order to compare the results of the SequenceL Answer Set Solver to the current state of the art, the solver was tested against the default CLASP, DLV, and SMODELS answer set solvers. SMODELS was included in an attempt to compare with one of the older solvers. Test cases were selected and the time necessary for the system to solve the grounded input was recorded (by grounded input, we mean the output of GRINGO that SLASP, CLASP, and Smodels all take as input).

The Potsdam group, who are the creators of CLASP, have a suite of benchmark problems on their website that range from toy problems like *Drosophila* to complicated real-world problems. Problems for our experiment were chosen randomly chosen from the set of problems in the Potsdam benchmarks satisfying two criteria: (1) the programs could be understood quickly, and (2) their solutions contained no choice rules. The reason for the omission of choice rules was the fact that our solver did not explicitly support them.

The following test cases were chosen:

- RedvsBlue
- Stable Marriage
- Hamiltonian Cycle
- Same Generation
- Reachability
- Ramsey Numbers
- Schur Decomposition

Test Results

On the whole the SequenceL solver ran slower than the mainstream solvers. This was to be expected considering that we implemented without optimizations. However, the SequenceL solver was able to outperform the mainstream solvers on one input program, called *RedBlue*. This ASP program, using pseudo-disjunction, resulted in a large number of possible answer sets, all of which were valid. This allowed the SequenceL solver to make better use of parallelization, and was not effected by heuristics. Since the heuristics used in the established solvers did not affect this problem, it was the only problem for which the algorithms were essentially equivalent, allowing a head to head comparison of language efficiency (SequenceL vs. C).

In most cases, though the SequenceL ASP Solver did not perform as well as the mainstream solvers, it still executed within a reasonable amount of time. For example, in the Hamiltonian Cycle problem the SequenceL ASP Solver performed considerably slower than the other solvers, but it still finished in a quarter of a second on average.

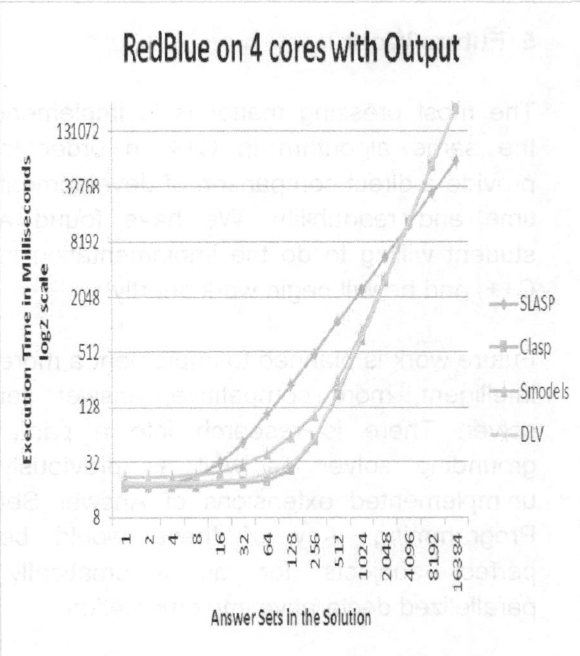

Source Code Comparison

The source code of the ASP Solver was presented to the Knowledge Representation group, a group of ASP experts, at Texas Tech University during an hour long seminar intended to be an introduction to SequenceL. The members of the audience had little to no knowledge of SequenceL. At the end of this seminar persons in the audience were able to make changes to the code that had significant positive effects on the performance of the solver.

The SequenceL solver was developed by two graduate students in less than a week. The total time spent in both planning and development was 25 hours. The first thing that had to be done was to convert the definitions from the algorithm that were not presented as effective definitions to such. This conversion took 3 hours to complete with both graduate students working at the same computer. Once all definitions were presented effectively implementation began, this is where the majority of time was spent. The implementation of the solver, in total, took 9 hours, of which 1 hour was spent on separate computers and 8 hours were spent on the same computer. It took one of the graduate students another 2 hours to write the necessary parsing and formatting functions. Finally, another 3 hours were spent debugging and error correcting. Debugging was also performed with both graduate students working at the same computer. The total time was calculated by weighting the joint efforts of the students on one computer by 1.5.

The final version of the solver consisted of less than 400 executable lines, in a single file of less than 29 kilobytes. This includes the code required to parse the output from GRINGO and format the output of the solver. In comparison, the SMODELS source consists of 32 files totaling over 150 kilobytes and the CLASP source consists of over 100 files totaling more than 1.5 megabytes.

Impact of Parallelization

Overall, in every test we ran on our solver that took longer than a second to execute, there was an average 15 times speed increase when going from 4 to 16 cores. This greater-than-linear speedup still remains to be explained.

The graph below shows the execution time of the SequenceL ASP Solver vs. the number of answer sets in the solution for the 4 core counts on which we tested. With 32763 answer sets, there was a 10-fold improvement between 4 cores and 16. It also shows a slowdown on small numbers of answer sets. This is because the overhead of setting up the threads outweighs the actual execution time.

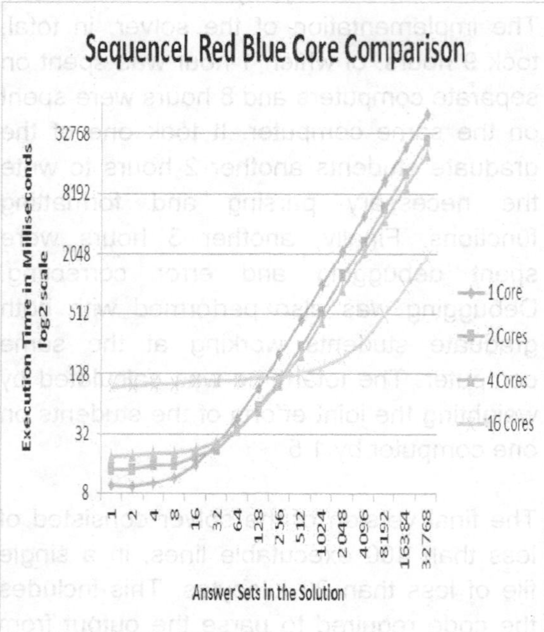

4. Conclusions

Due to the subjective nature of our hypothesis regarding simplicity and readability, we will present the results we collected and leave it to the reader to draw conclusions. We will also make available the source code of the SequenceL ASP Solver for closer inspection. We feel this experiment supports the claims made by Hughes and others that functional programming has a great positive impact on development time and readability. With regard to the hypothesis about automatic parallelizations, we feel that this experiment shows that automatic parallelizations allow a naïve algorithm implemented in SequenceL to perform within a range acceptable for a significant number of commercial applications.

5. Future Work

The most pressing matter is to implement the same algorithm in C++ in order to provide a direct comparison of development time and readability. We have found a student willing to do the implementation in C++, and he will begin work shortly.

Future work is planned to implement a more intelligent, more competitive, answer set solver. There is research into a partial grounding solver as well as previously unimplemented extensions of Answer Set Programming. Any of these would be perfect subjects for an automatically-parallelized declarative implementation.

There is also a continuing effort to apply SequenceL to other fields. Currently these fields include Bioinformatics, Language Parsing and Compilation, and Numerical Analysis.

6. Bibliography

[Gelfond 2013] Michael Gelfond and Yulia Kahl. *Knowledge Representation, Reasoning, and the Design of Intelligent Agents*. 2013.

Lag-based Load Balancing for Linux-based Multiprocessor Systems

Dongwon Ok[1], Byeonghun Song[1], Hyunmin Yoon[1], Peng Wu[1], Jaesoo Lee[2], Jungkeun Park[3], and Minsoo Ryu[4]
[1]Department of Electronics and Computer Engineering, Hanyang University, Seoul, Korea
[2]The-AiO, Seongnam, Gyoenggi, Korea
[3]Department of Aerospace Information Engineering, Konkuk University, Seoul, Korea
[4]Department of Computer Science and Engineering, Hanyang University, Seoul, Korea

Abstract - *In this paper, we present a lag-based load balancing approach to achieve global fairness with the Linux CFS (Completely Fair Scheduler). Lag of each task is defined as the ideal CPU time it should have received minus the actual CPU time it has received. The proposed approach monitors the lag of each task at runtime and moves tasks to under-loaded processors so that each task can bound its lag. We implemented the proposed approach in the Linux kernel and experimentally evaluated it. The results demonstrate that our algorithm shows significant fairness improvements.*

Keywords: Linux, Multi-core scheduling, Completely Fair Scheduler, Fairness, Load balancing

1 Introduction

The goal of fair scheduling is to share CPU resources among tasks so that each task receives CPU time proportional to its weight. Perfect fairness is generally impossible since it requires infinitesimal CPU quanta for scheduling. Most fair schedulers can provide approximate fairness attempting to minimize the gap between the ideal GPS (generalized processor sharing) [2] scheme and their actual one.

Since the Linux 2.6.23 kernel release, Linux introduced a fair scheduler, CFS (completely fair scheduler), replacing the O(1) scheduler. CFS is the first fair scheduler implemented in general purpose operating systems. Previously, most operating systems such as Windows and earlier Linux versions provide round-robin style sharing of CPU resources rather than weight-based proportional sharing. In contrast, CFS associates each task with a specific weight value determined by the task's nice value and attempts to assign CPU time proportionally. CFS uses the notion of virtual runtime to track the ratio of the actual CPU time each task has received and the ideal CPU time each task should have received. Scheduling decisions are made by finding one that has the minimum virtual runtime and thus CFS can guarantee proportional sharing of CPU time among tasks.

Unfortunately, CFS does not ensure global fairness for multiprocessor systems as Linux uses partitioned scheduling. Linux maintains a separate run queue for each processor and each run queue is scheduled by a separate CFS. Therefore, local fairness can be achieved by the CFS scheme on each processor while global fairness across multiple processors cannot be guaranteed by the CFS scheme. The Linux kernel attempts to mitigate this problem by balancing workload among processors, but this approach often results in unacceptable global fairness.

In this paper, we present a lag-based load balancing approach to achieve global fairness with CFS. We define lag as the ideal CPU time each task should have received minus the actual CPU time each task has received. Our proposed approach monitors the lag of each task at runtime and moves tasks across processors whenever their lag values seem to exceed a specified upper bound. By moving such tasks to under-loaded processors that are able to bound their lag values, our approach can provide global fairness on multiprocessor Linux systems.

The remainder of this paper is organized as follows. Section 2 describes the Linux CFS (completely fair scheduler), its load balancing mechanism and its limitation. Section 3 describes the lag-based load balancing algorithm. Section 4 concludes this paper.

2 Completely Fair Scheduler

Completely Fair Scheduler (CFS) has been employed as the Linux scheduler since Linux 2.6.23 to provide weighted fairness for task scheduling. The weight of each task is the function of its nice value, integer value from -20 to 19, where a small nice value corresponds to a large weight value. Linux creates a separate run queue for each CPU and keeps track of virtual runtime for each task to represent the ratio of the actual CPU time the task has received and the ideal CPU time the task should have received. A smaller virtual runtime value indicates that the task has received less CPU time.

A red-black tree is used to find a task that has the smallest virtual runtime. The red-black tree places the task of the smallest virtual runtime at its leftmost leaf. Whenever CFS makes a scheduling decision, it selects the leftmost task from the red-black tree.

Let w^0 be the weight of nice value 0, w_i be the weight of task τ_i and $PR(\tau_i, t)$ be the CPU time consumed by task τ_i by time t. The virtual time of task τ_i by time t is defined as below.

$$\mathrm{VR}(\tau_i, t) = \frac{PR(\tau_i, t)}{w_i} \times w^0 \quad (1)$$

Note that w^0 and w_i are determined from nice values, as shown in Figure 1 taken from ``sched.c'' in the Linux kernel source code.

```
static const int prio_to_weight[40] = {
/* -20 */   88761,   71755,   56483,   46273,   36291,
/* -15 */   29154,   23254,   18705,   14949,   11916,
/* -10 */    9548,    7620,    6100,    4904,    3906,
/* -5 */     3121,    2501,    1991,    1586,    1277,
/* 0 */      1024,     820,     655,     526,     423,
/* 5 */       335,     272,     215,     172,     137,
/* 10 */      110,      87,      70,      56,      45,
/* 15 */       36,      29,      23,      18,      15,
};
```

Figure 1. Mapping between nice values and weight values.

The main idea behind CFS is to achieve fairness by using virtual runtime values. However, in the current Linux kernel, virtual runtime values are not examined across CPUs, thus leading to unfairness from a global point of view. CFS performs weight-based load balancing to mitigate this problem, but this approach often results in unacceptable global fairness.

For load balancing, Linux defines the load of run queue as the sum of all task weights in a run queue and keeps its value as `load` in `struct rq`. It also specifies when to perform load balancing, usually every k scheduling ticks for a certain positive integer k in each scheduling domain. Scheduling domain is a set of CPUs that are managed by a single scheduling policy. Each scheduling domain may contain one or more CPU groups and each group may contain one or more CPUs. Linux tries to balance the load across CPU groups within a domain. At every scheduling tick, CFS checks if it needs to perform load balancing. If so, it starts load balancing by calling `load_balance()`. For each scheduling domain with `SD_LOAD_BALANCE` flag, it finds the busiest group by calling `find_busiest_group()`. Before finding the busiest one among the CPU groups, it checks again whether to proceed load balancing or not. The kernel performs load balancing only when the load of current group is sufficiently low. To do so, `find_busiest_group()` examines two cases. The first case is when the load of the current group is no less than the average load of scheduling domain. The second case is when the difference of the load of the current group and the maximum load in the scheduling domain does not exceed a certain imbalance value defined by `imbalance_pct` in `struct sched_domain`. When the load of current group is sufficiently low, `find_busiest_group()` function calculates the amount of load to move using the following imbalance metric.

$$L_{imbal} = \min(L_{max} - L_{avg}, L_{avg} - L_k) \quad (2)$$

where L_{max} is the maximum load of the busiest group in the scheduling domain, L_{avg} is an average load in the system and L_k is the load of the current group. Linux checks again if the imbalance L_{imbal} is greater than twice of the smallest weight in the busiest run queue. If so, Linux moves tasks from the busiest group to the current under-loaded group.

3 Lag-based Load Balancing

In this section, we propose a lag-based load balancing approach to achieve global fairness for CFS on multiprocessor hardware. The proposed approach relies on the notion of lag. The lag is defined as the ideal CPU time each task should have received minus the actual CPU time each task has received [1]. Suppose that task τ is runnable and have a fixed weight in the interval $[t_1, t_2]$. Let $S_{\tau,A}(t_1, t_2)$ denotes the CPU time that task τ receives in $[t_1, t_2]$ under a certain scheduling scheme A, and $S_{\tau,GPS}(t_1, t_2)$ denotes the CPU time under the Generalized Processor Sharing (GPS) [2] scheme; an idealized scheduling model which achieves perfect fairness. For any interval $[t_1, t_2]$, the lag of task τ at time $t \in [t_1, t_2]$ is formally defined as

$$lag_\tau(t) = S_{\tau,GPS}(t_1, t_2) - S_{\tau,A}(t_1, t_2). \quad (3)$$

A positive lag at time t implies that the task has received less CPU time than under GPS, and a negative lag indicates that the task has received more CPU time than required. If all tasks in a run queue have positive lags, then this implies that the load of the run queue is relatively higher. Similarly, negative lags imply lower load. Let T_i be the time slice that task τ_i can consume without preemption. When task τ_i is not scheduled for T_i, the lag of task τ_i will increase by the amount of Δlag_i.

$$\Delta lag_i = T_i \times \frac{Weight_i}{\sum_{j\in\Phi} Weight_j} \times N \quad (4)$$

where $Weight_i$ is the weight of task τ_i, Φ is the set of all the runnable tasks in the entire system, and N is the number of CPUs. As the average load of the entire system is

$$Average\ Load = \frac{\sum_{j\in\Phi} Weight_j}{N}, \quad (5)$$

Δlag_i can also be defined as below.

$$\Delta lag_i = T_i \times \frac{Weight_i}{Average\ Load} \quad (6)$$

Since the lag increases consistently unless the task is scheduled, the time that the task should be scheduled can be calculated back from lag_i and Δlag_i. Let $laxity_i$ denote the remaining time until task τ_i exceeds a certain specified lag bound without being scheduled. The $laxity_i$ for any task τ_i is defined by

$$laxity_i = \left\lfloor \frac{lag\ bound - lag_i}{\Delta lag_i} \right\rfloor . \quad (7)$$

Note that tasks tend to have large lag values in a high load run queue. As time progresses, the lag values of one or more tasks will exceed a specified bound. To avoid this, we need to constantly monitor the lag values and check in advance if they will exceed the bound or not. Specifically, whenever the Linux kernel makes a scheduling decision for each run queue, the proposed approach checks if there exist more than one tasks that will have zero laxity at some identical time point. If found, only one of those tasks remains in the original run queue and other tasks are moved to less-loaded run queues. Figure 2 shows this algorithm in flowchart where count_laxity_zero(τ) checks if there exists more than one tasks that will have zero laxity at some identical time point, min_vruntime(CPU) is the value of minimum virtual runtime for the given CPU, and vruntime(τ) is the virtual runtime of the given task.

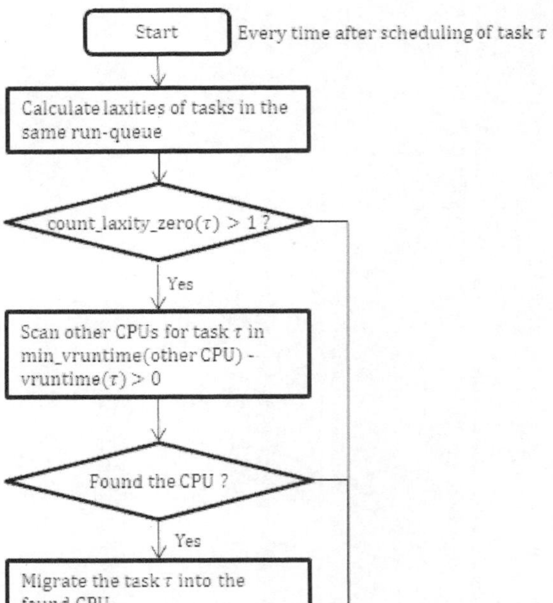

Figure 2. Flowchart of lag-based load balancing algorithm.

Whenever virtual runtime of the task is calculated, lag-based load balancing performs as follows:

(i) Lag-based load balancing algorithm calculates laxities of tasks in the same run queue.
(ii) If there are two or more tasks with laxity 0, tasks should be migrated.
(iii) The algorithm scans run queues of the other CPUs in min_vruntime(other CPU) – vruntime(τ) > 0. The virtual runtime of task τ should be lower than the minimum virtual runtime of other run queue, so the task τ will get chance to be scheduled right after migration.

If the suitable CPU is found, move the task τ into the run queue of the CPU.

4 Experimental Evaluation

We conducted to evaluate proposed load balancing algorithm in terms of the fairness. The algorithm was implemented in the Linux kernel 2.6.34.13. We used `ideal_time` value, which is calculated by Linux kernel to measure a dynamic time slice to check preemption, as a lag bound. Our experiments were performed on Ubuntu 10.10. In order to evaluate the fairness of the proposed algorithm, we ran four compute-intensive tasks with different weights, 1024, 335, 335 and 335. Let $D_{max}(t)$ be difference in virtual runtime of two tasks, between the task with the largest virtual runtime and the one with the smallest at time t. Since the virtual runtime of task has a concept of weighted CPU time, $D_{max}(t)$ represents unfairness; the lower $D_{max}(t)$ is, the fairer the algorithm is. The experimental result represented by the graph in Figure 3 shows that our approach enhances the fairness.

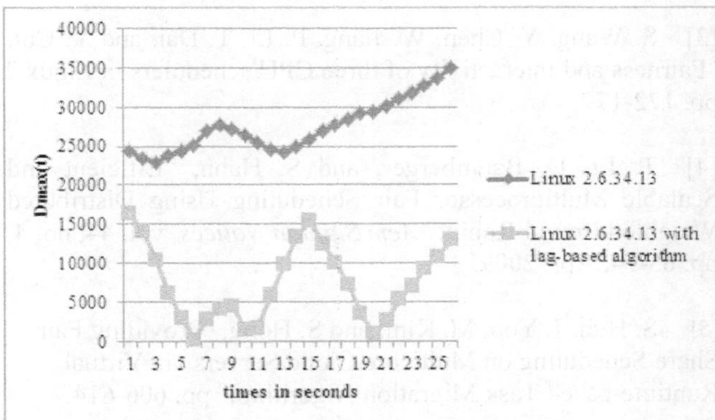

Figure 3. Comparison of $D_{max}(t)$ between legacy Linux 2.6.34.13 and the one with lag-based algorithm.

5 Conclusions

In this paper, we proposed a lag-based load balancing scheme to guarantee global fairness in Linux-based multiprocessor systems. The proposed approach introduces the notion of lag and provides fairness across multiple processors through lag-based load balancing. We also implemented the proposed approach in the Linux kernel and experimentally evaluated it. The results demonstrate that our algorithm shows significant improvement in terms of fairness.

6 Acknowledgement

This work was supported partly by Seoul Creative Human Development Program (HM120006), partly by Mid-career Researcher Program through NRF (National Research Foundation) grant funded by the MEST (Ministry of Education, Science and Technology) (NRF-2011-0015997), partly by the IT R&D Program of MKE/KEIT [10035708, "The Development of CPS (Cyber-Physical Systems) Core Technologies for High Confidential Autonomic Control Software"], and partly by the MSIP(Ministry of Science, ICT&Future Planning), Korea, under the CITRC(Convergence Information Technology Research Center) support program (NIPA-2013-H0401-13-1008) supervised by the NIPA(National IT Industry Promotion Agency).

7 References

[1] S. K. Baruah, N. K. Cohen, C. G. Plaxton, and D. A. Varvel, "Proportionate progress: A notion of fairness in resource allocation," *Algorithmica,* vol. 15, no. 6, pp. 600-625, 1996.

[2] A. K. Parekh, and R. G. Gallager, "A generalized processor sharing approach to flow control in integrated services networks: the single-node case," *IEEE/ACM Transactions on Networking (TON),* vol. 1, no. 3, pp. 344-357, 1993.

[3] S. Wang, Y. Chen, W. Jiang, P. Li, T. Dai, and Y. Cui, "Fairness and interactivity of three CPU schedulers in Linux." pp. 172-177.

[4] T. Li, D. Baumberger, and S. Hahn, "Efficient and Scalable Multiprocessor Fair Scheduling Using Distributed Weighted Round-Robin," *Acm Sigplan Notices,* vol. 44, no. 4, pp. 65-74, Apr, 2009.

[5] S. Huh, J. Yoo, M. Kim, and S. Hong, "Providing Fair Share Scheduling on Multicore Cloud Servers via Virtual Runtime-based Task Migration Algorithm." pp. 606-614.

SESSION

GRAPH BASED METHODS + RELATED ISSUES

Chair(s)

TBA

Generating edge covers of path graphs

J. Raymundo Marcial-Romero, J. A. Hernández, Vianney Muñoz-Jiménez and Héctor A. Montes-Venegas
Facultad de Ingeniería, Universidad Autónoma del Estado de México, UAEM, Toluca, México

Abstract—*It is known that the edge cover problem is #P complete. Even for path graphs with m edges it has been shown that the set of edge covers is equal to $fibonnaci(m)$. As a consequence, generating the set of edge covers of a given path graph is an exponential combinatorial problem. In this paper we show that the set of edge covers of a given path graph can be generated by what we call a set of kernel strings. Even more, we show that both the set of kernel strings is bounded by a quadratic polynomial and also there is a quadratic polynomial algorithm which generates kernel strings. As a consequence, a particular edge cover can be recovered from a kernel string in polynomial time.*

Keywords: Edge Covers, Graph Theory, Algorithms, Binary Patterns

1. Introduction

An edge cover of an undirected graph is a subset of its edges such that every vertex of the graph is incident to at least one edge of the subset. It is well known that the *edge cover problem* is #P complete. So, heuristic and exact methods have been proposed to count the number of edge covers for classes of graphs. For example, Bezáková et. al. [1] have shown that a Glauber dynamics Markov chain for edge covers mixes rapidly for graphs with degree at most three. De Ita et. al. [2] have shown that the number of edge covers for path graphs with m edges corresponds to $fibonacci(m)$. Although there is a polynomial time algorithm which computes the number of edge covers of a given path graph, generating the set of edge covers of a given path graph is an exponential combinatorial problem. For example a path graph with 60 edges has 1,548,008,755,920 edge covers. All of them are unthinkable useful for any real application. Even more, assuming that we can encode each edge cover on a byte, the storage space needed will be approximately 1TB for a 60 edges path graph. Instead of generating the whole set of edge covers, in this paper we show how to generate what we call kernel edge covers. Kernel edge covers means that any other edge cover can be generated from them. We show that the number of kernel edge covers is quadratic with respect to the number of edges in the graph. Additionally, we present an algorithm which generates the set of kernel edge covers also in quadratic time.

The set of kernel edge covers for path graphs is generated using an efficient algorithm for generating ascending compositions of an integer n in m parts based in the diagram structure proposed by [3]. The technique uses a binary pattern to map integer partitions into binary strings to represent edge covers.

The paper is organized as follow. Section 2 presents the preliminaries. Section 3 deals with generating partitions of an integer n in m parts, Section 4 presents the generation of edge covers of path graphs. Section 5 concludes the paper and future work is presented.

2. Preliminaries

An undirected graph G (i.e. finite, loopless and with no parallel edges) is defined as a tuple (V, E), where V is the set of *vertices* (or *nodes*) and E the set of *edges*. A vertex and an incident edge are said to *cover* each other.

A path graph $P = (V, E)$ consists of a set of nodes $V = \{a_1, a_2, \ldots a_n\}$ and edges built as $e_i = a_{i-1}a_i$, $1 \le i \le n$, i.e a path graph has $m = n - 1$ edges.

The neighborhood of a vertex $v \in V$ is the set $N(v) = \{w \in V : vw \in E\}$ and its degree, denoted as $d_G(v)$, is the number of neighbors that v has. The cardinality of a set A will be denoted as $|A|$. Given a graph $G = (V, E)$, $S = (V', E')$ is called a subgraph of G if $V' \subseteq V$ and $E' \subseteq E$. $G - v$ denotes the subgraph obtained from G by deleting v and all incidents edges to v whereas $G\backslash e$ is the subgraph obtained by simply deletion of the edge e.

An *edge cover* for a graph $G = (V, E)$ is a subset of edges $E' \subseteq E$ that covers all nodes of G, that is, for each $u \in V$ there is a $v \in V$ such that $e = uv \in E'$. Let $\mathcal{E}_G = \{E' \subseteq E : E'$ is an edge cover of $G\}$ be the set of *edge covers* for G, and $|\mathcal{E}_G|$ be the number of *edge covers* of G.

3. Partitions of Integers

In this section we introduce partitions of integers and give and efficient algorithm to compute them. In the following section, the use of partition of integers to generate edge covers will be discussed.

Let n be a positive integer. A composition of n is a way of writing n as the sum of positive integers denoted as $n = y_1 + y_2 + \ldots + y_k$. If the order of integers y_j is irrelevant, this representation is an *integer partition*. When $y_1 \le y_2 \le \ldots \le y_k$ we have an ascending composition. Algorithms for enumerating all the partitions of an integer or only the partitions with a restriction have been extensively studied [4], [5].

A data structure called *partition diagram* for storing all the partitions of an integer is proposed in [3]. In Merca [6], [7] improvements are proposed which, to date, are the most adequate data structures for generating integer partitions. We use the data structure proposed by Merca to present an efficient algorithm for generating ascending compositions of an integer n in m parts (See Algorithm 1). This algorithm is the foundation to generate edge covers of a path graph.

3.1 Partition Diagram

The partition diagram of an integer n is a directed acyclic graph. Fig. 1 shows a partition diagram of integer $i = 6$. A node in a partition diagram is denoted by (y, Y), where y is an element of a partition and Y is a number to be divided into parts that are not smaller than y. A node (y, Y) that has no predecessor is called a *anchored node* (*root node*) in a partition diagram. A node (y, Y) which has no succesor and $Y = 0$ is called a *terminal node*. A node (y, Y) with $Y > 0$ and $y \leq Y$ is called an *internal node*. For example, in Fig. 1 the node $(1, 6)$ is an *anchored node* and also *internal node*, whereas node $(5, 0)$ is a *terminal node* (*leaf node*). Fig. 1 shows a path pointing from $(2, 4)$ to $(2, 2)$ and $(4, 0)$, it means that the nodes $(2, 2)$ and $(4, 0)$ are the succesor of $(2, 4)$.

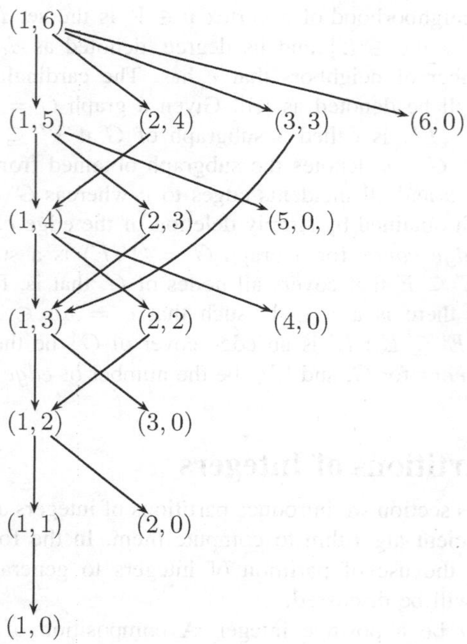

Fig. 1: Partition diagram needed to generate the integer partitions of the number 6. The diagram represents a directed acyclic graph.

Given a partition diagram of an integer n, a path from an anchored node to a terminal node defines a unique partition of n. The partition is formed during a path traversal by recovering all the first parts of the tuples excluding the anchored node and nodes of the form $(1, r)$ if its predecessor is of the form (y, r), where $y > 1$. For example, the path $(1, 6)$ $(1, 5)$ $(1, 4)$ $(2, 2)$ $(1, 2)$ $(2, 0)$ defines partition $\langle 1, 1, 2, 2\rangle$ since the nodes $(1, 6)$ and $(1, 2)$ are excluded. Traversing all the paths, the partitions of 6 are $\langle 1, 1, 1, 1, 1, 1\rangle$, $\langle 1, 1, 1, 1, 2\rangle$, $\langle 1, 1, 1, 3\rangle$, $\langle 1, 1, 2, 2\rangle$, $\langle 1, 1, 4\rangle$, $\langle 1, 2, 3\rangle$, $\langle 1, 5\rangle$, $\langle 2, 2, 2\rangle$, $\langle 2, 4\rangle$, $\langle 3, 3\rangle$, and $\langle 6\rangle$.

Although the partition diagram shown in Fig. 1 is created for integer $i = 6$, it also consists of all the partition diagrams of any integer smaller than 6. The partition diagram of any integer r smaller than n is anchored at node $(1, r)$. For example, the node $(1, 5)$ is the anchored node of the partition diagram of 5. In the next subsection we presented an efficient algorithm to generate the ascending composition of an integer n in m parts.

3.2 Algorithm for generating ascending composition of an integer n in m parts

To obtain all the ascending composition of integer n in m parts, we can generate all paths from the root node to the leaf nodes whose deep is $m + 1$ using the partition diagram. To achieve this, we present a variant of Merca algorithm for traversing all the paths with the constraint of m parts. We represent each level of the partition diagram as a dynamic vector, i.e. $diagram[0] = \{(1, 6)\}$, $diagram[1] = \{(1, 5), (2, 4), (3, 3), (6, 0)\}$ and so on. Particular elements of the diagram can be recovered as $diagram[row][column]$ where row represent the level of the diagram and $column$ the position in the level.

The required variables should be initialized as follows. Variables $row \leftarrow 1$ and $colum \leftarrow 0$, these values represent their position in the diagram. The variable $part \leftarrow 0$, is the number of parts in which n has been already divided. Finally, $partition \leftarrow \{\}$ has the elements of a partition. When a partition is formed, the set $partition$ is stored and modified to generate a new partition.

4. Computing edge covers for path graphs

In this section we show how to generate the set of *edge covers* of a path graph using 3.2. Firstly we present how to encode edge covers for path graphs as binary strings.

4.1 Binary strings to represent edge covers

A binary pattern can be used to represent an *edge cover* of a path graph. Let $b_1 b_2 \ldots b_m$ be a binary sequence. If $b_i = 1$ then the edge (a_i, a_{i+1}) belongs to the *edge cover* otherwise (i.e. $b_i = 0$) the edge (a_i, a_{i+1}) does not belong to the *edge cover*.

Let G be a path graph with n nodes. A binary sequence $b_1 b_2 \ldots b_m$, $m = n - 1$ represents an *edge cover* for G if the following conditions hold:

Algorithm 1 Parts (Generating ascending composition de n in m parts)

Require: *diagram* (Diagram structure of n)
Require: $m, row, column, part, partition$
for all $i = 0$; $i \leq length(diagram[row] - 1)$; $i = i + 1$ **do**
  $partition = partition \cup$ *first component* $(diagram[row][i])$;
  $part \leftarrow part + 1$;
  if *second component* $(diagram[row][i])! = 0$ and $part < m$ **then**
    Parts (*n-second component* $(diagram[row][i]) + 1$, 0, *part*,m,n)
  else
    if *second component* $(diagram[row][i] = 0)$ and $part == m$ **then**
      store *partition*;
    end if
  end if
  partition = *partition-last component(partition)*;
  $part \leftarrow part - 1$;
end for

1) $\nexists\ b_i, b_{i+1}$ such that $b_i = 0$ and $b_{i+1} = 0$.
2) $b_1 = 1$ and $b_m = 1$.

An *edge cover* representation, does not admit a sequence of consecutive zeros. So, a binary sequence is represented as
$1^{p_0}01^{p_1}\cdots01^{p_{l-1}}01^{p_l}$ for some $l \in \mathbb{N}$ and $p_0, p_1, \ldots p_l > 0$.

Lemma 1: Let ω be a binary sequence which represents an edge cover of a path graph with n nodes. The maximum number s_n of zeros appearing in ω is given by
$s_n = \frac{n-2}{2}$; if n is even and
$s_n = \frac{n-1}{2}$; if n is odd.

Proof:
It is obvious that, when each $p_i = 1$, $1 \leq i \leq n$, the string ω has the maximum number of zeros. Since the one's appearing at the extrema of ω are fixed, then a string of length $n-2$ is left where half of the symbols are zero if n is even or half of $n-1$ symbols are zero if n is odd. ■

Corollary 1: Let P be a path graph such that the number of nodes of P is n. If ω is a binary string which represents an edge cover for P then
1) if n is even there are $0 \leq s \leq \frac{n-2}{2}$ zeros on ω;
2) if n is odd there are $0 \leq s \leq \frac{n-1}{2}$ zeros on ω.

Example 1: : If a path graph with $n = 10$ nodes is given, then $0 \leq s \leq 4$ zeros are allowed in a binary string to represent an *edge cover*. If $s = 0$ then, there is only one binary string $\langle 1111111111 \rangle$, if $s = 1$ then there are eight binary strings $\langle 1011111111 \rangle$, $\langle 1101111111 \rangle$, $\langle 1110111111 \rangle$, $\langle 1111011111 \rangle$, $\langle 1111101111 \rangle$, $\langle 1111110111 \rangle$, $\langle 1111111011 \rangle$, $\langle 1111111101 \rangle$ and so on.

It is easy to see that there is only one string without zeros that represent an *edge cover* of a path graph with n nodes. In fact, it is the string with $n-1$ ones (each one represents an edge). The strings with one zero that represent *edge covers* are also easily counted and generated as the following lemma shows.

Lemma 2: Let P be a path graph with m edges ordered as $a_1, a_2, \ldots, a_m$. There are $m-2$ strings of length m with one zero that represent edge covers of P.

Proof: Let $b_1b_2\ldots b_m$ be an arbitrary string which represent the edges of the path graph P. It is obvious that b_1 and b_m should be one since each of them cover the nodes a_1 and a_n respectively. So the string where $b_2 = 0$ and $b_i = 1$, $i = 1, 3, 4, \ldots m$ represents an edge cover of P with one zero. If we shift the value of b_2 to b_3 and assign to b_2 the value one, we have the second string that represents an edge cover of P with one zero. In general if $b_i = 0$, $2 \leq i \leq m-2$ then shifting the value of b_i with b_{i+1} gives a new edge cover of P with one zero. ■

The generation of some strings with more that one zero which represent *edge covers* can be determined via the correspondence with the integer partitions of a number n.

Definition 1: A kernel string is a binary string of the form $01^{p1}01^{p2}\cdots1^{pl}0$, $l \geq 1$ where $0 < pl \leq p2 \leq \cdots \leq pl$.

Proposition 1: There are $n-4$ kernel strings with two zeros of length at most $n-2$.

Proof: A kernel string with two zeros is of the form $01^{p1}0$. In fact, if $1 \leq p1 \leq n-4$ the kernel strings $01^{p1}0$ have length at most $n-2$. ■

An ascending integer partition can be used to generate kernel strings.

Lemma 3: Let $p(n, m)$ be the set of ascending integer partitions of n in m parts. If $l_1 + l_2 + \cdots + l_m \in p(n, m)$, then $01^{l_1}01^{l_2}\cdots1^{l_m}0$ is a kernel string with $m+1$ zeros whose length is $l_1 + l_2 + \cdots + l_m + m + 1$.

Proof: That $01^{l_1}01^{l_2}\cdots1^{l_m}0$ is a kernel string is easily verified since each $l_i \neq 0$ and the ascending condition means that $l_1 \leq l_2 \leq \cdots \leq l_m$. The number of zeros is also straightforward computed. ■

Lemma 4: There are $\sum_{i=r}^{n-r-3} |p(i, r)|$ kernel strings with $r+1$ zeros for all $n \geq 5$.

Proof: The proof is by induction over n. ■

The following example shows how to generate a kernel string from an ascending integer partition $p(n, m)$.

Example 2: The partitions of four in two part are p(4,2)={2+2, 1+3}. Since the cardinality of the set is two, this means that there are two kernel strings with three zeros and four ones. The kernel string are of the form $01^{p1}01^{p2}0$. Each element of a partition is the value of a p_i. So one kernel string is formed when $p1 = p2 = 2$ and the other kernel string is formed when $p1 = 1$ and $p2 = 3$ which are the kernel strings 0110110 and 0101110, respectively. From lemma 4, if $n = 9$ there are four kernel strings with three zeros because

$$\begin{aligned}\sum_{i=2}^{9-2-3} p(i,2) &= \sum_{i=2}^{4} p(i,2)\\ &= p(2,2)+p(3,2)+(4,2)\\ &= 1+1+2\\ &= 4\end{aligned}$$

The kernel strings are shown in the following table.

$p(2,2)=1+1$	01010
$p(3,2)=1+2$	010110
$p(4,2)=\{2+2,1+3\}$	0110110, 0101110

It is well known that if $l_1+l_2+\cdots+l_m$ is an integer partition of a number n then a combination of the number, i.e., $l_2+l_1+\cdots+l_m$, represents the same integer partition of n. However, if they are used to generate kernel strings, those strings are different. We can not call both of them kernel strings since, if $l_1 \leq l_2$, it is not the case that $l_1 > l_2$, so the second is not a kernel string. We introduce another definition to include those strings.

Definition 2: A combined string is a binary string of the form $01^{p1}01^{p2}\cdots 1^{pl}0$, $l \geq 1$ where each $pi \neq 0$, $1 \leq i \leq l$.

Now, combined strings can be generated from integer partitions also. However, we do not want to count combinations of ascending integer partitions that are identical, i.e., if $l_1+l_2+\cdots+l_m$ is a partition which represent a combined string and $l_1 = l_2$ then, $l_2+l_1+\cdots+l_m$ will represent the same string. We use λ_{l_i} to denote the number of times the value l_i is repeated in the partition.

Let $t = l_1+l_2+\cdots+l_m$ be an ascending integer partition of the number t. It is well known that the total number of non-repeated combinations of the partition t is given by $(\sum_{i=1}^{m}\lambda_{l_i})!/\prod_{i=1}^{m}(\lambda_{l_i})!$. Algorithms which efficiently built these kind of integer partition combinations have long been studied, a survey can be found in Knuth [8]. What is important to point out is that combined strings can de generated from kernel string since combined integer partitions can be generated form integer partitions.

Corollary 2: Each combined string can be generated from a kernel string.

Corollary 3: The set of kernel strings is a subset of the set of combined strings.

Lemma 5: Let P be a path graph with m edges. If w is a combined string such that $|w| \leq m-2$ then $1w1^l$ represents an edge cover of P where $l = m-|w|-1$.

Proof: By definition, a combined string does not have two consecutive zeros. That the length of $1w1^l$ is m is establish by the condition $l = m-|w|-1$. ■

Theorem 1: Let P be a path graph with $m \geq 4$ edges.

1) If m is even then $(\frac{m}{2}-2)(\frac{m}{2}-1)$ kernel strings are needed to generate combined strings that represent edge covers.

$p(1,1)$		
$p(2,1)$	$p(2,2)$	
$p(3,1)$	$p(3,2)$	$p(3,3)$
$p(4,1)$	$p(4,2)$	$p(4,3)$
$p(5,1)$	$p(5,2)$	
$p(6,1)$		

Table 1: Ascending integer partitions calculated from Algorithm 2 for $n = 10$

2) If m is odd then $\frac{(m-3)^2}{4}$ kernel strings are needed to generate combined strings that represent edge covers.

Proof: We first prove the case where m is even. By lemma 1, it suffices to generate kernel strings with s zeros, $2 < s < (n-2)/2$. By proposition 1 there are $m-4$ kernel strings with two zeros. In the same way, there are $n-3$ kernel strings with three zeros. In general, there are $(n/2)+1$ kernel strings with $(n-2)/2$ zeros. Adding the number of string we have $\sum_{i=4,even}^{m-2}(m-i)$ kernel strings. $\sum_{i=4,even}^{m-2}(m-i) = (\frac{m}{2}-2)(\frac{m}{2}-1)$. Similarly, if m is odd, there are $\sum_{i=4,odd}^{m-3}(m-i)$ kernel strings and $\sum_{i=4,odd}^{m-3}(m-i) = \frac{(m-3)^2}{4}$. ■

Algorithm 2 Increasing integer partitions needed to generate kernel strings

Require: Integer $m \geq 4$ which represent the number of edges of P

```
if m odd then
    l = (m-3)/2
    p(l, l)
else
    l = (m-2)/2
end if
for all j = 1; j <= l; j++ do
    for all i = j; i < 2l - j; i++ do
        p(i, j)
    end for
end for
```

Let P be a path graph with $m \geq 4$ edges, algorithm 2 calculates the ascending integer partitions of l in r parts needed to generate kernel strings based on the number of edges m. For example, if $n = 10$, Table 1 shows which ascending integer partitions are needed. We use a tThe integer partitions are presented in rows and columns to see its correspondence with the previous results. For example, the second component of the elements in row one are 1. Those partitions represent the kernel strings with two zeros needed (lemma 4).

Although we known how to compute the set of combined string from kernel strings, there is a last set of strings which represent *edge covers* of path graphs that are not included in lemma 5. For example, the string 10110101111 represents an *edge cover* of a path graph with eleven edges, the combined string which generates such a string is 011010 based on a combination of the ascending partition $1+2$, i.e. $2+1$. However, the string 11011010111 which also represents an *edge cover* of a path graph with eleven edges is not generated from the result of lemma 5. Those strings can be obtained by shiftings to the right combined strings in the whole string. In our example, if the combined string 011010 is shifted one position to the right in the string 10110101111, the string 11011010111 is generated.

Lemma 6: Let P be a path graph with m edges. If $1w1^l$ represents an edge cover for P where w is a combined string and $l > 1$ then, $l-1$ different strings which represent edge covers of P can be generated from $1w1^l$.

Proof: Since $l > 1$ then, shifting one place to the right the combined string w generates a new string $11w1^{l-1}$ which also represents an edge cover of P. It is straightforward to notice that the shifting can be done $l-1$ times. ∎

We are now in a position to present the algorithm to generate the strings that represent *edge covers* for a path graph with at least four edges. *Edge covers* for path graphs with less than four edges are straightforward calculated.

Algorithm 3 Generating the edge covers of a path graph P

Require: Integer $m \geq 4$ which represent the number of edges of P

Generate *diagram structure* of m
Include the string without zeros, i.e., 1^m
Include $m-2$ *edge covers* with one zero
Compute kernel strings
Generate combined strings
for all combined string w **do**
  $p = m - |w| - 1$
  for all $i = 0$; $i < p$; $i++$ **do**
    add $11^i w 1^{p-i}$
  end for
end for

5. Conclusions and future work

A procedure to compute *edge covers* for *path graphs* using an efficient algorithm for generating ascending compositions of an integer n in m parts has been presented. Although the number of edge covers grows exponentially [2], the space and time needed to store either the partition diagram or the set of kernel strings is quadratic. The implication of this result is that, in practical applications, we can efficiently recover subsets of edge covers for a given path graph as kernel strings are the base to generate combined strings. We believe that the procedure presented will be the foundation to generate edge covers for simple graphs, i.e., acyclic and cyclic.

References

[1] I. Bezáková and W. Rummler, "Sampling edge covers in 3-regular graphs," in *Mathematical Foundations of Computer Science 2009*, ser. Lecture Notes in Computer Science, R. Královic and D. Niwiński, Eds. Springer Berlin Heidelberg, 2009, vol. 5734, pp. 137–148.

[2] G. D. Ita, J. R. Marcial-Romero, and H. A. Montes-Venegas, "Estimating the relevance on communication lines based on the number of edge covers," *Electronic Notes in Discrete Mathematics*, vol. 36, no. 0, pp. 247 - 254, 2010. [Online]. Available: http://www.sciencedirect.com/science/article/pii/S1571065310000338

[3] R.-B. Lin, "Efficient data structure for storing the partitions of integers," *The 22nd Workshop on Combinatorics and Computation Theory*, pp. 349–354, 2005.

[4] D. Stanton and D. White, "Constructive combinatorics," *Springer-Verlang, Berling*, 1986.

[5] C. L. Liu, "Introduction to combinatorial mathematics," *MacGraw-Hill College*, 1986.

[6] M. Merca, "Binary diagrams for storing ascending compositions," *The Computer Journal Advance Access*, 2012.

[7] ——, "Fast algorithm for generating ascending compositions," *Journal of Mathematical Modelling and Algorithms*, vol. 11, pp. 89–104, 2012. [Online]. Available: http://dx.doi.org/10.1007/s10852-011-9168-y

[8] D. E. Knuth, *The Art of Computer Programming, Volume 4A: Combinatorial Algorithms, Part 1.* Addison Wesley, 2011.

Finding Paths with Minimum Shared Edges in Graphs with Bounded Treewidth

Z.-Q. Ye[1], Y.-M. Li[2], H.-Q. Lu[3] and X. Zhou[4]
[1]Zhejiang University, Hanzhou, Zhejiang, China
[2]Wenzhou University, Wenzhou, Zhejiang, China
[3]Zhejiang University of Technology, Hangzhou, Zhejiang, China
[4]Tohoku University, Sendai, Japan

Abstract—*Given a positive integer p, a graph G and a pair of two terminals s and t in G, the minimum shared-edge paths problem is to find p paths connecting s and t so as to minimize the number of edges shared among the paths. This is a generalization of the well-known edge-disjoint paths problem which asks whether there exist p pairwise edge-disjoint paths connecting the terminals. The edge-disjoint paths problem is NP-complete for given many pairs of terminals even for graphs with treewidth at most two. In this paper we show that the minimum shared-edge paths problem for a given pair of two terminals can be solved in polynomial time for graphs with bounded treewidth.*

Keywords: Dynamic programming algorithm, Tree-decomposition, Treewidth

1. Introduction

Given a number p, a graph G and a pair of two terminals s and t in G, the *minimum shared-edge paths problem* is to find p paths connecting s and t so as to minimize the number of shared edges. This problem, introduced in [7], has an application for a security assurance demand in a geographic information system setting. Suppose that a security organization is hired to do planning for a VIP who wishes to travel safely between two locations. Given the security concerns, p paths are determined in pre-trip planning and then, just prior to actual travel, randomly one path among the p paths is chosen. The fewer edges, that are shared among the pre-trip paths, are to make the higher level of perceived security. However, if it becomes unavoidable to share edges among the paths, guards are employed on those shared edges. Since guards take some costs, we want to reduce their total number, that is, to minimize the number of shared edges.

For the special case where the number of shared edges is required to be zero, the minimum shared-edge paths problem is reduced to the "edge-disjoint paths" problem, which is to find p edge-disjoint paths connected s and t and can be solved in polynomial time using standard maximum flow algorithms. However the minimum shared-edge paths problem is NP-hard for gernal graphs [7].

The class of graphs with treewidth k includes trees ($k = 1$), series-parallel graphs ($k = 2$) [11], Halin graphs ($k = 3$), and k-terminal recursive graphs. Many problems can be solved efficiently for graphs with treewidth bounded by a constant k by a dynamic programming algorithm based on the tree-decomposition [1], [2], [5], [6], [8], [9], [10], [15], while the edge-disjoint paths problem for many pairs of terminals is NP-complete even for $k = 2$ [13].

In this paper we give a polynomial-time algorithm to solve the minimum shared-edge paths problem for graphs with treewidth bounded by a constant k. Our idea is to formulate the minimum shared-edge paths problem as a new type of an edge-coloring problem, and to bound the size of a dynamic programming (DP) table by $O((p+1)^{(k+4)^{2k+8}})$, applying and extending techniques developed for the ordinary edge-coloring problem [3], [12], [14]. We use the fact that when doing dynamic programming upward in a tree-decomposition only certain informations of the partial solutions must be kept. These informations concern basically the connectivity amongst the vertices of a basis graph inside a solution. So the state space that is to be remembered is in a sense given by the partitions of the vertex set of a basis graph.

The paper is organized as follows. In Section 2 we present some preliminary definitions. In Section 3 we give a simple algorithm, that cannot always run in polynomial time, for the minimum shared-edge paths problems on graphs with treewidth bounded by a constant k. In Section 4 we modify it to a polynomial-time algorithm. In Section 5 we conclude with a generalization of our algorithm.

2. Terminology and Definitions

In this section we give some definitions. Let $G = (V, E)$ denote a graph with vertex set V and edge set E. We often denote by $V(G)$ and $E(G)$ the vertex set and the edge set of G, respectively. We denote by n the number of vertices in G. The paper deals with *simple undirected* graphs without multiple edges or self-loops. An edge joining vertices u and v is denoted by (u, v). For $E' \subseteq E(G)$, $G[E']$ denotes the subgraph of G induced by the edges in E'; $G[E']$ contains every vertex of G to which at least one edge in E' is incident, and hence $G[E']$ contains no isolated vertex.

We will use notions as: *leaf*, *node*, *child* and *root* in their usual meaning. A *tree-decomposition* $T = (V_T, E_T)$ of a graph G is a rooted tree such that the following conditions (A1)–(A6) hold [3]:

(A1) each $X \in V_T$ is a subset of $V(G)$;

(A2) $\bigcup_{X \in V_T} X = V(G)$;

(A3) for each edge $(u,v) \in E(G)$, there is a leaf node $X \in V_T$ such that $u, v \in X$;

(A4) for any three nodes $X_1, X_2, X_3 \in V_T$, if node X_2 lies on the path between X_1 and X_3, then $X_1 \cap X_3 \subseteq X_2$;

(A5) $|V_T| = O(n)$; and

(A6) every internal node X_i in T has exactly two children X_l and X_r such that $X_i = X_l$ or $X_i = X_r$.

The *width* of T is defined as $\max\{|X| - 1 : X \in V_T\}$, and the *treewidth*, denoted by $\mathrm{tw}(G)$, of G is the minimum k such that G has a tree-decomposition of width k. We denote by X_{01} the root of a tree-decomposition. Assume that k is a bounded positive integer. Since a tree-decomposition T of a graph with treewidth k can be found in linear time [3], [4], we may assume that its tree-decomposition T are given.

We next recursively define an edge-set $E_i \subseteq E$ for each node X_i of T as follows. Let $rep : E \rightarrow V_T$ such that $rep(e)$ is a leaf node of T and the two ends of the edge e is in $rep(e)$. If X_i is a leaf of T, then let $E_i = \{e \in E |\ rep(e) = X_i\}$; if X_i is an internal node of T having two children X_l and X_r, then let $E_i = E_l \cup E_r$. Thus node X_i of T corresponds to a subgraph $G[E_i]$ of G induced by the edges in E_i. The subgraph $G[E_i]$ is often denoted simply by G_i. Then G_i is an edge-disjoint union of two subgraphs G_l and G_r, which share common vertices only in X_i.

3. Simple Algorithm

In this section we give a straightforward dynamic programming algorithm. Although all our algorithms only compute the minimum number $\omega(G,p)$ of shared edges among all p paths connecting s and t, they can be easily modified so that they actually find such p paths connecting s and t with minimum number of shared edges.

The main result of this section is the following theorem.

Theorem 3.1: Let $G = (V, E)$ be a graph with n vertices given by its tree-decomposition with width $\leq k$. Let (s,t) be a pair of two vertices in G, and let p be a positive integer. Then one can compute $\omega(G,p)$ in time

$$O\left(n\left\{p2^{pk(k+1)/2} + p(k+4)^{2(k+4)p+3}\right\}\right).$$

If k is bounded, the first term in the braces above, $p2^{pk(k+1)/2}$, is bounded by a polynomial in n if $p = O(\log n)$. The second term $p(k+4)^{2(k+4)p+3}$ is also bounded by a polynomial if $p = O(\log n)$ since p is in the single exponent over a constant $k+4$. On the other hand, both of the terms are bounded by a constant if $p = O(1)$. Thus we have the following corollary.

Corollary 3.2: If $p = O(\log n)$, then the minimum shared-edge paths problem can be solved for graphs with bounded treewidth in polynomial time. If $p = O(1)$, then the problem can be solved for graph with bounded treewidth in linear time.

In the remainder of this section we will give a proof of Theorem 3.1. Our idea is to formulate the minimum shared-edge paths problem as a new type of an edge-coloring problem, and then to solve the coloring problem using dynamic programming with a table of size at most $(k+4)^{(k+4)p}$. We employ techniques developed for the ordinary edge-coloring problem and the edge-disjoint paths problem [3], [14], [16].

Let $G = (V, E)$ be a graph, and let (s,t) be a pair of two vertices in V called *terminals*. Let p be a positive integer, and let $C = \{1, 2, \cdots, p\}$ be the set of colors. Any mapping $f : E \rightarrow 2^C$ is called a *coloring* of graph G. For a color $c \in C$, we denote by $G(f,c)$ the so-called *"color class"* for c, that is, the subgraph of G induced by the edges which are colored by a set of colors including c. We call f a *correct coloring* of G if, for each color $c \in C$, $G(f,c)$ has a connected component containing both terminals s and t.

Let $\omega(G,f)$, called the *cost* of f, be the number of edges which are in at least two graphs $G(f,c)$, $c \in C$. Let $\omega(G,p)$ be the minimum cost among all correct colorings of G. The *minimum shared-edge paths problem* is to compute $\omega(G,p)$ for a given graph G.

Let X_i be a node of a tree-decomposition T of a graph G. We say that a coloring of graph $G_i = G[E_i]$ is *extensible* if it can be extended to a correct coloring of $G = G[E_{01}]$ without changing the coloring of any edge in E_i, where X_{01} is the root of T.

When doing dynamic programming upward in a tree-decomposition, only certain informations of all extensible colorings must be kept in a DP table. The informations are called "color vectors," and the number of distinct color vectors is bounded by $(k+4)^{(k+4)p}$, as we show below.

For a set X we denote by $\mathcal{F}(X)$ the set of all families of pairwise disjoint subsets of X. If $x = |X| \geq 1$, then

$$|\mathcal{F}(X)| \leq (x+1)^{x+1}. \tag{1}$$

For a node X_i of T we call a p-tuple $\mathbf{C}(X_i) = (\mathcal{Y}_1, \mathcal{Y}_2, \cdots, \mathcal{Y}_p)$ a *color vector* on X_i, where $\mathcal{Y}_c$, $1 \leq c \leq p$, is a family in $\mathcal{F}(X_i \cup \{s,t\})$. Simply we define $\mathcal{F}_{st}(X_i) = \mathcal{F}(X_i \cup \{s,t\})$. We say that a color vector $\mathbf{C}(X_i) = (\mathcal{Y}_1, \mathcal{Y}_2, \cdots, \mathcal{Y}_p)$ on X_i is *active* if $G_i = G[E_i]$ has a coloring f such that $\mathcal{Y}_c = \mathcal{Y}(X_i; f, c)$ for each color $c \in C$, where

$$\mathcal{Y}(X_i; f, c) = \{V(D) \cap (X_i \cup \{s,t\}) \mid D \text{ is a connected component of } G_i(f,c)\}.$$

Such a vector $\mathbf{C}(X_i)$ is called the *color vector of the coloring* f. (Thus a color vector indicates which vertices in X_i are connected to each other or are reachable from terminals in a color class. Observe that there is a special case where one of the sets in $\mathcal{Y}_c$ is just $\{s,t\}$. This encodes the fact that the color c already connects terminals s and t entirely in G_i without using any vertex in X_i except s and t.)

We now have the following lemma.

Lemma 3.3: Let X_i be any node of a tree-decomposition T of a graph G. Let two colorings f and g of $G_i = G[E_i]$ have the same color vector. Then f is extensible if and only if g is extensible.

Proof: It suffices to prove that if f is extensible then g is also extensible. Suppose that f is extensible. Then f can be extended to a correct coloring f^* of $G = (V,E)$, where $f^*(e) = f(e)$ for $e \in E_i$. Let g^* be a coloring of G extended from g as follows: $g^*(e) = g(e)$ for $e \in E_i$, and $g^*(e) = f^*(e)$ for $e \in E - E_i$. Since the subgraph G_i of G is connected to other parts of G only through vertices in X_i and f and g have the same color vector and f^* is a correct coloring, g^* is a correct coloring. ■

Thus a color vector on X_i characterizes an equivalence class of extensible colorings of G_i. Since $|X_i| \le k+1$, $|X_i \cup \{s,t\}| \le k+3$. Therefore by Eq. (1) we have $|\mathcal{F}(X_i \cup \{s,t\})| \le (k+4)^{k+4}$. Hence there are at most

$$(k+4)^{(k+4)p} \tag{2}$$

color vectors $\mathbf{C}(X_i) = (\mathcal{Y}_1, \mathcal{Y}_2, \cdots, \mathcal{Y}_p)$ on X_i. Let

$$\omega(X_i, \mathbf{C}) = \min\{\omega(G_i, f) \mid f \text{ is a coloring of } G_i \text{ with the color vector } \mathbf{C}\},$$

and let $\omega(X_i, \mathbf{C}) = \infty$ if no such coloring f. Then clearly we have the following lemma.

Lemma 3.4: Let $\mathbf{C}$ be any color vector on a node X_i of T. Then $\mathbf{C}$ is active if and only if $\omega(X_i, \mathbf{C}) \ne \infty$.

The main step of our algorithm is to compute a table of all $\omega(X_i, \mathbf{C})$ for all active color vectors $\mathbf{C}$ on each node of T from leaves to the root X_{01} of T by means of dynamic programming. From the table on X_{01} one can easily compute $\omega(G,p)$, as follows.

Lemma 3.5: Let G be a graph with a tree-decomposition T rooted at X_{01}. Then

$$\omega(G,p) = \min_{\mathbf{C}} \omega(X_{01}, \mathbf{C}), \tag{3}$$

where the minimum is taken over all active color vectors $\mathbf{C} = (\mathcal{Y}_1, \mathcal{Y}_2, \cdots, \mathcal{Y}_p)$ on X_{01} such that, for each color $c \in C$, there is a set in $\mathcal{Y}_c$ containing both s and t. Furthermore Eq. (3) can be computed in time $O((k+4)^{(k+4)p})$.

We first compute the table of $\omega(X_i, \mathbf{C})$ for all active color vectors $\mathbf{C}$ on each leaf X_i of T as follows:

(1) enumerate all colorings $f : E_i \to 2^C$ of G_i; and

(2) compute all active color vectors $\mathbf{C}(X_i) = (\mathcal{Y}_1, \mathcal{Y}_2, \cdots, \mathcal{Y}_p)$ on X_i from the colorings f of G_i.

Since $|C| = p$ and $|E_i| \le k(k+1)/2$ for leaf X_i, the number of distinct colorings $f : E_i \to 2^C$ is at most $2^{pk(k+1)/2}$. For each coloring f of G_i, one can compute the color vector of f in time $O(p)$. Note that $k = O(1)$. Therefore, steps (1) and (2) above and hence all $\omega(G_i, \mathbf{C})$ can be compute for a leaf in time $O(p2^{pk(k+1)/2})$. Since T has $O(n)$ leaves, the tables on all leaves can be computed in time $O(np2^{pk(k+1)/2})$, which corresponds to the first term in the braces of the complexity mentioned in Theorem 3.1.

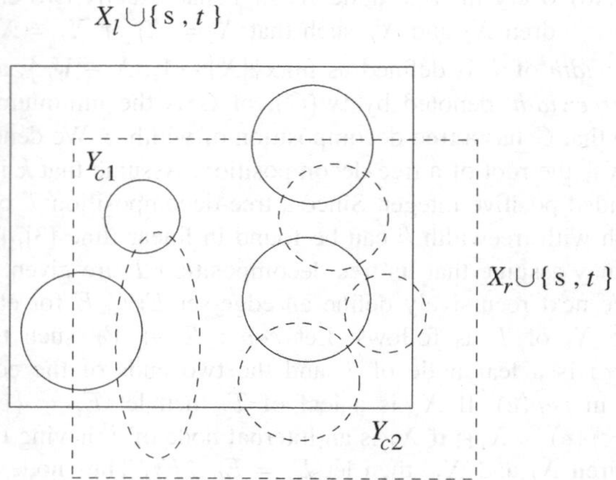

Fig. 1: Venn diagrams of $\mathcal{Y}_{lc}$ and $\mathcal{Y}_{rc}$ with two clusters Y_{c1} and Y_{c2}.

We next compute $\omega(X_i, \mathbf{C})$ for all active color vectors $\mathbf{C}$ on each internal node X_i of T from leaves to the root. Lemma 3.6 below shows how to compute them on X_i from all active color vectors on the left and right children X_l and X_r of X_i. We now introduce a notion of a family $\mathcal{U}(\mathcal{Y}_{lc}, \mathcal{Y}_{rc}; W)$ for families $\mathcal{Y}_{lc}, \mathcal{Y}_{rc}$ and a set $W \subseteq V$. Let $\mathbf{C}(X_l) = (\mathcal{Y}_{l1}, \mathcal{Y}_{l2}, \cdots, \mathcal{Y}_{lp})$ be an active color vector on X_l, and let $\mathbf{C}(X_r) = (\mathcal{Y}_{r1}, \mathcal{Y}_{r2}, \cdots, \mathcal{Y}_{rp})$ be an active color vector on X_r. Figure 1 illustrates Venn diagrams of $\mathcal{Y}_{lc}$ and $\mathcal{Y}_{rc}$, $c \in C$, where the sets in $\mathcal{Y}_{lc}$ are indicated by circles of solid lines and the sets in $\mathcal{Y}_{rc}$ by circles of dotted lines. All vertices shared by graphs G_l and G_r are contained in X_i, and $X_i \subseteq X_l \cup X_r$. Therefore each family $\mathcal{Y}_c$ in a color vector $\mathbf{C}(X_i)$ on X_i corresponds to a "cluster" in Fig. 1, formally defined as follows. For each color $c \in C$, let $G_{Bc} = (\mathcal{Y}_{lc} \cup \mathcal{Y}_{rc}, E_{B_c})$ be a bipartite graph with partite sets $\mathcal{Y}_{lc}$ and $\mathcal{Y}_{rc}$, where a vertex $Y_{lc} \in \mathcal{Y}_{lc}$ and a vertex $Y_{rc} \in \mathcal{Y}_{rc}$ are joined by an edge in E_{B_c} iff $Y_{lc} \cap Y_{rc} \ne \emptyset$. Let $D_{c1}, D_{c2}, \cdots, D_{cb}$ be the connected components of G_{Bc}, and for each j, $1 \le j \le b$, let $Y_{cj} = \bigcup_{Y \in V(D_{cj})} Y$. Then Y_{cj} is the "cluster" mentioned above, and corresponds to the vertex set of a connected component of $G_i(f,c)$ for the coloring f of G_i extended from the colorings of G_l and G_r having color vectors $\mathbf{C}(X_l)$ and $\mathbf{C}(X_r)$, respectively. For a set $W \subseteq V$ we define a family $\mathcal{U}(\mathcal{Y}_{lc}, \mathcal{Y}_{rc}; W)$ of vertex sets, as follows:

$$\mathcal{U}(\mathcal{Y}_{lc}, \mathcal{Y}_{rc}; W) = \{Y_{cj} \cap W \mid 1 \leq j \leq b\}.$$

We have the following lemma.

Lemma 3.6: Let an internal node X_i of T have two children X_l and X_r. Then, for any color vector $\mathbf{C}_i = (\mathcal{Y}_1, \mathcal{Y}_2, \cdots, \mathcal{Y}_p)$ on X_i,

$$\omega(X_i, \mathbf{C}_i) = \min_{\mathbf{C}', \mathbf{C}''} \omega(X_l, \mathbf{C}') + \omega(X_r, \mathbf{C}''), \quad (4)$$

where the minimum is taken over all color vectors $\mathbf{C}' = (\mathcal{Y}_{l1}, \mathcal{Y}_{l2}, \cdots, \mathcal{Y}_{lp})$ on X_l and $\mathbf{C}'' = (\mathcal{Y}_{r1}, \mathcal{Y}_{r2}, \cdots, \mathcal{Y}_{rp})$ on X_r satisfying

$$\mathcal{Y}_c = \mathcal{U}(\mathcal{Y}_{lc}, \mathcal{Y}_{rc}; X_i \cup \{s, t\}) \quad (5)$$

for each color $c \in C$.

Proof: We first prove that

$$\omega(X_i, \mathbf{C}_i) \geq \min_{\mathbf{C}', \mathbf{C}''} \omega(X_l, \mathbf{C}') + \omega(X_r, \mathbf{C}''). \quad (6)$$

If $\mathbf{C}_i$ is not active on X_i, then by Lemma 3.4 $\omega(X_i, \mathbf{C}_i) = \infty$ and hence Eq. (6) holds. Therefore one may assume that $\mathbf{C}_i$ is active and hence G_i has a coloring f with the active color vector $\mathbf{C}_i = (\mathcal{Y}_1, \mathcal{Y}_2, \cdots, \mathcal{Y}_p)$ such that $\omega(G_i, f) = \omega(X_i, \mathbf{C}_i)$. Let f_l and f_r be restrictions of f to E_l and E_r, respectively. Let $\mathbf{C}_l = (\mathcal{Y}_{l1}, \mathcal{Y}_{l2}, \cdots, \mathcal{Y}_{lp})$ be the active color vector of the coloring f_l, and let $\mathbf{C}_r = (\mathcal{Y}_{r1}, \mathcal{Y}_{r2}, \cdots, \mathcal{Y}_{rp})$ be the active color vector of the coloring f_r. Clearly $E_i = E_l \cup E_r$ and $E_l \cap E_r = \emptyset$. Furthermore all vertices shared by graphs G_l and G_r are contained in set $X_l \cap X_r \subseteq X_i$. Moreover $X_i \subseteq X_l \cup X_r$ since either $X_i = X_l$ or $X_i = X_r$. Therefore one can easily observe that $\mathcal{Y}_c = \mathcal{U}(\mathcal{Y}_{lc}, \mathcal{Y}_{rc}; X_i \cup \{s, t\})$ for each color $c \in C$, and hence $\mathbf{C}_l$ and $\mathbf{C}_r$ satisfy Eq. (5). We thus we have

$$\begin{aligned} \omega(X_i, \mathbf{C}_i) &= \omega(G_i, f) \\ &= \omega(G_l, f_l) + \omega(G_r, f_r) \\ &\geq \omega(G_l, \mathbf{C}_l) + \omega(G_r, \mathbf{C}_r) \\ &\geq \min_{\mathbf{C}', \mathbf{C}''} \omega(X_l, \mathbf{C}') + \omega(X_r, \mathbf{C}''), \end{aligned} \quad (7)$$

completing to prove Eq. (6).

We then prove that

$$\omega(X_i, \mathbf{C}_i) \leq \min_{\mathbf{C}', \mathbf{C}''} \omega(X_l, \mathbf{C}') + \omega(X_r, \mathbf{C}''). \quad (8)$$

If $\min_{\mathbf{C}', \mathbf{C}''} \omega(X_l, \mathbf{C}') + \omega(X_r, \mathbf{C}'') = \infty$, then Eq. (8) holds. Therefore one may assume $\min_{\mathbf{C}', \mathbf{C}''}\{\omega(X_l, \mathbf{C}') + \omega(X_r, \mathbf{C}'')\} \neq \infty$, and hence G_l and G_r have colorings g_l and g_r, respectively, with the active color vectors $\mathbf{C}_l = (\mathcal{Y}_{l1}, \mathcal{Y}_{l2}, \cdots, \mathcal{Y}_{lp})$ and $\mathbf{C}_r = (\mathcal{Y}_{r1}, \mathcal{Y}_{r2}, \cdots, \mathcal{Y}_{rp})$ such that $\omega(G_l, g_l) = \omega(X_r, \mathbf{C}_l)$, $\omega(G_r, g_r) = \omega(X_r, \mathbf{C}_r)$ and

$$\omega(X_r, \mathbf{C}_l) + \omega(X_r, \mathbf{C}_r) = \min_{\mathbf{C}', \mathbf{C}''} \omega(X_l, \mathbf{C}') + \omega(X_r, \mathbf{C}'').$$

Since $E_i = E_l \cup E_r$ and $E_l \cap E_r = \emptyset$, the following extension g of g_l and g_r

$$g(e) = \begin{cases} g_l(e) & \text{if } e \in E_l, \text{ and} \\ g_r(e) & \text{if } e \in E_r \end{cases}$$

is a coloring of G_i. Since by Eq. (5) $\mathcal{Y}_c = \mathcal{U}(\mathcal{Y}_{lc}, \mathcal{Y}_{rc}; X_i \cup \{s_c, t_c\})$ for each color $c \in C$, one can observe that $\mathbf{C}_i = (\mathcal{Y}_1, \mathcal{Y}_2, \cdots, \mathcal{Y}_p)$ is the color vector of g. Hence $\mathbf{C}_i$ is an active color vector on X_i. Furthermore we have

$$\begin{aligned} \omega(X_i, \mathbf{C}_i) &\leq \omega(G_i, g) \\ &= \omega(G_l, g_l) + \omega(G_r, g_r) \\ &= \omega(X_l, \mathbf{C}_l) + \omega(X_r, \mathbf{C}_r) \\ &= \min_{\mathbf{C}', \mathbf{C}''} \omega(X_l, \mathbf{C}') + \omega(X_r, \mathbf{C}''), \end{aligned}$$

completing to prove Eq. (8).

By Eqs. (6) and (8) we have verified Eq. (4). ■

Since $|\mathcal{Y}_{lc}|, |\mathcal{Y}_{rc}| \leq k + 4$, the bipartite graph $G_{Bc} = (\mathcal{Y}_{lc} \cup \mathcal{Y}_{rc}, E_{B_c})$ has at most $(k+4)^2$ edges, that is, $|E_{B_c}| \leq (k+4)^2$. Clearly one can check in time $O(k+4)$ whether $Y_{lc} \cap Y_{rc} \neq \emptyset$. Therefore each bipartite graph G_{Bc} can be constructed in time $O((k+4)^3)$, and hence all p bipartite graphs can be constructed in time $O(p(k+4)^3)$. Thus one can compute $\omega(X_i, \mathbf{C})$ of each active color vectors $\mathbf{C}$ on X_i from a pair of active color vectors on X_l and on X_r in time $O(p(k+4)^3)$. By Eq. (2) there are at most $(k+4)^{(k+4)p}$ active color vectors on X_l and at most $(k+4)^{(k+4)p}$ active color vectors on X_r. Therefore there are at most $(k+4)^{2(k+4)p}$ pairs of active color vectors on X_l and on X_r. Thus one can compute all $\omega(X_i, \mathbf{C})$ of active color vectors $\mathbf{C}$ on X_i in time $O(p(k+4)^{2(k+4)p+3})$. Since T has $O(n)$ internal nodes, one can compute the tables for all internal nodes in time $O(np(k+4)^{2(k+4)p+3})$, which corresponds to the second term of the complexity in Theorem 3.1.

This completes a proof of Theorem 3.1.

4. Polynomial-Time Algorithm

The main result of this section is the following theorem.

Theorem 4.1: Let $G = (V, E)$ be a graph of n vertices given by its tree-decomposition with width $\leq k$. Let (s, t) be a pair of two vertices in G, and let p be the positive integer. Then one can compute $\omega(G, p)$ in time

$$O\left(n(p+1)^{2^{k(k+1)/2}} + n(p+1)^{(k+4)^{2k+8}}\right).$$

If k is a bounded constant, then we have the following corollary.

Corollary 4.2: The minimum shared-edge paths problem can be solved in polynomial time for graph with bounded treewidth.

In the remainder of this section we will give a proof of Theorem 4.1. Our idea is to reduce the size of a DP table to

$O((p+1)^{(k+4)^{k+8}})$ by considering "correct colorings within a permutation," "counts" and "pair-counts" defined below.

Clearly the following lemma holds.

Lemma 4.3: Let f be a coloring of $G_i = G[E_i]$ for a node X_i, and let $\varphi : C \rightarrow C$ be any permutation (bijection) of C. Then the composite $\varphi \circ f : E_i \rightarrow 2^C$ of f and φ is extensible if and only if f is extensible, where $\varphi \circ f(e) = \{\varphi(c) \mid c \in f(e)\}$.

As known from Eq. (2), the number of distinct color vectors on X_i is not polynomially bounded unless $p = O(\log n)$. However, the number of distinct "counts" classifying all colorings of G_i is polynomially bounded even if $p = O(n)$, as follows.

We call a mapping $\gamma : \mathcal{F}_{st}(X_i) \rightarrow \{0, 1, 2, \cdots, p\}$ a *count on a node* X_i. A count γ on X_i is defined to be *active* if G_i has a coloring f with a color vector $\mathbf{C}(X_i) = (\mathcal{Y}_1, \mathcal{Y}_2, \cdots, \mathcal{Y}_p)$ such that γ satisfies

$$\gamma(\mathcal{A}) = |\{c \in C \mid \mathcal{A} = \mathcal{Y}_c\}|$$

for each $\mathcal{A} \in \mathcal{F}_{st}(X_i)$. Such a count γ is called the *count of the coloring* f. Clearly, for any active count γ,

$$\sum_{\mathcal{A} \in \mathcal{F}_{st}(X_i)} \gamma(\mathcal{A}) = |C| = p.$$

We now have the following lemma.

Lemma 4.4: Let two colorings f and g of $G_i = G[E_i]$ for a node X_i have the same count on X_i. Then f is extensible if and only if g is extensible.

Proof: It suffices to prove that if f is extensible then g is also extensible. Assume that f is extensible. Then f can be extended to a correct coloring f^* of G. Since f and g have the same count, the following equation holds for any families $\mathcal{A} \in \mathcal{F}_{st}(X_i)$:

$$|\{c \in C \mid \mathcal{A} = \mathcal{Y}(X_i; f, c)\}| = |\{c \in C \mid \mathcal{A} = \mathcal{Y}(X_i; g, c)\}|.$$

Therefore there exists a permutation $\varphi : C \rightarrow C$ such that

$$\mathcal{Y}(X_i; \varphi \circ f, c) \quad = \quad \mathcal{Y}(X_i; g, c)$$

for each color $c \in C$. Let g^* be a coloring of G extended from g as follows:

$$g^*(e) = \begin{cases} g(e) & \text{if } e \in E_i, \\ \varphi(f^*(e)) & \text{otherwise.} \end{cases}$$

We then claim that g^* is a correct coloring of G and hence g is extensible. It suffices to prove that for each color $c \in C$ graph $G(g^*, c)$ contains the terminals s and t, both in the same connected component of $G(g^*, c)$. Let c be any color in C. Since f^* is a correct coloring of G, graph $G(f^*, c)$ contains the terminals s and t, both in the same connected component of $G(f^*, c)$. Therefore graph $G(\varphi \circ f^*, \varphi(c))$ contains the terminals s and t, both in the same connected component of $G(\varphi \circ f^*, \varphi(c))$. The coloring $\varphi \circ f^*$ is the same as the coloring g^* for the edges in $E - E_i$. Furthermore $\mathcal{Y}(X_i; \varphi \circ f, c) = \mathcal{Y}(X_i; g, c)$. Therefore graph $G(g^*, \varphi(c))$ contains s and t, both in the same connected component of $G(g^*, \varphi(c))$. Thus we have proved that g^* is a correct coloring of G. ■

By Lemma 4.4 an active count γ characterizes an equivalence class of extensible colorings of G_i. Since $|X_i| \leq k+1$, by Eq. (1) $|\mathcal{F}_{st}(X_i)| \leq (k+4)^{k+4}$. Therefore there are at most $(k+4)^{k+4}$ distinct $\mathcal{A} \in \mathcal{F}_{st}(X_i)$. Thus the number n_γ of distinct active counts $\gamma : \mathcal{F}_{st}(X_i) \rightarrow \{0, 1, \cdots, p\}$ is at most

$$n_\gamma \leq (p+1)^{(k+4)^{k+4}}. \quad (9)$$

The number n_γ is bounded by a polynomial in p. For a count γ on X_i, let

$$\omega(X_i, \gamma) = \min\{\omega(G_i, f) \mid f \text{ is a coloring of } G_i \text{ with the count } \gamma\},$$

and let $\omega(X_i, \gamma) = \infty$ if no such a coloring exists.

From the table on the root X_{01} containing all $\omega(X_{01}, \gamma)$ of all active counts γ, one can easily compute $\omega(G, p)$, as follows:

$$\omega(G, p) = \min_\gamma\{\omega(X_{01}, \gamma)\} \quad (10)$$

where the minimum is taken over all counts γ on the root X_{01}. By Eqs. (9) and (10), $\omega(G, p)$ can be computed in time $O((p+1)^{(k+4)^{k+4}})$. We thus need to compute a table of all $\omega(X_i, \gamma)$ on each X_i by means of dynamic programming, described below.

We first compute the table of $\omega(X_i, \gamma)$ for all active counts γ on each leaf X_i of T. Since the number of all colorings $f : E_i \rightarrow 2^C$ of G_i is $2^{p|E_i|}$, it is not polynomial in p. We do not need to enumerate all colorings of G_i as the following lemma.

Lemma 4.5: Let X_i be a leaf of T. Let γ be a count on X_i. Then

$$\omega(X_i, \gamma) = \min_\xi \left| \left\{ e \in E_i : \sum_{S \subseteq E_i, S \ni e} \xi(S) \geq 2 \right\} \right|, \quad (11)$$

where the minimum is taken over all mappings $\xi : 2^{E_i} \rightarrow \{0, 1, \cdots, p\}$ such that for each $\mathcal{A} \in \mathcal{F}_{st}(X_i)$

$$\gamma(\mathcal{A}) = \sum_S \xi(S), \quad (12)$$

where the summation above is taken over all $S \subseteq E_i$ such that

$$\mathcal{A} = \{V(D) \cap \mathcal{F}_{st}(X_i) \mid D \text{ is a connected component of } G[S]\}. \quad (13)$$

Proof: We first prove

$$\omega(X_i, \gamma) \geq \min_\xi \left| \left\{ e \in E_i : \sum_{S \subseteq E_i, S \ni e} \xi(S) \geq 2 \right\} \right|. \quad (14)$$

If $\omega(X_i, \gamma) = \infty$, then Eq. (14) holds true. Therefore we may assume $\omega(X_i, \gamma) \neq \infty$ and hence γ is active on X_i. Then G_i has a coloring f with the count γ. For each $\mathcal{A} \in \mathcal{F}_{st}(X_i)$, let

$$C_f(\mathcal{A}) = \{c \in C \mid \mathcal{A} = \mathcal{Y}(X_i; f, c)\}, \quad (15)$$

then

$$\gamma(\mathcal{A}) = |C_f(\mathcal{A})|. \quad (16)$$

Let

$$E_i(f, c) = \{e \in E_i \mid f(e) \ni c\}, \quad (17)$$

for each color $c \in C$ and we define

$$C_g(S) = \{c \in C \mid S = E_i(f, c)\}$$

and

$$\xi(S) = |C_g(S)| \quad (18)$$

for each $S \subseteq E_i$. Then ξ is a mapping $2^{E_i} \to \{0, 1, \cdots, p\}$. We now prove that ξ satisfies Eq. (12). Since $\gamma(\mathcal{A}) = |C_f(\mathcal{A})|$ for each $\mathcal{A} \in \mathcal{F}_{st}(X_i)$ and $C_g(S_1) \cap C_g(S_2) = \emptyset$ for each pair of distinct $S_1, S_2 \subseteq E_i$, by Eqs. (16) and (18) it suffices to show

$$C_f(\mathcal{A}) = \bigcup_S C_g(S) \quad (19)$$

where the union is taken over all $S \subseteq E_i$ satisfying Eq. (13).

We first prove that

$$C_f(\mathcal{A}) \subseteq \bigcup_S C_g(S). \quad (20)$$

It suffices to prove that any color $c \in C_f(\mathcal{A})$ is contained in $C_g(S)$ for some S satisfying Eq. (13). Since $c \in C_f(\mathcal{A})$, we have

$$\mathcal{A} = \mathcal{Y}(X_i; f, c).$$

By Eq. (17), choose $S' = E_i(f, c)$, then $c \in C_g(S')$ and hence we should prove that S' satisfies Eq. (13). By Eq. (17), clearly

$$\begin{aligned} \mathcal{A} &= \{V(D) \cap \mathcal{F}_{st}(X_i) \mid \\ &\qquad D \text{ is a connected component of } G[E_i(f, c)]\} \\ &= \{V(D) \cap \mathcal{F}_{st}(X_i) \mid \\ &\qquad D \text{ is a connected component of } G[S']\}, \end{aligned}$$

and hence S' satisfies Eq. (13).

We next prove that

$$C_f(\mathcal{A}) \supseteq \bigcup_S C_g(S). \quad (21)$$

Let c be any color $c \in C_g(S)$ for S satisfying Eq. (13). Clearly $S = E_i(f, c)$. By the definition of $\mathcal{Y}(X_i; f, c)$, we have

$$\begin{aligned} \mathcal{A} &= \{V(D) \cap \mathcal{F}_{st}(X_i) \mid \\ &\qquad D \text{ is a connected component of } G[E_i(f, c)]\}, \end{aligned}$$

and hence $\mathcal{A} = \mathcal{Y}(X_i; f, c)$. By Eq. (15) we thus have $c \in C_f(\mathcal{A})$. Thus we have proved Eq. (14).

By Eqs. (20) and (21) we have verified Eq. (19).

Similarly as above, we can prove

$$\omega(X_i, \gamma) \leq \min_{\xi} \left| \left\{ e \in E_i : \sum_{S \subseteq E_i, S \ni e} \xi(S) \geq 2 \right\} \right|.$$

■

By Lemma 4.5, a mapping $\xi : 2^{E_i} \to \{0, 1, \cdots, p\}$ such that $\xi(S) = |\{c \in C \mid S = E_i(f, c)\}|$ for each $S \in E_i$ characterizes an equivalence class of colorings f of G_i. Since $|C| = p$ and $|E_i| \leq k(k+1)/2$ for leaf X_i, the number of distinct such mappings $\xi : 2^{E_i} \to \{0, 1, \cdots, p\}$ is at most $(p+1)^{2^{k(k+1)/2}}$ which is polynomial in p. Note that $k = O(1)$. Therefore, all $\omega(X_i, \gamma)$ can be computed for a leaf in time $O((p+1)^{2^{k(k+1)/2}})$. Since T has $O(n)$ leaves, the tables on all leaves can be computed in time $O(n(p+1)^{2^{k(k+1)/2}})$, which corresponds to the first term in the braces of the complexity mentioned in Theorem 4.1.

We now compute all $\omega(X_i, \gamma)$ of all active counts γ on an internal node X_i from all active counts of its children X_l and X_r. Note that $E_i = E_l \cup E_r$ and $E_l \cap E_r = \emptyset$. We call a mapping $\rho : \mathcal{F}_{st}(X_l) \times \mathcal{F}_{st}(X_r) \to \{0, 1, 2, \cdots, p\}$ a *pair-count* on X_i. We define a pair-count ρ to be *active* if G_i has a coloring f such that, for each pair of $\mathcal{A}_l \in \mathcal{F}_{st}(X_l)$ and $\mathcal{A}_r \in \mathcal{F}_{st}(X_r)$

$$\begin{aligned} \rho(\mathcal{A}_l, \mathcal{A}_r) = |\{c \in C \ :\ & \mathcal{A}_l = \mathcal{Y}(X_l; f_l, c), \\ & \mathcal{A}_r = \mathcal{Y}(X_r; f_r, c)\}|, \end{aligned}$$

where $f_l = f|G_l$ is the restriction of f to E_l and $f_r = f|G_r$ is the restriction of f to E_r. Such a pair-count ρ is called the *pair-count of the coloring* f of G_i. Let

$$\begin{aligned} \omega_{\text{pair}}(X_i, \rho) = \min_f \{ & \omega(G_i, f) \mid \\ & f \text{ is a coloring of } G_i \text{ with the pair-count } \rho \}, \end{aligned}$$

and let $\omega_{\text{pair}}(X_i, \rho) = \infty$ if no such a coloring exists. Then we have the following lemma.

Lemma 4.6: Let an internal node X_i of T have two children X_l and X_r, and let ρ be any pair-count on X_i. Then

$$\omega_{\text{pair}}(X_i, \rho) = \min_{\gamma_l, \gamma_r} \omega(X_l, \gamma_l) + \omega(X_r, \gamma_r), \quad (22)$$

where the minimum is taken over all pairs of active counts γ_l on X_l and γ_r on X_r satisfying

(B1) $\gamma_l(\mathcal{A}_l) = \sum_{\mathcal{A} \in \mathcal{F}_{st}(X_r)} \rho(\mathcal{A}_l, \mathcal{A})$ for each $\mathcal{A}_l \in \mathcal{F}_{st}(X_l)$; and

(B2) $\gamma_r(\mathcal{A}_r) = \sum_{\mathcal{A} \in \mathcal{F}_{st}(X_l)} \rho(\mathcal{A}, \mathcal{A}_r)$ for each $\mathcal{A}_r \in \mathcal{F}_{st}(X_r)$.

Using Lemma 4.6, we compute all $\omega_{\text{pair}}(X_i, \rho)$ of all active pair-counts ρ on X_i from all pairs of active counts γ_l on X_l and γ_r on X_r. Since there are at most $(k+4)^{2k+8}$

pairs $(\mathcal{A}_l, \mathcal{A}_r)$ for which $\rho(\mathcal{A}_l, \mathcal{A}_r) \geq 1$, there are at most $(p+1)^{(k+4)^{2k+8}}$ possible distinct active counts ρ. For each ρ of them, we check in time $O((k+4)^{k+4}) = O(1)$ whether ρ satisfies Conditions (B1) and (B2) in Lemma 4.6. Checking Conditions (B1) and (B2) for all possible ρ's can be done in time $O((p+1)^{2(k+4)^{k+4}})$. Thus we have shown that all active pair-counts ρ and $\omega_{\rm pair}(X_i, \rho)$ on X_i can be computed in time

$$O((p+1)^{(k+2)^{2k+8}}).$$

We now show how to compute all $\omega(X_i, \gamma)$ of all active counts γ on an internal node X_i from all active pair-counts on X_i as in the following lemma.

Lemma 4.7: Let an internal node X_i of T have two children X_l and X_r, and let γ be any count on X_i. Then

$$\omega(X_i, \gamma) = \min_{\rho'}\{\omega_{\rm pair}(X_i, \rho')\}, \quad (23)$$

where the minimum is taken over all active pair-counts ρ' on X_i such that for each pair $\mathcal{A} \in \mathcal{F}_{st}(X_i)$

$$\gamma(\mathcal{A}) = \sum \rho(\mathcal{A}_l, \mathcal{A}_r), \quad (24)$$

where the summation above is taken over all pairs of $\mathcal{A}_l \in \mathcal{F}_{st}(X_l)$ and $\mathcal{A}_r \in \mathcal{F}_{st}(X_r)$ satisfying

$$\mathcal{A} = \mathcal{U}(\mathcal{A}_l, \mathcal{A}_r; X_i), \quad (25)$$

where $\mathcal{U}$ has been defined in the previous section.

Using Lemma 4.7, we compute all $\omega(X_i, \gamma)$ of all active counts γ on X_i from all active pair-counts ρ on X_i. There are at most $(p+1)^{(k+4)^{2k+8}}$ distinct active pair-counts ρ. From each ρ of them, we compute γ satisfying Eq. (24) in time $O(1)$. Since $|\mathcal{A}_l| \leq k+4$, the bipartite graph $G_{Bc} = (\mathcal{A}_l \cup \mathcal{A}_r, E_c)$ defined in the previous section contains at most $(k+4)^2 = O(1)$ edges. Therefore one can check in time $O(1)$ for $\mathcal{A}$, $\mathcal{A}_l$ and $\mathcal{A}_r$ whether $\mathcal{A} = \mathcal{U}(\mathcal{A}_l, \mathcal{A}_r; X_i)$, and hence one can check Eq. (25) in time $O(1)$. Thus one can compute all $\omega(X_i, \gamma)$ of all active counts γ on X_i in time

$$O((p+1)^{(k+4)^{2k+8}}).$$

Since T has $O(n)$ internal nodes, one can compute the tables for all internal nodes in time $O(n(p+1)^{(p+1)^{2k+8}})$, which corresponds to the second term in the braces of the complexity mentioned in Theorem 4.1.

This completes a proof of Theorem 4.1.

5. Conclusion

In this paper we gave a polynomial-time algorithm for the minimum shared-edge paths problem on graphs with bounded treewidth. Our algorithms can be extended to more than one terminal pair as follows. Let $(s_1, t_1), (s_2, t_2), \cdots, (s_\alpha, t_\alpha)$ be α pairs of two terminals in G, and for each i, $1 \leq i \leq \alpha$, let p_i be a positive integer. Then the problem is to find $\sum_{1 \leq i \leq \alpha} p_i$ paths such that there are p_i paths connecting s_i and t_i for each i, $1 \leq i \leq \alpha$, so as to minimize the number of edges shared among the paths. If α is bounded, our algorithm can be extended to solve the problem in polynomial time for graphs with bounded treewidth.

Acknowledgments

This work is partially supported by the Japan Society for the Promotion of Science (JSPS), Grant-in-Aid for Scientific Research, Grant Numbers 23500001.

References

[1] S. Arnborg, B. Courcelle, A. Proskurowski and D. Seese. An algebraic theory of graph reduction. *Journal of the Association for Computing Machinery*, Vol. 40, No. 5, pp. 1134–1164, 1993.

[2] S. Arnborg, J. Lagergren and D. Seese. Easy problems for tree-decomposable graphs. *Journal of Algorithms*, Vol. 12, No. 2, pp. 308–340, 1991.

[3] H. L. Bodlaender. Polynomial algorithms for graph isomorphism and chromatic index on partial k-trees. *Journal of Algorithms*, Vol. 11, No. 4, pp. 631–643, 1990.

[4] H. L. Bodlaender. A linear time algorithm for finding tree-decompositions of small treewidth. *SIAM Journal on Computing*, Vol. 25, pp. 1305–1317, 1996.

[5] R. B. Borie, R. G. Parker and C. A. Tovey. Automatic generation of linear-time algorithms from predicate calculus descriptions of problems on recursively constructed graph families. *Algorithmica*, Vol. 7, pp. 555–581, 1992.

[6] B. Courcelle. The monadic second-order logic of graphs I: Recognizable sets of finite graphs. *Information and Computation*, Vol. 85, pp. 12–75, 1990.

[7] M.T. Omran, J.-R. Sack and H. Zarrabi-Zadeh. Finding paths with minimum shared edges *Journal of Combinatorial Optimization*, to appear.

[8] N. Robertson and P.D. Seymour. Graph minors. II. Algorithmic aspects of tree-width. *Journal of Algorithms*, Vol. 7, pp. 309–322, 1986.

[9] N. Robertson and P.D. Seymour. Graph minors. XIII. The disjoint paths problem. *J. of Combin. Theory, Series B*, Vol. 63, No. 1, pp. 65–110, 1995.

[10] P. Scheffler. A practial linear time algorithm for disjoint paths in graphs with bounded tree-width. Technical Report, 396, Dept. of Mathematics, Technische Universität Berlin, 1994.

[11] K. Takamizawa, T. Nishizeki and N. Saito. Linear-time computability of combinatorial problems on series-parallel graphs. *Journal of ACM*, Vol. 29, No. 3, pp. 623–641, 1982.

[12] X. Zhou and T. Nishizeki. Optimal parallel algorithms for edge-coloring partial k-trees with bounded degrees. *IEICE Trans. on Fundamentals of Electronics, Communication and Computer Sciences*, Vol. E78-A, pp. 463–469, 1995.

[13] T. Nishizeki, J. Vygen and X. Zhou. The edge-disjoint paths problem is NP-complete for series-parallel graphs. *Discrete Applied Mathematics*,115, pp. 177-186, 2001.

[14] X. Zhou, S. Nakano and T. Nishizeki. Edge-coloring partial k-trees. *Journal of Algorithms*, Vol. 21, pp. 598–617, 1996.

[15] X. Zhou, H. Suzuki and T. Nishizeki. A linear algorithm for edge-coloring series-parallel multigraphs. *Journal of Algorithms*, Vol. 20, pp. 174–201, 1996.

[16] X. Zhou, S. Tamura and T. Nishizeki. Finding edge-disjoint paths in partial k-trees. *Algorithmica*, 26, pp. 3-30, 2000.

Labeling for Vertices in Strict 2-Threshold Graphs

Wei-Da Hao
Department of Electrical Engineering and Computer Science, Texas A&M University-Kingsville
Kingsville, TX 78363, U.S.A.

Abstract *- In this paper, we show a labeling scheme for a class of graphs named Strict 2-Threshold that have threshold dimension 2. The labeling scheme characterizes the structural properties of neighborhood of each vertex. As a consequence, $O(n)$ variation of a known $O(m)$ recognition algorithm by Rossella Petreschi and Andrea Sterbini published in 1995 is presented, where n is the number of nodes, and m is the number of edges in the graph.*

Keywords: *strict 2-threshold, recognition, labeling scheme*

1 Introduction

We consider finite undirected graphs with no loops or multiple edges. Let $G = (V, E)$ be such a graph, where V is the set of vertex of G with magnitude $|V| = n$ and E is the set of edges of G with magnitude $|E| = m$. Strict 2-threshold (S2T[1]) graphs are a subset of 2-threshold graphs. A graph $G = (V, E)$ is called a 2-threshold graph, if it is edge-coverable with two threshold graphs, $T_1 = (V_1, E_1)$ and $T_2 = (V_2, E_2)$. An example of threshold graph is illustrated in Figure 1-a. T_1 and T_2 are called the threshold components, and constitute a threshold configuration of G. The threshold dimension is defined to be the minimum number of threshold sub-graphs to cover the edges. So, 2-threshold graphs are of threshold dimension 1 or 2. The set of vertices that contains the intersection of the vertex sets of T_1 and T_2 is V_C, i.e. $V_C = V_1 \cap V_2$. The sub-graph induced by V_C is called connection graph, G_V. Vertices of T_1 can be partitioned to K_1 and I_1, i.e. $V_1 = K_1 + I_1$, where K_1 is a clique and I_1 is a stable set. Similarly, vertices of T_2 can be partitioned to K_2 and I_2, i.e. $V_2 = K_2 + I_2$, where K_2 is a clique and I_2 is a stable set. The neighbors of $v \in V$ in G are the union of neighbors of v in T_1 and neighbors of v in T_2, i.e. $adj_G(v) = adj_{T_1}(v) \cup adj_{T_2}(v)$.

A graph G is called a S2T graph if it is a 2-threshold graph, and exists at least one threshold configuration such that every triangle of G is also a triangle in one of its threshold components. Examples of S2T graphs are illustrated in Figure 1-b and 1-c. Some properties and characterization of S2T graphs can be found in [1, 3]. In [1] an algorithm published in 1995 to recognize and decompose strict 2-threshold graphs in $O(m)$ time is presented. This algorithm uses adjacency lists as data structure for input graph, and its design is based on the neighbors of the maximum-degree vertices. A $O(m^2)$ time algorithm based on the conflict graph and related signed graph was known for recognition of S2T graphs and published in 1988 [3]. A $O(\log n)$ time CRCW parallel algorithm using $O(n^3/\log n)$ processor based on standard representation to recognize S2T graphs was published in 1991 [4].

In section 2, labeling scheme for S2T graphs is addressed. In section 3, we show a $O(n)$ variation in time of the existing recognition algorithm of time complexity $O(m)$ proposed in [1], as a result of the labeling scheme. Section 4 contains summary of the works achieved in this paper and future research.

2 Labeling for strict 2-threshold (S2T) graphs

In the proposed labeling scheme, the label for each vertex is composed of two parts. The first part of the label is assigned based on if it is in the connection graph. For vertex not belonging to connection graph, NC is assigned to the first part, otherwise C is assigned. The second part of the label indicates the status of the vertex in the threshold configuration. Based on whether the vertex belongs to a clique or independent set in the threshold components, K, I, I^2, K^2 or IK are assigned as the second part of the label. Thus, each vertex has one of the following labels: NC-K, NC-I, C-I^2, C-K^2, and C-IK. Figure 1-b and 1-c illustrate the labeling scheme. $L(v)$ indicates the label of v.

Lemma 1:
If $G = (V, E)$ is a S2T graph, and $v \in V$, then $adj_{T_1}(v) \cap adj_{T_2}(v) = \emptyset$. And, if $L(v)$ is C-I^2, C-K^2 or C-IK, then $ab \notin E$, where $a \in adj_{T_1}(v)$ and $b \in adj_{T_2}(v)$.
Proof: To prove $adj_{T_1}(v) \cap adj_{T_2}(v) = \emptyset$ by contradiction, we assume $\exists u \in adj_{T_1}(v) \cap adj_{T_2}(v)$. As a result, $uv \in E_1 \cap E_2$, which is against the definition of S2T graphs that $E = E_1 + E_2$. So, the assumption is not correct, and thus $adj_{T_1}(v) \cap adj_{T_2}(v) = \emptyset$ is true.
To prove $ab \notin E$ by contradiction, we assume $\exists ab \in E$, where $a, b \in V$ such that $a \in adj_{T_1}(v)$ and $b \in adj_{T_2}(v)$. Under the assumption, Δvab exists in G with $va \in E_1$ and $vb \in E_2$, which is against the definition of S2T graphs that the edges of triangle of G belong to the same threshold component . So, the assumption is not correct, and thus it is true that $ab \notin E$. Q.E.D.

[1] S2T is abbreviation for Strict 2-threshold graphs throughout this article.

1-a

1-b

1-c

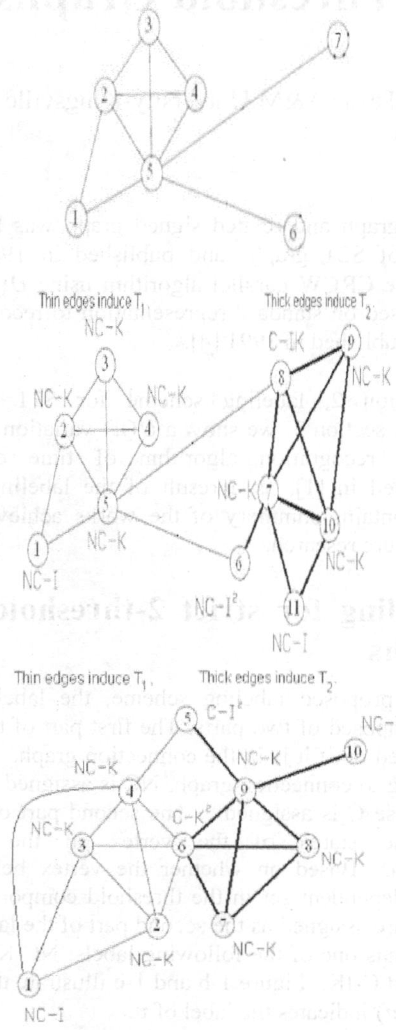

Figure 1 1-a Illustration of threshold graph. The clique is composed of vertices 2, 3, 4 and 5. The independent set is composed of vertices 1, 6 and 7; 1-b Illustration of labeling for strict 2-threshold (S2T) graphs. Clique of $T_1$is composed of vertices 2, 3, 4 and 5. Independent set of $T_1$is composed of vertices 1, 6 and 8; Clique of T_2 is composed of vertices 7, 8, 9 and 10. Independent set of T_2 is composed of vertices 6 and 11; 1-c Illustration of labeling for strict 2-threshold (S2T) graphs. Clique of $T_1$is composed of vertices 2, 3, 4 and 6. Independent set of $T_1$is composed of vertices 1 and 5; Clique of T_2 is composed of vertices 6, 7, 8 and 9. Independent set of T_2 is composed of vertices 5 and 10.

With Lemma 1, the correctness of the following theorem is straightforward. The proof is thus skipped.

Theorem 1 $G = (V, E)$ is a S2T graph, and $v \in V$. Characterization of sub-graph $G_{v'}$, where $v' = adj_G(v)$:

1. If $L(v)$ = NC-K, $G_{v'}$ is a threshold graph.
2. If $L(v)$ = NC-I, $G_{v'}$ is a clique.
3. If $L(v)$ = C-I^2, $G_{v'}$ is two independent cliques.
4. If $L(v)$ = C-K^2, $G_{v'}$ is two independent threshold graphs.
5. If $L(v)$ = C-IK, $G_{v'}$ is two separated components, where one is a clique and the other is a threshold graph.

3 *O(n)* variation in time of the existing recognition algorithm

Execution of the *O (m)* algorithm to recognize S2T graph in [1] has two phases. The input to this algorithm is the graph $G = (V, E)$ represented by its adjacency list.

In the first phase, a vertex of maximum degree, v_{max}, and its neighboring vertices $adj_G(v_{max})$ are selected. Let $N_1 = \{v_{max}\} \cup adj_G(v_{max})$. Then, S is derived as those vertices in N_1 which have different degree in N_1 and G. Finally, N_2 is derived as the vertices not belonging to N_1 and belonging to S, *i.e.* $N_2 = V - N_1 + S$. Sub-graph induced by N_1 is G_{N_1}, and sub-graph induced by N_2 is G_{N_2}.

Then, the algorithm tests if G_{N_1} and $G_{N_2}$are threshold graphs, and if S is an independent set. If any of the tests on G_{N_1}, $G_{N_2}$and S fails, second phase takes place. Otherwise, G is a S2T graph with G_{N_1} and G_{N_2}as its threshold components. In recognition of threshold graphs, the authors of the paper in [1] choose Orlin's algorithm [6] of *O(m)* complexity.

In the second phase, a maximum degree vertex, $v'_{max}$is selected in $adj_G(v_{max})$. Then, repeat the steps in phase one with v_{max} replaced by v'_{max} to generate G_{N_1}, $G_{N_2}$and S. Then, the algorithm tests if G_{N_1} and $G_{N_2}$are threshold graphs, and if S is an independent set. If any of the tests on G_{N_1}, $G_{N_2}$and S fail, G is not a S2T graph.

In current paper, Chvátal and Hammer's recognition algorithm for threshold graphs [5] is selected to recognize threshold graphs in phase 1, which is an implementation of Theorem 2 in the following.

Theorem 2 [5]
Let $G = (V, E)$ be an undirected graph with degree sequence $d_1 < d_2 < \cdots < d_k$. Define d_0 and $d_{k+1} = |V| - 1$. B_i contains vertices of degree d_i, where $i = 0 \cdots k$. $V = B_0 + B_1 + \cdots + B_k$. G is a threshold graph if and only if the recursions below are satisfied: $d_{i+1} = d_i + |B_{k-i}|$, where $i = 0, 1, \cdots, \lfloor k/2 \rfloor - 1$, and $d_i = d_{i+1} - |B_{k-i}|$, where $i = k, k-1, \cdots, \lfloor k/2 \rfloor + 1$.

Lemma 2
Let $G = (V, E)$ be a graph with a universal vertex v_{max} , and G' is induced by $V - V_{\deg\_1}$, where $V_{\deg\_1} = \{v | v \in V, vv_{max} \in E \text{ and } deg_G(v) = 1\}$. Then, G is a threshold graph if and only if $G'$is a threshold graph.
Proof: ($\Rightarrow$) If G is a threshold graph, its sub-graph G' is also a threshold graph.

($\Leftarrow$) If G' is a threshold graph, its vertex set can be partitioned to an independent set and a clique, i.e. $V(G') = I_{G'} + K_{G'}$. From the definition of threshold graph, we know

$$adj_{K_{G'}}(v) \subseteq adj_{K_{G'}}(w) \text{ or } adj_{K_{G'}}(w) \subseteq adj_{K_{G'}}(v), \text{ for } v, w \in I_G. \quad (1)$$

Since v_{max} is universal in G, it is still a universal vertex in G'. So,

$$\{v_{max}\} \subset adj_{K_{G'}}(v) \qquad \text{for } \forall v \in I_{G'} \quad (2)$$

Let $I = I_{G'} + V_{\deg\_1}$ and $K = K_{G'}$. By (1), (2) and the definition of $V_{\deg\_1}$, $adj_K(v) \subseteq adj_K(w)$ or $adj_K(w) \subseteq adj_K(v)$, for $v, w \in I_G$. Thus, G is a threshold graph with $I_G = I$ and $K_G = K$. Q.E.D.

Based on lemma 2, the algorithm implementation of Theorem 2 is revised and listed in the following to recognize thresholdness of G_{N_1}.

Algorithm 1 Recognize if G_{N_1} is a threshold graph
Input: Adjacency list of G_{N_1}
Output: Yes. G_{N_1} is a threshold graph. Or, no, G_{N_1} is not a threshold graph.
Begin

1. Identify $V_{\deg\_1} = \{v | v \in V, vv_{max} \in E \text{ and } deg_G(v) = 1\}$.
2. Generate degree sequence:
   $d_1(G_{N_1-V_{\deg\_1}}) < d_2(G_{N_1-V_{\deg\_1}}) < \cdots < d_{k'}(G_{N_1-V_{\deg\_1}})$
3. Define $d_0 = 0$ and $d_{k'+1} = |N_1 - V_{\deg\_1}| - 1$.
4. i= 0; j= k';
6. **WHILE** ($i < \lfloor k'/2 \rfloor$)
   if $d_{i+1}(G_{N_1-V_{\deg\_1}}) \neq (d_i(G_{N_1-V_{\deg\_1}}) + |B_{k'-i}(G_{N_1-V_{\deg\_1}})|)$
   { G_{N_1} is not a threshold graph. **STOP**.};
   i = i+1;
   END WHILE
7. **WHILE** ($j \geq \lfloor k'/2 \rfloor + 1$)
   if $d_j(G_{N_1-V_{\deg\_1}}) \neq (d_{j+1}(G_{N_1-V_{\deg\_1}}) - |B_{k'-j}(G_{N_1-V_{\deg\_1}})|)$
   { G_{N_1} is not a threshold graph. STOP.};
   j= j-1;
   END WHILE
8. G_{N_1} is a threshold graph.

End

Lemma 3
G is a S2T graph. Let the graph induced by $N_G[v] = adj_G(v) \cup \{v\}$, where $v \in V_C$, by $G_{N_G[v]}$, and its degree sequence is $d_1(G_{N_G[v]}) < d_2(G_{N_G[v]}) < \cdots < d_l(G_{N_G[v]})$. Define $d_0(G_{N_G[v]}) = 0$ and $d_{l+1}(G_{N_G[v]}) = |N_G[v]| - 1$. Then, when $d_1(G_{N_G[v]}) = 1$ and $d_l(G_{N_G[v]}) - |B_1(G_{N_G[v]})| = d_{l-1}(G_{N_G[v]})$, $G_{N_G[v]}$ is a threshold graph.

Proof: Sub-graph induced by $adj_G(v)$ is two separate non-empty components, C_1 and C_2, according to 3, 4 and 5 of Theorem 1. We first show the necessary condition for $d_1(G_{N_G[v]}) = 1$ and $d_l(G_{N_G[v]}) - |B_1(G_{N_G[v]})| = d_{l-1}(G_{N_G[v]})$ are: C_1 or C_2 is a stable set. Let $V(C_1)$ and $V(C_2)$ be the set of vertex of C_1 and C_2 respectively. Since $v \in V_C$, v is adjacent to every vertex of C_1 and C_2, and the following are true:

1. $l \geq 2$.
2. $B_l(G_{N_G[v]}) = \{v\}$.
3. $d_l(G_{N_G[v]}) = |V(C_1) - B_1(G_{N_G[v]})| + |V(C_2) - B_1(G_{N_G[v]})| + |B_1(G_{N_G[v]})|$

By moving $|B_1(G_{N_G[v]})|$ to left hand side in 3 above, we obtain

$$d_l(G_{N_G[v]}) - |B_1(G_{N_G[v]})| = |V(C_1) - B_1(G_{N_G[v]})| + |V(C_2) - B_1(G_{N_G[v]})| \quad (3)$$

When neither C_1 nor C_2 is stable set, both C_1 and C_2 contain K_2(clique of two vertices). This implies $|V(C_1) - B_1(G_{N_G[v]})| \geq 2$ and $|V(C_2) - B_1(G_{N_G[v]})| \geq 2$ (4)

When $d_1(G_{N_G[v]}) = 1$, $d_{l-1}(G_{N_G[v]}) =$

$$\max\,[|V(C_1) - B_1(G_{N_G[v]})| + 1,\ |V(C_2) - B_1(G_{N_G[v]})| + 1] \quad (5)$$

Using (4) and (5) in (3), we have the following derivation

1. If $d_{l-1}(G_{N_G[v]}) = |V(C_1) - B_1(G_{N_G[v]})| + 1$, then $d_l(G_{N_G[v]}) - |B_1(G_{N_G[v]})| \geq |V(C_1) - B_1(G_{N_G[v]})| + 2 > d_{l-1}(G_{N_G[v]})$.
2. If $d_{l-1}(G_{N_G[v]}) = |V(C_2) - B_1(G_{N_G[v]})| + 1$, then $d_l(G_{N_G[v]}) - |B_1(G_{N_G[v]})| \geq |V(C_2) - B_1(G_{N_G[v]})| + 2 > d_{l-1}(G_{N_G[v]})$.

And it leads to the inference:

$[d_1(G_{N_G[v]}) = 1] \wedge \sim[C_1 \text{ or } C_2 \text{ is stable set.}] \Rightarrow d_l(G_{N_G[v]}) - |B_1(G_{N_G[v]})| \neq d_{l-1}(G_{N_G[v]})$

And, the contra-positive equivalence of the inference is $d_l\left(G_{N_{G[v]}}\right) - \left|B_1\left(G_{N_{G[v]}}\right)\right| = d_{l-1}\left(G_{N_{G[v]}}\right) \Rightarrow \sim[d_1(G_{N_G[v]}) = 1] \vee [C_1 \text{ or } C_2 \text{ is stable set.}]$

So, the necessary condition for $d_1\left(G_{N_{G[v]}}\right) = 1$ and $d_l\left(G_{N_{G[v]}}\right) - \left|B_1\left(G_{N_{G[v]}}\right)\right| = d_{l-1}\left(G_{N_{G[v]}}\right)$ is: C_1 or C_1 is a stable set.

When both C_1 and C_2 are stable sets, $G_{N_{G[v]}}$ is a star graph, which belongs to the class of threshold graphs. And, when one of C_1 and C_2 is stable set and the other is not, according to 3, 4 and 5 of Theorem 1, the other is a clique or threshold graph. In this situation, $G_{N_{G[v]}}$ is a threshold graph. Thus, we have proved when $d_1\left(G_{N_{G[v]}}\right) = 1$ and $d_l\left(G_{N_{G[v]}}\right) - \left|B_1\left(G_{N_{G[v]}}\right)\right| = d_{l-1}\left(G_{N_{G[v]}}\right)$, $G_{N_{G[v]}}$ is a threshold graph. Q.E.D.

Theorem 3
Let G be a S2T graph. The outcome of applying algorithm 1 is either the algorithm runs to the end (line 8), or the algorithm stops in the first iteration of while loop.
Proof: Suppose T_1, T_2 is a threshold configuration of G. Let the degree sequence of T_1 be $d_1(T_1) < d_2(T_1) < \cdots < d_{k\_1}(T_1)$, and the degree sequence of T_2 be $d_1(T_2) < d_2(T_2) < \cdots < d_{k\_2}(T_2)$. Based on lemma 3 in [1], each maximum degree vertex, v_{max}, in G is located in one of the following locations: 1. v_{max} is in $B_{k\_1}(T_1) - V_C$. 2. v_{max} is in $B_{k\_2}(T_2) - V_C$. 3. v_{max} is in V_C.

In cases 1 and 2, G_{N_1} is an induced sub-graph of T_1 or T_2, and thus is a threshold graph. According to lemma 2, algorithm 1 will run to the end (line 8) and recognize G_{N_1} as a threshold graph.

In case 3, the label for v_{max} is C-I^2, C-K^2 or C-IK. According to 3, 4 and 5 of Theorem 1, $G_{N_1-\{v_{max}\}}$ is two separate components, C_1 and C_2. Let the degree sequence of G_{N_1} be $d_0(G_{N_1}) < d_1(G_{N_1}) < \cdots < d_l(G_{N_1})$, and $B_i(G_{N_1})$ contains vertex of degree $d_i(G_{N_1})$ for $0 \le i \le l$, where $l \ge 2$, $d_0(G_{N_1}) = 0$, $|B_0(G_{N_1})| = 0$, $d_l(G_{N_1}) = |V(C_1)| + |V(C_2)|$ and $B_l(G_{N_1}) = \{v_{max}\}$.

If $d_1(G_{N_1}) \neq 1$, i.e. $d_1(G_{N_1}) \ge 2$, $G_{N_1-V_{\deg\_1}}$ is the same as G_{N_1}. Thus,

$$B_{k'}\left(G_{N_1-V_{\deg\_1}}\right) = B_l(G_{N_1}) = \{v_{max}\}$$

The algorithm will stop at the first iteration of the while loop beginning at line 6, since the condition of if statement is true.

If $d_1(G_{N_1}) = 1$, $B_1(G_{N_1})$ contains vertex of degree 1 in G_{N_1}. Algorithm 1 will delete $V_{\deg\_1} = B_1(G_{N_1})$ from G_{N_1} and generate degree sequence $d_0\left(G_{N_1-V_{\deg\_1}}\right) < d_1\left(G_{N_1-V_{\deg\_1}}\right) < \cdots < d_{k'}\left(G_{N_1-V_{\deg\_1}}\right)$ where $k' = l-1$, $d_0\left(G_{N_1-V_{\deg\_1}}\right) = 0$ and $d_i\left(G_{N_1-V_{\deg\_1}}\right) = d_{i+1}(G_{N_1})$ for $i = 1 \cdots k'-1$.

1. When $d_l(G_{N_1}) - |B_1(G_{N_1})| > d_{l-1}(G_{N_1})$:
   $d_{k'}\left(G_{N_1-V_{\deg\_1}}\right) = d_l(G_{N_1}) - |B_1(G_{N_1})|$. In the first iteration of the while loop on line 6, the condition of the if statement "if $d_{i+1}\left(G_{N_1-V_{\deg\_1}}\right) \neq d_i\left(G_{N_1-V_{\deg\_1}}\right) + |B_{k'-i}\left(G_{N_1-V_{\deg\_1}}\right)|$ ..." is true, since $d_1\left(G_{N_1-V_{\deg\_1}}\right) \neq d_0\left(G_{N_1-V_{\deg\_1}}\right) + |B_{k'}(G_{N_1-V_{\deg\_1}})|$ can be justified from the facts that $d_1\left(G_{N_1-V_{\deg\_1}}\right) = d_2(G_{N_1}) \ge 2$, $d_0\left(G_{N_1-V_{\deg\_1}}\right) = 0$ and $|B_{k'}\left(G_{N_1-V_{\deg\_1}}\right)| = 1$.

This indicates the recursion for threshold graph in Theorem 2 is not satisfied, the algorithm stops.

2. When $d_l(G_{N_1}) - |B_1(G_{N_1})| < d_{l-1}(G_{N_1})$:
   This condition never exists.
3. When $d_l(G_{N_1}) - |B_1(G_{N_1})| = d_{l-1}(G_{N_1})$:
   According to lemma 3, $G_{N_1-V_{\deg\_1}}$ is a threshold graph. Algorithm 1 will run to the end (line 8) and claim G_{N_1} as a threshold graph. Q.E.D.

The $O(n)$ variation on the S2T recognition algorithm proposed in 1995 is stated in the following corollary.

Corollary
In the first phase of the algorithm in [1], if the test of thresholdness of the sub-graph induced by $N_1 = \{v_{max}\} \cup adj_G(v_{max})$. is negative, the execution of second phase takes place, which has time complexity $O(n)$. However, by using algorithm listed in Figure 2, we know G is not a S2T graph, if it stops not in the first iteration of the while loop. And thus the execution of phase 2 is waived. As a consequence, $O(n)$ variation in time complexity is generated.

4 Conclusion

We have presented vertex labeling scheme for the class of perfect graphs known as strict 2-threshold (S2T) graphs. The adjacent set of vertex in S2T graph has been shown to have specific structure according to its assigned label. The *O(m)* recognition algorithm for S2T graph in [1] can be refined with the outcome enabled by the proposed labeling scheme. As a consequence, many non-S2T graphs can be identified as early as in phase 1, instead of proceeding to phase 2, and thus $O(n)$ variation in time is obtained. Labeling scheme can extend its application further to other algorithmic development for S2T graphs and other classes of graphs coverable by threshold graphs.

5 References

[1] Rossella Petreschi, Andrea Sterbini, Recognizing strict 2-threshold graphs in O(m) time, Information Processing Letters 54 (1995) 193 – 198.
[2] Frank Harry, Uri Peled, Hamiltonian Threshold Graphs, Discrete Applied Mathematics 16 (1987) 11-15.
[3] N.V.R. Mahadev, U.N. Peled, Strict 2-threshold graphs, Discrete Appl. Math. 21 (1988) 113-131.
[4] Lin Yu Tseng, W. D. Hao, An NC Algorithm for Recognizing Strict 2-threshold Graphs, Int'l Conference on Parallel Processing 3 (1991) 296-297.
[5] Martin Charles Golumbic, Algorithmic Graph Theory and Perfect Graphs, Elsevier, 2004, Chapter 10 Threshold Graphs.
[6] James Orlin, The minimal integral separator of a threshold graph, Annals of Discrete mathematics 1 (1977) 415-419.
[7] N.V.R. Mahadev, U.N. Peled, Threshold Graphs and Related Topics, Annnals of Discrete Mathematics 56, North-Holland, Amsterdam, 1995.

Weak Convex Restrained Dominating Critical Graphs

P.J.A. Alphonse [1] and T.N. Janakiraman [2]
[1] *Department of Computer Applications, National Institute of Technology, Tiruchirappalli, India.*
[2] *Department of Mathematics, National Institute of Technology, Tiruchirappalli, India.*

Abstract: - *In a graph G = (V, E), a set D⊆ V is a weak convex set if $d_{<D>}(u, v) = d_G(u, v)$ for any two vertices u, v in D. A weak convex set D is called as a weak convex dominating (WCD) set if each vertex of V-D is adjacent to at least one vertex in D. A weak convex dominating set D is called weak convex restrained dominating (WCRD) set if every vertex in V(G)-D is adjacent to a vertex in D and another vertex in V(G)-D.*

Consider a network contains transceivers that are capable of broadcasting either a primary signal or an auxiliary signal but not both and capable of receiving both a primary signal and an auxiliary signal. Now the problem under consideration is that finding a delay preserving sub network that broadcasts the primary signal such that the transceivers not broadcasting the primary signal requires to receive the auxiliary signal. Problem of finding such a sub network is equivalent to finding a weak convex restrained dominating set in the underlying graph of the network.

In this paper we study the structure of the network/sub network with respect to WCRD set and addition of new links in the network.

Keywords: *domination number, distance, neighbourhood, weak convex set, weak convex dominating set, weak convex restrained dominating set.*

1. INTRODUCTION

Graphs discussed in this paper are undirected and simple. Unless otherwise stated the graphs which we consider are connected graphs only. For a graph G, let V(G) and E(G) denote its vertex and edge set respectively and p and q denote the cardinality of those sets respectively. The *degree* of a vertex *v* in a graph G is denoted by $deg_G(v)$. The minimum and maximum degree in a graph is denoted by δ and Δ respectively. The length of any shortest path between any two vertices *u* and *v* of a connected graph G is called the *distance between u and v* and is denoted by $d_G(u, v)$. The distance between two vertices in different components of a disconnected graph is defined to be ∞. For a connected graph G, the *eccentricity* $e_G(v) = \max\{d_G(u, v): u \in V(G)\}$. If there is no confusion, we simply use the notion deg(*v*), d(*u*, *v*) and e(*v*) to denote degree, distance and eccentricity respectively for the concerned graph. The minimum and maximum eccentricities are the *radius* and *diameter* of G, denoted r(G) and diam(G) respectively. When these two are equal, the graph is called *self-centered* graph with radius r, equivalently is *r self-centered*. A vertex *u* is said to be an *eccentric vertex* of *v* in a graph G, if d(*u*, *v*) = e(*v*). In general, *u* is called an eccentric vertex, if it is an eccentric vertex of some vertex. For *v*∈ V(G), the *neighbourhood* $N_G(v)$ of *v* is the set of all vertices adjacent to *v* in G. The set $N_G[v] = N_G(v) \cup \{v\}$ is called the *closed neighbourhood* of *v*. A set S of edges in a graph is said to be *independent* if no two of the edges in S are adjacent. An edge e = (*u*, *v*) is a *dominating edge* in a graph G if every vertex of G is adjacent to at least one of *u* and *v*.

The concept of domination in graphs was introduced by Ore. A set D⊆ V(G) is called *dominating set* of G if every vertex in V(G)-D is adjacent to some vertex in D. D is said to be a *minimal* dominating set if D-{*v*} is not a dominating set for any *v*∈ D. The *domination number* γ(G) of G is the minimum cardinality of a dominating set. We call a set of vertices a γ-set if it is a dominating set with cardinality γ(G). Different types of dominating sets have been studied by imposing conditions on the dominating sets. A dominating set D is called *connected* (*independent*) dominating set if the induced subgraph <D> is connected (independent). D is called a *total dominating set* if every vertex in V(G) is adjacent to some vertex in D.

A cycle of D of a graph G is called a *dominating cycle* of G, if every vertex in V – D is adjacent to some vertex in D. A dominating set D of a graph G is called a *clique dominating set* of G if <D> is complete. A set D is called an *efficient dominating set* of G if every vertex in V – D is adjacent to exactly one vertex in D. A set D ⊆ V is called a *global dominating set* if D is a dominating set in G and $\overline{G}$. A set D is called a *restrained dominating set* if every vertex in V(G)-D is adjacent to a vertex in D and another vertex in V(G)-D. A set D is a *weak convex dominating set* if each vertex of V-D is adjacent to at least one vertex in D and $d_{<D>}(u,v) = d_G(u,v)$ for any two vertices u, v in D. By $\gamma_c, \gamma_i, \gamma_t, \gamma_o, \gamma_k, \gamma_e, \gamma_g, \gamma_r$ and γ_{wc}, we mean the minimum cardinality of a connected dominating set, independent dominating set, total dominating set, cycle dominating set, clique dominating set, efficient dominating set, global dominating set, restrained dominating set and weak convex dominating set respectively.

Consider a network contains transceivers that are capable of broadcasting either a primary signal or an auxiliary signal but not both and capable of receiving both a primary signal and an auxiliary signal. Now the problem under consideration is that finding a delay preserving sub network that broadcasts the primary signal such that the transceivers not broadcasting the primary signal requires to receive the auxiliary signal. Problem of finding such a sub network is equivalent to finding a weak convex restrained dominating set in the underlying graph of the network. This problem is introduced and well addressed in [1], [4] and [5].

In this paper we study the change in the behaviour of weak convex restrained domination number with respect to addition of new edges in the respective graph. In this paper we define a graph called k – Weak Convex Restrained Domination critical graph and study the properties possessed by the graph with respect to k = 2 and 3. Also we studied several interesting properties with respect to the diameter and radius of the graph.

2. MAIN RESULTS

Definition 1 :[4]

A dominating set D with $d_{<D>}(u, v) = d_G(u, v)$ for any two vertices u, v in D is called as a Weak Convex Dominating (W.C.D) set.

Definition 2 :[5]

A weak convex dominating set D is called **W**eak **C**onvex **R**estrained **D**ominating set (WCRD) if every vertex in V(G)-D is adjacent to a vertex in D and another vertex in V(G)-D.

The cardinality of the minimum weak convex restrained dominating set is called Weak Convex restrained domination number and is denoted by $\gamma_{rc}(G)$.

Definition 3:

A graph G is said to be a k-**W**eak **C**onvex **R**estrained **D**ominating(k-WCRD) critical graph if $\gamma_{rc}(G + e) < \gamma_{rc}(G)$ and $\gamma_{rc}(G) = k$, for any edge $e \notin E(G)$.

Proposition 1:

A graph G is 1-W.C.R.D critical ⇔ $G = K_p$.

Proposition 2:

G is 2- W.C.R.D critical ⇔ the following hold good;

(i) G is 2-domination; and

(ii) For any two non-adjacent vertices one of them is of degree (n-2).

Proposition 3:

In a 2- W.C.R.D critical graph there cannot be two vertices of degree less than or equal to n-3.

Proof:

If there exist, two vertices u and v of degree less than or equal to n-3. Join u and v. Then G + uv must have a dominating set, which is either {u} or {v}. But both u and v are of degree less than or equal to n-2 in G + uv, which is a contradiction. Hence there exists only one vertex of degree less than or equal to n-3.

Theorem 1:

Let G be any 2-W.C.R.D critical graph on n vertices. Then G must be any one of the following graph:

(1) (n-2)-regular graph

(2) a bi-regular graph with degree sequence (k, n-2), $2 \le k \le n-3$.

(3) A tri-regular graph with degree sequence (1, n-2, n-1).

Proof:

Let G be a 2- W.C.R.D critical graph on n vertices. Let u be a vertex of G.

Case 1: If deg(u) = 1.

Since G is 2-dominating, the set {u, v} will form a dominating set, where v is the support of u. This implies that v must be adjacent to all the vertices and hence deg(v) = n-1. Also all the vertices except u will form a clique. If any two vertices x and y other than u are not adjacent, then the graph G + xy is still going to have {u, v} as the only dominating set, which is a contradiction to G is critical. Hence degree of the vertices other than u and v will be n-2. Hence G is a tri-regular graph with degree sequence (1, n-2, n-1). In this case the number of edges in G is $\dfrac{1 + (n-1) + (n-2)^2}{2}$

$$= \frac{n^2 - 3n + 4}{2}.$$

Case 2: Let deg(u) = k, $2 \le k \le n-3$.

From proposition 3, there be no other vertex other than u which is of degree less than or equal to n-3. Since G is 2-domination, there cannot be a vertex of degree n-1. Hence all the vertices except u are of degree n-2. Thus G is bi-regular graph with degree sequence (k, n-2), where $2 \le k \le n-3$. In this case $\dfrac{k(n-2) + k(n-k)}{2}$.

Case 3: If deg(u) ≥ n-2, for all $u \in V(G)$.

Clearly as G is 2-dominating graph there cannot be any vertex of degree n-1. Hence G is (n-2)-regular graph.

Proposition 4:

Any 2-W.C.R.D critical graph has diameter equal to two.

Proof:

Let u and v be any two non-adjacent vertices of G. Then G+uv has either {u} or {v} as a W.C.R.D set. Without loss of generality assume that {u} form a W.C.R.D set. This implies that {u} is adjacent with the neighbours of v, that is d(u, v) = 2 . Hence the diameter of any 2-critical graph is equal to two.

Theorem 2:

Any 2-W.C.R.D critical graph with $\delta \geq 2$, is a block.

Proof:

Let u be a cut vertex of a 2-critical graph G. Then in G-u, at least in one component there exist a vertex which is of distance 2 from u(otherwise G is dominated by u itself). Then that vertex and any vertex in some other component must be at distance at least three in G, which is a contradiction to the proposition 4. Hence G is a block. Clearly in this case, G is self-centered with diameter 2.

Corollary 1:

There exists no graph G for which both G and $\overline{G}$ are 2- W.C.R.D critical.

Proof:

Proof follows from Proposition 2 and Theorem 2.

Theorem 3:

The diameter of a 3- W.C.R.D critical graph is at most 3.

Proof:

Let G be a 3- W.C.R.D critical graph.

Case 1: If G has two pendant vertices u and v.

Then u and v have a common neighbour w(since $\gamma_{rc}(G) = 3$). This implies that {u, v, w} be the only minimum W.C.R.D set.

- $\Rightarrow$ all the vertices other than u and v are also adjacent with w(to maintain the domination).
- $\Rightarrow$ d(x, y) = 2, for any x, y $\in$ V(G)
- $\Rightarrow$ diameter = 2.

Case 2: Suppose G has only one pendant vertex u with a support v.

Claim 1: Any two vertices other than u and v are adjacent.

If x and y are any two non-adjacent vertices of G, then joining of x and y by an edge will not reduce the domination number. That is, still $\gamma_{rc}(G+xy) = 3$ with dominating set containing u, v and either x or y. Therefore, any two vertices other than u and v must be adjacent.

Claim 2: There cannot be more than one vertex, which is not adjacent with v.

If there exist two vertices x and y, which are not adjacent with v, then still $\gamma_{rc}(G+xv) = 3$ (That is, to dominate G+xy, we require u, v and some vertex to dominate y). Hence the claim 2.

Thus from claim 1 and claim 2, we get for any x, y $\in$ V(G), d(x, y) $\leq$ 3.

Hence the diameter of G is at most 3.

Case 2: Suppose G has no pendant vertex.

Let x and y be any two non-adjacent vertices. Now G+xy has a two dominating set with one vertex as x or y. Without loss of generality let {x, z} form a two dominating set for G+xy. If x dominates some vertex in $N_1(y)$, then we get d(x, y) = 2 in G. If not, then z must dominate all of $N_1(y)$ in G+xy, and hence in G also. This implies that d(x,y) $\leq$ 3.

Hence the diameter of G is less than or equal to 3.

Theorem 4:

Any cut vertex of a 3- W.C.R.D critical graph is adjacent with a vertex of degree 1.

Proof:

Let u be a cut vertex of a 3- W.C.R.D critical graph G. Suppose u is not adjacent with any pendant vertex. Let $C_1, C_2, \ldots, C_n$ be the components of G-u with $|C_i| \geq 2$.

Claim 1: There cannot be two vertices v_i and v_j from two different C_i and C_j respectively such that $d(u, v_i)$ and $d(u, v_j) \geq 2$.

Suppose there exist two v_i and v_j from C_i and C_j respectively with $d(u, v_i)$ and $d(u, v_j)$ greater than or equal to 2 in G. Then $d(v_i, v_j) \geq 4$ in G. This is a contradiction to the fact that diameter of G is less than or equal to 3 for a 3- W.C.R.D critical graph.

Hence we have, if there exists a vertex v in a component, say C_1 which is at distance 2 from u in G, then all the vertices of the other components $C_2, C_3, \ldots, C_n$ must be adjacent to u.

Claim 2: Each of the components $C_2, \ldots, C_n$ forms a clique individually.

Suppose any of the component C_i(i=2 to n) has two non-adjacent vertices, then the join of those vertices will not reduce the W.C.R.D number (since they are not pendant vertices of G) and hence the claim 2.

Claim 3: n = 2.

Suppose n $\geq$ 3, then joining of any two vertices of C_2 and C_3 will not affect the domination number of G as they do not have any pendant vertex of G. Hence,

$n < 3$ and u is a cut vertex implies $n = 2$. Thus G-u has two components such that $diam(C_1) = 2$ and $diam(C_2) = 1$.

Claim 4: $|C_2| = 1$.

Suppose $|C_2| \geq 2$. Let v and w be two vertices in C_2. Join any x in C_1 and v in C_2.

Subclaim: $\{x, y / y \neq u\}$ cannot be a 2-dominating set of G+xv.

Clearly, for any y in C_1, xy is not a dominating edge of G+xv, since the edge xy cannot dominate w in C_2. If y is in C_2 so that xy dominates G+xv, then the edge xu will become a dominating set for G, which is a contradiction to $\gamma_{rc}(G) = 3$.

Therefore, sub claim implies that xu is the only dominating edge of G+xv. This also not admissible as early we discussed. Hence $|C_2| = 1$. Thus, we have proved that G-u has two components in which one is trivial. Hence u is adjacent to a pendant vertex.

Theorem 5:

Any 3- W.C.R.D critical graphs has at most one cut vertex.

Proof:

This is trivial (since if it has two cut vertices then the contradiction follows directly from the previous Theorem 4 and the logic that W.C.R.D set contains all the pendant vertices).

Corollary 2:

If G is a 3- W.C.R.D critical graph with $\delta \geq 2$, then G is a block.

Theorem 6:

Let u be a cut vertex of a 3- W.C.R.D critical graph G, then $|N_2(u)| \leq 1$.

Proof: Let u be a cut point of a 3- W.C.R.D critical graph G. Let us suppose u is adjacent to exactly one pendant vertex v. If $|N_2(u)| \geq 2$ and $x, y \in N_2(u)$, then it is clear that any W.C.R.D set of G must contain {u, v, w}, where w is a vertex from $N_1(u)$. If we join u and x then clearly {u, v} can be the only dominating edge for G+ux. But it cannot dominate y. Which is a contradiction to G is 3- W.C.R.D critical. Hence $|N_2(u)| \leq 1$.

Theorem 7:

Let G be a 3- W.C.R.D critical graph with exactly one pendant vertex v, then $|N_3(v)| = 1$.

Proof:

From the previous Theorem 6, we have $|N_3(v)| \leq 1$. Clearly $N_3(v)$ is non-empty. If not, that is if $N_2(u)$ is empty, where u is the support of v. This implies that uv will dominate the entire graph G. This is a contradiction to the assumption that G is 3- W.C.R.D critical. Hence $|N_3(v)|=1$.

Theorem 8:

Let G be a 3- W.C.R.D critical graph with two pendant vertices x and y then $N_3(x) \cup N_3(y) = \phi$.

Proof:

Let G be a 3- W.C.R.D critical graph with two pendant vertices, say x and y. Let u be the support of both x and y. Then {u, x, y} will be the only W.C.R. dominating set of G. This implies that u is adjacent to all the remaining vertices. Thus, $N_2(u) = \phi$. Hence $N_3(x) \cup N_3(y) = \phi$.

Theorem 9:

Let G be a 3- W.C.R.D critical graph with exactly one pendant vertex, then $q = \binom{p-1}{2} + 1$.

Proof:

Let u be a support of a pendant vertex v in G. Therefore, from Theorem 7, $|N_3(v)| = 1$.

Claim : $\langle N_1(u) \cup N_2(u) - \{v\} \rangle$ is a clique.

Let x and y be any two non-adjacent vertices of $\langle N_1(u) \cup N_2(u) - \{v\} \rangle$. If we join x and y, then G+xy is dominated only by a 3-dominating set. This is a contradiction to the critical property of G. Therefore, x and y must be adjacent. Hence $\langle N_1(u) \cup N_2(u) - \{v\} \rangle$ is a clique. Hence the claim.

Also u is adjacent to (p-2) number of vertices. Hence from the claim we have

$$q = \binom{p-2}{2} + (p-2) + 1$$

$$= \frac{(p-2)(p-3)}{2} + (p-2) + 1$$

$$= \frac{(p-2)(p-3+2)}{2} + 1$$

$$= \frac{(p-1)(p-2)}{2} + 1$$

$$= \binom{p-1}{2} + 1$$

Theorem 10:

Let G be a 3- W.C.R.D critical graph with two pendant vertices, then $q = \binom{p-2}{2} + 2$.

Proof:

Let u be a support of the two pendant vertices x and y.

Claim : G-{x, y} will form a clique.

Let v, w be any two non-adjacent vertices of G-{x, y}. If we join v and w, then still G+vw will have the minimum W.C.R.D set {u, x, y} only, which is a contradiction to the criticality of G. Therefore, v and w are adjacent. As v and w are arbitrary, G-{x, y} will form a clique and hence q = $\binom{p-2}{2} + 2$.

References:

[1] Alphonse P.J.A. (2002). *On Distance, Domination and Related Concepts in Graphs and their Applications*. Doctoral Dissertation, Bharathidasan University, Tamilnadu, India.

[2] Cockayne, E.J., and S.T. Hedetniemi, *Optimal Domination in Graphs,*. IEEE Trans. On Circuits and Systems, CAS-22(11)(1973), 855-857.

[3] Cockayne, E.J., and S.T. Hedetniemi. *Towards a theory of domination in graphs*. Networks, 7:247-261, 1977.

[4] Janakiraman, T.N., and Alphonse, P.J.A.,, *Weak Convex Domination in Graphs*, International Journal of Engineering Science, Advanced Computing and Bio-Technology., Vol.1, No.1, 1-13, 2010,.

[5] Janakiraman, T.N., and Alphonse, P.J.A.,, *Weak Convex Restrained Domination in Graphs*, International Journal of Engineering Science, Advanced Computing and Bio-Technology., Vol.2, No.1, 01-10, 2011,.

[6] Janakiraman, T.N., (1991). *On some eccentricity properties of the graphs*. Thesis, Madras University, Tamilnadu, India.

[7] Mulder, H.M., (1980). *Interval function of a graph*. Thesis, Verije University, Amsterdam.

[8] Teresa W. Haynes, Stephen T. Hedetniemi, Peter J. Slater: *Fundamentals of domination in graphs*. Marcel Dekker, New York 1998.

[9] O. Ore: *Theory of Graphs*, Amer. Soc. Colloq. Publ. vol. 38. Amer. Math. Soc., Providence, RI 1962.

SESSION

FORMAL VERIFICATION + AUTOMATA

Chair(s)

TBA

Formalization Description of Huffman Coding Trees Using Mizar

Takaya Ido[1], Hiroyuki Okazaki[1], and Yasunari Shidama[1]
[1]Shinshu University, 4-17-1 Wakasato Nagano-city, Nagano 380-8553, Japan

Abstract—*Mizar is a type of system known as a "proof checker," which automatically inspects the validity of formal mathematical proofs. Mizar, designed for computational descriptions of mathematics, was developed by Professor A. Trybulec et al. at the University of Bialystok, in Poland [1]. Various theorems can be formulated using the Mizar programming language, and their validity is automatically checked by Mizar's proof checker. The Mizar system contains a library known as the Mizar Mathematical Library, a repository of many formally described theorems and definitions whose validity has been already inspected, from which various applications can be sourced. In this report, we examine the future direction of formal definitions of source coding using Mizar, and as a specific example, we report on the formal description of Huffman coding [2].*

Keywords: Formal Verification, Mizar, Huffman trees

1. Formalization of tree structures

The so-called tree_* series in the Mizar Mathematical library (code abridged), known as a tree structure in Mizar, is expressed as a set of finite sequences of natural numbers. For example the set of finite sequences

$$\{\{\}, <*0*>, <*1*>, <*1,0*>, <*1,1*>\} \quad (1)$$

represents the tree shown in Figure 1. The top (or root) of

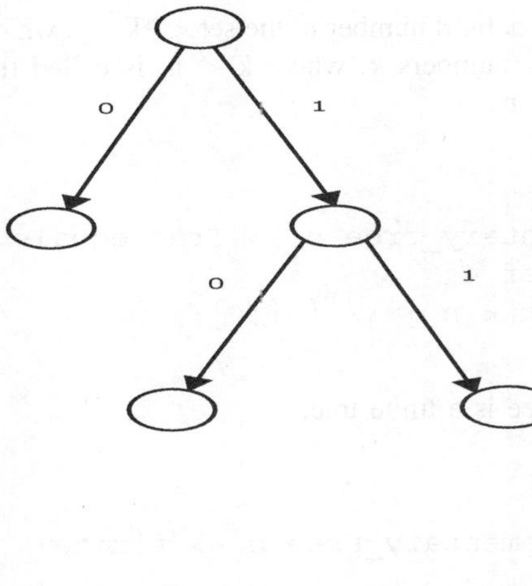

Fig. 1: Tree

the tree is represented by "," and a number is assigned to each branch. The terminating leaves and intermediate nodes are represented by the number sequence of their preceding branches

$$<*0*>,<*1*>,<*1,0*>,<*1,1*> \quad (2)$$

In general, a tree is a set X of finite sequences of natural numbers that satisfy conditions (1) and (2) mentioned below.

1.1 Conditions of a tree

Consider a finite sequence of natural numbers belonging to set X, of arbitrary length m,

$$q = <*q_1, q_2, \cdots q_m*> \quad (3)$$

Condition 1: For an arbitrary natural number n, where n $\leq$ m, the subsequence

$$p = <*q_1, q_2, \cdots q_n*> \quad (4)$$

including the elements from the leading element of q to the nth element also belongs to set X. Condition 2: If a finite sequence of length m + 1, obtained by adding 1 to the end of q,

$$q\hat{\ } <*l*> = <*q_1, q_2, \cdots q_m, l*> \quad (5)$$

belongs to set X, the finite sequence of length m + 1 obtained by adding an arbitrary natural number k (where k $\leq$ 1),

$$q\hat{\ } <*k*> = <*q_1, q_2, \cdots q_m, k*> \quad (6)$$

also belongs to set X. The above-mentioned conditions (1) and (2) can be formalized as follows. The predicate specifying whether p is the leading element to the nth element (n $\leq$ m) extracted from the finite sequence q is

```
notation
  let p,q be FinSequence;
  synonym p is_a_prefix_of q for p c= q;
end;

definition
  let p,q be FinSequence;
  redefine pred p is_a_prefix_of q means
:: TREES_1:def 1
  ex n st p = q|Seg n;
end;
```

Here, Seg n is the set of natural numbers N $\neq$ 0 and N $\leq$ n .

```
definition
  let n be Nat;
  func Seg n -> set equals
```

```
:: FINSEQ_1:def 1
  { k where k is Nat: 1 <= k & k <= n };
end;
```

A proper subsequence is defined by

```
notation
 let p,q be FinSequence;
 synonym p is_a_proper_prefix_of
                         q for p c < q;
end;
```

The set of this proper subsequence is defined by

```
definition
  let p be FinSequence;
  func ProperPrefixes p -> set means
:: TREES_1:def 2
  for x being element holds
  x in it iff ex q being FinSequence
  st x = q & q is_a_proper_prefix_of p;
end;
```

In terms of the above definitions, conditions (1) and (2) are expressed as attributes (attr) of set X and also as a variable type definition as follows:

```
definition
  let X;
  attr X is Tree-like means
:: TREES_1:def 3
  X c= NAT* & (for p st p in
  X holds ProperPrefixes p c= X) &
  for p,k,n st p^<*k*>
  in X & n <= k holds
  p^<*n*> in X;
end;
definition
 mode Tree is Tree-like non empty set;
end;
```

In the tree shown in Figure 1, "" corresponds to the top of the tree. The nodes descending left and right from the top are denoted as " < *1* > " and " < *0* > ," respectively. Continuing this pattern, the nodes descending left and right from the preceding right node on the right are denoted as "< *1, 0* >" and "< *1, 1* >," respectively.

2. Root nodes and empty sequences

An empty finite sequence expressed as "" or "< * >" NAT represents the root node at the top of the tree structure. By definition, this node constitutes an element of the tree and is formalized in the following proposition.

```
reserve T,T1 for Tree;
theorem :: TREES_1:22
  {} in T & <*> NAT in T;
```

Furthermore, an empty set of finite sequences also satisfies the conditions of a tree.

```
theorem :: TREES_1:23
  { {} } is Tree;
```

2.1 Sum and intersection of two trees

Because the sets of two trees comprise finite sequences of natural numbers, their intersection and sum also comprise finite sequences of natural numbers; thus, both operations generate trees. A formalized description of this statement is

```
reserve T,T1 for Tree;
registration
  let T,T1;
  cluster T \/ T1
   -> Tree-like;
  cluster T /\ T1
   -> Tree-like non empty;
end;
theorem :: TREES_1:24
  T \/ T1 is Tree;
theorem :: TREES_1:25
  T /\ T1 is Tree;
```

2.2 Finite trees

If tree T comprises a finite set of sequences, then it is said to be finite. The sum and intersection of two finite trees are also finite.

```
reserve fT,fT1 for finite Tree;
theorem :: TREES_1:26
  fT \/ fT1 is finite Tree;
theorem :: TREES_1:27
  fT /\ T is finite Tree;
```

2.3 Elementary trees

For an arbitrary natural number n, the set < *k* >, which consists of natural numbers k, where k < n, is called the elementary tree of n.

```
definition
  let n;
  func elementary_tree n -> Tree equals
:: TREES_1:def 4
  { <*k*> : k < n } \/ { {} };
end;
```

The elementary tree is a finite tree.

```
registration
  let n;
  cluster elementary_tree n -> finite;
end;
```

Also, given that < *k* >, where k < n, is an element of elementary_tree n, the following proposition can be established:

```
theorem :: TREES_1:28
 k < n implies <*k*>
 in elementary_tree n;
theorem :: TREES_1:29
 elementary_tree 0 = { {} };
theorem :: TREES_1:30
 p in elementary_tree n implies p =
     {} or ex k st k < n & p = <*k*>;
```

2.4 Leaf nodes

Because the leaf nodes lie at the bottom level of the tree structure, they possess no child nodes. If the finite sequence p is a leaf node of tree T, then the finite sequence q-an element of T-can never contain p as a proper subsequence. The formal definition is

```
definition
  let T;
  func Leaves T -> Subset of T means
:: TREES_1:def 5
  p in it iff p in T & not ex q st q in
          T & p is_a_proper_prefix_of q;
end;
```

For the tree shown in Figure 1,

$$\{\{\}, <*0*>, <*1*>, <*1,0*>, <*1,1*>\} \quad (7)$$

the leaves are

$$\{<*1,0*>, <*1,1*>\} \quad (8)$$

The set of all leaf nodes is defined as a variable, as shown below.

```
definition
  let T;
  assume
 Leaves T <> {};
  mode Leaf of T -> Element of T means
:: TREES_1:def 7
  it in Leaves T;
end;
```

2.5 Subtrees

If T is a tree and a finite sequence p is an element of T, then a finite sequence q may be connected to the end of p to create the finite sequence pq̂. Note that pq (expressed as T|p) is also an element of T, and q is also a tree.

```
definition
  let T;
  let p such that
 p in T;
  func T|p -> Tree means
:: TREES_1:def 6  ::
  q in it iff p^q in T;
end;
```

For the tree shown in Figure 1,

$$T = \{\{\}, <*0*>, <*1*>, <*1,0*>, <*1,1*>\} \quad (9)$$

if p = < *1* >, then,

$$\begin{aligned} p\hat{}\{\} &= <*1*> \\ p\hat{}<*0*> &= <*1,0*> \\ p\hat{}<*1*> &= <*1,1*> \end{aligned} \quad (10)$$

so,

$$T|p = \{\{\}, <*0*>, <*1*>\}. \quad (11)$$

Therefore, T|p is a subtree of T as shown in Figure 2. From the above analysis, a subtree can be defined using

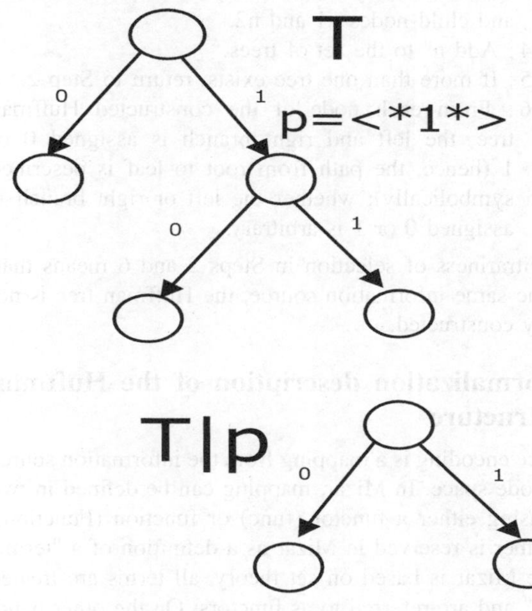

Fig. 2: Subtrees

the following variable type:

```
definition
  let T;
  mode Subtree of T -> Tree means
:: TREES_1:def 8
    ex p being Element of T st it = T|p;
end;
```

3. Huffman trees

Huffman coding is a type of entropy encoding from which an optimum code may always be constructed. A binary Huffman tree is based on the frequency of information symbols. The leaves of this tree correspond to information symbols, and the binary sequences denoting the paths from root to leaves are the code language. Here we outline a Huffman tree construction method.

3.1 Construction method for a Huffman tree

Step 1 : Every information symbol corresponds to a tree with a single node; the value of the node is the appearance frequency of the symbol. This step generates a set of trees in which all information symbols are either a root or leaf.

Step 2 : From the set of trees, select two nodes n1 and n2 with roots of least value. If multiple roots have the second lowest value, an arbitrary selection is made.

Step 3 : A new node n′ with its value equal to the sum of the values of nodes n1 and n2 is created. The resulting binary tree n" comprises a parent node n' and child nodes n1 and n2.

Step 4 : Add n" to the set of trees.

Step 5 : If more than one tree exists, return to Step 2.

Step 6 : From each node of the constructed Huffman tree, the left and right branch is assigned 0 or 1 (hence, the path from root to leaf is described symbolically); whether the left or right branch is assigned 0 or 1 is arbitrary.

The arbitrariness of selection in Steps 2 and 6 means that, given the same information source, the Huffman tree is not uniquely constructed.

3.2 Formalization description of the Huffman tree structure

Source encoding is a mapping from the information source to the code space. In Mizar, mapping can be defined in two ways; using either a functor (func) or function (Function). The former is reserved in Mizar as a definition of a "term." Because Mizar is based on set theory, all terms are treated as "sets" and are referred to as functors. On the other hand, functions can also be treated as a set, with a family of functions constituting a new data type, "mode." As stated in Section 3.1 , the construction method for Huffman trees is not uniquely determined. Thus, in this report, a family of Huffman trees is defined as a "mode" of functions. The encoder is similarly defined in terms of functions or families of functions. Furthermore (although this is outside the scope of the present report), we consider that larger classes of code, such as entropy encoding and compact code, can be formalized in a manner similar to the Huffman code in Mizar.

In this section, a formal description of the construction method outlined in Section 2.1 is presented. We consider a binary tree with values (binary DecoratedTree) described in Section 1. A Huffman tree is defined as a binary tree i.e., a finite set of binary sequences, with the binary tree function as its domain and the direct products of sources and their occurrence probabilities as its range. Because a binary tree is a code space, the function is a decoder, and a one-to-one mapping exists between them. Therefore, the definition for encoding should be derivable from the binary tree definition. First, we define the predicate that must be satisfied by the Huffman tree construction method.

```
definition
let SOURCE be non empty finite set;
let p be Probability of
      (Trivial-SigmaField SOURCE);
let Tseq be  FinSequence
         f BoolBinFinTrees ExtSOURCE ;
let q being FinSequence of NAT;
pred Tseq,q,SOURCE,
p is_constructingHuffman
 means
:: HUFFMAN:def 12
Tseq.1 = Initial-Trees(SOURCE,p)
 & len Tseq = card (SOURCE)
 & ( for i be Nat st 1<= i
 & i < len Tseq
  holds
  ex X,Y  be non empty finite
          Subset of BinFinTrees
     ExtSOURCE
  st
  ex s,t,v be  finite  binary
    DecoratedTree of ExtSOURCE
  st
  Tseq.i = X
  & s is_MinValueTree_of X
  & Y = X \ {s}
  & t is_MinValueTree_of Y
  & v in
   {MakeTree (t,s,MaxVl(X) + 1),
    MakeTree (s,t,MaxVl(X) + 1) }
  & Tseq.(i+1) = (X \ {t,s}) \/ {v})
  & ( ex T be finite  binary
  DecoratedTree of ExtSOURCE
     st {  T  } = Tseq.(len Tseq) )
  & dom q = Seg  card (SOURCE)
  & (for k be Nat st k
    in Seg card (SOURCE)
    holds q.k = card(Tseq.k)
    & q.k <> 0 )
  & (for k be Nat holds
    (k  < card (SOURCE)  implies
     q.(k+1) = q.1 - k))
  & (for k be Nat
    st 1<=k & k < card (SOURCE)
    holds  2 <= q.k );
end;
definition
let SOURCE be non empty finite set;
let p be Probability of
       (Trivial-SigmaField SOURCE);
```

```
let T be  finite  binary
      DecoratedTree of ExtSOURCE ;
pred T,p,SOURCE is_HuffmanCode-Like
 means
:: HUFFMAN:def 13
ex  Tseq be  FinSequence
      of BoolBinFinTrees ExtSOURCE,
    q being FinSequence of NAT
st Tseq,q,SOURCE,
p is_constructingHuffman
   & {T} = Tseq.( (len Tseq) ) ;
end;
```

The following is an explanatory outline. In HUFFMAN:def 12 from above,

1) Step 1 is the processing step. In the initial set of trees, all information symbols correspond to trees with a single node, and the node values are the frequencies of the information symbols. Steps 2 to 4 are iterative steps. Two trees are selected from the set of trees in an intermediate process and combined into a new tree. The selected trees are then removed, and the new tree is added to the tree set. This serial process is represented formally by introducing the finite sequence of the set of binary trees (Tseq) with values in ExtSOURCE.
2) For the set of given information sources SOURCE and its appearance probability distribution p, the following proposition guarantees that Tseq (the finite sequence of the set of binary trees) exists.

```
theorem :: HUFFMAN:3
for  SOURCE be non empty finite set,
     p be Probability of
     (Trivial-SigmaField SOURCE)
     st 2 <= card (SOURCE)
holds
ex  Tseq be  FinSequence
    of BoolBinFinTrees ExtSOURCE,
    q being FinSequence of NAT
st
    Tseq,q,SOURCE,
    p is_constructingHuffman;
```

3) ExtSOURCE is the set of all pairings between the numbers (natural numbers) attached to the nodes of the sequentially generated Huffman trees and their appearance probabilities (real numbers) given by probability p.

```
definition
func  ExtSOURCE  -> non empty set
  equals
:: HUFFMAN:def 2
   [:NAT,REAL:] ;
end;
```

By formalizing a Huffman tree as a binary tree with a value in ExtSOURCE, a unique pairing of number and appearance probability can be mapped to each node.

4) The initial tree set is the initial value of Tseq, (Tseq.1), defined as Initial-Trees(SOURCE,p). The iterations proceed through Tseq.i to process the ith set of trees. The final iteration of Tseq is expressed as Tseq.(lenTseq) (determined by the length lenTseq of Tseq). Tseq.(lenTseq) comprises a single Huffman tree expressed as

```
{T} = Tseq.( (len Tseq) ) ;
```

5) The set of initial trees Initial-Trees(SOURCE,p) is a set of trees each with a single node, in which appearance probability p.x, given by the information number x and its probability, is mapped to an elementary tree elementarytree0 = (as described in Section 1), elementary tree0 - - > [(canFSSOURCE)."x,p.x] and is defined as follows:

```
definition
let SOURCE be non empty finite set;
let p be Probability
    of (Trivial-SigmaField SOURCE);
func  Initial-Trees(SOURCE,p)
-> non empty finite Subset of
             BinFinTrees ExtSOURCE
equals
:: HUFFMAN:def 5
{T where T is Element of
     FinTrees ExtSOURCE :
  T is finite  binary
    DecoratedTree of ExtSOURCE
  & ex x be Element of SOURCE st
    T =  elementary_tree 0 -->
    [(canFS SOURCE)".x , p.{x}]} ;
end;
```

Here,(canFS SOURCE)" is a mapping that uniquely corresponds natural numbers to elements x from the set of information sources SOURCE.

Among the set of trees in the ith iteration of Tseq.i, the two trees rooted by the lowest appearance probability (the second coordinate of their attached value) are selected (according to the predicate "is MinValueTree of"). The formal procedure by which s and t are removed from Tseq.1 and the synthesized tree is added to construct Tseq.(i + 1) is shown below. This formulation includes Step 3.

```
Tseq.i = X
& s is_MinValueTree_of X
& Y = X \ {s}
& t is_MinValueTree_of Y
& v in {MakeTree (t,s,MaxVl(X) + 1),
        MakeTree (s,t,MaxVl(X) + 1) }
& Tseq.(i+1) = (X \ {t,s} ) \/ {v})
```

The action of fetching the first and second

coordinates of the value corresponding to the binary tree, which has a value in ExtSOURCE, is described below.

```
definition
let p be DecoratedTree of ExtSOURCE;
func  Vrootr p ->Real
 equals
:: HUFFMAN:def 6
     (p.{}) `2 ;
end;
```

```
definition
let p be DecoratedTree of ExtSOURCE;
func  Vrootl p -> Nat
 equals
:: HUFFMAN:def 7
     (p.{}) `1 ;
end;
```

The predicate "is MinValueTree of" is hence formalized as

```
definition
let X be non empty finite Subset of
       BinFinTrees ExtSOURCE;
let p be   finite binary
       DecoratedTree of ExtSOURCE ;
pred  p  is_MinValueTree_of X
means
:: HUFFMAN:def 10
p in X & for q be finite binary
       DecoratedTree of ExtSOURCE
st
q in X holds (Vrootr p) <= Vrootr q;
end;
```

and MakeTree is defined as follows.

```
definition
let p,q be finite binary
    DecoratedTree of ExtSOURCE;
let k be Nat;
func MakeTree (p,q,k)
   -> finite  binary
   DecoratedTree of ExtSOURCE
 equals
:: HUFFMAN:def 9
 [k, (Vrootr p) +(Vrootr q)]
  -tree (p,q);
end;
```

MakeTree (t, s, MaxVl(X) + 1) generates a new tree from s and t, as described in Section 1. The maximum value MaxVl(X) of all numbers attached to the roots of the trees belonging to X = Tseq.i is increased by 1 and paired with the sum of appearance probabilities of the roots of s and t. This pairing then corresponds to the root of the newly synthesized tree.

Maximum value MaxVl is formalized as shown below. The second coordinate of the value corresponding to the root of tree p, belonging to the set T of binary trees with values in ExtSOURCE, is defined as

```
definition
let T be   finite  binary
        DecoratedTree of ExtSOURCE;
let p be Element of (dom T) ;
func  Vtree (T,p) -> Real
 equals
:: HUFFMAN:def 8
   (T.p) `2 ;
end;
```

by which the number assigned to the root of the tree in X = Tseq.i is fetched.

Next, we describe how the largest of these numbers is fetched.

```
definition
let X be non empty finite Subset of
      BinFinTrees ExtSOURCE;
func MaxVl(X)  -> Nat
 means
:: HUFFMAN:def 11
 ex L be non empty
 finite Subset of NAT
 st L = {Vrootl p where p
 is Element of
 BinFinTrees ExtSOURCE: p in X }
 & it = max L ;
end;
```

The processing of Step 6 can be encompassed in a definition that clearly expresses (including the existence of the mapping itself) the mapping that corresponds each node of the processed Huffman tree to a finite sequence of 0,1.

```
definition
let SOURCE be non empty finite set;
let p be Probability of
        (Trivial-SigmaField SOURCE);
mode entropyCode-encoder of SOURCE,p
     -> Function of SOURCE, BOOLEAN*
 means
:: HUFFMAN:def 19
 it is one-to-one
 & ex T be  finite  binary
         DecoratedTree of ExtSOURCE
  st
 sT,p,SOURCE is_HuffmanCode-Like
 & rng it = Leaves (dom T)
 & for x be Element of SOURCE
   holds
   T.(it.x)
```

```
  = [(canFS(SOURCE))".x ,p.{x}];
end;
```

The appearance probability of each node that is not a leaf of the final Huffman tree is the sum of the appearance probabilities of each of its child nodes.

This is expressed in the following proposition:

```
theorem :: HUFFMAN:19
for SOURCE be non empty finite set,
 p be Probability of
      (Trivial-SigmaField SOURCE),
 T be  finite  binary
      DecoratedTree of ExtSOURCE
st  T,p,SOURCE is_HuffmanCode-Like
holds
 for  t,s,r be Element of dom T
  st
  t in ( dom T \ (Leaves (dom T)) )
  & s = (t^<* 0 *> )
  & r = (t^<* 1 *> )
  holds
   Vtree (T,t) =
    Vtree (T,s) + Vtree (T,r);
```

To prove this proposition, we must show that a similar proposition holds for the trees in Tseq.i, the set of trees in the ith iteration. This is achieved by mathematical induction involving i, as follows.

```
theorem :: HUFFMAN:18
 for SOURCE be non empty finite set,
   p be Probability of
      (Trivial-SigmaField SOURCE),
   Tseq be  FinSequence
      of BoolBinFinTrees ExtSOURCE,
   q being FinSequence of NAT
  st  Tseq,q,SOURCE,
      p is_constructingHuffman
 holds
  for i be Nat st 1 <=i
     & i <=len Tseq
   holds
     for  T be  finite  binary
      DecoratedTree of ExtSOURCE
     for  t,s,r be Element of dom T
       st T in Tseq.i & t in
         ( dom T \ (Leaves (dom T)) )
       & s = (t^<* 0 *> )
       & r = (t^<* 1 *> )
      holds
      Vtree (T,t)
      = Vtree (T,s) + Vtree (T,r);
```

4. Closing remarks

In this report, we propose a series of formal definitions for source coding in Mizar. Specifically, we reported a formal definition of Huffman coding. First, we defined a method of constructing a Huffman tree. From this definition, we defined the encoder connecting the information source to the code space and the coding scheme. Proofs of definitions and theorems relating to the Huffman code were formulated in Mizar and verified using Mizar's checker. Future work will address proofs on the characteristics of Huffman encoding, such as length of code, the sibling property [3], and optimality.

Acknowledgment

This study was partly supported by JSPS KAKENHI 21240001 and 22300285.

References

[1] Mizar System: Available at http://mizar.org/.

[2] D.A. Huffman, A method for the construction of minimum-redundancy codes, Proceedings of the I.R.E. September, pp.1098-1102, 1952.

[3] R.G. Gallager, Variations on a Theme by Huffman, IEEE Transactions on Information Theory,Vol. IT- 24,NO. 6, pp. 668-674, 1978.

Extended Timed Alternating Finite Automata: Revisited

A. Fellah
Dept. of Computer Science & Applied Statistics
University of New Brunswick
Saint John, NB, E2L 4L5, Canada
Email: fellah@unb.ca

Abstract—**In this paper, we continue to investigate timed alternating finite automata (TAFA), in particular we generalize the existing theory to the case of extended timed alternating finite automata (ETAFA). We define a framework extension of TAFA, study their power and properties. We develop an algebraic treatment of such ETAFA, along the lines of the algebraic treatment of systems of equations based on timed alternating finite automata. We present an equational language representation for ETAFA which parallels that of languages equations for TAFA. The power of these machines is discussed, as well as some of their fundamental properties. Moreover, we consider timed ϵ-transitions and clock precisions, and discuss their interpretations in ETAFA.**

I. Introduction

The power of timed alternating finite automata (TAFA) lies in its natural alternation between existential and universal transitions during the course of a computation. Their power lies not only exclusively in automata theory, but they become an efficient framework in many applications, ranging from proving properties of real time systems and specifying their behaviors to verifying and model checking software systems. Moreover, they provide a succinct representation for regular languages, but are double-exponentially more succinct than deterministic finite automata. Time alternating finite automata have been independently introduced in [8], [10] and thoroughly investigated in literature. Since their introduction, these models have been largely investigated under several theoretical and practical aspects. TAFA have been extended with clock variables, in almost the same way that time finite automata (TFA) [4].

Classical automata are traditionally untimed or asynchronous models of computation in which only the ordering of events, not the time at which events occurs, would affect the result of a computation. Timed automata received their first seminal treatment in [4], since then they have become a powerful canonical model for describing time to model and verify embedded systems with real-time constraint computations. In timed automata the value of a clock depends on the path taken by the automaton are determined by transition relations. Clocks were also extended to alternating finite automata to justify timed transitions and sequences in these models. A comprehensive analysis of the theory of timed alternating finite automata (TAFA) based upon a hybrid combination of alternating finite automata and timed automata models were proposed in [8], [10], [11]. In addition, deterministic timed alternating finite automata (DTAFA) were introduced in [12] as the first determinizable subclass of alternating timed automata by restricting the use of clocks. Moreover, they have been shown to be more expressive and powerful than timed automata and TAFA. Unlike timed automata model, the key for the determinization of TAFA is the property that each computation step, all clock values are determined only by the input timed word. DTAFA are characterized by a fixed, predefined association between the clocks and the symbols of the input alphabet.

The aim of this paper is to propose a formalism which is sufficiently general for modeling all variants of timed alternating finite automata for which the Boolean operations can be effectively defined. In this paper, we introduce extended timed alternating finite automata (ETAFA), a general class of automata that includes all restricted versions of timed AFA. Moreover, we present a general equational language representation for ETAFA which parallels that of timed languages for TAFA. We also give some fundamental properties of ETAFA.

This paper is organized as follows. Section II is devoted to notations and preliminaries. Section III introduces extended timed alternating finite automata (ETAFA) – a general framework for several types of timed alternating finite automata. In addition in Section IV, we develop an algebraic treatment of such ETAFA, along the lines of the algebraic treatment of systems of equations based on timed alternating finite automata. The solutions for such equations over time languages parallel that of language equations for TAFA. Section V describes the transformation between an equational language representation and ETAFA. Closure properties and some results of ETAFA are stated in Sections VI, VII, and VIII. In Section IX, we consider the clock precision and discuss timed ϵ-transitions. Finally, in Section X we draw some concluding remarks.

II. Preliminaries

We denote by $\mathbb{R}$ the set of all non-negative reels including 0. The cardinality of a finite set A is $|A|$. An *alphabet* Δ is a finite, nonempty set whose elements are called *symbols* or *letters*. A *timed word*, w_t over Δ is a finite sequence $w_t = (a_1, t_1)(a_2, t_2) \cdots (a_i, t_i)$ where the $a_i's$ are symbols of Δ and the $t_i's$ are in $\mathbb{R}$ such that for all $i \geq 1$, $t_i < t_{i+1}$. The first element, $a_i's$, of each pair are the input symbols, and the second element, $t_i's$, are the *time elapsed* with respect to the $a_i's$ since the previous symbol reading. We assume that $t_1 = 0$. Thus, $t_1 \cdots t_i$ is a finite monotonically non-decreasing time sequence of $\mathbb{R}$. The time language $(\Delta \times \mathbb{R})^*$

is the set of all timed words over Δ where λ denotes the empty timed word. Recall that classical words over Δ form the free monoid $(\Delta^*, \cdot, \lambda)$ generated be Δ, where "·" is the classical concatenation operator (we write either *ab* or $a \cdot b$ for the concatenation). For any timed language $\mathcal{L}_t \subseteq (\Delta \times \mathbb{R})^*$, $\overline{\mathcal{L}_t} = \Delta^* \backslash \mathcal{L}_t$, is the complement of $\mathcal{L}_t$ with respect to Δ^*. For languages $\mathcal{L}_{t1}$ and $\mathcal{L}_{t2}$ over Δ, the union and intersection are denoted by $\mathcal{L}_{t1} \cup \mathcal{L}_{t2}$ and $\mathcal{L}_{t1} \cap \mathcal{L}_{t2}$, respectively.

Given a finite set $\mathcal{X}$ of clock variables, a *clock constraint* ψ over $\mathcal{X}$ on a given input symbol $a \in \Delta$ can be generated by the following grammar.

$$\psi := x \leq c \mid x < c \mid c \leq x \mid c < x \mid \psi_1 \vee \psi_2 \mid \psi_1 \wedge \psi_2$$

where x is any clock in $\mathcal{X}$ and $c \in \mathbb{R}$ such that $c \geq 0$. The operators $\vee$ and $\wedge$ stands for the logical-*or* and logical-*and*, respectively. A *clock interpretation (valuation)* ν for $\mathcal{X}$ is a mapping from $\mathcal{X}$ to $\mathbb{R}$. That is, ν assigns to each clock $x \in \mathcal{X}$ the value $\nu(x)$. A clock interpretation represents the values of all clocks in $\mathcal{X}$ at a given snapshot in time. The length of a timed word w_t, denoted by $|w_t|$, is the total number of symbols in w_t.

III. Extended Timed Alternating Finite Automata

Let $\mathbb{B}$ denote the two-element Boolean algebra $\mathbb{B} = (\{0,1\}, \vee, \wedge, \neg, 0, 1)$. $\mathbb{B}^Q$ is a vector with $|Q|$ elements referring to all the Boolean functions from Q to $\mathbb{B}$ where $\vee$, $\wedge$, $\neg$ (interchangeably $^-$) denote the "or", "and" and "not", respectively. Let $\mathbb{R}^{\mathcal{X}}$ is a vector over $\mathbb{R}$ with $|\mathcal{X}|$ elements referring to all real functions from $\mathcal{X}$ to $\mathbb{R}$. For notation convenience, let $\mathbb{X}$ denote a value vector over $\mathbb{R}^{\mathcal{X}}$.

Definition 3.1: An extended timed alternating finite automaton (ETAFA) is a sept-tuple $A = (Q, \Delta, s, \mathcal{X}, g, h, F)$, where (a) Q is a finite set, the set of *states,* (b) Δ is the alphabet, the *input alphabet,* (c) $s \in Q$ is the *starting state,* (d) $\mathcal{X}$ is a finite set, the set of clocks, (e) h is the time transition function, $h : (\mathbb{R}^{\mathcal{X}} \times \mathbb{R}) \mapsto \mathbb{R}^{\mathcal{X}}$; (f) g is the letter transition function from $(Q \times \mathbb{R}^{\mathcal{X}})$ into the set of all functions $(\mathbb{B}^Q)^{\mathbb{R}^{\mathcal{X}}}$ into $\mathbb{B}$. (g) $F \subseteq Q$ is the set of *final states.*

The function h is specifically defined as:

$$h((x_1, x_2, \ldots, x_{|\mathcal{X}|}), t) = ((x_1 + t, x_2 + t, \ldots, x_{|\mathcal{X}|} + t))$$

where $x_i \in \mathcal{X}$ for $1 \leq i \leq |\mathcal{X}|$ and $t \in \mathbb{R}$ such that $t \geq 0$. For convenience, the definition of the function h can be rewritten as $h(\mathbb{X}, t) = \mathbb{X}'$, where for all $x \in \mathcal{X}$, $\mathbb{X}' = \mathbb{X} + t$ where t is the time associated with the word that has been read.

For each state $q \in Q$ and with each vector $\mathbb{X} \in \mathbb{R}^{\mathcal{X}}$, $g(q, \mathbb{X})$ is a function from $(\mathbb{B}^Q)^{\mathbb{R}^{\mathcal{X}}} \times (\Delta \times \mathbb{R})$ into $\mathbb{B}$, which we denote as $g_q(\mathbb{X})$. For each $q \in Q$ with each $\mathbb{X} \in \mathbb{R}^{\mathcal{X}}$ and for each $a \in (\Delta \times \mathbb{R})$, we define $g_q(\mathbb{X})(a)$ to be the Boolean function $(\mathbb{B}^Q)^{\mathbb{R}^{\mathcal{X}}} \mapsto \mathbb{B}$ such that:

$$g_q(\mathbb{X})(a)(u) = g_q(\mathbb{X})(a, u)$$

where $u \in (\mathbb{B}^Q)^{\mathbb{R}^{\mathcal{X}}}$. Thus, for any $u \in (\mathbb{B}^Q)^{\mathbb{R}^{\mathcal{X}}}$, the value of $g_q(\mathbb{X})(a)(u)$, also $g_q(\mathbb{X})(a, u)$ is either 1 or 0.

We define the function $g_{Q \times \mathbb{R}^{\mathcal{X}}_{\geq 0}} : (\mathbb{B}^Q)^{\mathbb{R}^{\mathcal{X}}} \times (\Delta \times \mathbb{R}) \mapsto \mathbb{B}$ by putting together the $|Q \times \mathbb{R}^{\mathcal{X}}|$ functions $g_q(\mathbb{X}) : (\mathbb{B}^Q)^{\mathbb{R}^{\mathcal{X}}} \times (\Delta \times \mathbb{R}) \mapsto \mathbb{B}$ for each $q \in Q$ and with each $\mathbb{X} \in \mathbb{R}^{\mathcal{X}}$ as follows:

For $a \in (\Delta \times \mathbb{R})$ and $u, v \in (\mathbb{B}^Q)^{\mathbb{R}^{\mathcal{X}}}$, $g_{Q \times \mathbb{R}^{\mathcal{X}}}(u, a) = v$ if and only if $g_a(\mathbb{X})(u, a) = v_{(q,\mathbb{X})}$, for each $q \in Q$ and with each $\mathbb{X} \in \mathbb{R}^{\mathcal{X}}$, where $v_{(q,\mathbb{X})}$ indexes the q element of the $\mathbb{X}$ vector in $(\mathbb{B}^Q)^{\mathbb{R}^{\mathcal{X}}}$. For convenience, we write $g(u, q)$ instead of $g_{Q \times \mathbb{R}^{\mathcal{X}}}$ when there is no confusion.

Now, we extend g to a function of $Q \times \mathbb{R}^{\mathcal{X}}$ into the set of all functions $(\mathbb{B}^Q)^{\mathbb{R}^{\mathcal{X}}} \times (\Delta \times \mathbb{R})^* \mapsto \mathbb{B}$ as follows:

$$g_q(\mathbb{X})(u, w_t) = \begin{cases} u_{(q,\mathbb{X})} & \text{if} \quad w_t = \epsilon \\ g_q(\mathbb{X})((u, w_t'), a) & \text{if} \quad w_t = a w_t' \end{cases}$$

where $a \in (\Delta \times \mathbb{R})$, $w_t, w_t' \in (\Delta \times \mathbb{R})^*$ and $u \in (\mathbb{B}^Q)^{\mathbb{R}^{\mathcal{X}}}$. Note that $\epsilon \in (\Delta \times \mathbb{R})$ is the timed null word where $\epsilon = (\lambda, 0)$ such that $w_t \cdot \epsilon = w_t \epsilon = w_t$.

For all $q \in Q$ and with each $\mathbb{X} \in \mathbb{R}^{\mathcal{X}}$, we define the *characteristic vector* $f \in (\mathbb{B}^Q)^{\mathbb{R}^{\mathcal{X}}}$ of F as follows:

$$f_{(q,\mathbb{X})} = 1 \iff q \in F$$
$$f_{(q,\mathbb{X})} = 0 \iff q \in Q \backslash F$$

Definition 3.2: A word $w_t \in (\Delta \times \mathbb{R})^*$ is accepted by a ETAFA M if and only if $g_s(h(\mathbf{0}, t))(f, w_t) = 1$, where s is the starting state, f is the characteristic vector of F, t is the time associated with the word that has been read, and $\mathbf{0} \in \mathbb{R}^{\mathcal{X}}$ is the zero-valued vector (*i.e.,* $0 = 0$ for all $x \in \mathcal{X}$).

The language accepted by a ETAFA $A = (Q, \Delta, s, \mathcal{X}, g, h, F)$ is defined as follows:

$$\mathcal{L}_t(A) = \{w_t \in (\Delta \times \mathbb{R})^* \mid g_s(h(\mathbf{0}, t))(f, w_t) = 1\}$$

Note that $w_t = (a, t) w_t'$ for some $a \in \Delta$, $t \in \mathbb{R}$, and $w_t' \in (\Delta \times \mathbb{R})^*$.

Example 3.1: Consider the following ETAFA $A = (Q, \Delta, q_0, \mathcal{X}, g, h, F)$ where $Q = \{q_0, q_1, q_2\}$, $\Delta = \{a\}$, h is given as in the ETAFA's definition. $\mathcal{X} = \{x\}$, and $F_2 = \{q_2\}$. Thus, the characteristic vector f and the function g are as follows:

$$f = (0,0,1), (0,0,1), \ldots, (0,0,1) = (0,0,1)^{\mathbb{R}^{\mathcal{X}}} = (0,0,1)$$

g	a
q_0	$q_0 \vee (q_1[x := 0])$
q_1	$((x \neq 1) \wedge q_1) \vee ((x = 1) \wedge q_2)$
q_2	q_2

Analyzing the definition of the function g in the ETAFA A, we can see how to trace one of the $|Q \times \mathbb{R}^{\mathcal{X}}|$ functions for every $g_q(\mathbb{X})$ transition that is made while tracing the word. In addition the notation $[x := 0]$ denotes a "reset" of the clock x and $(x = 1)$ indicates a comparison.

For example, tracing the timed word $w_t =< a,1/2 >< a,0 >< a,1 >$ assuming $\epsilon =< \lambda, 0 >$ is:

$$
\begin{aligned}
& g_{q_0}(h(0,1/2))((0,0,1), <a,1/2><a,0><a,1>) \\
= \; & g_{q_0}(1/2)((0,0,1), <a,1/2><a,0><a,1>) \\
= \; & g_{q_0}(h(1/2,0))((0,0,1), <a,0><a,1>) \\
& \vee g_{q_0}(h(0,0))((0,0,1), <a,0><a,1>) \\
= \; & g_{q_0}(1/2)((0,0,1), <a,0><a,1>) \\
& g \vee_{q_0}(0)((0,0,1), <a,0><a,1>) \\
= \; & g_{q_0}(h(1/2,1))((0,0,1), <a,1>) \\
& \vee g_{q_1}(h(0,1))((0,0,1), <a,1>) \\
& \vee g_{q_1}(h(0,1))((0,0,1), <a,1>) \\
= \; & g_{q_0}(h(1\,1/2,1))((0,0,1), <a,1>) \\
& \vee g_{q_1}(1)((0,0,1), <a,1>) \vee g_{q_1}(1)((0,0,1), <a,1>) \\
= \; & g_{q_0}(h(1\,1/2,0))((0,0,1), <\lambda,0>) \\
& \vee g_{q_1}(h(0,0))((0,0,1), <\lambda,0>) \\
& g_{\vee q2}(h(1,0))((0,0,1), <\lambda,0>) \\
& \vee g_{q_2}(h(1,0))((0,0,1), <\lambda,0>) \\
= \; & g_{q_1}(1\,1/2)((0,0,1), <\lambda,0>) \\
& \vee g_{q_0}(0)((0,0,1), <\lambda,0>) \vee g_{q_2}(1)((0,0,1), <\lambda,0>) \\
& \vee g_{q_2}(1)((0,0,1), <\lambda,0>) \\
= \; & 0 \vee 0 \vee 1 \vee 1 \\
= \; & 1.
\end{aligned}
$$

Therefore the timed word $w_t < a,1/2 >< a,0 >< a,1 >$ is accepted.

Because ETAFA only considers passage of time between two input symbols (with the h function) by adding the elapsed time to the current clock values, a change in either the ETAFA, or the format of an input word is required. This can be accomplished in one of the following two methods: (1) Adding a *universal clock* to the ETAFA. This is a clock that never resets and contains the value of the total elapsed time since the start of a word. (2) Choosing the representation of a timed word so that each time value of the $(a,t) \in (\Delta \times \mathbb{R})$ would be the time since the last symbol was read as opposed to the time since the start of the word. We have chosen the second method in the previous tracing example. Either method will work fine as there would be no change to the current ETAFA definition.

IV. Equational Language Representation of ETAFA

The theory of classical language equations received its formal treatment in the seminal paper of [6]. Most of the subsequent research focused on restricted various types of language equations and their different solution techniques. (See for example, [10], [12], [13]). However, language equation solutions still suffer from a lack of generality. In this section, we define a general framework class of language equations and relate them to extended alternating timed finite automata.

Let $A = (Q, \Delta, s, \mathcal{X}, g, h, F)$ be a ETAFA. For all $q \in Q$, A can be represented by the following system of equations.

$$\widehat{X}_{(q,\mathbb{X})} = \left\{ \sum_{a \in \Delta} a \cdot g_q(\mathbb{X})(\widehat{X}, a) + \epsilon_{(q,\mathbb{X})} \right\}_{q \in Q, \mathbb{X} \in \mathbb{R}^{\mathcal{X}}} \quad (1)$$

for all $\mathbb{X} \in \mathbb{R}^{\mathcal{X}}$ and where "." is the concatenation operation. $\widehat{X}$ is a vector of $|Q \times \mathbb{R}^{\mathcal{X}}|$ variables $\widehat{X}_{(q,\mathbb{X})}$ indexedm/cmr5.pfb¿¡/usr/share/texmf-texlive/fonts/type1/public/amsfonts/c m/cmr7.pfb¿¡ by the states $q \in Q$ and vectors $\mathbb{X} \in \mathbb{R}^{\mathcal{X}}$ and

$$\epsilon_{(q,\mathbb{X})} = \begin{cases} \lambda & \text{if } q \in F \\ 0 & \text{otherwise} \end{cases}$$

for each $q \in Q$ with each $\mathbb{X} \in \mathbb{R}^{\mathcal{X}}$.
Note all terms of the form $a.0$, $a \in \Delta$ can be omitted as can the term $\epsilon_{(q,\mathbb{X})}$ if $q \in Q \backslash F$.

The following theorems are the most important results relating timed alternating finite automata and their equational representations. The second theorem gives a sufficient condition for the uniqueness of the solution of the system of equations (1).

Theorem 4.1: [11] Let $A = (Q, \Delta, s, \mathcal{X}, g, h, F)$ be a ETAFA represented by the system of language equations $\widehat{X}_{(q,\mathbb{X})}$ of the form (1) whose solution is $\{\widehat{X}_q\}_{q \in Q}$. Let s be the starting state of A. Then $\mathcal{L}_t(A) = \widehat{X}_s$.

Theorem 4.2: [11], [12] Any system of language equations of the form of (1) has a unique solution for each $\{\widehat{X}_q\}_{q \in Q}$. Furthermore, the solution for each $\{\widehat{X}_q\}$ is regular.

The following system of equations represents the ETAFA A given in Example 3.1.

$$
\begin{aligned}
\widehat{X}_{q_0} &= a \cdot (\widehat{X}_{q_0} \vee (\widehat{X}_{q_1}[x := 0])) \\
\widehat{X}_{q_1} &= a \cdot (x \neq 1) \wedge \widehat{X}_{q_1}) \vee ((x = 1) \wedge \widehat{X}_{q_2})) \\
\widehat{X}_{q_2} &= a \cdot \widehat{X}_{q_2} + \lambda
\end{aligned}
$$

Note that $\widehat{X}_{(q_0,\mathbb{X})}$ for all $\mathbb{X} \in \mathbb{R}^{\mathcal{X}}$ can be written as $\widehat{X}_{q_0}$ for convenience.

Lemma 4.1: Let $\widehat{X}_{(q,\mathbb{X})}$ be an equational representation of a given ETAFA $A = (Q, \Delta, s, \mathcal{X}, g, h, F)$, then $\widehat{X}_{(q,\mathbb{X})}$ and A are equivalent in terms of language acceptance.

Proposition 1: The family of languages accepted by ETAFA is the class of timed regular languages.

V. From the Equational Representation to ETAFA

Given the equational representation of ETAFA, we should be able to construct the corresponding ETAFA. For example, given the following system of equations:

$$
\begin{aligned}
\widehat{X}_{q_0} &= a \cdot \widehat{X}_{q_0} + b \cdot (\widehat{X}_{q_1} \wedge \neg(\widehat{X}_{q_2}[y := 0]) \\
\widehat{X}_{q_1} &= a \cdot (x \leq 2) \wedge \widehat{X}_{q_1}) + b \cdot \widehat{X}_{q_2} + \lambda \\
\widehat{X}_{q_2} &= a + b \cdot (y = 1/2)
\end{aligned}
$$

We will assume that q_0 is the starting state, but this may not always be the case. We also assume that h is defined the usual way unless explicitly told so. X Thus, the ETAFA $A = (Q, \Delta, q_0, g, h, \mathcal{X}, F)$ where $Q = \{q_0, q_1, q_2\}$, $\Delta = \{a, b\}$, $X = \{x, y\}$, $F = \{q_1\}$, and g is given as:

g	a	b
q_0	q_0	$q_1 \wedge \neg(q_2[y := 0])$
q_1	$(x \leq 2) \wedge q_1$	q_2
q_2	1	$(y = 1/2)$

VI. Boolean Operations on ETAFA

Given the equational representation of a ETAFA $A = (Q, \Delta, s, \mathcal{X}, g, h, F)$:

$$\widehat{X}_{(s,\mathbb{X})} = \left\{ \sum_{a\in\Delta} a \cdot g_s(\mathbb{X})(\widehat{X}, a) + \epsilon_{(s,\mathbb{X})} \right\}_{s \in Q, \mathbb{X} \in \mathbb{R}^{\mathcal{X}}}$$

We construct the complement $\overline{A} = (Q', \Delta, s', \mathcal{X}, g', h', F')$ as follows:

$$\widehat{X}_{(\overline{s},\mathbb{X})} = \left\{ \overline{\sum_{a\in\Delta} a \cdot g_s(\mathbb{X})(\widehat{X}, a) + \overline{\epsilon_{(s,\mathbb{X})}}} \right\}_{s \cup \overline{s} \in Q'}$$

where $\mathbb{X} \in \mathbb{R}^{\mathcal{X}} s$ and $\overline{s}$ are the starting states of A and $\overline{A}$ such that

$$\overline{\epsilon_{(s,\mathbb{X})}} = \begin{cases} 0 & \text{if} \quad \epsilon_{(s,\mathbb{X})} = \lambda \\ \lambda & \text{if} \quad \epsilon_{(s,\mathbb{X})} = 0 \end{cases}$$

Theorem 6.1: Let $A^1 = (Q^1, \Delta^1, s^1, \mathcal{X}^1, g^1, h^1, F^1)$ and $A^2 = (Q^2, \Delta^2, s^2, \mathcal{X}^2, g^2, h^2, F^2)$ two ETAFA represented by their equations $\widehat{X}^1_{(q^1,\mathbb{X}^1)}$ and $\widehat{X}^2_{(q^2,\mathbb{X}^2)}$ and accepting the languages $\mathcal{L}_t(A^1)$ and $\mathcal{L}_t(A^2)$, respectively. Then, there exists a ETAFA represented by its language equation $\widehat{X}_{(s,\mathbb{X})} =$ such that $\mathcal{L}_t(A) = \mathcal{L}_t(A^1) \cup \mathcal{L}_t(A^2)$, $\mathcal{L}_t(A) = \mathcal{L}_t(A^1) \cap \mathcal{L}_t(A^2)$, and $\mathcal{L}_t(A) = \mathcal{L}_t(A^1) \cdot \mathcal{L}_t(A^2)$.

Proof: The proof is constructive and follows the same steps as in the complement operation. Moreover and due to space constraint, we summarize the results as follows: □

Theorem 6.2: Extended timed alternating finite automata are closed under all Boolean operations, including the intersection and composition.

In the following section we show that timed finite automaton (TFA) can be converted into an extended timed finite automata (ETAFA).

VII. TFA - ETAFA Transformation

Timed finite automata (TFA) are are finite state automata extended with a set of clocks. Whenever the automaton is in state q, it can change to state q' by reading a symbol while the time constraints are satisfied. A state of a timed finite automaton can be considered as a tuple containing the current state of the automaton and the current values of the clocks. Clocks are used to justify timed transitions and sequences in TFA. These clocks can either progress synchronously and uniformly, or they can be reset to zero. There are two types of clock constraints – *invariants* labeling states, and *guards* labeling transitions.

Definition 7.1: A timed finite automaton (TFA) is a six-tuple $A' = (Q', \Delta', s', \mathcal{X}', \delta', F')$, where (a) Q' is a finite set, the set of *states;* (b) Δ' is an alphabet, the *input alphabet;* (c) $s' \in Q'$ is the *starting state;* (d) $\mathcal{X}'$ is a finite set, the set of *clocks;* (e) $F' \subseteq Q'$ is a finite set, the set *final states;* (f) δ' is a time transition function of the form (q, ϕ, ρ, a, q') where $q, q' \in Q'$, $a \in \Delta' \cup \{\epsilon\}$, $\rho \in \mathcal{X}'$, ϕ is the transition guard, it is a boolean combination of the form $\mathcal{X} \in I$ for some clock $\mathcal{X}'$ and some bound interval I. q is the current state, q' is the next state, a is the letter read, ρ is the set of clocks to be reset.

Corollary 7.1: Let $A' = (Q', \Delta', s', \mathcal{X}', \delta', F')$ be a TFA, we can construct a ETAFA $A = (Q, \Delta, s, \mathcal{X}, g, h, F)$ where $Q = Q'$, $\Delta = \Delta'$, $s = s'$, h is defined the usual way, $\mathcal{X} = \mathcal{X}'$, $F = F'$, and g is given by the equational language representation $\widehat{X}$ as follows: For each $(q, \phi, \rho, a, q') \in \delta'$ where $a \neq \epsilon$.

$$\widehat{X}_q := \widehat{X}_q \vee (\emptyset \wedge (\widehat{X}_{q'}[p := 0]))$$

for all $p \in \mathcal{P}(\mathcal{X})$.

The proof is straightforward. Simply perform an "or" operator with the current boolean expression terms and $(\emptyset \wedge (\widehat{X}_{q'}[p := 0]))$.

Example 7.1: Consider $A' = (Q', \Delta', s', \mathcal{X}', \delta', F')$ be a TFA where $Q' = \{q_0, q_1, q_2\}$, $\Delta' = \{a, b\}$, $s' = \{q_0\}$, $\mathcal{X}' = \{x, y\}$, $(x, y) \in \mathbb{R}$, $F' = \{q_2\}$, and $\delta' = \{(q_0, (x, y), \{x\}, a, q_1), (q_1, (x, y), \emptyset, b, q_1)$, $(q_1, x \in [2, 2] \vee y \in \mathbb{R}, \emptyset, b, q_1), (q_1, x \in \mathbb{R} \vee y \in [0, 2), \emptyset, a, q_2), (q_2, (x, y), \{x\}, a, q_2), (q_2, (x, y), \emptyset, b, q_0)\}$

The ETAFA equivalent is $A = (Q, \Delta, s, \mathcal{X}, g, h, F)$ where $Q = \{q_0, q_1, q_2\}$, $\mathcal{X} = \{x, y\}$, $\Delta = \{a, b\}$, $s = \{q_0\}$, h is defined as $h((x, y), t) = (x + t, y + t)$, $F = \{q_2\}$, and g is given by the equation $\widehat{X}$ as follows.

$$\begin{aligned}
\widehat{X}_{q_0} &= a \cdot (\widehat{X}_{q_1}[x := 0]) \\
\widehat{X}_{q_1} &= a \cdot (y \in [0, 2)) \wedge \widehat{X}_{q_2}) + \\
& \quad b \cdot (\widehat{X}_{q_1} \vee (x \in [2, 2]) \wedge \widehat{X}_{q_0}) \\
\widehat{X}_{q_2} &= a \cdot (\widehat{X}_{q_2}[x := 0]) + b \cdot \widehat{X}_{q_0} + \epsilon
\end{aligned}$$

VIII. Untimed ϵ-transitions and ϵ-transitions with no guards

So far, we have not considered TFA with ϵ-transitions for changing to ETAFA. The discussion of ϵ-transitions can break down into two categories, ones with no time constraint of guard, and ones that have constraints or guards. The type of ϵ-transitions are actually fairly easy to simulate in ETAFA. Consider the transition $(q, x \in \mathbb{R}, \{\mathcal{X}\}, \epsilon, q')$, for every transition $(q', x \in I, \mathcal{X}^0, a, q)$ for some interval I, some $a \in \Sigma$, some $q' \in Q$, and $\mathcal{X}^0 \subseteq \mathcal{X}$, add the transition $(q', x \in I, \mathcal{X}^0 \cup \{x\}, \epsilon, q')$. After all transitions have been added, delete the edge $(q, x \in \mathbb{R}, \{x\}, \epsilon, q')$.

The TFA can be transformed to a ETAFA. Formally, we have the following theorem:

Theorem 8.1: For every ϵ-transitions TFA M' there exists a ETAFA M such that $\mathcal{L}_t(M') = \mathcal{L}_t(M)$.

Proof: Due to space constraint we present a constructive proof. Consider each transition $(q, x \in \mathbb{R}, \mathcal{X}', \epsilon, q') \in M'$ for some $q, q' \in Q'$, and $\mathcal{X}^0 \subseteq \mathcal{X}$. Now for each transition $(q', \phi, \mathcal{X}^0, a, q)$ for some $q' \in Q', \mathcal{X}^0 \subseteq \mathcal{X}, a \in \Delta'$, add the edge $(q, \phi, \mathcal{X}^0 \cup \mathcal{X}', a, q')$. Finally, delete the edge $(q', x \in \mathbb{R}, \mathcal{X}', \epsilon, q')$, If $q = s$ for some $(q, x \in \mathbb{R}, \mathcal{X}', \epsilon, q')$, then we notice that we cannot reduce this yet, but the ETAFA equation $\widehat{X}_q$ for the starting state q is as follows:

$$\widehat{X}_{(q,\mathbb{X})} = \left\{ \sum_{a \in \Delta} a \cdot g_q(\mathbb{X})(\widehat{X}, a) \vee g_{q'}(\mathbb{X})(\widehat{X}, a) \right\}_{q \in Q}$$

□

IX. Discrete Clock and Clock Precision

In the previous section we discuss timed ϵ-transitions, in this section we consider another clock metric, *clock precision*. Let $\mathcal{X}$ be the finite set of clocks and $x \in \mathcal{X}$. We may ask the following question what is the smallest possible values of $x \in \mathcal{X}$ that satisfies $x > 2$? If $x \in \mathbb{R}$, then we can only say that x approaches 2 from the positive side, but this is a poorly defined way of describing the clock value. Instead, we will define the *precision* as some positive number in $\mathbb{R}$ such that a clock value may only be multiples of this value., *i.e.,* if the precision is 10^{-3}, then the smallest value of x for $x > 2$ is 2.001.

To simulate an ϵ-transition, we must redefine $g_q(\mathbb{X})(a, u)$ for $a \in \Delta$ as defined in Section III to $g_q(\mathbb{X})(a, u)$ for $a \in \Delta \cup \{\lambda\}$ and its extension over $(\Delta \times \mathbb{R})^*$ becomes $(\Delta \cup \{\lambda\} \times \mathbb{R})^*$. There is a potential problem because our current definition for g is

$$g_q(\mathbb{X})(u, w_t) = \begin{cases} u_{(q,\mathbb{X})} & \text{if} \quad w_t = \epsilon = (\lambda, 0) \\ g_q(\mathbb{X})((u, w_t'), a) & \text{if} \quad w_t = a w_t' \end{cases}$$

However, since we are now considering λ, a readable letter, we don't want to collapse the g_q function to $u_{(q,\mathbb{X})}$ because we might not be at the end of the word. Therefore, we define $\overline{\epsilon} = (\overline{\lambda}, 0)$ to denote the *word terminator* that is read at the end of each word and collapse g to $u_{(q,\mathbb{X})}$ if $a = \overline{\epsilon}$ is read. Now, the equation becomes how to interpret these new ϵ-transition in ETAFA. This is best illustrated by the following example:

$$\widehat{X}_{(q,\mathbb{X})} = a \cdot (\widehat{X}_{(q',\mathbb{X})}[y := 0]) + \lambda \cdot ((\widehat{X}_{(q',\mathbb{X})} \wedge (y > 2) + \overline{\lambda}$$

Note that $\overline{\lambda}$ indicates that q is a final state. Now if we consider the expression $g_q(h((0,1), 3)(u, a)$ for clock $\mathcal{X} = (x, y) = (0, 1)$, we notice that the time expression function $h((0, 1), 3)$ will result in $y > 2$ being satisfied. In this case we chose the minimum value in the range [0,3] $=\mu$ that will satisfy $1+\mu > 2$ since $\mu \in \mathbb{R}$, then there is no adequate way to properly write what μ is. However, if we consider the precision (*i.e.,* 10^{-3}), then 1,001 will work, therefore $1 + |1, 001| > 2$ is the least value that we can choose for this example.

X. Conclusion

We investigated extension of timed alternating finite automata with ϵ-transitions and presented is presented a general framework for this class of automata. We further extended the equational representation of TAFA to represent ETAFA and explore solutions and properties for such equations over time languages. Timed ϵ-transitions and clock precisions need further investigation. There are several future directions worth mentioning, including the relationship between extended timed regular expressions and extended timed alternating finite automata which are being investigated.

References

[1] F. Baader, A. Okhotin. Solving Language Equations and Disequations with Applications to Disunification in Description Logics and Monadic Set Constraints. *Logic for Programming, Artificial Intelligence, and Reasoning,* (LPAR-18), LNCS 7180, pp 107-121, 2012.

[2] M. Ackerman, J. Shallit. Efficient Enumeration of Regular Languages. *Proc. of the 12th Internat. Conference on Implementation and Application of Automata,* Springer-Verlag, 2007.

[3] E. Carta-Gerardino, P. Babaali. Weighted Automata and Recurrence Equations for Regular Languages *arXiv preprint arXiv:1007.1045, arxiv.org,* 2010.

[4] R. Alur, D. Dill, A Theory of Timed Automata. *Theoretical Computer Science,* 126 (2), pp. 183-235, 1994.

[5] R. Alur, L. Fix, T.A. Henzinger. Event-clock Automata: A Determinizable Class of Timed Automata. *Theoretical Computer Science,* 211 (1-2), pp. 253-273, 1999.

[6] J.A. Brzozowski, E. Leiss, On Equations for Regular Languages, Finite Automata, and Sequential Networks, *Theoret. Comput. Sci.* 10, pp. 19-35. 1980.

[7] E. Asarin, P. Caspi, and O. Maler. Timed Regular Expressions. *JACM,* 49(2): 172-206, 2002.

[8] Lasota, S. and Walukiewicz, I. Alternating Timed Automata. *ACM Trans. Comput. Logic,* 9(2), 2008.

[9] A.K. Chandra, D.C. Kozen, L.J. Stockmeyer, Alternation, *J. Assoc. Comput,* 28, 1981, pp. 114-133, 1981.

[10] A. Fellah, C. Harding, Language Equations for Timed Alternating Finite Automata, *Internat. J. Comput. Math.* 80,2, pp. 1075-1091, 2003.

[11] A. Fellah, Generalized Timed Alternating Finite Automata. *7th Intl Workshop on Boolean Problems,* Freiberg, Sachsen, Germany, pp. 159-164, 2006.

[12] A. Fellah, A. Fellah, Z. Friggstad and S. Noureddine, Deterministic Timed AFA: A New Class of Timed Alternating Finite Automata. *Journal of Computer Science,* Vol. 5. No. 1, pp. 18, 2007.

[13] E. Leiss, Succinct Representation of Regular Languages by Boolean automata II. *Theoret. Comput. Sci.* 38, pp. 133-136, 1985.

[14] O. Kupferman, M. Vardi, Weak Alternating Automata are not that Weak. *ACM Trans. Comput. Log.* 2(3), pp. 408-429, 2001.

[15] K. Salomaa, X. Wu, S. Yu, Efficient Implementation of Regular Languages using Reversed Alternating Finite Automata, *Theoret. Comput. Sci.* 231, pp. 103-111, 2000.

[16] E. Leiss, Language Equations, Springer-Verlag, New York, 1999.

[17] T.A. Henzinger, B. Horowitz, C.M. Kirsch. Giotto: A Time-triggered Language for Embedded Programming. *Proceedings of EMSOFT,* pp. 166-184, 2001.

[18] E. Fersman, P. Pettersson, W. Yi. Timed Automata with Asynchronous Processes: Schedulability and Decidability. In Tools and Algorithms for the Construction and Analysis of Systems, Vol 2280 of Lecture Notes in Computer Science. Springer-Verlag. 2002.

[19] C.L. Oding, W. Thomas. Alternating Automata and Logics over infinite words. In IFIP TCS'00, Vol. 1872 of LNCS, pp. 521-535, 2000.

Formalization of Binary Fields and N-dimensional Binary Vector Spaces Using the Mizar Proof Checker

Kenichi Arai[1] and Hiroyuki Okazaki[2]
[1]Tokyo University of Science, 2641 Yamazaki Noda-City, Chiba 278-8510, Japan
[2]Shinshu University, 4-17-1 Wakasato Nagano-city, Nagano 380-8553, Japan

Abstract— *Binary fields and n-dimensional binary vector spaces play important roles in practical computer science, for example, coding theory and cryptology. In this paper, we introduce our formalization of binary fields and n-dimensional binary vector spaces. We then prove some theorems about subspaces and bases of n-dimensional binary vector spaces. We prove the correctness of our formalization using the Mizar proof checking system as a formal verification tool. Mizar is a project that formalizes mathematics with a computer-aided proving technique and is a universally accepted proof checking system. The main objective of this study is to prove the security of cryptographic systems using the Mizar proof checker.*

Keywords: Formal Verification, Proof Checker, Mizar, Binary Field, N-dimensional Binary Vector Space

1. Introduction

Mizar[1] is a project that formalizes mathematics with a computer-aided proving technique. The objective of this study is to prove the security of cryptographic systems using the Mizar proof checker. To this end, we intend to formalize several topics concerning cryptology. As a part of this effort, we have previously introduced our formalization of the Advanced Encryption Standard (AES) at FCS'12[2].

The binary set $\{0, 1\}$ together with modulo-2 addition and multiplication is called a binary field, which is denoted by $\mathbb{F}_2$. A vector space over $\mathbb{F}_2$ is called a binary vector space. The set of all binary vectors of length n forms an n-dimensional vector space V_n over $\mathbb{F}_2$. Binary fields and n-dimensional binary vector spaces play important roles in practical computer science, for example, coding theory[3] and cryptology. In cryptology, binary fields and n-dimensional binary vector spaces are very important in proving the security of cryptographic systems[4].

In this paper, we introduce our formalization of binary fields, n-dimensional binary vector spaces, and their algebraic structures using the Mizar proof checker. We then prove some theorems about subspaces and bases of n-dimensional binary vector spaces.

The remainder of this paper is organized as follows. In Section 2, we briefly introduce the Mizar project. In Section 3, we briefly introduce binary fields and n-dimensional binary vector spaces. In Section 4, we introduce our formalization of binary fields and their algebraic structures. In Section 5, we introduce our formalization of n-dimensional binary vector spaces and their algebraic structures. We then prove some theorems about subspaces and bases of n-dimensional binary vector spaces. We conclude our discussion in Section 6. The definitions and theorems in this paper have been verified for correctness using the Mizar proof checker.

2. Mizar

Mizar[1] is an advanced project of the Mizar Society led by A.Trybulec, which formalizes mathematics with a computer-aided proving technique. The Mizar project describes mathematical proofs in the Mizar language, which was created to formally describe mathematics. The Mizar proof checker operates in both Windows and UNIX environments, and registers the proven definitions and theorems in the Mizar Mathematical Library (MML). Mizar is one of the proof assistants that can mechanically check proofs written in the Mizar language.

The text that formalizes and describes the proof of mathematics by Mizar is called an "article". When an article is newly described, it is possible to advance it by referring to articles registered in the MML that have already been inspected as proof. Likewise, other articles can refer to an article after it has been registered in the MML. Although the Mizar language is based on a descriptive method for general mathematical proofs, a reader should consult the references for its grammatical details because Mizar uses a specific, unique notation[5], [6], [7], [8].

3. Outline of Binary Fields and N-dimensional Binary Vector Spaces

In this section, we review binary fields, n-dimensional binary vector spaces, and vector subspaces[3].

3.1 Binary Fields

The binary field $\mathbb{F}_2$ (a so-called Galois field and written GF(2)) is a finite field with two elements: 0 and 1. The operations defined over the binary field $\mathbb{F}_2$ are binary addition and multiplication. Binary addition "+" and multiplication "•" are defined by the rules of modulo-2 arithmetic, as shown in Figure 1.

+	0	1
0	0	1
1	1	0

Binary Addition

•	0	1
0	0	0
1	0	1

Binary Multiplication

Figure 1: Binary Addition and Binary Multiplication

Here, 0 is the additive identity and 1 is the multiplicative identity. Binary addition and multiplication correspond to the XOR (exclusive OR) and AND operations, respectively. Because $\mathbb{F}_2$ is a field, many of the familiar properties of number systems such as rational numbers and real numbers are retained; these include associativity, commutativity, and distributivity.

3.2 N-dimensional Binary Vector Spaces

The vector space V consists of a set of elements over which the binary addition operation, denoted by the XOR operation "$\oplus$," is defined. If $\mathbb{F}$ is a field, the binary multiplication operation, denoted by the AND operation "$\bullet$," is defined between an element of the field $\mathbb{F}$ and the vectors of the space V. Thus, V is called a vector space over the field $\mathbb{F}$ if it satisfies the following conditions:

(i) V is a commutative group for the binary addition operation.
(ii) For any $x \in \mathbb{F}$ and any $\boldsymbol{u} \in V$, $x \bullet \boldsymbol{u} \in V$.
(iii) For any $\boldsymbol{u}, \boldsymbol{v} \in V$ and any $x \in \mathbb{F}$, $x \bullet (\boldsymbol{u} + \boldsymbol{v}) = x \bullet \boldsymbol{u} + x \bullet \boldsymbol{v}$.
(iv) For any $\boldsymbol{u} \in V$ and any $x, y \in \mathbb{F}$, $(x + y) \bullet \boldsymbol{u} = x \bullet \boldsymbol{u} + y \bullet \boldsymbol{u}$.
(v) For any $\boldsymbol{u} \in V$ and any $x, y \in \mathbb{F}$, $(x \bullet y) \bullet \boldsymbol{u} = x \bullet (y \bullet \boldsymbol{u})$.
(vi) If 1 is the unit element in $\mathbb{F}$, then $1 \bullet \boldsymbol{u} = \boldsymbol{u}$ for any $\boldsymbol{u} \in V$.

Here, the elements of V and $\mathbb{F}$ are called vectors and scalars, respectively.

Consider an ordered sequence of n components $(x_1, x_2, \dots, x_n)$ where each component x_i is an element of the binary field $\mathbb{F}_2$. This sequence is called an n-component vector. There are a total of 2^n vectors. The corresponding vector space for this set of vectors is denoted as V_n, a vector space of dimension n.

The binary addition operation $\oplus$ for this vector space is defined as follows: if $\boldsymbol{u} = (u_1, u_2, \dots, u_n)$ and $\boldsymbol{v} = (v_1, v_2, \dots, v_n)$ are vectors in V_n, then

$$\boldsymbol{u} \oplus \boldsymbol{v} = (u_1 \oplus v_1, u_2 \oplus v_2, \dots, u_n \oplus v_n).$$

Since the sum vector is also an n-component vector, this vector also belongs to the vector space V_n, and so the vector space is said to be closed under the addition operation $\oplus$.

The addition of any two vectors of a given vector space is also another vector of the same vector space.

Furthermore, V_n is a commutative group under the addition operation. The all-zero vector $\boldsymbol{0} = (0, 0, \dots, 0)$ is also in the vector space and is the identity for the addition operation:

$$\boldsymbol{u} \oplus \boldsymbol{0} = (u_1 \oplus 0, u_2 \oplus 0, \dots, u_n \oplus 0) = \boldsymbol{u},$$
$$\boldsymbol{u} \oplus \boldsymbol{u} = (u_1 \oplus u_1, u_2 \oplus u_2, \dots, u_n \oplus u_n) = \boldsymbol{0}.$$

Each vector of a vector space defined over the binary field is its own additive inverse. It can be shown that the vector space defined over $\mathbb{F}_2$ is a commutative group, so that associative and commutative laws are satisfied. The multiplication between a vector of the vectorial space $\boldsymbol{u} \in V$ and a scalar of the binary field $x \in \mathbb{F}_2$ can be defined as

$$x \bullet \boldsymbol{u} = (x \bullet u_1, x \bullet u_2, \dots, x \bullet u_n).$$

It can be shown that addition and scalar multiplication obey the associative, commutative, and distributive laws, so the set of vectors V_n is a vector space defined over the binary field $\mathbb{F}_2$. In addition, a vector space over $\mathbb{F}_2$ is a binary vector space; therefore, it is called an n-dimensional binary vector space V_n.

3.3 Vector Subspaces

A subset S of the vector space V is called a subspace of the vector space V. A non-empty subset S of V is a subspace if it satisfies the following conditions:

- For any two vectors in S, $\boldsymbol{u}, \boldsymbol{v} \in S$, the sum vector $(\boldsymbol{u} + \boldsymbol{v}) \in S$.
- For any element of the field $x \in \mathbb{F}$ and any vector $\boldsymbol{u} \in S$, the scalar multiplication $x \bullet \boldsymbol{u} \in S$.

If $\{\boldsymbol{v_1}, \boldsymbol{v_2}, \dots, \boldsymbol{v_k}\}$ is a set of vectors of the vector space V defined over $\mathbb{F}$ and $x_1, x_2, \dots, x_k$ are scalar numbers of the field $\mathbb{F}$, the sum $x_1 \bullet \boldsymbol{v_1} \oplus x_2 \bullet \boldsymbol{v_2} \oplus \cdots \oplus x_k \bullet \boldsymbol{v_k}$ is called a linear combination of the vectors $\{\boldsymbol{v_1}, \boldsymbol{v_2}, \dots, \boldsymbol{v_k}\}$. A set of k vectors $\{\boldsymbol{v_1}, \boldsymbol{v_2}, \dots, \boldsymbol{v_k}\}$ is said to be linearly dependent if and only if there exist k scalars of $\mathbb{F}$, not all equal to zero, such that a linear combination is equal to the all-zero vector:

$$x_1 \bullet \boldsymbol{v_1} \oplus x_2 \bullet \boldsymbol{v_2} \oplus \cdots \oplus x_k \bullet \boldsymbol{v_k} = \boldsymbol{0}.$$

If the set of vectors is not linearly dependent, then this set is said to be linearly independent.

A set of vectors is said to generate (span) a vector space V if each vector in that vector space is a linear combination of the vectors of the set. In any vector space or subspace, there exists a set of at least linearly independent vectors that generate such a vectorial space or subspace.

For a given n-dimensional binary vector space V_n, the set of vectors $\{\boldsymbol{e_1}, \boldsymbol{e_2}, \dots, \boldsymbol{e_n}\}$ =

$\{(1,0,\ldots,0),(0,1,\ldots,0),\ldots,(0,0,\ldots,1)\}$ is the set of vectors $\boldsymbol{e_i}$ that has a non-zero component only at position i. This set of vectors is linearly independent.

This set of linearly independent vectors $\{\boldsymbol{e_1},\boldsymbol{e_2},\ldots,\boldsymbol{e_n}\}$ generates the n-dimensional binary vector space V_n, whose dimension is n and is called a basis of the n-dimensional binary vector space V_n. If $k < n$, the set of linearly independent vectors $\{\boldsymbol{v_1},\boldsymbol{v_2},\ldots,\boldsymbol{v_k}\}$ generates S of the n-dimensional binary vector space V_n through all their possible linear combinations:

$$\boldsymbol{c} = y_1 \bullet \boldsymbol{v_1} \oplus y_2 \bullet \boldsymbol{v_2} \oplus \cdots \oplus y_k \bullet \boldsymbol{v_k}.$$

The subspace formed is of dimension k and consists of 2^k vectors. The number of combinations is 2^k because the coefficients $y_i \in \mathbb{F}_2$ adopt only one of the following two possible values: 0 or 1.

4. Binary Fields and their Algebraic Structures

In this section, we formalize the binary field $\mathbb{F}_2$ as an algebraic structure. First, we define "BinaryField" as a structure that has BOOLEAN as its carrier and that includes the following two binary operations on BOOLEAN: "XORB1" and "MLB1." Next, we prove that BinaryField has the attributes of a field.

We define binary addition and multiplication as follows:

```
definition
  func XORB1 -> BinOp of BOOLEAN
  means
  for x,y be Element of BOOLEAN
  holds it.(x,y) = x 'xor' y;
end;
```

```
definition
  func MLB1 -> BinOp of BOOLEAN
  means
  for x,y be Element of BOOLEAN
  holds it.(x,y) = x '&' y;
end;
```

"BOOLEAN" denotes the binary set {0, 1} in the Mizar language. Here, each of the operations, XORB1 and MLB1, is defined as a "BinOp of BOOLEAN," which is a function from (BOOLEAN, BOOLEAN) into BOOLEAN[9], [10]. Thus, the definitions of both XORB1 and MLB1 ensure that their outputs are elements of BOOLEAN.

We can now define an algebraic structure that has BOOLEAN as its carrier, two binary operations, and two identity elements [1]:

```
definition
  func BinaryField ->
    strict non empty doubleLoopStr
  equals
  doubleLoopStr(# BOOLEAN,XORB1,MLB1,
    TRUE,FALSE #);
end;
```

Here, BinaryField has TRUE (1) and FALSE (0) as the identities of MLB1 and XORB1, respectively.

In the Mizar language, "Field" denotes a field as follows[11]:

```
definition
  mode Field is add-associative
    right_zeroed right_complementable
    Abelian commutative associative
    well-unital distributive
    almost_left_invertible
    non degenerated doubleLoopStr;
end;
```

Data types are constructed as "modes" in the Mizar language. We can construct new modes in the Mizar language using existing modes and attributes, which are characteristics of modes and other objects.

Now, we explain attributes of "doubleLoopStr" $(\mathcal{F},f,g,e_g,e_f)$, where $\mathcal{F}$ is BOOLEAN, f is XORB1, g is MLB1, e_g is TRUE, and e_f is FALSE. Here, "add-associative right_zeroed ... almost_left_invertible non degenerated" are attributes. The attribute "add-associative" means that $(\mathcal{F},f)$ holds the associative law:

$$\forall a,b,c \in \mathcal{F},\ f(f(a,b),c) = f(a,f(b,c)).$$

The attribute "right_zeroed" means that e_f is an additive identity in $\mathcal{F}$, that is, $\forall a \in \mathcal{F},\ f(a,e_f) = a$. The attribute "right_complementable" means that for any $a \in \mathcal{F}$, there exists an additive inverse b of a in $\mathcal{F}$, that is, $f(a,b) = e_f$. The attribute "Abelian" means that $(\mathcal{F},f)$ holds the commutative law: $\forall a,b \in \mathcal{F},\ f(a,b) = f(b,a)$. The attribute "commutative" means that $(\mathcal{F},g)$ holds the commutative law: $\forall a,b \in \mathcal{F},\ g(a,b) = g(b,a)$. The attribute "associative" means that $(\mathcal{F},g)$ holds the associative law:

$$\forall a,b,c \in \mathcal{F},\ g(g(a,b),c) = g(a,g(b,c)).$$

The attribute "well-unital" means that e_g is a multiplicative identity in $\mathcal{F}$, that is, $\forall a \in \mathcal{F},\ g(a,e_g) = g(e_g,a) = a$.

[1] An algebraic structure "doubleLoopStr" is a set for which two binary operations and two elements are defined.

The attribute "distributive" means that $(\mathcal{F}, f, g)$ holds the distributive law:

$$\forall a, b, c \in \mathcal{F},\ g(a, f(b, c)) = f(g(a, b), g(a, c)),$$
$$\forall a, b, c \in \mathcal{F},\ g(f(a, b), c) = f(g(a, c), g(b, c)).$$

The attribute "almost_left_invertible" means that for any $a \in \mathcal{F} \setminus \{0\}$, there exists a multiplicative inverse b of a in $\mathcal{F} \setminus \{0\}$, that is, $g(b, a) = e_g$. The attribute "non degenerated" means that there exists non-zero divisor $a(\neq 0) \in \mathcal{F}$, where $g(a, b) = 0$ for some element $b(\neq 0) \in \mathcal{F}$. Then, if "doubleLoopStr" $(\mathcal{F}, f, g, e_g, e_f)$ has all the above attributes, the algebraic structure is a field.

Next, we introduce the following "cluster" for BinaryField:

```
registration
  cluster BinaryField ->
    add-associative right_zeroed
    right_complementable Abelian
    commutative associative
    well-unital distributive
    almost_left_invertible
    non degenerated;
end;
```

This cluster is equivalent to the following theorem:

```
theorem
  BinaryField is add-associative
    right_zeroed right_complementable
    Abelian commutative associative
    well-unital distributive
    almost_left_invertible
    non degenerated doubleLoopStr;
```

In the Mizar system, a cluster captures some properties of an expression, for example, its attributes. Once a cluster has been registered, these properties can be derived automatically from the expression, although it is always necessary to refer to theorems.

Finally, we prove the following theorem:

```
theorem
  BinaryField is Field;
```

5. N-dimensional Binary Vector Spaces and their Algebraic Structures

In this section, we formalize the n-dimensional binary vector space V_n as an algebraic structure. We then prove some theorems about subspaces and bases of n-dimensional binary vector spaces.

5.1 Formalization of N-dimensional Binary Vector Spaces

In this section, we explain the definition of a vector space V as an algebraic structure that has already been formalized in Mizar. Then, we define "n-BinaryVectSp" as the structure that has n-tuples on BOOLEAN as its carrier and that includes addition and scalar multiplication on n-tuples on BOOLEAN, "XORB n" and "MLTB n."

In Mizar, the vector space algebraic structure, "VectSpStr over F," has already been formalized as follows[11]:

```
definition
  let F be 1-sorted;
  struct(addLoopStr) VectSpStr over F
    (# carrier -> set,
    addF -> BinOp of the carrier,
    ZeroF -> Element of the carrier,
    lmult ->
      Function of
        [:the carrier of F,
        the carrier:], the carrier #);
end;
```

Mizar supports multiple inheritance of structures, making a whole hierarchy of interrelated structures available in the MML. In that hierarchy, the "1-sorted" structure is the common ancestor of almost all other structures[12].

The definition of a vector space, "VectSp of F," has already been formalized as follows[11]:

```
definition
  let F be add-associative
    right_zeroed right_complementable
    Abelian associative well-unital
    distributive non empty
    doubleLoopStr;
  mode VectSp of F is
    vector-distributive
    scalar-distributive
    scalar-associative
    scalar-unital
    add-associative right_zeroed
    right_complementable Abelian
    non empty VectSpStr over F;
end;
```

Here, "vector-distributive," "scalar-distributive," "scalar-associative," and "scalar-unital" are attributes and correspond to (iii), (iv), (v), and (vi) of Section 3.2, respectively. This definition also satisfies (i) from VectSpStr over F. See the Appendix for details of this definition. If VectSpStr over F has all the above attributes, the algebraic structure is a vector space V. Thus, we will use VectSpStr over F and VectSp of F to formalize the n-dimensional binary vector space V_n, "n-BinaryVectSp."

We define addition and scalar multiplication on n-tuples on BOOLEAN, "XORB n" and "MLTB n," as follows:

```
definition
  let n be non zero Element of NAT;
  func XORB n ->
    BinOp of n-tuples_on BOOLEAN
  means
  for x,y being
    Element of n-tuples_on BOOLEAN
  holds it.(x,y) = Op-XOR(x,y);
end;
```

```
definition
  let n be non zero Element of NAT;
  func MLTB n ->
    Function of
      [:the carrier of BinaryField,
      n-tuples_on BOOLEAN:],
      n-tuples_on BOOLEAN
  means
  for a be Element of BOOLEAN,
  x be Element of n-tuples_on BOOLEAN,
  i be set st i in Seg n
  holds (it.(a,x)).i = a '&' x.i;
end;
```

"NAT" denotes the set of natural numbers with 0 in the Mizar language. Here, Op-XOR is a bitwise XOR function and Seg n = [1, n].

The additive identity, the all-zero vector, for n-tuples on BOOLEAN is defined as follows:

```
definition
  let n be non zero Element of NAT;
  func ZeroB n ->
    Element of n-tuples_on BOOLEAN
  equals
  n |-> 0;
end;
```

Here, n |-> 0 is the all-zero n-tuples $(0, 0, \ldots, 0)$.

The following theorem can then be proved:

```
theorem
  VectSpStr(# n-tuples_on BOOLEAN,
    XORB n,ZeroB n,MLTB n #) is
  VectSp of BinaryField;
```

We now define an algebraic structure that has n-tuples on BOOLEAN as its carrier, addition, scalar multiplication, and the additive identity, as follows:

```
definition
  let n be non zero Element of NAT;
  func n-BinaryVectSp ->
    VectSp of BinaryField
  equals
  VectSpStr(# n-tuples_on BOOLEAN,
    XORB n,ZeroB n,MLTB n #);
end;
```

Finally, we prove the following theorem:

```
theorem
  n-BinaryVectSp is
    VectSp of BinaryField;
```

5.2 Theorems about Subspaces and Bases of N-dimensional Binary Vector Spaces

In this section, we prove some theorems about subspaces and bases of n-dimensional binary vector spaces. Definitions of linear independence, bases, dimension, and subspace have already been formalized in Mizar[13], [14], [15]. Therefore, we use those definitions to prove some theorems.

First, we formalize the theorem about linear independence as follows:

```
theorem
  for n,m be non zero Element of NAT,
  A be FinSequence of
    n-tuples_on BOOLEAN,
  B be finite Subset of n-BinaryVectSp
  st rng A = B & m <= n & len A = m &
  A is one-to-one &
  (for i,j be Nat st i in Seg n &
    j in Seg m holds
    (i = j implies (A.i).j = TRUE) &
    (i <> j implies (A.i).j = FALSE))
  holds B is linearly-independent;
```

Here, rng A of A that holds "(for i,j be Nat st i in Seg n & ··· & (i <> j implies (A.i).j = FALSE))" is a basis of n-BinaryVectSp. Because this rng A is linearly independent, any subset B of rng A is also linearly independent.

Second, we formalize the following theorem that relates to the above theorem:

```
theorem
  for n be non zero Element of NAT,
  A be FinSequence of
    n-tuples_on BOOLEAN,
  B be finite Subset of n-BinaryVectSp
  st rng A = B & len A = n &
  A is one-to-one &
  (for i,j be Nat st i in Seg n &
    j in Seg n holds
    (i = j implies (A.i).j = TRUE) &
    (i <> j implies (A.i).j = FALSE))
  holds Lin B = VectSpStr
    (# the carrier of n-BinaryVectSp,
    the addF of n-BinaryVectSp,
    the ZeroF of n-BinaryVectSp,
    the lmult of n-BinaryVectSp #);
```

Here, Lin B means the space generated (spanned) by B. The space generated by B has an algebraic structure equal to n-BinaryVectSp.

We can then formalize the following theorem about the basis:

```
theorem
  for n be non zero Element of NAT
  holds
  ex B be finite Subset of
    n-BinaryVectSp st B is Basis of
    n-BinaryVectSp &
  card B = n &
  ex A be FinSequence of
    n-tuples_on BOOLEAN st len A = n &
  A is one-to-one & card (rng A) = n &
  rng A = B &
  (for i,j be Nat st i in Seg n &
    j in Seg n holds
    (i = j implies (A.i).j = TRUE) &
    (i <> j implies (A.i).j = FALSE));
```

If B is a basis of n-BinaryVectSp, this theorem means that B, which is a finite subset of n-BinaryVectSp, exists.

Next, we formalize a theorem about dimension as follows:

```
theorem
  for n be non zero Element of NAT
  holds
  n-BinaryVectSp is finite-dimensional
  & dim (n-BinaryVectSp) = n;
```

Here, dim (n-BinaryVectSp) means the dimension of n-BinaryVectSp.

Finally, we formalize a theorem about the subspace as follows:

```
theorem
  for n be non zero Element of NAT,
  A be FinSequence of
    n-tuples_on BOOLEAN,
  C be Subset of n-BinaryVectSp
  st len A = n & A is one-to-one &
  card (rng A) = n &
  (for i,j be Nat st i in Seg n &
    j in Seg n holds
    (i = j implies (A.i).j = TRUE) &
    (i <> j implies (A.i).j = FALSE))
  & C c= rng A
  holds
  Lin C is Subspace of n-BinaryVectSp
  & C is Basis of Lin C &
  dim (Lin C) = card C;
```

Here, c= means $\subseteq$. This theorem means that the space generated by C, which is a subset of rng A, is a subspace of n-BinaryVectSp. In that case, C is a basis of the space generated by C and the dimension of Lin C is equal to the cardinal number of C.

6. Conclusion

In this paper, we introduced our formalization of binary fields, n-dimensional binary vector spaces, and their algebraic structures in Mizar. We also proved some theorems about subspaces and bases of the n-dimensional binary vector spaces using the Mizar proof checking system as a formal verification tool. Currently, we are analyzing the cryptographic systems using our formalization in order to achieve the security proof of cryptographic systems.

Acknowledgments

This work was supported by JSPS KAKENHI Grant Numbers 21240001 and 22300285. We would like to sincerely thank Prof. Shidama at Shinshu University for his helpful advice.

References

[1] *Mizar Proof Checker*. [Online]. Available: http://mizar.org/.

[2] H.Okazaki, K.Arai, and Y.Shidama, "Formal Verification of AES Using the Mizar Proof Checker," Proceedings of the 2012 International Conference on Foundations of Computer Science (FCS'12), pp.78–84, 2012.

[3] J.C.Moreira and P.G.Farrell, *Essentials of Error-Control Coding*, John Wiley & Sons Ltd, The Atrium, Southern Gate, Chichester, 2006.

[4] X.Lai, "Higher Order Derivatives and Differential Cryptanalysis," Communications and Cryptography, pp.227–233, Kluwer Academic Pablishers, 1994.

[5] E.Bonarska, *An Introduction to PC Mizar*, Mizar Users Group, Fondation Philippe le Hodey, Brussels, 1990.

[6] M.Muzalewski, *An Outline of PC Mizar*, Fondation Philippe le Hodey, Brussels, 1993.

[7] Y.Nakamura, T.Watanabe, Y.Tanaka, and P.Kawamoto, *Mizar Lecture Notes (4th Edition)*, Shinshu University, Nagano, 2001. [Online]. Available: http://markun.cs.shinshu-u.ac.jp/kiso/projects/proofchecker/mizar/index-e.html.

[8] A.Grabowski, A.Kornilowicz, and A.Naumowicz, "Mizar in a Nutshell," Journal of Formalized Reasoning, 3(2), pp.153–245, 2010.

[9] C.Bylinski, "Binary Operations," Formalized Mathematics, 1(1), pp.175–180, 1990.

[10] Library Committee of the Association of Mizar Users, "Binary Operations on Numbers," To appear in Formalized Mathematics, 2004.

[11] E.Kusak, W.Leonczuk, M.Muzalewski, "Abelian Groups, Fields and Vector Spaces," Formalized Mathematics, 1(2), pp.335–342, 1990.

[12] Library Committee of the Association of Mizar Users, "Preliminaries to Structures," To appear in Formalized Mathematics, 1995.

[13] A.Trybulec, "Basis of Vector Space," Formalized Mathematics, 1(5), pp.883–885, 1990.

[14] J.C.Chen, "The Steinitz Theorem and the Dimension of a Real Linear Space," Formalized Mathematics, 6(3), pp.411–415, 1997.

[15] A.Trybulec, "Subspaces and Cosets of Subspaces in Real Linear Space," Formalized Mathematics, 1(2), pp.297–301, 1990.

Appendix

(ii) is formalized as follows:

```
definition
  let F be non empty 1-sorted,
  V be non empty VectSpStr over F;
  let x be Element of F;
  let v be Element of V;
  func x*v -> Element of V
  equals (the lmult of V).(x,v);
end;
```

(iii) is formalized as follows:

```
definition
  let F be non empty doubleLoopStr;
  let IT be non empty VectSpStr over F;
  attr IT is vector-distributive
  means
  for x being Element of F
  for v,w being Element of IT
  holds x*(v+w) = x*v+x*w;
end;
```

(iv), (v), and (vi) are formalized as follows:

```
definition
  let F be non empty doubleLoopStr;
  let IT be non empty VectSpStr over F;
  attr IT is scalar-distributive
  means
  for x,y being Element of F
  for v being Element of IT
  holds (x+y)*v = x*v+y*v;

  attr IT is scalar-associative
  means
  for x,y being Element of F
  for v being Element of IT
  holds (x*y)*v = x*(y*v);

  attr IT is scalar-unital
  means
  for v being Element of IT
  holds (1.F)*v = v;
end;
```

Moreover, the elements of V and $\mathbb{F}$ are called vectors and scalars, respectively; they are formalized as follows:

```
definition
  let F be 1-sorted;
  let VS be VectSpStr over F;
  mode Vector of VS is Element of VS;
  mode Scalar of F is Element of F;
end;
```

SESSION

ENCRYPTION + CALCULUS + TESTING METHODS AND NEW METHODOLOGIES

Chair(s)

TBA

On the Expressiveness of Monadic Higher Order Safe Ambient Calculus

Zining Cao[1,2]
[1]State Key Laboratory for Civil Aircraft Flight Simulation
Shanghai Aircraft Design and Research Institute
Shanghai 201210, China
[2]Department of Computer Science and Technology
Nanjing University of Aeronautics & Astronautics
Nanjing 210016, China
Email: caozn@nuaa.edu.cn

Abstract—*In this paper, we propose a monadic higher order safe ambient calculus. The expressiveness of this calculus is studied. We showed that polyadic higher order safe ambient calculus, first order safe ambient calculus with capability-passing, first order safe ambient calculus with name-passing, and polyadic π-calculus can all be encoded in monadic higher order ambient calculus. At last, we show that synchronous monadic higher order ambient calculus can be encoded in asynchronous monadic higher order ambient calculus.*

Keywords: Process Calculus; Higher Order Safe Ambient Calculus; Expressiveness.

1. Introduction

Mobile Ambients was proposed and studied intensively in [3]. The calculus of Mobile Ambients (MA) is proposed both as a core programming language for the Web and as a model for reasoning about properties of mobile processes, including security. In contrast with previous formalisms for mobile processes such as the π-calculus, whose computational model is based on the notion of communication, the MA computational model is based on the notion of movement. An ambient, which may be thought of as a named location, is the unit of movement. Processes within the same ambient may exchange messages; ambients may be nested, so to form a hierarchical structure. The three primitives for movement allow: an ambient to enter another ambient; an ambient to exit another ambient; a process to dissolve an ambient boundary thus obtaining access to its content. Elegant type systems for MA have been given; they control the type of values exchanged within an ambient and the mobility of ambients. A few variants of MA were proposed in literatures [1], [5], [8]. In the Safe Ambients calculus (SA) [8], for example, CCS-style co-actions are introduced into the calculus to control potential interferences from other ambients. Recently, there are several works about MA with higher order communication. In [2], authors proposed an extension of the ambient calculus in which processes can be passed as values. A filter model for this calculus was presented. This model was proved to be fully abstract with respect to the notion of contextual equivalence where the observables are ambients at top level. In [4], we present a higher order ambient calculus, which is a higher order extension of Safe Ambients calculus with passwords [10]. Furthermore, we present late bisimulation, quasi late bisimulation, concise quasi late bisimulation and quasi normal bisimulation for the higher order ambient calculus and study the relation between these bisimulations. In this paper, we propose a higher order extension of Safe Ambients calculus, named MHSA, and study its expressive power.

This paper is organized as follows: Section 2 gives a brief view of syntax and operational semantics of higher order ambient calculus. Then we also give the reduction barbed congruence. Section 3 we show that polyadic higher order ambient calculus can be encoded in monadic higher order ambient calculus. In Section 4 we show that first order ambient calculus with capability-passing can be encoded in monadic higher order ambient calculus. In Section 5 we show that first order ambient calculus with name-passing can be encoded in monadic higher order ambient calculus. In Section 6, we show that polyadic π-calculus can be encoded in monadic higher order ambient calculus. In Section 7, we show that the synchronous monadic higher order ambient calculus can be encoded in the asynchronous monadic higher order ambient calculus, which means that all process calculi in this paper can be encoded in the asynchronous monadic higher order ambient calculus. The paper is concluded in Section 8.

2. Monadic Higher Order Safe Ambient Calculus

In this section, we present a monadic higher order safe ambients calculus (named as MHSA), which is an extension of safe ambients by adding capability of higher order communication. Mobile capabilities (in, out, open and their co-capabilities) make ambient calculi in born with the higher order property. But these mobile capabilities are linear, i.e., only one copy of a process can move, whereas higher order communication ((X) and $\langle P\rangle$) are non-linear higher order operators since more than one copy of a process can be communicated. Therefore MHSA extends SA with non-linear higher order communication capabilities.

2.1 Syntax and Labelled Transition System of MHSA

The formal definition of process is given as follows:

$P ::= 0 \mid X \mid (X).P \mid \langle P_1\rangle.P_2 \mid in\langle n\rangle.P \mid out\langle n\rangle.P \mid open\langle n\rangle.P \mid \overline{in}\langle n\rangle.P \mid \overline{out}\langle n\rangle.P \mid \overline{open}\langle n\rangle.P \mid P_1|P_2 \mid (\nu n)P \mid n[P] \mid recX.P$, where $n \in$ set N of names, $X \in$ set Var of process variables.

Informally, 0 denotes inaction. X is a process variable. $c.P$ can perform action c, where c is in the form of $in\langle n\rangle$, $out\langle n\rangle$, $open\langle n\rangle$, $\overline{in}\langle n\rangle$, $\overline{out}\langle n\rangle$, $\overline{open}\langle n\rangle$, (X), $\langle Q\rangle$, then continues as P. $P_1|P_2$ is a parallel composition of two processes P_1 and P_2. In each process of the form $(\nu n)P$ the occurrence of n is bound within the scope of P. $n[P]$ denotes process P in an ambients n. $recX.P$ is a recursive definition of process. An occurrence of n in P is said to be free iff it does not lie within the scope of a bound occurrence of n. The set of names occurring free in P is denoted $fn(P)$. An occurrence of a name in P is said to be bound if it is not free, we write the set of bound names as $bn(P)$. $n(P)$ denotes the set of names of P, i.e., $n(P) = fn(P) \cup bn(P)$. We use $n(P,Q)$ to denote $n(P) \cup n(Q)$. A process is closed if it has no free variable; it is open if it may have free variables. Processes P and Q are α-convertible, $P \equiv_\alpha Q$, if Q can be obtained from P by a finite number of changes of bound names and bound variables. The class of the processes is denoted as Pr. The class of the closed processes is denoted as Pr^c.

The formal definition of indexed context is given below:

$C[\,] ::= [\,] \mid 0 \mid X \mid (X).C \mid \langle P\rangle.C \mid \langle C\rangle.P \mid in\langle n\rangle.C \mid out\langle n\rangle.C \mid open\langle n\rangle.C \mid \overline{in}\langle n\rangle.C \mid \overline{out}\langle n\rangle.C \mid \overline{open}\langle n\rangle.C \mid P|C \mid C|P \mid (\nu n)C \mid n[C] \mid recX.C$

Structural congruence of MHSA is a congruence relation including the following rules:

$P \equiv Q$ if $P \equiv_\alpha Q$; $P|Q \equiv Q|P$; $(P|Q)|R \equiv P|(Q|R)$; $P|0 \equiv P$; $(\nu n)0 \equiv 0$; $(\nu m)(\nu n)P \equiv (\nu n)(\nu m)P$; $(\nu n)(P|Q) \equiv P|(\nu n)Q$ if $n \notin fn(P)$; $(\nu n)(m[P]) \equiv m[(\nu n)P]$ if $n \neq m$.

The operational semantics of MHSA is given in Table 1. We have omitted the symmetric of the parallelism and interaction.

Table 1: Labelled transition system of MHSA

$$STRUC: \frac{P \longrightarrow P'}{Q \longrightarrow Q'} P \equiv Q, P' \equiv Q'$$

$$COM: (X).P|\langle Q\rangle.R \longrightarrow P\{Q/X\}|R$$

$$IN: n[in\langle m\rangle.P_1|P_2]|m[\overline{in}\langle m\rangle.Q_1|Q_2] \longrightarrow m[n[P_1|P_2]|Q_1|Q_2]$$

$$OUT: m[n[out\langle m\rangle.P_1|P_2]|P_3]|\overline{out}\langle m\rangle.Q \longrightarrow n[P_1|P_2]|m[P_3]|Q$$

$$OPEN: open\langle n\rangle.P|n[\overline{open}\langle n\rangle.Q_1|Q_2] \longrightarrow P|Q_1|Q_2$$

$$PAR: \frac{P \longrightarrow P'}{P|Q \longrightarrow P'|Q} \qquad RES: \frac{P \longrightarrow P'}{(\nu n)P \longrightarrow (\nu n)P'}$$

$$AMB: \frac{P \longrightarrow P'}{n[P] \longrightarrow n[P']}$$

$$REC: \frac{P\{recX.P/X\} \longrightarrow P'}{recX.P \longrightarrow P'}$$

2.2 Reduction Barbed Congruence of MHSA

Now we can give the concept of reduction barbed congruence for higher order ambients. Reduction barbed congruence is a behavioural equivalence defined as the largest equivalence that is preserved by all the constructs of the language, is preserved by the reduction semantics of the language, and preserves barbs, which are simple observables of terms.

Now we review the concept of reduction barbed congruence for SA. In the remainder of this paper, we abbreviate $P\{R/U\}$ as $P\langle R\rangle$. In the following, we use $P \Longrightarrow P'$ to abbreviate $P \longrightarrow ... \longrightarrow P'$.

Definition 1. For each name n, the observability predicate $\Downarrow_n$ is defined by

$P \Downarrow_n$ if $\exists P'$, $P \Longrightarrow P' \equiv (\nu\widetilde{k})(n[c.P_1|P_2]|P_3)$, where $c \in \{\overline{in}\langle n\rangle, \overline{open}\langle n\rangle\}$ and $n \notin \{\widetilde{k}\}$;

Definition 2. A symmetric relation $R \subseteq Pr^c \times Pr^c$ is a weak reduction barbed congruence if $P\ R\ Q$ implies:

(1) $C[P]\ R\ C[Q]$ for any $C[\,]$;

(2) whenever $P \Longrightarrow P'$ then there exists Q' such that $Q \Longrightarrow Q'$ and $P'\ R\ Q'$;

(3) $P \Downarrow_n$ implies $Q \Downarrow_n$.

We write $P \approx_{Ba} Q$ if P and Q are weakly reduction barbed congruent.

3. Encoding of Polyadic Higher Order Safe Ambient Calculus

Now we introduce a polyadic higher order safe ambient calculus, then give an encoding which transforms this polyadic higher order safe ambient calculus into the monadic calculus. At last, we prove the full abstraction property of this encoding.

3.1 Syntax and Labelled Transition System

Intuitively, polyadic higher order safe ambients are ambients which can send or receive many processes contemporaneously. The formal definition of processes of polyadic higher order safe ambients is given as follows:

$P ::= 0 \mid X \mid (X_1, ..., X_k).P \mid \langle P_1, ..., P_k\rangle.P \mid in\langle n\rangle.P \mid out\langle n\rangle.P \mid open\langle n\rangle.P \mid \overline{in}\langle n\rangle.P \mid \overline{out}\langle n\rangle.P \mid \overline{open}\langle n\rangle.P \mid P_1|P_2 \mid (\nu n)P \mid n[P] \mid recX.P$, where $n \in$ set N of names, $X \in$ set Var of process variables.

The operational semantics of processes is similar as Table 1 except that COM is replaced by the following rule:

$$COM : (X_1, ..., X_k).P|\langle Q_1, ..., Q_k\rangle.R \longrightarrow P\{Q_1/X_1, ..., Q_k/X_k\}|R$$

3.2 Encoding Polyadic Higher Order Safe Ambient Calculus in MHSA

Now we show that polyadic higher order safe ambients can be simulated by monadic higher order safe ambients.

Definition 3. We give a mapping $Tr_{PS}\{\}^a$ with respect to name a which transforms every polyadic higher order safe ambient P into the monadic higher order safe ambient $Tr_{PS}\{P\}^a$. The mapping is defined inductively on the structure of P.

(1) $Tr_{PS}\{0\}^a = 0$;
(2) $Tr_{PS}\{X\}^a = X$;
(3) $Tr_{PS}\{(X_1, ..., X_k).P\}^a = (X).a[X|\overline{open}\langle a\rangle.(X_1)...(X_k).Tr_{PS}\{P\}^a]$;
(4) $Tr_{PS}\{\langle P_1, ..., P_k\rangle.P\}^a = (\nu p)((\langle in\langle p\rangle.0\rangle.p[\overline{in}\langle p\rangle.open\langle a\rangle.\langle Tr_{PS}\{P_1\}^a\rangle...\langle Tr_{PS}\{P_k\}^a\rangle.\overline{open}\langle p\rangle.Tr_{PS}\{P\}^a] |open\langle p\rangle.0)$;
(5) $Tr_{PS}\{in\langle n\rangle.P\}^a = in\langle n\rangle.Tr_{PS}\{P\}^a$;
(6) $Tr_{PS}\{out\langle n\rangle.P\}^a = out\langle n\rangle.Tr_{PS}\{P\}^a$;
(7) $Tr_{PS}\{open\langle n\rangle.P\}^a = open\langle n\rangle.Tr_{PS}\{P\}^a$;
(8) $Tr_{PS}\{\overline{in}\langle n\rangle.P\}^a = \overline{in}\langle n\rangle.Tr_{PS}\{P\}^a$;
(9) $Tr_{PS}\{\overline{out}\langle n\rangle.P\}^a = \overline{out}\langle n\rangle.Tr_{PS}\{P\}^a$;
(10) $Tr_{PS}\{\overline{open}\langle n\rangle.P\}^a = \overline{open}\langle n\rangle.Tr_{PS}\{P\}^a$;
(11) $Tr_{PS}\{P_1|P_2\}^a = Tr_{PS}\{P_1\}^a|Tr_{PS}\{P_2\}^a$;
(12) $Tr_{PS}\{(\nu n)P\}^a = (\nu n)Tr_{PS}\{P\}^a$;
(13) $Tr_{PS}\{n[P]\}^c = n[Tr_{PS}\{P\}^a]$;
(14) $Tr_{PS}\{recX.P\}^a = recX.Tr_{PS}\{P\}^a$.

Now we can give the full abstraction property of encoding $Tr_{PS}\{\}^a$.

Lemma 1. For any polyadic higher order ambients P and $Q_1, ..., Q_k$, $Tr_{PS}\{P\}^a\{Tr_{PS}\{Q_1\}^a/X_1, ..., Tr_{PS}\{Q_k\}^a/X_k\} \approx_{Ba} Tr_{PS}\{P\{Q_1/X_1, ..., Q_k/X_k\}\}^a$, where $a \notin fn(P, Q_1, ..., Q_k)$.

Lemma 2. For any polyadic higher order ambients P and Q, $P \Longrightarrow Q \Leftrightarrow (\nu a)Tr_{PS}\{P\}^a \Longrightarrow\approx_{Ba} (\nu a)Tr_{PS}\{Q\}^a$, where $a \notin fn(P) \cup fn(Q)$.

Lemma 3. For any polyadic higher order ambient P, $P \Downarrow n \Leftrightarrow (\nu a)Tr_{PS}\{P\}^a \Downarrow n$, where $a \notin fn(P)$.

The definition of (weak) reduction barbed congruence $\approx_{Ba}$ for polyadic higher order ambients calculus is the same as Definition 2.

Proposition 1. For any polyadic higher order ambients P and Q, $P \approx_{Ba} Q \Leftrightarrow (\nu a)Tr_{PS}\{P\}^a \approx_{Ba} (\nu a)Tr_{PS}\{Q\}^a$, where $a \notin fn(P) \cup fn(Q)$.

Proof : By Lemmas 1, 2 and 3.

The above results show that the polyadic higher order ambients calculus can be encoded in the monadic higher order ambients calculus.

4. Encoding of First Order Ambient Calculus with Capability-Passing

For first order ambient calculus with communication, there are two kinds of communication, one is capability-passing, i.e., processes can send or receive capabilities; another is name-passing, i.e., processes can send or receive names. We will prove that both these calculus can be encoded in monadic higher order safe ambient calculus.

In this section, we prove that ambient calculus with capability-passing can be encoded in monadic higher order safe ambient calculus.

4.1 Syntax and Labelled Transition System of Polyadic Calculus and Monadic Calculus

The formal definition of processes of polyadic first order ambient calculus with capability-passing is given as follows: $P ::= 0 \mid X \mid (x_1, ..., x_k).P \mid \langle c_1, ..., c_k\rangle.P \mid x.P \mid in\langle n\rangle.P \mid out\langle n\rangle.P \mid open\langle n\rangle.P \mid \overline{in}\langle n\rangle.P \mid \overline{out}\langle n\rangle.P \mid \overline{open}\langle n\rangle.P \mid P_1|P_2 \mid (\nu n)P \mid n[P] \mid recX.P$, where $n \in$ set N of names, x_i is a variable, c_i is a capability.

The operational semantics of processes is similar as Table 1 except that COM is replaced by the following rule:

$$COM : (x_1, ..., x_k).P|\langle c_1, ..., c_k\rangle.Q \longrightarrow P\{c_1/x_1, ..., c_k/x_k\}|Q$$

Monadic calculus is a subcalculus of polyadic calculus where only one parameter can be communicated. The syntax and labelled transition system of monadic calculus is similar to polyadic calculus except that the number of parameters in communications is one.

4.2 Encoding Polyadic Ambient Calculus in Monadic Ambient Calculus

To prove that polyadic first order ambient calculus can be encoded by polyadic higher order ambient calculus, we approach this aim by two steps: firstly, we show that polyadic first order ambient calculus can be encoded by monadic first order ambient calculus; secondly, we show that monadic first order ambient calculus can be encoded by monadic higher order ambient calculus.

Now we first prove that polyadic first order ambient calculus can be simulated by monadic first order ambient calculus.

Definition 4. We give an encoding of the polyadic ambient calculus in the monadic ambient calculus. The mapping is defined inductively on the structure of P, where a ia a fresh name.

(1) $Tr_{PFC}\{0\}^a = 0$;
(2) $Tr_{PFC}\{X\}^a = X$;
(3) $Tr_{PFC}\{(x_1, ..., x_k).P\}^a = (x).a[x.\overline{open}\langle a\rangle.(x_1)...(x_k).Tr_{PFC}\{P\}^a]$;
(4) $Tr_{PFC}\{\langle c_1, ..., c_k\rangle.P\}^a = (\nu p)(\langle in\langle p\rangle\rangle.p[\overline{in}\langle p\rangle.open\langle a\rangle.\langle c_1\rangle...\langle c_k\rangle.\overline{open}\langle p\rangle.Tr_{PFC}\{P\}^a]|open\langle p\rangle.0)$;

(5) $Tr_{PFC}\{\alpha.P\}^a = \alpha.Tr_{PFC}\{P\}^a$, where α is not in the form of $(x_1, ..., x_k)$ and $\langle c_1, ..., c_k\rangle$;

(6) $Tr_{PFC}\{P_1|P_2\}^a = Tr_{PFC}\{P_1\}^a|Tr_{PFC}\{P_2\}^a$;

(7) $Tr_{PFC}\{(\nu n)P\}^a = (\nu n)Tr_{PFC}\{P\}^a$;

(8) $Tr_{PFC}\{n[P]\}^a = n[Tr_{PFC}\{P\}^a]$;

(9) $Tr_{PFC}\{recX.P\}^a = recX.Tr_{PFC}\{P\}^a$.

In the following, we give the full abstraction property of $Tr_{PFC}\{\}^a$.

Lemma 4. For any polyadic ambient P, $Tr_{PFC}\{P\}^a \{c_1/x_1, ..., c_k/x_k\} \approx_{Ba} Tr_{PFC}\{P\{c_1/x_1, ..., c_k/x_k\}\}^a$, where $a \notin fn(P, c_1.0, ..., c_k.0)$.

Lemma 5. For any polyadic ambients P and Q, $P \Longrightarrow Q \Leftrightarrow (\nu a)Tr_{PFC}\{P\}^a \Longrightarrow\approx_{Ba} (\nu a)Tr_{PFC}\{Q\}^a$, where $a \notin fn(P) \cup fn(Q)$.

Lemma 6. For any polyadic ambient P, $P \Downarrow n \Leftrightarrow (\nu a)Tr_{PFC}\{P\}^a \Downarrow n$, where $a \notin fn(P)$.

The definition of (weak) reduction barbed congruence $\approx_{Ba}$ for polyadic/monadic ambients with capability-passing is the same as Definition 2.

Proposition 2. For any polyadic ambients P and Q, $P \approx_{Ba} Q \Leftrightarrow (\nu a)Tr_{PFC}\{P\}^a \approx_{Ba} (\nu a)Tr_{PFC}\{Q\}^a$, where $a \notin fn(P) \cup fn(Q)$.

Proof : By Lemmas 4, 5 and 6.

4.3 Encoding Monadic Ambient Calculus in MHSA

Now we show that every monadic ambient can be encoded in a monadic higher order safe ambient.

Definition 5. We give a mapping $Tr_{FC}\{\}^a$ with respect to name a which transforms every monadic ambient P into monadic higher order safe ambient $Tr_{FC}\{P\}^a$. The mapping is defined inductively on the structure of P.

(1) $Tr_{FC}\{0\}^a = 0$;

(2) $Tr_{FC}\{X\}^a = X$;

(3) $Tr_{FC}\{(x).P\}^a = (X).Tr_{FC}\{P\}^a$;

(4) $Tr_{FC}\{\langle in\langle n\rangle\rangle.P\}^a = \langle in\langle n\rangle.open\langle a\rangle.0\rangle.Tr_{FC}\{P\}^a$;

(5) $Tr_{FC}\{\langle out\langle n\rangle\rangle.P\}^a = \langle out\langle n\rangle.open\langle a\rangle.0\rangle.Tr_{FC}\{P\}^a$;

(6) $Tr_{FC}\{\langle open\langle n\rangle\rangle.P\}^a = \langle open\langle n\rangle.open\langle a\rangle.0\rangle.Tr_{FC}\{P\}^a$;

(7) $Tr_{FC}\{\langle \overline{in}\langle n\rangle\rangle.P\}^a = \langle \overline{in}\langle n\rangle.open\langle a\rangle.0\rangle.Tr_{FC}\{P\}^a$;

(8) $Tr_{FC}\{\langle \overline{out}\langle n\rangle\rangle.P\}^a = \langle \overline{out}\langle n\rangle.open\langle a\rangle.0\rangle.Tr_{FC}\{P\}^a$;

(9) $Tr_{FC}\{\langle \overline{open}\langle n\rangle\rangle.P\}^a = \langle \overline{open}\langle n\rangle.open\langle a\rangle.0\rangle.Tr_{FC}\{P\}^a$;

(10) $Tr_{FC}\{x.P\}^a = X|a[\overline{open}\langle a\rangle.Tr_{FC}\{P\}^a]$;

(11) $Tr_{FC}\{in\langle n\rangle.P\}^a = in\langle n\rangle.Tr_{FC}\{P\}^a$;

(12) $Tr_{FC}\{out\langle n\rangle.P\}^a = out\langle n\rangle.Tr_{FC}\{P\}^a$;

(13) $Tr_{FC}\{open\langle n\rangle.P\}^a = open\langle n\rangle.Tr_{FC}\{P\}^a$;

(14) $Tr_{FC}\{\overline{in}\langle n\rangle.P\}^a = \overline{in}\langle n\rangle.Tr_{FC}\{P\}^a$;

(15) $Tr_{FC}\{\overline{out}\langle n\rangle.P\}^a = \overline{out}\langle n\rangle.Tr_{FC}\{P\}^a$;

(16) $Tr_{FC}\{\overline{open}\langle n\rangle.P\}^a = \overline{open}\langle n\rangle.Tr_{FC}\{P\}^a$;

(17) $Tr_{FC}\{P_1|P_2\}^a = Tr_{FC}\{P_1\}^a|Tr_{FC}\{P_2\}^a$;

(18) $Tr_{FC}\{(\nu n)P\}^a = (\nu n)Tr_{FC}\{P\}^a$;

(19) $Tr_{FC}\{n[P]\}^a = n[Tr_{FC}\{P\}^a]$;

(20) $Tr_{FC}\{recX.P\}^a = recX.Tr_{FC}\{P\}^a$.

The following lemmas and propositions state the full abstraction property of $Tr_{FC}\{\}^a$.

Lemma 7. For any monadic ambient P, $Tr_{FC}\{P\}^a\{c.open\langle a\rangle.0/X\} \approx_{Ba} Tr_{FC}\{P\{c/x\}\}^a$, where $a \notin fn(P, c.0)$.

Lemma 8. For any monadic ambients P and Q, $P \Longrightarrow Q \Leftrightarrow (\nu a)Tr_{FC}\{P\}^a \Longrightarrow\approx_{Ba} (\nu a)Tr_{FC}\{Q\}^a$, where $a \notin fn(P) \cup fn(Q)$.

Lemma 9. For any monadic ambient P, $P \Downarrow n \Leftrightarrow (\nu a)Tr_{FC}\{P\}^a \Downarrow n$, where $a \notin fn(P)$.

Proposition 3. For any monadic ambients with capability-passing P and Q, $P \approx_{Ba} Q \Leftrightarrow (\nu a)Tr_{FC}\{P\}^a \approx_{Ba} (\nu a)Tr_{FC}\{Q\}^a$, where $a \notin fn(P) \cup fn(Q)$.

Proof : By Lemmas 7, 8 and 9.

We can indirectly encode polyadic first order ambient calculus with capability-passing in monadic higher order ambient calculus since polyadic first order ambient calculus with capability-passing can be encoded in monadic first order ambient calculus with capability-passing and monadic first order ambient calculus with capability-passing can be encoded in monadic higher order safe ambient calculus.

5. Encoding of First Order Ambient Calculus with Name-Passing

In this section, we will give an encoding of ambient calculus with name-passing, then we will prove the full abstraction of this encoding.

5.1 Syntax and Labelled Transition System of Polyadic Calculus and Monadic Calculus

The formal definition of processes of polyadic first order ambient calculus with name-passing is given as follows:

$P ::= 0 \mid X \mid (x_1, ..., x_k).P \mid \langle n_1, ..., n_k\rangle.P \mid in\langle n\rangle.P \mid out\langle n\rangle.P \mid open\langle n\rangle.P \mid \overline{in}\langle n\rangle.P \mid \overline{out}\langle n\rangle.P \mid \overline{open}\langle n\rangle.P \mid P_1|P_2 \mid (\nu n)P \mid n[P] \mid recX.P \mid x[P] \mid in\langle x\rangle.P \mid out\langle x\rangle.P \mid open\langle x\rangle.P \mid \overline{in}\langle x\rangle.P \mid \overline{out}\langle x\rangle.P \mid \overline{open}\langle x\rangle.P$, where $n \in$ set N of names, x_i is a variable.

The operational semantics of processes is similar as Table 1 except that COM is replaced by the following rule:

$$COM : (x_1, ..., x_k).P|\langle n_1, ..., n_k\rangle.R \longrightarrow P\{n_1/x_1, ..., n_k/x_k\}|R$$

Similarly, monadic calculus is a subcalculus of polyadic calculus where only one parameter can be exchanged in one communication. The syntax and labelled transition system of monadic calculus is similar to polyadic calculus except that the number of parameters in communications is one.

5.2 Encoding Polyadic Ambient Calculus with Name-Passing in Monadic Calculus

At first we show that the polyadic ambient calculus with name-passing can be simulated by the monadic ambient calculus with name-passing.

Definition 6. We give an encoding of the polyadic ambient calculus with name-passing in the monadic ambient calculus with name-passing. The mapping is defined inductively on the structure of P, where a is a fresh name.

(1) $Tr_{PFN}\{0\}^a = 0$;

(2) $Tr_{PFN}\{X\}^a = X$;

(3) $Tr_{PFN}\{(x_1, ..., x_k).P\}^a = (x).a[in\langle x\rangle.\overline{open}\langle a\rangle.(x_1)...(x_k).Tr_{PFN}\{P\}^a]$;

(4) $Tr_{PFN}\{\langle n_1, ..., n_k\rangle.P\}^a = \nu p(\langle p\rangle.p[\overline{in}\langle p\rangle.open\langle a\rangle.\langle n_1\rangle...\langle n_k\rangle.\overline{open}\langle p\rangle.Tr_{PFN}\{P\}^a]|open\langle p\rangle.0)$;

(5) $Tr_{PFN}\{\alpha.P\}^a = \alpha.Tr_{PFN}\{P\}^a$, where α is not in the form of $(x_1, ..., x_k)$ and $\langle n_1, ..., n_k\rangle$;

(6) $Tr_{PFN}\{P_1|P_2\}^a = Tr_{PFN}\{P_1\}^a|Tr_{PFN}\{P_2\}^a$;

(7) $Tr_{PFN}\{(\nu n)P\}^a = (\nu n)Tr_{PFN}\{P\}^a$;

(8) $Tr_{PFN}\{n[P]\}^a = n[Tr_{PFN}\{P\}^a]$;

(9) $Tr_{PFN}\{x[P]\}^a = x[Tr_{PFN}\{P\}^a]$;

(10) $Tr_{PFN}\{recX.P\}^a = recX.Tr_{PFN}\{P\}^a$.

The full abstraction property of this encoding can be given similar to Proposition 2.

5.3 Encoding Monadic Ambient Calculus with Name-Passing in Polyadic Higher Order Safe Ambient Calculus

Now we show that every monadic ambient with name-passing can be encoded in a polyadic higher order safe ambient.

Definition 7. We give a mapping $Tr_{FN}\{\}^a$ with respect to name a which transforms every monadic ambient P into polyadic higher order safe ambient $Tr_{FN}\{P\}^a$. The mapping is defined inductively on the structure of P.

(1) $Tr_{FN}\{0\}^a = 0$;

(2) $Tr_{FN}\{X\}^a = X$;

(3) $Tr_{FN}\{in\langle n\rangle.P\}^a = in\langle n\rangle.Tr_{FN}\{P\}^a$;

(4) $Tr_{FN}\{out\langle n\rangle.P\}^a = out\langle n\rangle.Tr_{FN}\{P\}^a$;

(5) $Tr_{FN}\{open\langle n\rangle.P\}^a = open\langle n\rangle.Tr_{FN}\{P\}^a$;

(6) $Tr_{FN}\{\overline{in}\langle n\rangle.P\}^a = \overline{in}\langle n\rangle.Tr_{FN}\{P\}^a$;

(7) $Tr_{FN}\{\overline{out}\langle n\rangle.P\}^a = \overline{out}\langle n\rangle.Tr_{FN}\{P\}^a$;

(8) $Tr_{FN}\{\overline{open}\langle n\rangle.P\}^a = \overline{open}\langle n\rangle.Tr_{FN}\{P\}^a$;

(9) $Tr_{FN}\{P_1|P_2\}^a = Tr_{FN}\{P_1\}^a|Tr_{FN}\{P_2\}^a$;

(10) $Tr_{FN}\{(\nu n)P\}^a = (\nu n)Tr_{FN}\{P\}^a$;

(11) $Tr_{FN}\{n[P]\}^a = n[Tr_{FN}\{P\}^a]$;

(12) $Tr_{FN}\{recX.P\}^a = recX.Tr_{FN}\{P\}^a$;

(13) $Tr_{FN}\{(x).P\}^a = (Z_1^x, Z_2^x, Z_3^x, Z_4^x, Z_5^x, Z_6^x, Z_7^x, Z_8^x).Tr_{FN}\{P\}^a$;

(14) $Tr_{FN}\{\langle n\rangle.P\}^a = \langle n[\overline{in}\langle n\rangle.open\langle a\rangle.0], in\langle n\rangle.0, in\langle n\rangle.open\langle a\rangle.0, out\langle n\rangle.open\langle a\rangle.0, open\langle n\rangle.open\langle a\rangle.0, \overline{in}\langle n\rangle.open\langle a\rangle.0, \overline{out}\langle n\rangle.open\langle a\rangle.0, \overline{open}\langle n\rangle.open\langle a\rangle.0\rangle.Tr_{FN}\{P\}^a$;

(15) $Tr_{FN}\{x[P]\}^a = Z_1^x|a[Z_2^x|\overline{open}\langle a\rangle.Tr_{FN}\{P\}^a]$;

(16) $Tr_{FN}\{in\langle x\rangle.P\}^a = Z_3^x|a[\overline{open}\langle a\rangle.Tr_{FN}\{P\}^a]$;

(17) $Tr_{FN}\{out\langle x\rangle.P\}^a = Z_4^x|a[\overline{open}\langle a\rangle.Tr_{FN}\{P\}^a]$;

(18) $Tr_{FN}\{open\langle x\rangle.P\}^a = Z_5^x|a[\overline{open}\langle a\rangle.Tr_{FN}\{P\}^a]$;

(19) $Tr_{FN}\{\overline{in}\langle x\rangle.P\}^a = Z_6^x|a[\overline{open}\langle a\rangle.Tr_{FN}\{P\}^a]$;

(20) $Tr_{FN}\{\overline{out}\langle x\rangle.P\}^a = Z_7^x|a[\overline{open}\langle a\rangle.Tr_{FN}\{P\}^a]$;

(21) $Tr_{FN}\{\overline{open}\langle x\rangle.P\}^a = Z_8^x|a[\overline{open}\langle a\rangle.Tr_{FN}\{P\}^a]$.

The full abstraction of $Tr_{FN}\{\}^a$ is stated in the following lemmas and propositions.

Lemma 10. For any monadic ambient P, $Tr_{FN}\{P\}^a \{n[\overline{in}\langle n\rangle.open\langle a\rangle.0]/Z_1^x, in\langle n\rangle.0/Z_2^x, in\langle n\rangle.open\langle a\rangle.0/Z_3^x, out\langle n\rangle.open\langle a\rangle.0/Z_4^x, open\langle n\rangle.open\langle a\rangle.0/Z_5^x, \overline{in}\langle n\rangle.open\langle a\rangle.0/Z_6^x, \overline{out}\langle n\rangle.open\langle a\rangle.0/Z_7^x, \overline{open}\langle n\rangle.open\langle a\rangle.0/Z_8^x\} \approx_{Ba} Tr_{FN}\{P\{n/x\}\}^a$, where $a \notin fn(P) \cup \{n\}$.

Lemma 11. For any monadic ambients P and Q, $P \Longrightarrow Q \Leftrightarrow (\nu a)Tr_{FN}\{P\}^a \Longrightarrow\approx_{Ba} (\nu a)Tr_{FN}\{Q\}^a$, where $a \notin fn(P) \cup fn(Q)$.

Lemma 12. For any monadic ambient P, $P \Downarrow n \Leftrightarrow (\nu a)Tr_{FN}\{P\}^a \Downarrow n$, where $a \notin fn(P)$.

The definition of (weak) reduction barbed congruence $\approx_{Ba}$ for monadic ambients with name-passing is the same as Definition 2.

Proposition 4. For any monadic ambients with name-passing P and Q, $P \approx_{Ba} Q \Leftrightarrow (\nu a)Tr_{FN}\{P\}^a \approx_{Ba} (\nu a)Tr_{FN}\{Q\}^a$, where $a \notin fn(P) \cup fn(Q)$.

Proof : By Lemmas 10, 11 and 12.

We can indirectly encode polyadic first order ambient calculus with name-passing in monadic higher order ambient calculus since polyadic first order ambient calculus with name-passing can be encoded in monadic first order ambient calculus with name-passing, monadic first order ambient calculus with name-passing can be encoded in polyadic higher order safe ambient calculus, and polyadic higher order safe ambient calculus can be encoded in monadic higher order safe ambient calculus.

6. Encoding of Polyadic π-Calculus

In this section, we will show that polyadic π-calculus can be encoded in monadic higher order ambient calculus.

6.1 Syntax and Labelled Transition System of Polyadic π-Calculus

Now we briefly recall the syntax and labelled transition system of the polyadic π-calculus.

We use $a, b, c, ..., x, y, z, ...$ to range over the class of names. The class Pr of the polyadic π-calculus processes is built up using the operators of prefixing, sum, parallel composition, restriction and replication in the grammar below:

$P ::= 0 \mid x(y_1, ..., y_k).P \mid \overline{x}\langle y_1, ..., y_k\rangle.P \mid P_1|P_2 \mid (\nu x)P \mid\ !P$

In each process of the form $(\nu y)P$ or $x(y).P$ the occurrence of y is bound within the scope of P. An occurrence of y in a process is said to be free iff it does not lie within the scope of a bound occurrence of y. The set of names occurring free in P is denoted $fn(P)$. An occurrence of a name in a process is said to be bound if it is not free, we write the set of bound names as $bn(P)$. Process P and Q are α-convertible, $P \equiv_\alpha Q$, if Q can be obtained from P by a finite number of changes of bound names. The set of all processes is denoted as Pr^c_π.

Structural congruence of polyadic π-calculus is a congruence relation including the following rules:

$P \equiv Q$ if $P \equiv_\alpha Q$; $P|Q \equiv Q|P$; $(P|Q)|R \equiv P|(Q|R)$; $P|0 \equiv P$; $(\nu n)0 \equiv 0$; $(\nu m)(\nu n)P \equiv (\nu n)(\nu m)P$; $(\nu n)(P|Q) \equiv P|(\nu n)Q$ if $n \notin fn(P)$.

The operational semantics of processes is given in Table 2. We have omitted the symmetric of the parallelism and communication.

Table 2: Labelled transition system of polyadic π-calculus

$$COM : \overline{x}\langle y_1, ..., y_k\rangle.P|x(z_1, ..., z_k).Q \longrightarrow P|Q\{y_1/z_1, ..., y_k/z_k\}$$

$$ALP : \frac{P \longrightarrow P'}{Q \longrightarrow Q'} P \equiv Q, P' \equiv Q'$$

$$PAR : \frac{P \longrightarrow P'}{P|Q \longrightarrow P'|Q}$$

$$RES : \frac{P \longrightarrow P'}{(\nu x)P \longrightarrow (\nu x)P'}$$

$$REP : \frac{P|!P \longrightarrow P'}{!P \longrightarrow P'}$$

6.2 Encoding Polyadic π-Calculus in First Order Ambient Calculus with Name-Passing

Now we show that polyadic π-calculus [12] can be encoded in first order ambient calculus with name-passing.

Definition 8. We give a mapping $Tr_\pi\{\}$ which transforms every polyadic π-calculus process P into the first order ambient calculus with name-passing process $Tr_\pi\{P\}$. The mapping is defined inductively on the structure of P.

(1) $Tr_\pi\{0\} = 0$;

(2) $Tr_\pi\{x(y_1, ..., y_k).P\} = x[\overline{in}\langle x\rangle.open\langle\overline{x}\rangle.(y_1, ..., y_k).\overline{open}\langle x\rangle.Tr_\pi\{P\}]|open\langle x\rangle.0$;

(3) $Tr_\pi\{\overline{x}\langle y_1, ..., y_k\rangle.P\} = \overline{x}[in\langle x\rangle.\langle y_1, ..., y_k\rangle.Tr_\pi\{P\}|\overline{open}\langle\overline{x}\rangle.0]$;

(4) $Tr_\pi\{P_1|P_2\} = Tr_\pi\{P_1\}|Tr_\pi\{P_2\}$;

(5) $Tr_\pi\{(\nu x)P\} = (\nu x)Tr_\pi\{P\}$;

(6) $Tr_\pi\{!P\}^n = !Tr_\pi\{P\}^n$.

By the above Proposition 4, we can also get a full abstract encoding from polyadic π-calculus in the monadic higher order ambient calculus. Therefore, π-calculus can be expressed in the monadic higher order ambient calculus.

Reduction barbed congruence for polyadic π-calculus is defined as follows:

Definition 9. A symmetric relation $R \subseteq Pr^c_\pi \times Pr^c_\pi$ is a weakly reduction barbed congruence if $P\ R\ Q$ implies:

(1) $P|C\ R\ Q|C$ for any C;

(2) Whenever $P \Longrightarrow P'$ then $Q \Longrightarrow Q'$ and $P'\ R\ Q'$;

(3) For any name n, if $P \Downarrow n$, then also $Q \Downarrow n$. Here $P \Downarrow n$ means $\exists P'$, $P \Longrightarrow P' \equiv (\nu\widetilde{k})(\alpha.P_1|P_2)$ where $n = x$ if $\alpha = x(y_1, ..., y_k)$, $n = \overline{x}$ if $\alpha = \overline{x}\langle y_1, ..., y_k\rangle\}$ and $\{n, \overline{n}\} \cap \widetilde{k} = \emptyset$.

We write $P \approx_{Ba} Q$ if P and Q are weakly reduction barbed congruent.

Now we can give the full abstraction of $Tr_\pi\{\}$.

Lemma 13. For any polyadic π-calculus process P, $Tr_\pi\{P\}\{z_1/y_1, ..., z_k/y_k\} \approx_{Ba} Tr_\pi\{P\{z_1/y_1, ..., z_k/y_k\}\}$.

Lemma 14. For any polyadic π-calculus processes P and Q, $P \Longrightarrow Q \Leftrightarrow Tr_\pi\{P\} \Longrightarrow\approx_{Ba} Tr_\pi\{Q\}$.

Lemma 15. For any polyadic π-calculus process P, $P \Downarrow n \Leftrightarrow Tr_\pi\{P\} \Downarrow n$.

Proposition 5. For any polyadic π-calculus processes P and Q, $P \approx_{Ba} Q \Leftrightarrow Tr_\pi\{P\} \approx_{Ba} Tr_\pi\{Q\}$.

Proof : By Lemmas 13, 14 and 15.

7. Asynchronous vs. Synchronous Communication

In the above sections, we study the expressiveness of synchronous calculi. But many ambients calculi are asynchronous calculi [3], [9]. So in this section, we will exploit the expressiveness of asynchronous calculus.

For asynchronous calculus, message emission is non-blocking. Asynchronous communications are interesting from the point of view of concurrent and distributed programming languages, because they are closer to the communication primitives offered by available distributed systems. Asynchronous calculi are usually achieved, syntactically, by disallowing output prefix (that is, continuations underneath output messages) and choice. In [7], authors showed that synchronous higher order π-calculus can be encoded in asynchronous higher order π-calculus.

In this section, we show that the similar result also holds for ambient calculus: synchronous monadic higher order safe ambient calculus can be encoded in asynchronous monadic higher order safe ambient calculus, named asynchronous MHSA. This result implies that all process calculi in this paper can be encoded in asynchronous monadic higher order ambient calculus.

7.1 Syntax and Labelled Transition System of Asynchronous MHSA

The formal definition of processes of asynchronous monadic higher order safe ambients is given as follows:

$P ::= 0 \mid X \mid (X).P \mid \langle P\rangle \mid in\langle n\rangle.P \mid out\langle n\rangle.P \mid open\langle n\rangle.P \mid \overline{in}\langle n\rangle.P \mid \overline{out}\langle n\rangle.P \mid \overline{open}\langle n\rangle.P \mid P_1|P_2 \mid (\nu n)P \mid n[P] \mid recX.P$, where $n \in$ set N of names, $X \in$ set Var of process variables.

The operational semantics of processes is similar as Table 1 except that COM is replaced by the following rule:

$$COM : (X).P|\langle Q\rangle \longrightarrow P\{Q/X\}$$

7.2 Encoding MHSA in Asynchronous MHSA

In this section we present an encoding from synchronous monadic higher order safe ambients to asynchronous monadic higher order safe ambients, then prove the full abstraction property of this encoding.

Definition 10. We give a mapping $Trs_S\{\}^{a,b,c}$ with respect to names a, b, c which transforms every synchronous monadic higher order safe ambient P into the asynchronous monadic higher order safe ambient $Trs_S\{P\}^{a,b,c}$. The mapping is defined inductively on the structure of P.

(1) $Trs_S\{0\}^{a,b,c} = 0$;

(2) $Trs_S\{X\}^{a,b,c} = X$;

(3) $Trs_S\{(X).P\}^{a,b,c} = a[\overline{in}\langle a\rangle.open\langle b\rangle.(X).open\langle c\rangle.\overline{open}\langle a\rangle.Trs_S\{P\}^{a,b,c}]|open\langle a\rangle.0$;

(4) $Trs_S\{\langle P_1\rangle.P_2\}^{a,b,c} = b[in\langle a\rangle.\overline{open}\langle b\rangle.\langle Trs_S\{P_1\}^{a,b,c}\rangle|c[\overline{open}\langle c\rangle.Trs_S\{P_2\}^{a,b,c}]]$;

(5) $Trs_S\{in\langle n\rangle.P\}^{a,b,c} = in\langle n\rangle.Trs_S\{P\}^{a,b,c}$;

(6) $Trs_S\{out\langle n\rangle.P\}^{a,b,c} = out\langle n\rangle.Trs_S\{P\}^{a,b,c}$;

(7) $Trs_S\{open\langle n\rangle.P\}^{a,b,c} = open\langle n\rangle.Trs_S\{P\}^{a,b,c}$;

(8) $Trs_S\{\overline{in}\langle n\rangle.P\}^{a,b,c} = \overline{in}\langle n\rangle.Trs_S\{P\}^{a,b,c}$;

(9) $Trs_S\{\overline{out}\langle n\rangle.P\}^{a,b,c} = \overline{out}\langle n\rangle.Trs_S\{P\}^{a,b,c}$;

(10) $Trs_S\{\overline{open}\langle n\rangle.P\}^{a,b,c} = \overline{open}\langle n\rangle.Trs_S\{P\}^{a,b,c}$;

(11) $Trs_S\{P_1|P_2\}^{a,b,c} = Trs_S\{P_1\}^{a,b,c}|Trs_S\{P_2\}^{a,b,c}$;

(12) $Trs_S\{(\nu n)P\}^{a,b,c} = (\nu n)Trs_S\{P\}^{a,b,c}$;

(13) $Trs_S\{n[P]\}^{a,t,c} = n[Trs_S\{P\}^{a,b,c}]$;

(14) $Trs_S\{recX.P\}^{a,b,c} = recX.Trs_S\{P\}^{a,b,c}$.

In the following, we aim to prove the full abstraction property of encoding $Trs_S\{\}^{a,b,c}$.

Lemma 16. For any synchronous monadic higher order ambients P and Q, $Trs_S\{P\}^{a,b,c}\{Trs_S\{Q\}^{a,b,c}/X\} \approx_{Ba} Trs_S\{P\{Q/X\}\}^{a,b,c}$, where $a, b, c \notin fn(P, Q)$.

Lemma 17. For any synchronous monadic higher order ambients P and Q, $P \Longrightarrow Q \Leftrightarrow (\nu a, b, c) Trs_S\{P\}^{a,b,c} \Longrightarrow\approx_{Ba} (\nu a, b, c)Trs_S\{Q\}^{a,b,c}$, where $a, b, c \notin fn(P) \cup fn(Q)$.

Lemma 18. For any synchronous monadic higher order ambient P, $P \Downarrow n \Leftrightarrow (\nu a, b, c)Trs_S\{P\}^{a,b,c} \Downarrow n$, where $a, b, c \notin fn(P)$.

The definition of (weak) reduction barbed congruence $\approx_{Ba}$ for asynchronous monadic higher order ambient calculus is the same as Definition 2.

Proposition 6. For any synchronous monadic higher order ambients P and Q, $P \approx_{Ba} Q \Leftrightarrow (\nu a, b, c)Trs_S\{P\}^{a,b,c} \approx_{Ba} (\nu a, b, c)Trs_S\{Q\}^{a,b,c}$, where $a, b, c \notin fn(P) \cup fn(Q)$.

Proof: By Lemmas 16, 17 and 18.

The above results show that the synchronous monadic higher order ambient calculus can be encoded in asynchronous monadic higher order ambient calculus.

8. Conclusions

In this paper, we studied the expressive power of monadic higher order safe ambient calculus. We showed that polyadic higher order safe ambient calculus, first order safe ambient calculus with capability-passing, first order safe ambient calculus with name-passing, and polyadic π-calculus can all be encoded in monadic higher order ambient calculus. At last, we also showed that synchronous monadic higher order ambient calculus can be encoded in asynchronous monadic higher order ambient calculus. Therefore, all process calculi in this paper can be encoded in asynchronous monadic higher order ambient calculus. In [6], authors showed that a higher order π-calculus with n-adic communication cannot be encoded in a calculus with $n-1$-adic communication. We have showed that polyadic π-calculus can be encoded in monadic higher order ambient calculus in this paper. Since it was proved that higher order π-calculus can be encoded in π-calculus in [11], we can conclude that the monadic higher order ambient calculus cannot be encoded in higher order π-calculus with n-adic communication for any n. Therefore, this result means that the expressive power of monadic higher order ambient calculus is strictly stronger than higher order π-calculus.

Acknowledgment

This work was supported by the Aviation Science Fund of China under Grant No. 20128052064 and the National Natural Science Foundation of China under Grant No. 60873025.

References

[1] M. Bugliesi, G. Castagna, and S. Crafa. Boxed ambients. In Proc. 4th TACS. LNCS, vol. 2215. Springer Verlag. 2001.

[2] M. Coppo and M. Dezani-Ciangcaglini. A fully abstract model for higher-order ambients. Proceedings of VMCAI 2002. LNCS 2294. 255-271.

[3] L. Cardelli, and A. Gordon. Mobile ambients. Theoretical Computer Science 240, 1, 177-213. 2000. An extended abstract appeared in Proc. of FoSSaCS98.

[4] Z. Cao. A Calculus of Higher Order Safe Ambients and Its Bisimulations. Proceedings of TASE, 93-100, 2012.

[5] Y. Fu. Fair ambients. Acta Inf., 43(8):535-594, 2007.

[6] I. Lanese, J. A. Perez, D. Sangiorgi, and A. Schmitt. On the Expressiveness of Polyadicity in Higher-Order Process Calculi. In Proceedings of ICTCS'09, 7 pages, 2009.

[7] I. Lanese, J. A. Perez, D. Sangiorgi, and A. Schmitt. On the Expressiveness of Polyadic and Synchronous Communication in Higher-Order Process Calculi. In Proc. ICALP'10, LNCS, 2010.

[8] F. Levi, and D. Sangiorgi. Controlling interference in ambients. An extended abstract appeared in Proc. 27th POPL, ACM Press, 2000.

[9] F. Levi, and D. Sangiorgi. Mobile safe ambients. ACM Transactions on Programming Languages and Systems 25(1), 1-69, 2003.

[10] M. Merro, M. Hennessy. A Bisimulation-based Semantic Theory of Safe Ambients. ACM Transactions on Programming Languages and Systems, 28(2):290-330, 2006.

[11] D. Sangiorgi. Expressing mobility in process algebras: first-order and higher-order paradigms, Ph.D thesis, University of Einburgh, 1992.

[12] D. Sangiorgi, D. Walker. The π-calculus: a theory of mobile processes, Cambridge University Press, 2001.

Test Case Generation and Execution based on Record-Replayer Mechanism

Jinyoung Kim[1], Hyunmin Yoon[1], and Minsoo Ryu[2]
[1]Department of Electronics Computer Engineering, Hanyang University, Seoul, Korea
[2]Department of Computer Science and Engineering, Hanyang University, Seoul, Korea

Abstract - *In this paper, we present a novel testing approach using deterministic replay. Deterministic replay is a technology that records nondeterministic events during a normal computer execution and deterministically replays the computer system's execution along with the recorded events. We apply this deterministic replay technology to event-driven embedded system testing. The proposed approach works in three steps. First, we run an initial test using a sequence of "essential'' events and obtain an event history that contains enough information needed for deterministic replay. Second, we create a number of variants of event history, i.e., test cases, by mutating the event history and/or adding more event records into the event history. Third, we execute the variants of event history emulating all recorded I/O events. This approach has two important advantages. It allows us to easily and efficiently generate a lot of effective test cases that can exhibit subtle bugs like races. It also provides an efficient means for automated test case execution since we do not need any arrangement of external entities like users and other systems.*

Keywords: Embedded system testing, Record-Replay, Automated test execution, Event-driven test

1 Introduction

Event-driven embedded software places significant challenges on test case creation and execution. Event-driven embedded software involves many sources of events including users and a variety of physical devices such as NICs(network interface cards) and storage devices. These sources may generate a lot of events that lead us to consider numerous combinations of events for testing, and thus make the creation of test cases very difficult. Furthermore, such events may occur in a complicated fashion; sequentially or concurrently, with or without interdependencies among them. Therefore, to detect some hard bugs such as races and time-sensitive bugs, we should be able to control the precise timing of event occurrences during the test process. Unfortunately, the operating environment for event-driven software involves a lot of entities such as users, physical devices and other external embedded systems, which are hard to arrange for precise event simulation during the testing process.

In this paper, we present a novel testing approach using deterministic replay. Deterministic replay is a technology that records nondeterministic events during a normal computer execution and deterministically replays the computer system's execution along with the recorded events. Since deterministic replay can re-produce identical behavior during re-execution, it has shown very effective in many areas including debugging [1, 2, 3], fault tolerance [4, 5], security [6] and post-mortem analysis [7]. In this work, we use RT-Replayer, a software-based replayer that can capture and replay I/O events with instruction level accuracy, to support test case creation and execution for event-driven embedded software. RT-Replayer is a software component that is installed inside an operating system kernel. It has two execution modes, record and replay. In record mode, it monitors I/O interrupts and records them in an event history. In replay mode, it disables all interrupts and emulates the recorded events at the same time points and locations as those in record mode.

The proposed testing approach using RT-Replayer works in three steps. First, we run an initial test using a sequence of "essential'' events with RT-Replayer enabled in record mode, and obtain an event history that contains enough information needed for deterministic replay. Specifically, each event record in the event history contains the type and source of event, the program counter value where the event occurred, the instruction count when it occurred, and the data content that accompanied the event. Second, we create a number of variants of event history, i.e., test cases, by varying program counter values, instruction counts and data content that satisfy certain testing criteria. In doing so, we may change the order of events or even their timings so that subtle program bugs like races can be detected. We may also add some other events into the event history. This manipulation of event history allows us to efficiently generate a series of effective test cases. Third, we execute the variants of event history with RT-Replayer enabled in replay mode. Since RT-Replay is able to emulate events with all I/O interrupt disabled, we do not need any arrangement of external entities like users and other systems since RT-Replayer emulates all I/O events. Therefore, the use of RT-Replayer can be used as an efficient vehicle for automated test case execution.

2 Overview of RT-Replayer

RT-Replayer consists of three major components, event recorder, event history and event replayer, as shown in Figure 1. During the record phase, the event recorder logs interrupts and I/O data into a special data structure, called event log. When the kernel terminates, the event recorder stores the event history in safe non-volatile storage. During the replay phase, the event replayer emulates the interrupts stored in the event history.

In order to efficiently record interrupts and I/O data, the event recorder is implemented within OS interrupt handlers and I/O device drivers. By using hardware performance counters, it records the following important information for deterministic replay.

- Event type and source (who)
- Data (what)
- Program counter value or I/O address (where)
- Instruction count (when)

The first element represents the type and source of event. It is used to distinguish between interrupts and I/O data access. It is also used to identify the source of interrupt or I/O address. The second element represents the data obtained by interrupt handling or I/O data access. The third element may represent the program counter (PC) address where an interrupt occurred or the I/O address from which an I/O operation read the data. The last element represents an instruction count. We use instruction counts to determine when interrupts occurred.

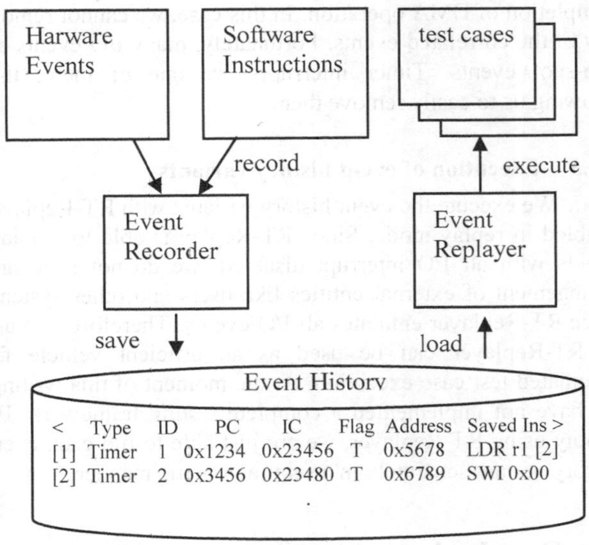

Figure 1. Overview of RT-Replayer

The event replayer performs full-system replay by appropriately handling the recorded events and data guided by the event log. In order to avoid any external disturbance during the replay phase, the event replay mechanism keeps all hardware interrupts disabled and prohibits I/O drivers from accessing real hardware. Instead, the event replay mechanism emulates hardware interrupts and supplies requested I/O data consulting the event history.

3 Replay Testing

3.1 Difficulties of testing embedded systems

Concurrency is one of important features in modern event-driven embedded systems for providing improved performance. However, concurrent behavior often causes delicate bugs such as race conditions and deadlocks. For example, a shared variable may exhibit non-deterministic behavior without proper synchronization using primitives like semaphores or mutexes. In general, race conditions and deadlocks are hard to track down and fix since they are not reproducible in most cases.

Time-sensitive operations are another source of bugs that make testing significantly difficult. For instance, most I/O controllers require a certain amount of time delay for subsequent I/O operations: HD44780 character LCD controller specifies that writing data into DDRAM takes 37 *us* to complete, which means a device driver must wait at least 37 *us* before it performs a subsequent I/O operation. If not, the character LCD device may not work correctly. Most practitioners implement such a time delay using idle loops with an appropriate safety margin, since the actual time delay is affected by many factors like processor's pipeline and cache behavior and/or some other events that may be interleaved between I/O operations. As a result, it is very hard to verify whether a device driver properly implements such a specified time delay or not.

Hardware failures are even harder to test than concurrent and time-sensitive software failures. There can be a lot of hardware failures due to factors such as bus conflict. One example is I^2C bus. The I^2C bus arbitration protocol specifies that only a single slave can send or receive through the bus. For some reasons, i.e., buggy device driver implementation or faulty hardware implementation, more than one slaves can use the bus simultaneously corrupting bus signals. In this case, the slave devices may not function well or crash. This type of hardware failures would be extremely hard to test and reproduce.

3.2 Replay testing process

As described earlier, the proposed testing approach using RT-Replayer works in three steps; (1) running an initial test to obtain an event history with RT-Replayer enabled in record mode; (2) create a number of variants of event history by mutating the event history and/or adding more event records into the event history, and (3) executing the variants of event history with RT-Replayer enabled in replay mode. In this subsection, we describe each step in detail.

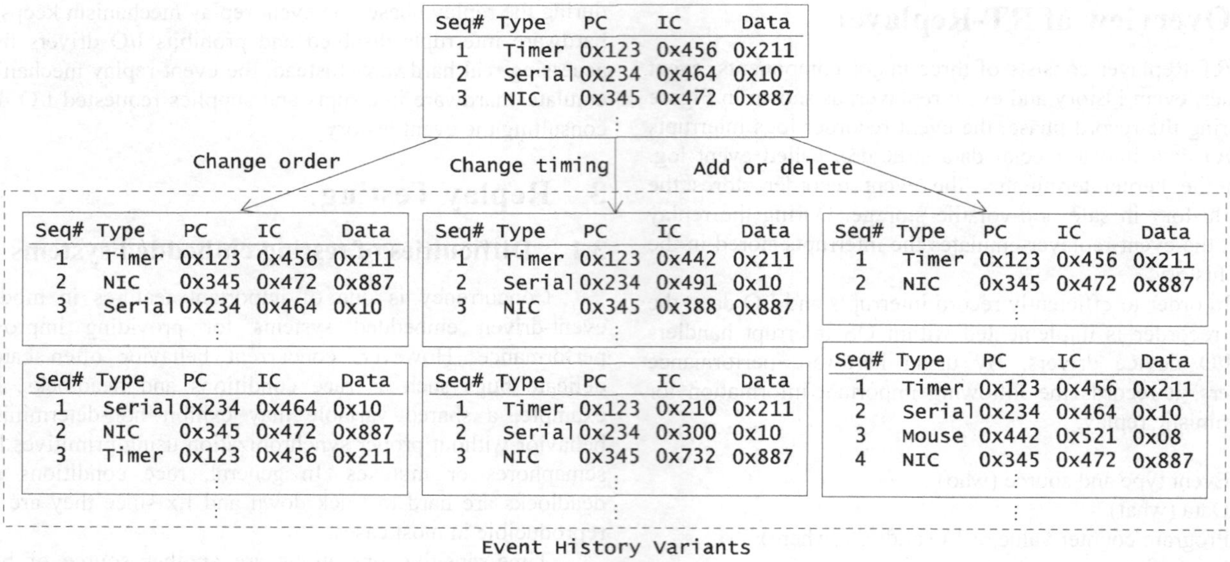

Figure 2. Creation of event history variants

3.2.1 Initial test case generation with RT-Replayer

We run an initial test using a sequence of "essential" events with RT-Replayer enabled in record mode. It is important to choose likely events that can exhibit certain bugs satisfying our testing criteria. For example, if we want to find time sensitive bugs for some I/O devices, we need to choose appropriate I/O events from those I/O devices and run a test generating and interleaving the I/O events. During the test execution, the I/O events are recoreded in the event history of RT-Replayer. RT-Replayer logs in the event history information needed for deterministic replay. Specifically, each event record in the event history contains the type and source of event, the program counter value where the event occurred, the instruction count when it occurred, and the data content that accompanied the event.

3.2.2 Creation of event history variants

Once we obtained an initial event history, we then create event history variants. We can create event history variants in three ways. First, we can modify some fields of event records. For example, we can modify intruction count values of event records so that events are generated at different time points during replay. Second, we can modify the order of events. Third, we can add or delete some events. Figure 2 shows an example of creating event history variants.

Note that we must use a valid event record when adding new one into the original event history. Every field of an event record must be consistent and follow the specification of the source I/O device. For example, when we create a new event record for an interrupt from NIC, we must use a legal network packet data that satisfies the network protocol format. For some I/O devices, this may not be easy since we should understand complex device specifications or I/O protocol specifications. In such cases, we may run record-mode tests multiple times so that we can obtain a valid event record for each type of I/O event.

Deleting some events from the event history also needs a special care. Some events can be correlated and must occur in a specific order. For example, DMA can use multiple interrupts for a single I/O data operation to send acknowledgement of DMA request and to notify the completion of DMA operation. In this case, we cannot remove any of the correlated events. Fortunately, many I/O events are one-shot events. Timer interrupts are one of them, thus allowing us to easily remove them.

3.2.3 Execution of event history variants

We execute the event history variants with RT-Replayer enabled in replay mode. Since RT-Replay is able to emulate events with all I/O interrupt disabled, we do not need any arrangement of external entities like users and other systems since RT-Replayer emulates all I/O events. Therefore, the use of RT-Replayer can be used as an efficient vehicle for automated test case execution. At the moment of this writing, we have not implemented a complete testing framework. By simply using RT-Replayer, we are just able to run each event history variant separately in a semi-automatic manner.

4 Conclusion

We proposed a testing method based on record-replay technology for event-driven embedded system. We believe that our method has two important advantages. It allows us to easily and efficiently generate a lot of effective test cases that can exhibit subtle bugs like races. It also provides an efficient means for automated test case execution since we do not need any arrangement of external entities like users and other systems.

5 Acknowledgement

This work was supported partly by Seoul Creative Human Development Program (HM120006), partly by the IT R&D Program of MKE/KEIT [10035708, "The Development of CPS (Cyber-Physical Systems) Core Technologies for High Confidential Autonomic Control Software"], partly by Mid-career Researcher Program through NRF (National Research Foundation) grant funded by the MEST (Ministry of Education, Science and Technology) (NRF-2011-0015997), and partly by Business for Cooperative R&D between Industry, Academy, and Research Institute funded Korea Small and Medium Business Administration in 2013 (Grants No. 00045488).

6 References

[1] Dennis Geels , Gautam Altekar , Scott Shenker , Ion Stoica "Replay debugging for distributed applications"; Proceedings of the annual conference on USENIX '06 Annual Technical Conference, p.27-27, May 30-June 03, 2006.

[2] T. J. LeBlanc, J. M. Mellor-Crummey. "Debugging parallel programs with instant replay"; IEEE Transactions on Computers, v.36 n.4, p.471-482, Apr 1987.

[3] Satish Narayanasamy, Gilles Pokam, Brad Calder. "BugNet: Continuously Recording Program Execution for Deterministic Replay Debugging"; Proceedings of the 32nd Annual International Symposium on Computer Architecture, p.284-295, Jun 2005.

[4] E. N. (Mootaz) Elnozahy , Lorenzo Alvisi , Yi-Min Wang , David B. Johnson "A survey of rollback-recovery protocols in message-passing systems"; ACM Computing Surveys (CSUR), v.34 n.3, p.375-408, Sep 2002.

[5] Daniel J. Sorin, Milo M. K. Martin, Mark D. Hill, David A. Wood. "SafetyNet: improving the availability of shared memory multiprocessors with global checkpoint/recovery"; Proceedings of the 29th annual international symposium on Computer architecture, p.123, May 2002

[6] George W. Dunlap, Samuel T. King, Sukru Cinar, Murtaza A. Basrai, Peter M. Chen. "ReVirt: enabling intrusion analysis through virtual-machine logging and replay"; ACM SIGOPS Operating Systems Review, v.36 n.SI, winter 2002.

[7] Jim Chow, Tal Garfinkel, Peter M. Chen. "Decoupling dynamic program analysis from execution in virtual environments"; USENIX 2008 Annual Technical Conference on Annual Technical Conference, p.1-14, Jun 2008.

[8] J.C. Maeng, J.-I. Kwon, M.-K. Sin, M.Ryu. "Rt-replayer: a record-replay architecture for embedded real-time software debugging"; SAC '09: Proceedings of the 2009 ACM Symposium on Applied Computing, p. 1670–1675, 2009.

[9] Jonathan Corbet, Alessandro Rubini, Greg Kroah-Hartman. "Linux Device Drives 3rd Edition"; O'REILLY media, 2005.

Normal Bisimulation for Higher Order π-Calculus with Passivation Revisited

Zining Cao[1,2]
[1]Department of Computer Science and Technology
Nanjing University of Aeronautics & Astronautics
Nanjing 210016, China
[2]State Key Laboratory for Civil Aircraft Flight Simulation
Shanghai Aircraft Design and Research Institute
Shanghai 201210, China
Email: caozn@nuaa.edu.cn

Abstract—*In this paper, we present late context bisimulation and normal bisimulation for higher order π-calculus with passivation and prove the coincidence between normal bisimulation, late context bisimulation, early context bisimulation and contextual barbed bisimulation for higher order π-calculus with passivation. Furthermore, we give a variant of normal bisimulation, called limited normal bisimulation, and prove the equivalence between limited normal bisimulation and other bisimulations. At last, we extend the definitions and propositions for weak bisimulations of HOπP to the case of strong bisimulations.*

Keywords: Process Calculus; Higher Order π-Calculus with Passivation; Bisimulation.

1. Introduction

Higher order π-calculus was proposed and studied intensively in Sangiorgi's dissertation [13]. It is an extension of the π-calculus [11] to allow communication of processes rather than names alone. In [13], some interesting bisimulations for higher order π-calculus were presented, such as barbed equivalence, context bisimulation and normal bisimulation. Barbed equivalence can be regarded as a uniform definition of bisimulation for a variety of concurrency calculi. Context bisimulation is a very intuitive definition of bisimulation for higher order π-calculus, but it is heavy to handle, due to the appearance of universal quantifications in its definition. In the definition of normal bisimulation, all universal quantifications disappeared, therefore normal bisimulation is a very economic characterisation of bisimulation for higher order π-calculus.

The definitions of context bisimulation and barbed equivalence involve quantification over contexts. So they are often awkward to work with directly. It is therefore important to look for more tractable characterisations of the bisimulations. In [13], [14], the equivalence between weak normal bisimulation, weak context bisimulation and weak barbed equivalence was proved for early and late semantics respectively.

In [8], higher order π-calculus was extended to a calculus with passivation (HOπP) and normal bisimulation for HOπP was studied. In [8], it was showed that a large class of test processes, i.e., abstraction-free process (which is a process built with the regular HOπP syntax but without message input $a(X).P$), cannot be used to derive a normal bisimilarity in HOπP. But it was showed that a form of normal bisimilarity can be defined for HOπP without restriction.

The main aim of this paper is to present a normal bisimulation for HOπP and give a proof for the equivalence between normal bisimulation and early context bisimulation for HOπP. To achieve this aim, we firstly introduce a late context bisimulation, then we study the relation between normal bisimulation, late context bisimulation and early context bisimulation for HOπP. As a corollary of this proposition, we get the equivalence between normal bisimulation and early context bisimulation for HOπP. Moreover, we present a variant of normal bisimulation, named limited normal bisimulation, and prove the equivalence between limited normal bisimulation and other bisimulations. Finally, we extend the definitions and propositions for weak bisimulations of HOπP to the case of strong bisimulations.

This paper is organized as follows: Section 2 gives a brief review of syntax and operational semantics of HOπP. Section 3 recalls the definitions of contextual barbed bisimulation and early context bisimulation. Then we present a late context bisimulation and a normal bisimulation for HOπP. In Section 4, the equivalence between contextual barbed bisimulation and early context bisimulation was given. Then we give a proof for the equivalence between normal bisimulation, late context bisimulation, early context bisimulation and contextual barbed bisimulation for HOπP. In Section 5, we give the definition of limited normal bisimulation, and prove the equivalence between limited normal bisimulation and other bisimulations. In Section 6, we give the definitions and propositions for strong bisimulations. The paper is concluded in Section 7.

2. Syntax and Labelled Transition System of Higher Order π-Calculus with Passivation

In this section we briefly recall the syntax and labelled transition system of the higher order π-calculus with passivation [8].

We assume a set N of names, ranged over by $a, b, c, ...$ and a set Var of process variables, ranged over by $X, Y, Z, U, ...$ We use $E, F, P, Q, ...$ to stand for processes. Pr denotes the set of all processes.

We first give the grammar for the higher order π-calculus processes as follows:

$P ::= 0 \mid U \mid \pi.P \mid P_1|P_2 \mid (\nu a)P \mid !P \mid a[P]$

π is called a prefix and can have one of the following forms:

$\pi ::= \tau \mid a(U) \mid \overline{a}\langle P\rangle$, where τ is a tau prefix; l is a first order input prefix; $\overline{l}$ is a first order output prefix; $a(U)$ is a higher order input prefix and $\overline{a}\langle P\rangle$ is a higher order output prefix.

In each process of the form $(\nu a)P$ the occurrence of a is bound within P. An occurrence of a in a process is said to be free iff it does not lie within the scope of a bound occurrence of a. The set of names occurring free in P is denoted $fn(P)$. An occurrence of a name in a process is said to be bound if it is not free, we write the set of bound names as $bn(P)$. $n(P)$ denotes the set of names of P, i.e., $n(P) = fn(P) \cup bn(P)$.

The set of all closed processes, i.e., the processes which have no free variable, is denoted as Pr^c.

The structural congruence relation is the smallest congruence generated by the following laws:

$P|0 \equiv P$, $P_1|P_2 \equiv P_2|P_1$, $P_1|(P_2|P_3) \equiv (P_1|P_2)|P_3$, $(\nu a)0 \equiv 0$, $(\nu a)(\nu b)P \equiv (\nu b)(\nu a)P$, $P|(\nu a)Q \equiv (\nu a)(P|Q)$ if $a \notin fn(P)$

A context is a term with a hole $\{\}$ in it:

$C\{\} ::= \{\} \mid \pi.C \mid C|P \mid P|C \mid (\nu a)C \mid !C \mid a[C]$

The operational semantics of higher order processes is given in Table 1. We have omitted the symmetric of the parallelism and communication rules.

Table 1: Labelled transition system of higher order π-calculus with passivation

$$ALP: \frac{P \xrightarrow{\alpha} P'}{Q \xrightarrow{\alpha} Q'} P \equiv Q, P' \equiv Q' \qquad TAU: \tau.P \xrightarrow{\tau} P$$

$$OUT: \overline{a}\langle E\rangle.P \xrightarrow{\overline{a}\langle E\rangle} P \qquad IN: a(U).P \xrightarrow{a\langle E\rangle} P\{E/U\}$$

$$SUM: \frac{P \xrightarrow{\alpha} P'}{P+Q \xrightarrow{\alpha} P'}$$

$$PAR: \frac{P \xrightarrow{\alpha} P'}{P|Q \xrightarrow{\alpha} P'|Q} bn(\alpha) \cap fn(Q) = \emptyset$$

$$COM: \frac{P \xrightarrow{(\nu\widetilde{b})\overline{a}\langle E\rangle} P' \quad Q \xrightarrow{a\langle E\rangle} Q'}{P|Q \xrightarrow{\tau} (\nu\widetilde{b})(P'|Q')} \widetilde{b} \cap fn(Q) = \emptyset$$

$$RES: \frac{P \xrightarrow{\alpha} P'}{(\nu a)P \xrightarrow{\alpha} (\nu a)P'} a \notin n(\alpha)$$

$$REP: \frac{P|!P \xrightarrow{\alpha} P'}{!P \xrightarrow{\alpha} P'}$$

$$OPEN: \frac{P \xrightarrow{(\nu\widetilde{c})\overline{a}\langle E\rangle} P'}{(\nu b)P \xrightarrow{(\nu b,\widetilde{c})\overline{a}\langle E\rangle} P'} a \neq b,\ b \in fn(E) - \widetilde{c}$$

$$LOC: \frac{P \xrightarrow{\alpha} P'}{a[P] \xrightarrow{\alpha} a[P']}$$

$$PASSIV: a[P] \xrightarrow{\overline{a}\langle P\rangle} 0$$

3. Bisimulations of Higher Order π-Calculus with Passivation

In [13], barbed equivalence was presented as a uniform definition of bisimulation for first order π-calculus and higher order π-calculus. In [6], a variant of barbed equivalence, called contextual barbed bisimulation, was presented.

Definition 1. For each name or co-name μ, the observability predicate $\downarrow_\mu$ is defined by

(1) $P \downarrow_a$ if there exist E, P' such that $P \xrightarrow{a\langle E\rangle} P'$;

(2) $P \downarrow_{\overline{a}}$ if there exist $\widetilde{b}, E, P'$ such that $P \xrightarrow{(\nu\widetilde{b})\overline{a}\langle E\rangle} P'$

Definition 2. A symmetric relation $R \subseteq Pr^c \times Pr^c$ is a weak contextual barbed bisimulation if $P\ R\ Q$ implies:

(1) $C\{P\}\ R\ C\{Q\}$ for any context C;

(2) whenever $P \stackrel{\varepsilon}{\Longrightarrow} P'$ there exists Q' such that $Q \stackrel{\varepsilon}{\Longrightarrow} Q'$ and $P'\ R\ Q'$;

(3) $P \Downarrow_\mu$ implies $Q \Downarrow_\mu$, where $P \Downarrow_\mu$ means $\exists P', P \stackrel{\varepsilon}{\Longrightarrow} P' \downarrow_\mu$.

We write $P \approx_{Ba} Q$ if P and Q are weakly contextual barbed bisimilar.

Context and normal bisimulations were presented in [13], [14] to describe the behavioral equivalences for higher order π-calculus. In [8], Context and normal bisimulations for HOπP were studied. In the following, we abbreviate $P\{E/U\}$ as $P\langle E\rangle$.

The grammar of HOπP evaluation contexts, which was introduced in [8], is:

$\mathbf{S} ::= \{\} \mid (\nu a)\mathbf{S} \mid \mathbf{S}|P \mid P|\mathbf{S} \mid a[\mathbf{S}]$

For HOπP evaluation contexts, the notations of free name and bound name are similar to the case of HOπP processes.

In the following, we use $\stackrel{\varepsilon}{\Longrightarrow}$ to abbreviate the reflexive and transitive closure of $\xrightarrow{\tau}$, and use $\stackrel{\alpha}{\Longrightarrow}$ to abbreviate $\stackrel{\varepsilon}{\Longrightarrow}\xrightarrow{\alpha}\stackrel{\varepsilon}{\Longrightarrow}$. By neglecting the tau action, we can get the following formal definitions of weak bisimulations:

Definition 3. ([8])Weak early context bisimilarity $\approx^E_{Ct}$ is the largest symmetric relation on closed processes R such that $P\ R\ Q$ implies:

(1) whenever $P \stackrel{\varepsilon}{\Longrightarrow} P'$, there exists Q' such that $Q \stackrel{\varepsilon}{\Longrightarrow} Q'$ and $P'\ R\ Q'$;

(2) whenever $P \overset{a\langle E\rangle}{\Longrightarrow} P'$, there exists Q' such that $Q \overset{a\langle E\rangle}{\Longrightarrow} Q'$ and $P' \; R \; Q'$;

(3) whenever $P \overset{(\nu\widetilde{b})\overline{a}\langle E\rangle}{\Longrightarrow} P'$, for all $C(U)$ with $fn(C(U)) \cap bn(P,Q) = \emptyset$, for all $\mathbf{S}\{\}$, there exist Q', F, $\widetilde{c}$ such that $Q \overset{(\nu\widetilde{c})\overline{a}\langle F\rangle}{\Longrightarrow} Q'$ and $(\nu\widetilde{b})(\mathbf{S}\{P'\}|C\langle E\rangle) \; R \; (\nu\widetilde{c})(\mathbf{S}\{Q'\}|C\langle F\rangle)$.

We write $P \approx^E_{Ct} Q$ if P and Q are weakly early context bisimilar.

In the following, we give the "late" variant of $\approx^E_{Ct}$, where the universal quantification is after the existential one.

Definition 4. Weak late context bisimilarity $\approx^L_{Ct}$ is the largest symmetric relation on closed processes R such that $P \; R \; Q$ implies:

(1) whenever $P \overset{\varepsilon}{\Longrightarrow} P'$, there exists Q' such that $Q \overset{\varepsilon}{\Longrightarrow} Q'$ and $P' \; R \; Q'$;

(2) whenever $P \overset{a(U)}{\Longrightarrow} P'$, there exists Q' such that $Q \overset{a(U)}{\Longrightarrow} Q'$ and for all E, $P'\{E/U\} \; R \; Q'\{E/U\}$;

(3) whenever $P \overset{(\nu\widetilde{b})\overline{a}\langle E\rangle}{\Longrightarrow} P'$,there exist Q', F, $\widetilde{c}$ such that $Q \overset{(\nu\widetilde{c})\overline{a}\langle F\rangle}{\Longrightarrow} Q'$ and for all $C(U)$ with $fn(C(U)) \cap \{\widetilde{b}, \widetilde{c}\} = \emptyset$, for all $\mathbf{S}\{\}$, $(\nu\widetilde{b})(\mathbf{S}\{P'\}|C\langle E\rangle) \; R \; (\nu\widetilde{c})(\mathbf{S}\{Q'\}|C\langle F\rangle)$.

We write $P \approx^L_{Ct} Q$ if P and Q are weakly late context bisimilar.

For some process calculi, late bisimulation was proved to be equivalent to early bisimulation [14]. The similar proposition also holds for HOπP. In the following, we will prove that $\approx^L_{Ct}$ is equivalent to $\approx^E_{Ct}$.

Distinguished from context bisimulation, normal bisimulation does not have universal quantifications in the clauses of its definition. In the following, a name is called fresh in a statement if it is different from any other name occurring in the processes of the statement. In [8], it was showed that a large class of test processes, i.e., abstraction-free process (which is a process built with the regular HOπP syntax but without message input $a(X).P$), cannot be used to derive a normal bisimilarity in HOπP.

In the following we give a normal bisimulation for HOπP.

Definition 5. Weak normal bisimilarity $\approx_{Nr}$ is the largest symmetric relation on closed processes R such that $P \; R \; Q$ implies:

(1) whenever $P \overset{\varepsilon}{\Longrightarrow} P'$, there exists Q' such that $Q \overset{\varepsilon}{\Longrightarrow} Q'$ and $P' \; R \; Q'$;

(2) whenever $P \overset{a\langle n(U).U\rangle}{\Longrightarrow} P'$, there exists Q' such that $Q \overset{a\langle n(U).U\rangle}{\Longrightarrow} Q'$ and $P' \; R \; Q'$, where n is a fresh name;

(3) whenever $P \overset{(\nu\widetilde{b})\overline{a}\langle E\rangle}{\Longrightarrow} P'$, there exist Q', F, $\widetilde{c}$ such that $Q \overset{(\nu\widetilde{c})\overline{a}\langle F\rangle}{\Longrightarrow} Q'$ and $(\nu\widetilde{b})(\overline{m}\langle P'\rangle.0|!\overline{n}\langle E\rangle.0) \; R \; (\nu\widetilde{c})(\overline{m}\langle Q'\rangle.0|!\overline{n}\langle F\rangle.0)$, where m, n are fresh names.

We write $P \approx_{Nr} Q$ if P and Q are weakly normal bisimilar.

In the above definition of normal bisimulation, we use the process in the form of $n(U).U$, which is not abstraction-free process mentioned in [8]. Therefore the equivalence between $\approx^E_{Ct}$ and $\approx_{Nr}$ does not conflict with the result in [8].

4. The Equivalence between Bisimulations

In [13], [14], the equivalence between weak context bisimulation and weak normal bisimulation was proved. In the proof, the factorisation theorem was firstly given. It allows us to factorise out certain subprocesses of a given process. Thus, a complex process can be decomposed into the parallel composition of simpler processes. Then the concept of triggered processes was introduced, which is the key step in the proof. Triggered processes represent a sort of normal form for the processes of the calculus. Most importantly, there is a very simple characterisation of context bisimulation on triggered processes, called triggered bisimulation. By the factorisation theorem, a process can be transformed to a triggered process. The transform allows us to use the simpler theory of triggered processes to reason about the set of all processes. In [13], [14], weak context bisimulation was firstly proved to be equivalent to weak triggered bisimulation on triggered processes, then by the transformation from processes to triggered processes, the equivalence between weak context bisimulation and weak normal bisimulation was proved.

To study the relation between bisimulations in the case of calculus with with passivation, we firstly give factorisation theorems for HOπP, furthermore we show that $\approx^L_{Ct} \subseteq \approx^E_{Ct}$, $\approx_{Nr} \subseteq \approx^L_{Ct}$ and $\approx^E_{Ct} \subseteq \approx_{Nr}$. At last we get the proposition: $P \approx^E_{Ct} Q \Leftrightarrow P \approx^L_{Ct} Q \Leftrightarrow P \approx_{Nr} Q$.

At first, we give the congruence of weak early context bisimulation.

Proposition 1. (Congruence of $\approx^E_{Ct}$) For all P, Q, $S \in Pr^c$, $P \approx^E_{Ct} Q$ implies:

1. $\pi.P \approx^E_{Ct} \pi.Q$;
2. $P|S \approx^E_{Ct} Q|S$;
3. $(\nu a)P \approx^E_{Ct} (\nu a)Q$;
4. $!P \approx^E_{Ct} !Q$;
5. $\overline{a}\langle P\rangle.S \approx^E_{Ct} \overline{a}\langle Q\rangle.S$;
6. $a[P] \approx^E_{Ct} a[Q]$.

Proof : Let $R = \{(C\{P\}, C\{Q\}) \mid P \approx^E_{Ct} Q\}$. It is enough to prove that $R \subseteq \approx^E_{Ct}$. Similar to the argument of the analogous result for context bisimulation in [13, Theorem 4.2.7]. ■

Now we give the equivalence of $\approx_{Ba}$ and $\approx^E_{Ct}$.

Proposition 2. For any $P, Q \in Pr^c$, $P \approx_{Ba} Q \Leftrightarrow P \approx^E_{Ct} Q$.

Proof : ($\Leftarrow$) Let $R = \{(P, Q) \mid P \approx^E_{Ct} Q\}$. It is enough to prove that $R \subseteq \approx_{Ba}$. It is trivial by the congruence of $\approx^E_{Ct}$.

($\Rightarrow$) Let $R = \{(P, Q) \mid P \approx_{Ba} Q\}$. It is enough to prove that $R \subseteq \approx^E_{Ct}$.

We discuss the following cases.

(1) Suppose $P \overset{\varepsilon}{\Longrightarrow} P'$. Since $P \approx_{Ba} Q$, we have $Q \overset{\varepsilon}{\Longrightarrow} Q'$ and $P' \approx_{Ba} Q'$. Therefore $Q \overset{\varepsilon}{\Longrightarrow} Q'$ and $(P', Q') \in R$.

(2) Suppose $P \stackrel{a\langle E\rangle}{\Longrightarrow} P'$. Since $P \approx_{Ba} Q$, we have $P|m(X).\overline{a}\langle E\rangle.n(Y).0|\overline{m}\langle 0\rangle.\overline{n}\langle 0\rangle.0 \approx_{Ba} Q|m(X).\overline{a}\langle E\rangle. n(Y).0|\overline{m}\langle 0\rangle.\overline{n}\langle 0\rangle.0$, where m, n, X, Y are fresh names and variables. Furthermore, we have $P|m(X).\overline{a}\langle E\rangle.n(Y) .0|\overline{m}\langle 0\rangle.\overline{n}\langle 0\rangle.0 \downarrow_m \not\downarrow_n \stackrel{\tau}{\longrightarrow} P|\overline{a}\langle E\rangle.n(Y).0|\overline{n}\langle 0\rangle.0 \not\downarrow_m \downarrow_n \stackrel{\tau}{\longrightarrow} P'|n(Y).0|\overline{n}\langle 0\rangle.0 \downarrow_n \stackrel{\tau}{\longrightarrow} P' \not\downarrow_n$, and $Q|m(X).\overline{a}\langle E\rangle. n(Y).0|\overline{m}\langle 0\rangle.\overline{n}\langle 0\rangle.0 \downarrow_m \not\downarrow_n \stackrel{\varepsilon}{\Longrightarrow} Q''|\overline{a}\langle E\rangle.n(Y).0|\overline{n}\langle 0\rangle.0 \not\downarrow_m \downarrow_n \stackrel{\varepsilon}{\Longrightarrow} Q'''|n(Y).0|\overline{n}\langle 0\rangle.0 \downarrow_n \stackrel{\varepsilon}{\Longrightarrow} Q' \not\downarrow_n$ and $P' \approx_{Ba} Q'$. Therefore $Q \stackrel{a\langle E\rangle}{\Longrightarrow} Q'$ and $(P', Q') \in R$.

(3) Suppose $P \stackrel{(\nu\widetilde{b})\overline{a}\langle E\rangle}{\Longrightarrow} P'$. Since $P \approx_{Ba} Q$, for any $C(U)$ with $fn(C(U)) \cap bn(P, Q) = \emptyset$, for any $\mathbf{S}\{\}$, we have $\mathbf{S}\{P\}|m(X).a(U).n(Y).C(U)|\overline{m}\langle 0\rangle.\overline{n}\langle 0\rangle.0 \approx_{Ba} \mathbf{S}\{Q\} |m(X).a(U).n(Y).C(U)|\overline{m}\langle 0\rangle.\overline{n}\langle 0\rangle.0$, where m, n, X, Y are fresh names and variables. Furthermore, we have $\mathbf{S}\{P\}|m(X).a(U).n(Y).C(U)|\overline{m}\langle 0\rangle.\overline{n}\langle 0\rangle.0 \downarrow_m \not\downarrow_n \stackrel{\tau}{\longrightarrow} \mathbf{S}\{ P\}|a(U).n(Y).C(U)|\overline{n}\langle 0\rangle.0 \not\downarrow_m \downarrow_n \stackrel{\tau}{\longrightarrow} (\nu\widetilde{b})(\mathbf{S}\{P'\}|n(Y) .C\langle E\rangle|\overline{n}\langle 0\rangle.0) \downarrow_n \stackrel{\tau}{\longrightarrow} (\nu\widetilde{b})(\mathbf{S}\{P'\}|C\langle E\rangle) \not\downarrow_n$, and $\mathbf{S}\{Q\}| m(X).a(U).n(Y).C(U)|\overline{m}\langle 0\rangle.\overline{n}\langle 0\rangle.0 \downarrow_m \not\downarrow_n \stackrel{\varepsilon}{\Longrightarrow} \mathbf{S}\{Q''\}| a(U).n(Y).C(U)|\overline{n}\langle 0\rangle.0 \not\downarrow_m \downarrow_n \stackrel{\varepsilon}{\Longrightarrow} (\nu\widetilde{c})(\mathbf{S}\{Q'''\}|n(Y). C\langle F\rangle|\overline{n}\langle 0\rangle.0) \downarrow_n \stackrel{\varepsilon}{\Longrightarrow} (\nu\widetilde{c})(\mathbf{S}\{Q'\}|C\langle F\rangle) \not\downarrow_n$ and $(\nu\widetilde{b}) (\mathbf{S}\{P'\}|C\langle E\rangle) \approx_{Ba} (\nu\widetilde{c})(\mathbf{S}\{Q'\}|C\langle F\rangle)$. Therefore $Q \stackrel{(\nu\widetilde{c})\overline{a}\langle F\rangle}{\Longrightarrow} Q'$ and $((\nu\widetilde{b})(\mathbf{S}\{P'\}|C\langle E\rangle), (\nu\widetilde{c})(\mathbf{S}\{Q'\}|C\langle F\rangle)) \in R$. ■

Proposition 3 states the easy part of the relation between $\approx^L_{Ct}$ and $\approx^E_{Ct}$.

Proposition 3. For any $P, Q \in Pr^c$, $P \approx^L_{Ct} Q \Rightarrow P \approx^E_{Ct} Q$.

Proof : It is trivial by the definition. ■

Now we give the factorisation theorem for process substitution, which states that, by means of triggers, a subprocess of a given process can be factorised out.

Proposition 4. For any processes P and E with $m \notin fn(P) \cup fn(E)$, it holds that $P\{\tau.E/X\} \sim^L_{Ct} (\nu m)(P\{m(U).U/X\}|!\overline{m}\langle E\rangle.0)$.

Proof : Similar to the proof of $P\{\tau.R/U\} \sim_{Ct} (\nu m)(P\{\overline{m}.0/U\}|!m.R)$ in [13], by induction on the structure of P. ■

Proposition 5. (Factorisation theorem) For any processes P and E with $m \notin fn(P) \cup fn(E)$, it holds that $P\{E/X\} \approx^L_{Ct} (\nu m)(P\{m(U).U/X\}|!\overline{m}\langle E\rangle.0)$.

Proof : By Proposition 4. ■

Now we give the factorisation theorem for evaluation contexts.

Proposition 6. For any evaluation context $\mathbf{S}\{\}$ and process E with $m \notin fn(\mathbf{S}) \cup fn(E)$, it holds that $\mathbf{S}\{\tau.E\} \sim^L_{Ct} (\nu m)(\mathbf{S}\{m(U).U\}|\overline{m}\langle E\rangle.0)$.

Proof : Similar to the proof of $P\{\tau.R/U\} \sim_{Ct} (\nu m) (P\{\overline{m}.0/U\}|!m.R)$ in [13], by induction on the structure of $\mathbf{S}\{\}$. ■

Proposition 7. (Factorisation theorem) For any evaluation context $\mathbf{S}\{\}$ and process E with $m \notin fn(\mathbf{S}) \cup fn(E)$, it holds that $\mathbf{S}\{E\} \approx^L_{Ct} (\nu m)(\mathbf{S}\{m(U).U\}|\overline{m}\langle E\rangle. 0)$.

Proof : By Proposition 6. ■

The following proposition states that $\approx_{Nr}$ is preserved by parallel composition and restriction.

Proposition 8. (Congruence of $\approx_{Nr}$) For all P, Q, $S \in Pr^c$, $P \approx_{Nr} Q$ implies:

1. $P|S \approx_{Nr} Q|S$;
2. $(\nu a)P \approx_{Nr} (\nu a)Q$.

Proof : Let $R = \{(C\{P\}, C\{Q\}) \mid P \approx_{Nr} Q\}$. It is enough to prove that $R \subseteq \approx_{Nr}$. Similar to the argument of the analogous result for triggered bisimulation in [13, Lemma 4.6.3]. ■

To prove Proposition 9, we need the following Definition 6 and Lemma 1.

Definition 6. A relation $R \subseteq Pr^c \times Pr^c$ is a weak late context bisimulation up to $\approx^L_{Ct}$, if there is a symmetric relation R:

(1) whenever $P \stackrel{\varepsilon}{\Longrightarrow} P'$, there exists Q' such that $Q \stackrel{\varepsilon}{\Longrightarrow} Q'$ and $P' \approx^L_{Ct} R \approx^L_{Ct} Q'$;

(2) whenever $P \stackrel{a\langle E\rangle}{\Longrightarrow} P'$, there exists Q' such that $Q \stackrel{a\langle E\rangle}{\Longrightarrow} Q'$ and $P' \approx^L_{Ct} R \approx^L_{Ct} Q'$;

(3) whenever $P \stackrel{(\nu\widetilde{b})\overline{a}\langle E\rangle}{\Longrightarrow} P'$,there exist Q', F, $\widetilde{c}$ such that $Q \stackrel{(\nu\widetilde{c})\overline{a}\langle F\rangle}{\Longrightarrow} Q'$ and for all $C(U)$ with $fn(C(U)) \cap \{\widetilde{b}, \widetilde{c}\} = \emptyset$, for all $\mathbf{S}\{\}$, $(\nu\widetilde{b})(\mathbf{S}\{P'\}|C\langle E\rangle) \approx^L_{Ct} R \approx^L_{Ct} (\nu\widetilde{c})(\mathbf{S}\{Q'\}|C\langle F\rangle)$.

Lemma 1. If R is a weak late context bisimulation up to $\approx^L_{Ct}$, then $R \subseteq \approx^L_{Ct}$.

Proof : The same argument of the analogous result for CCS bisimilarity in [10]: Use a diagram-chasing argument to show that $\approx^L_{Ct} R \approx^L_{Ct}$is a weak late context bisimulation. ■

The following proposition states that $\approx_{Nr}$ is included in $\approx^L_{Ct}$.

Proposition 9. For any $P, Q \in Pr^c$, $P \approx_{Nr} Q \Rightarrow P \approx^L_{Ct} Q$.

Proof : Let $R = \{(P, Q) \mid P \approx_{Nr} Q\}$. It is enough to prove that $R \subseteq \approx^L_{Ct}$.

We discuss the case of higher order input and output, other cases are trivial.

(1) Suppose $P \approx_{Nr} Q$ and $P \stackrel{a\langle E\rangle}{\Longrightarrow} P' \equiv P''\{E/X\}$. We have $P \stackrel{a\langle n(U).U\rangle}{\Longrightarrow} P''\{n(U).U/X\}$, then there exists Q'' such that $Q \stackrel{a\langle n(U).U\rangle}{\Longrightarrow} Q''\{n(U).U/X\}$ and $P''\{n(U).U/X\}\ R\ Q''\{n(U).U/X\}$. By the congurence of $\approx_{Nr}$, we have $(\nu n)(P''\{n(U).U/X\}|!\overline{n}\langle E\rangle.0) \approx_{Nr} (\nu n) (Q''\{n(U).U/X\}|!\overline{n}\langle E\rangle.0)$. By factorisation theorem, $P''\{E/X\} \approx^L_{Ct} (\nu n)(P''\{n(U).U/X\}|!\overline{n}\langle E\rangle.0)\ R\ (\nu n) (Q''\{n(U).U/X\}|!\overline{n}\langle E\rangle.0) \approx^L_{Ct} Q''\{E/X\}$. Therefore, we have $Q \stackrel{a\langle E\rangle}{\Longrightarrow} Q''\{E/X\}$ and $P''\{E/X\} \approx^L_{Ct} R \approx^L_{Ct} Q''\{E/X\}$. By Lemma 1, R is a weak late context bisimulation up to $\approx^L_{Ct}$, So we have $R \subseteq \approx^L_{Ct}$.

(2) Suppose $P \approx_{Nr} Q$ and $P \stackrel{(\nu\widetilde{b})\overline{a}\langle E\rangle}{\Longrightarrow} P'$, then there exist Q', F, $\widetilde{c}$ such that $Q \stackrel{(\nu\widetilde{c})\overline{a}\langle F\rangle}{\Longrightarrow} Q'$ and $(\nu\widetilde{b})(\overline{m}\langle P'\rangle.0|!\overline{n}\langle E\rangle.0)$

R $(\nu\widetilde{c})(\overline{m}\langle Q'\rangle.0|!\overline{n}\langle F\rangle.0)$, where m, n are fresh names. By the congruence of $\approx_{Nr}$, we have $(\nu m, n)((\nu\widetilde{b})(\mathbf{S}\{m(U).U\}|C\langle n(U).U\rangle)|\overline{m}\langle P'\rangle.0|!\overline{n}\langle E\rangle.0) \approx_{Nr} (\nu m, n)((\nu\widetilde{c})(\mathbf{S}\{m(U).U\}|C\langle n(U).U\rangle)|\overline{m}\langle Q'\rangle.0|!\overline{n}\langle F\rangle.0)$.

Furthermore, by Propositions 5 and 7, $(\nu\widetilde{b})(\mathbf{S}\{P'\}|C\langle E\rangle) \approx^L_{Ct} (\nu m, n)((\nu\widetilde{b})(\mathbf{S}\{m(U).U\}|C\langle n(U).U\rangle)|\overline{m}\langle P'\rangle.0|!\overline{n}\langle E\rangle.0)$ R $(\nu m, n)((\nu\widetilde{c})(\mathbf{S}\{m(U).U\}|C\langle n(U).U\rangle)|\overline{m}\langle Q'\rangle.0|!\overline{n}\langle F\rangle.0) \approx^L_{Ct} (\nu\widetilde{c})(\mathbf{S}\{Q'\}|C\langle F\rangle)$. By Lemma 1, R is a weak late context bisimulation up to $\approx^L_{Ct}$. So we have $R \subseteq \approx^L_{Ct}$. ■

The following lemma is used in the proof of Proposition 10.

Lemma 2. For any $P, Q, E, F \in Pr^c$, $(\nu\widetilde{b})(m[P]|E) \approx^E_{Ct} (\nu\widetilde{c})(m[Q]|F) \Rightarrow (\nu\widetilde{b})(\overline{n}\langle P\rangle.0|E) \approx^E_{Ct} (\nu\widetilde{c})(\overline{n}\langle Q\rangle.0|F)$, where m, n are fresh names.

Proof : Since $(\nu\widetilde{b})(m[P]|E) \approx^E_{Ct} (\nu\widetilde{c})(m[Q]|F)$, by the congruence of $\approx^E_{Ct}$, $(\nu\widetilde{b})(m[P]|E)|m(U).\overline{k}\langle U\rangle.0 \approx^E_{Ct} (\nu\widetilde{c})(m[Q]|F)|m(U).\overline{k}\langle U\rangle.0$. Therefore $(\nu\widetilde{b})(m[P]|E)|m(U).\overline{k}\langle U\rangle.0 \stackrel{\varepsilon}{\Longrightarrow} (\nu\widetilde{b})(\overline{k}\langle P'\rangle.0|E) \approx^E_{Ct} (\nu\widetilde{c})(\overline{k}\langle Q'\rangle.0|F) \stackrel{\varepsilon}{\Longleftarrow} (\nu\widetilde{c})(m[Q]|F)|m(U).\overline{k}\langle U\rangle.0$, where $P \approx^E_{Ct} P'$, $Q \approx^E_{Ct} Q'$. Furthermore, since $P \approx^E_{Ct} P'$, $Q \approx^E_{Ct} Q'$, by the congruence of $\approx^E_{Ct}$, we have $(\nu\widetilde{b})(\overline{k}\langle P\rangle.0|E) \approx^E_{Ct} (\nu\widetilde{b})(\overline{k}\langle P'\rangle.0|E)$ and $(\nu\widetilde{c})(\overline{k}\langle Q\rangle.0|F) \approx^E_{Ct} (\nu\widetilde{c})(\overline{k}\langle Q'\rangle.0|F)$. Hence we get $(\nu\widetilde{b})(\overline{k}\langle P\rangle.0|E) \approx^E_{Ct} (\nu\widetilde{c})(\overline{k}\langle Q\rangle.0|F)$. ■

Now we show that $\approx^E_{Ct}$ is included in $\approx_{Nr}$.

Proposition 10. For any $P, Q \in Pr^c$, $P \approx^E_{Ct} Q \Rightarrow P \approx_{Nr} Q$.

Proof : Let $R = \{(P, Q) \mid P \approx^E_{Ct} Q\}$. It is enough to prove that $R \subseteq \approx_{Nr}$.

We discuss the case of higher order output, other cases are trivial.

The only nontrivial case is to show how higher order output actions of P are matched by Q.

Suppose $P \stackrel{(\nu\widetilde{b})\overline{a}\langle E\rangle}{\Longrightarrow} P'$. By the definition of $\approx^E_{Ct}$, for all $C(U)$ with $fn(C(U)) \cap bn(P, Q) = \emptyset$, for all $\mathbf{S}\{\}$, there exist Q', F, $\widetilde{c}$ such that $Q \stackrel{(\nu\widetilde{c})\overline{a}\langle F\rangle}{\Longrightarrow} Q'$ and $(\nu\widetilde{b})(\mathbf{S}\{P'\}|C\langle E\rangle) \approx^E_{Ct} (\nu\widetilde{c})(\mathbf{S}\{Q'\}|C\langle F\rangle)$.

Let $\mathbf{S}\{\} = m[\{\}]$, $C(U) = !\overline{n}\langle U\rangle.0$, we have $(\nu\widetilde{b})(m[P']|!\overline{n}\langle E\rangle.0) \approx^E_{Ct} (\nu\widetilde{c})(m[Q']|!\overline{n}\langle F\rangle.0)$. By Lemma 2, we have $(\nu\widetilde{b})(\overline{m}\langle P'\rangle.0|!\overline{n}\langle E\rangle.0) \approx^E_{Ct} (\nu\widetilde{c})(\overline{m}\langle Q'\rangle.0|!\overline{n}\langle F\rangle.0)$. Therefore $R \subseteq \approx_{Nr}$. ■

The following proposition is the main result of this paper, which states the equivalence of bisimulations for HOπP.

Proposition 11. For any $P, Q \in Pr^c$, $P \approx_{Ba} Q \Leftrightarrow P \approx^E_{Ct} Q \Leftrightarrow P \approx^L_{Ct} Q \Leftrightarrow P \approx_{Nr} Q$.

Proof : By Propositions 2, 3, 9 and 10. ■

5. A Variant of Normal Bisimulation

Let us see the language of HOπP without replication operator defined by the following grammar:

$P ::= 0 \mid U \mid P_1|P_2 \mid (\nu a)P \mid a[P]$

$\pi_i ::= \tau \mid a(U) \mid \overline{a}\langle P\rangle$

We write the set of processes of this higher order π-calculus as Pr_p.

In [12], Parrow has shown that in higher order π-calculus, replication can be defined by inaction, prefix, sum, parallel and restriction under the sense of weak bisimulations. For example, $!P$ can be simulated by $R_P = (\nu a)(D|\overline{a}\langle P|D\rangle)$, where $D = a(X).(X|\overline{a}\langle X\rangle)$. Hence the expressive power of this HOπP without replication operator is equivalent to whole HOπP. In the definition of normal bisimulation, replication appears. Although we can translate replication into other operators, the form is somewhat complicated. In [2], we gave a variant of normal bisimulation, where parallel of any finitary copies is used as a limit form of replication. We proved it coincides with normal bisimulation for higher order π-calculus in [2].

In the following, we extend the variant of normal bisimulation in [2] to HOπP, and then prove the equivalence of the variant of normal bisimulation and other bisimulations.

Definition 7. A symmetric relation $R \subseteq Pr^c \times Pr^c$ is a weak limit normal bisimulation if P R Q implies:

(1) whenever $P \stackrel{\varepsilon}{\Longrightarrow} P'$, there exists Q' such that $Q \stackrel{\varepsilon}{\Longrightarrow} Q'$ and P' R Q';

(2) whenever $P \stackrel{a\langle n(U).U\rangle}{\Longrightarrow} P'$, there exists Q' such that $Q \stackrel{a\langle n(U).U\rangle}{\Longrightarrow} Q'$ and P' R Q', where n is a fresh name;

(3) whenever $P \stackrel{(\nu\widetilde{b})\overline{a}\langle E\rangle}{\Longrightarrow} P'$, there exist Q', F, $\widetilde{c}$ such that $Q \stackrel{(\nu\widetilde{c})\overline{a}\langle F\rangle}{\Longrightarrow} Q'$ and $(\nu\widetilde{b})(\overline{m}\langle P'\rangle.0|\Pi_k\overline{n}\langle E\rangle.0)$ R $(\nu\widetilde{c})(\overline{m}\langle Q'\rangle.0|\Pi_k\overline{n}\langle F\rangle.0)$ for all $k \in N = \{0, 1, 2, ...\}$, where m, n are fresh names. Here we write $\Pi_k P$ to denote the parallel of k copies of P, for example, $\Pi_3 P$ represents $P|P|P$.

We write $P \approx_{nor} Q$ if P and Q are weakly limit normal bisimilar.

Proposition 12. For any $P, Q \in Pr^c$, $P \approx^E_{Ct} Q \Rightarrow P \approx_{nor} Q$.

Proof : Similar to the proof of Proposition 10, just let $\mathbf{S}\{\} = m[\{\}]$, $C(U) = \Pi_k\overline{n}\langle U\rangle.0$. ■

Proposition 13. For any $P, Q \in Pr^c$, $P \approx_{nor} Q \Rightarrow P \approx_{Nr} Q$.

Proof : Let $R = \{((\nu\widetilde{b})(P|!\overline{n_1}\langle E_1\rangle.0|...|!\overline{n_m}\langle E_m\rangle.0), (\nu\widetilde{c})(Q|!\overline{n_1}\langle F_1\rangle.0|...|!\overline{n_m}\langle F_m\rangle.0)) : (\nu\widetilde{b})(P|\Pi_{k_1}\overline{n_1}\langle E_1\rangle.0|...|\Pi_{k_m}\overline{n_m}\langle E_m\rangle.0) \approx_{nor} (\nu\widetilde{c})(Q|\Pi_{k_1}\overline{n_1}\langle F_1\rangle.0|...|\Pi_{k_m}\overline{n_m}\langle F_m\rangle.0)$ for any $k_1, ..., k_m \in N$ with fresh names $n_1, ..., n_m.\}$. It is enough to prove that $R \subseteq \approx_{Nr}$.

We want to prove that

(1) If $(\nu\widetilde{b})(P|!\overline{n_1}\langle E_1\rangle.0|...|!\overline{n_m}\langle E_m\rangle.0)$ R $(\nu\widetilde{c})(Q|!\overline{n_1}\langle F_1\rangle.0|...|!\overline{n_m}\langle F_m\rangle.0)$ and $(\nu\widetilde{b})(P|!\overline{n_1}\langle E_1\rangle.0|...|!\overline{n_m}\langle E_m\rangle.0) \stackrel{\varepsilon}{\Longrightarrow} S$, then there exists T' such that $(\nu\widetilde{c})(Q|!\overline{n_1}\langle F_1\rangle.0|...|!\overline{n_m}\langle F_m\rangle.0) \stackrel{\varepsilon}{\Longrightarrow} T$ and S R T.

(2) if $(\nu\widetilde{b})(P|!\overline{n_1}\langle E_1\rangle.0|...|!\overline{n_m}\langle E_m\rangle.0)$ R $(\nu\widetilde{c})(Q|!\overline{n_1}\langle F_1\rangle.0|...|!\overline{n_m}\langle F_m\rangle.0)$ and $(\nu\widetilde{b})(P|!\overline{n_1}\langle E_1\rangle.0|...|!\overline{n_m}\langle E_m\rangle.0) \stackrel{a\langle n(U).U\rangle}{\Longrightarrow} S$, there exists T such that $(\nu\widetilde{c})(Q|!\overline{n_1}\langle F_1\rangle.0|...|!\overline{n_m}\langle F_m\rangle.0) \stackrel{a\langle n(U).U\rangle}{\Longrightarrow} T$ and S R T, where n

is a fresh name.

(3) if $(\nu\widetilde{b})(P|!\overline{n_1}\langle E_1\rangle.0|...|!\overline{n_m}\langle E_m\rangle.0)\ R\ (\nu\widetilde{c})(Q|!\overline{n_1}\langle F_1\rangle.0|...|!\overline{n_m}\langle F_m\rangle.0)$ and $(\nu\widetilde{b})(P|!\overline{n_1}\langle E_1\rangle.0|...|!\overline{n_m}\langle E_m\rangle.0) \stackrel{(\nu\widetilde{e})\overline{a}\langle E\rangle}{\Longrightarrow} S$, there exist T, F, $\widetilde{f}$ such that $(\nu\widetilde{c})(Q|!\overline{n_1}\langle F_1\rangle.0|...|!\overline{n_m}\langle F_m\rangle.0) \stackrel{(\nu\widetilde{f})\overline{a}\langle F\rangle}{\Longrightarrow} T$ and $(\nu\widetilde{e})(S|!\overline{n}\langle E\rangle.0)\ R\ (\nu\widetilde{f})(T|!\overline{n}\langle F\rangle.0)$, where n is a fresh name.

Case (1): We have $(\nu\widetilde{b})(P|!\overline{n_1}\langle E_1\rangle.0|...|!\overline{n_m}\langle E_m\rangle.0) \stackrel{\varepsilon}{\Longrightarrow} (\nu\widetilde{b})(P'|!\overline{n_1}\langle E_1\rangle.0|...|!\overline{n_m}\langle E_m\rangle.0) \equiv S$, hence $P \stackrel{\varepsilon}{\Longrightarrow} P'$. Since $(\nu\widetilde{b})(P|!\overline{n_1}\langle E_1\rangle.0|...|!\overline{n_m}\langle E_m\rangle.0)\ R\ (\nu\widetilde{c})(Q|!\overline{n_1}\langle F_1\rangle.0|...|!\overline{n_m}\langle F_m\rangle.0)$, $(\nu\widetilde{b})(P|\Pi_{k_1}\overline{n_1}\langle E_1\rangle.0|...|\Pi_{k_m}\overline{n_m}\langle E_m\rangle.0) \approx_{nor} (\nu\widetilde{c})(Q|\Pi_{k_1}\overline{n_1}\langle F_1\rangle.0|...|\Pi_{k_m}\overline{n_m}\langle F_m\rangle.0)$ for any $k_1, ..., k_m \in N$, hence $(\nu\widetilde{b})(P|\Pi_{k_1}\overline{n_1}\langle E_1\rangle.0|...|\Pi_{k_m}\overline{n_m}\langle E_m\rangle.0) \stackrel{\varepsilon}{\Longrightarrow} (\nu\widetilde{b})(P'|\Pi_{k_1}\overline{n_1}\langle E_1\rangle.0|...|\Pi_{k_m}\overline{n_m}\langle E_m\rangle.0) \equiv S'$, $(\nu\widetilde{c})(Q|\Pi_{k_1}\overline{n_1}\langle F_1\rangle.0|...|\Pi_{k_m}\overline{n_m}\langle F_m\rangle.0) \stackrel{\varepsilon}{\Longrightarrow} (\nu\widetilde{c})(Q'|\Pi_{k_1}\overline{n_1}\langle F_1\rangle.0|...|\Pi_{k_m}\overline{n_m}\langle F_m\rangle.0) \equiv T'$ and $S' \approx_{nor} T'$. Therefore $(\nu\widetilde{c})(Q|!\overline{n_1}\langle F_1\rangle.0|...|!\overline{n_m}\langle F_m\rangle.0) \stackrel{\varepsilon}{\Longrightarrow} (\nu\widetilde{c})(Q'|!\overline{n_1}\langle F_1\rangle.0|...|!\overline{n_m}\langle F_m\rangle.0) \equiv T$ and $S\ R\ T$.

Case (2): We have $(\nu\widetilde{b})(P|!\overline{n_1}\langle E_1\rangle.0|...|!\overline{n_m}\langle E_m\rangle.0) \stackrel{a\langle n(U).U\rangle}{\Longrightarrow} (\nu\widetilde{b})(P'|!\overline{n_1}\langle E_1\rangle.0|...|!\overline{n_m}\langle E_m\rangle.0) \equiv S$, where n is a fresh name, hence $P \stackrel{a\langle n(U).U\rangle}{\Longrightarrow} P'$. Since $(\nu\widetilde{b})(P|!\overline{n_1}\langle E_1\rangle.0|..|!\overline{n_m}\langle E_m\rangle.0)\ R\ (\nu\widetilde{c})(Q|!\overline{n_1}\langle F_1\rangle.0|...|!\overline{n_m}\langle F_m\rangle.0)$, $(\nu\widetilde{b})(P|\Pi_{k_1}\overline{n_1}\langle E_1\rangle.0|...|\Pi_{k_m}\overline{n_m}\langle E_m\rangle.0) \approx_{nor} (\nu\widetilde{c})(Q|\Pi_{k_1}\overline{n_1}\langle F_1\rangle.0|...|\Pi_{k_m}\overline{n_m}\langle F_m\rangle.0)$ for any $k_1, ..., k_m \in N$, hence $(\nu\widetilde{b})(P|\Pi_{k_1}\overline{n_1}\langle E_1\rangle.0|...|\Pi_{k_m}\overline{n_m}\langle E_m\rangle.0) \stackrel{a\langle n(U).U\rangle}{\Longrightarrow} (\nu\widetilde{b})(P'|\Pi_{k_1}\overline{n_1}\langle E_1\rangle.0|...|\Pi_{k_m}\overline{n_m}\langle E_m\rangle.0) \equiv S'$, $(\nu\widetilde{c})(Q|\Pi_{k_1}\overline{n_1}\langle F_1\rangle.0|...|\Pi_{k_m}\overline{n_m}\langle F_m\rangle.0) \stackrel{a\langle n(U).U\rangle}{\Longrightarrow} (\nu\widetilde{c})(Q'|\Pi_{k_1}\overline{n_1}\langle F_1\rangle.0|...|\Pi_{k_m}\overline{n_m}\langle F_m\rangle.0) \equiv T'$ and $S' \approx_{nor} T'$. Therefore $(\nu\widetilde{c})(Q|!\overline{n_1}\langle F_1\rangle.0|...|!\overline{n_m}\langle F_m\rangle.0) \stackrel{a\langle n(U).U\rangle}{\Longrightarrow} (\nu\widetilde{c})(Q'|!\overline{n_1}\langle F_1\rangle.0|...|!\overline{n_m}\langle F_m\rangle.0) \equiv T$ and $S\ R\ T$.

Case (3): We have $(\nu\widetilde{b})(P|!\overline{n_1}\langle E_1\rangle.0|...|!\overline{n_m}\langle E_m\rangle.0) \stackrel{(\nu\widetilde{e})\overline{a}\langle E\rangle}{\Longrightarrow} (\nu\widetilde{b})(P'|!\overline{n_1}\langle E_1\rangle.0|...|!\overline{n_m}\langle E_m\rangle.0) \equiv S$, hence $P \stackrel{(\nu\widetilde{e})\overline{a}\langle E\rangle}{\Longrightarrow} P'$. Since $(\nu\widetilde{b})(P|!\overline{n_1}\langle E_1\rangle.0|...|!\overline{n_m}\langle E_m\rangle.0)\ R\ (\nu\widetilde{c})(Q|!\overline{n_1}\langle F_1\rangle.0|...|!\overline{n_m}\langle F_m\rangle.0)$, $(\nu\widetilde{b})(P|\Pi_{k_1}\overline{n_1}\langle E_1\rangle.0|...|\Pi_{k_m}\overline{n_m}\langle E_m\rangle.0) \approx_{nor} (\nu\widetilde{c})(Q|\Pi_{k_1}\overline{n_1}\langle F_1\rangle.0|...|\Pi_{k_m}\overline{n_m}\langle F_m\rangle.0)$ for any $k_1, ..., k_m \in N$, hence $(\nu\widetilde{b})(P|\Pi_{k_1}\overline{n_1}\langle E_1\rangle.0|...|\Pi_{k_m}\overline{n_m}\langle E_m\rangle.0) \stackrel{(\nu\widetilde{e})\overline{a}\langle E\rangle}{\Longrightarrow} (\nu\widetilde{b})(P'|\Pi_{k_1}\overline{n_1}\langle E_1\rangle.0|...|\Pi_{k_m}\overline{n_m}\langle E_m\rangle.0) \equiv S'$, there exist T', F, $\widetilde{f}$ such that $(\nu\widetilde{c})(Q|\Pi_{k_1}\overline{n_1}\langle F_1\rangle.0|...|\Pi_{k_m}\overline{n_m}\langle F_m\rangle.0) \stackrel{(\nu\widetilde{f})\overline{a}\langle F\rangle}{\Longrightarrow} (\nu\widetilde{c})(Q'|\Pi_{k_1}\overline{n_1}\langle F_1\rangle.0|...|\Pi_{k_m}\overline{n_m}\langle F_m\rangle.0) \equiv T'$ and $(\nu\widetilde{e})(S'|!\overline{n}\langle E\rangle.0) \approx_{nor} (\nu\widetilde{f})(T'|!\overline{n}\langle F\rangle.0)$, where n is a fresh name. Therefore $(\nu\widetilde{c})(Q|!\overline{n_1}\langle F_1\rangle.0|...|!\overline{n_m}\langle F_m\rangle.0) \stackrel{(\nu\widetilde{f})\overline{a}\langle F\rangle}{\Longrightarrow} (\nu\widetilde{c})(Q'|!\overline{n_1}\langle F_1\rangle.0|...|!\overline{n_m}\langle F_m\rangle.0) \equiv T$ and $(\nu\widetilde{e})(S|!\overline{n}\langle E\rangle.0)\ R\ (\nu\widetilde{f})(T'!\overline{n}\langle F\rangle.0)$. ■

Proposition 14. For any $P, Q \in Pr^c$, $P \approx_{Ba} Q \Leftrightarrow P \approx^E_{Ct} Q \Leftrightarrow P \approx^L_{Ct} Q \Leftrightarrow P \approx_{Nr} Q \Leftrightarrow P \approx_{nor} Q$.

Proof : By Propositions 11, 12 and 13, we have the proposition holds. ■

6. Strong Bisimulations

We give the definitions and prove the propositions only for the case of weak bisimulations. The definitions and propositions for weak bisimulations of HOπP can be extended to the case of strong bisimulations.

Roughly speaking, to get the definition of strong bisimulations, we just need to replace $\stackrel{\varepsilon}{\Longrightarrow}$ by $\stackrel{\tau}{\longrightarrow}$, replace $\stackrel{\alpha}{\Longrightarrow}$ by $\stackrel{\alpha}{\longrightarrow}$, and replace $\Downarrow_\mu$ by $\downarrow_\mu$ in the definition of weak bisimulations. In the following, we give the definitions of strong bisimulations.

Definition 8. A symmetric relation $R \subseteq Pr^c \times Pr^c$ is a strong contextual barbed bisimulation if $P\ R\ Q$ implies:

(1) $C\{P\}\ R\ C\{Q\}$ for any context C;

(2) whenever $P \stackrel{\tau}{\longrightarrow} P'$ there exists Q' such that $Q \stackrel{\tau}{\longrightarrow} Q'$ and $P'\ R\ Q'$;

(3) $P \downarrow_\mu$ implies $Q \downarrow_\mu$.

We write $P \sim_{Ba} Q$ if P and Q are strongly contextual barbed bisimilar.

Definition 9. Strong early context bisimilarity $\sim^E_{Ct}$ is the largest symmetric relation on closed processes R such that $P\ R\ Q$ implies:

(1) whenever $P \stackrel{\tau}{\longrightarrow} P'$, there exists Q' such that $Q \stackrel{\tau}{\longrightarrow} Q'$ and $P'\ R\ Q'$;

(2) whenever $P \stackrel{a\langle E\rangle}{\longrightarrow} P'$, there exists Q' such that $Q \stackrel{a\langle E\rangle}{\longrightarrow} Q'$ and $P'\ R\ Q'$;

(3) whenever $P \stackrel{(\nu\widetilde{b})\overline{a}\langle E\rangle}{\longrightarrow} P'$ for all $C(U)$ with $fn(C(U)) \cap bn(P, Q) = \emptyset$, for all $\mathbf{S}\{\}$, there exist Q', F, $\widetilde{c}$ such that $Q \stackrel{(\nu\widetilde{c})\overline{a}\langle F\rangle}{\longrightarrow} Q'$ and $(\nu\widetilde{b})(\mathbf{S}\{P'\}|C\langle E\rangle)\ R\ (\nu\widetilde{c})(\mathbf{S}\{Q'\}|C\langle F\rangle)$.

We write $P \sim^E_{Ct} Q$ if P and Q are strongly early context bisimilar.

Definition 10. Strong late context bisimilarity $\sim^L_{Ct}$ is the largest symmetric relation on closed processes R such that $P\ R\ Q$ implies:

(1) whenever $P \stackrel{\tau}{\longrightarrow} P'$, there exists Q' such that $Q \stackrel{\tau}{\longrightarrow} Q'$ and $P'\ R\ Q'$;

(2) whenever $P \stackrel{a(U)}{\longrightarrow} P'$, there exists Q' such that $Q \stackrel{a(U)}{\longrightarrow} Q'$ and for all E, $P'\{E/U\}\ R\ Q'\{E/U\}$;

(3) whenever $P \stackrel{(\nu\widetilde{b})\overline{a}\langle E\rangle}{\longrightarrow} P'$,there exist Q', F, $\widetilde{c}$ such that $Q \stackrel{(\nu\widetilde{c})\overline{a}\langle F\rangle}{\longrightarrow} Q'$ and for all $C(U)$ with $fn(C(U)) \cap \{\widetilde{b}, \widetilde{c}\} = \emptyset$, for all $\mathbf{S}\{\}$, $(\nu\widetilde{b})(\mathbf{S}\{P'\}|C\langle E\rangle)\ R\ (\nu\widetilde{c})(\mathbf{S}\{Q'\}|C\langle F\rangle)$.

We write $P \sim^L_{Ct} Q$ if P and Q are strongly late context bisimilar.

Definition 11. Strong normal bisimilarity $\sim_{Nr}$ is the largest symmetric relation on closed processes R such that $P\ R\ Q$ implies:

(1) whenever $P \stackrel{\tau}{\longrightarrow} P'$, there exists Q' such that $Q \stackrel{\tau}{\longrightarrow} Q'$ and $P'\ R\ Q'$;

(2) whenever $P \stackrel{a\langle n(U).U\rangle}{\longrightarrow} P'$, there exists Q' such that $Q \stackrel{a\langle n(U).U\rangle}{\longrightarrow} Q'$ and $P'\ R\ Q'$, where n is a fresh name;

(3) whenever $P \overset{(\nu\widetilde{b})\overline{a}\langle E\rangle}{\longrightarrow} P'$, there exist Q', F, $\widetilde{c}$ such that $Q \overset{(\nu\widetilde{c})\overline{a}\langle F\rangle}{\longrightarrow} Q'$ and $(\nu\widetilde{b})(\overline{m}\langle P'\rangle.0|!\overline{n}\langle E\rangle.0)$ R $(\nu\widetilde{c})(\overline{m}\langle Q'\rangle.0|!\overline{n}\langle F\rangle.0)$, where m, n are fresh names.

We write $P \sim_{Nr} Q$ if P and Q are strongly normal bisimilar.

Definition 12. A symmetric relation $R \subseteq Pr^c \times Pr^c$ is a strong limit normal bisimulation if $P\ R\ Q$ implies:

(1) whenever $P \overset{\tau}{\longrightarrow} P'$, there exists Q' such that $Q \overset{\tau}{\longrightarrow} Q'$ and $P'\ R\ Q'$;

(2) whenever $P \overset{a\langle n(U).U\rangle}{\longrightarrow} P'$, there exists Q' such that $Q \overset{a\langle n(U).U\rangle}{\longrightarrow} Q'$ and $P'\ R\ Q'$, where n is a fresh name;

(3) whenever $P \overset{(\nu\widetilde{b})\overline{a}\langle E\rangle}{\longrightarrow} P'$, there exist Q', F, $\widetilde{c}$ such that $Q \overset{(\nu\widetilde{c})\overline{a}\langle F\rangle}{\longrightarrow} Q'$ and $(\nu\widetilde{b})(\overline{m}\langle P'\rangle.0|\Pi_k\overline{n}\langle E\rangle.0)$ R $(\nu\widetilde{c})(\overline{m}\langle Q'\rangle.0|\Pi_k\overline{n}\langle F\rangle.0)$ for all $k \in N = \{0, 1, 2, ...\}$, where m, n are fresh names.

We write $P \sim_{nor} Q$ if P and Q are strongly limit normal bisimilar.

By using the technique in [1], the equivalence of $\approx_{Ct}^{E}$, $\approx_{Ct}^{L}$, $\approx_{Nr}$ and $\approx_{nor}$ for HOπP can be extended to the case of strong bisimulations, i.e., the equivalence of $\sim_{Ct}^{E}$, $\sim_{Ct}^{L}$, $\sim_{Nr}$ and $\sim_{nor}$.

Proposition 15. For any $P, Q \in Pr^c$, $P \sim_{Ba} Q \Leftrightarrow P \sim_{Ct}^{E} Q \Leftrightarrow P \sim_{Ct}^{L} Q \Leftrightarrow P \sim_{Nr} Q \Leftrightarrow P \sim_{nor} Q$.

7. Conclusions

In [8], higher order π-calculus was extended to a calculus with passivation (HOπP) and bisimulations for HOπP were presented and studied. In [8], it was showed that abstraction-free process cannot be used to derive a normal bisimilarity in HOπP. But it was showed that a form of normal bisimilarity can be defined for HOπP without restriction.

The aim of this paper is to study the relation between bisimulations for HOπP. We proposed the concepts of normal bisimulation and late context bisimulation for HOπP. Then we prove the equivalence between normal bisimulation, late context bisimulation, early context bisimulation and contextual barbed bisimulation for HOπP. Furthermore, we give a variant of normal bisimulation, called limited normal bisimulation, and prove the equivalence between limited normal bisimulation and other bisimulations. At last, we extend the definitions and propositions for weak bisimulations of HOπP to the case of strong bisimulations.

Acknowledgment

This work was supported by the Aviation Science Fund of China under Grant No. 20128052064 and the National Natural Science Foundation of China under Grant No. 60873025.

References

[1] Z. Cao. More on bisimulations for higher-order π-calculus. In FOSSACS06, LNCS 3921, 63-78, 2006.

[2] Z. Cao, A Spatial Logical Characterisation of Context Bisimulation. In Proceeding of ASIAN 2006, Lecture Notes in Computer Science 4435, 232-240, 2006.

[3] J. C. Godskesen, T. Hildebrandt, and V. Sassone. A Calculus of Mobile Resources. In L. Brim, P. Jancar, M. Kretinsky, and A. Kucera, editors, Proceedings of the 13th International Conference on Concurrency Theory (CONCUR'02), volume 2421 of LNCS, pages 272–287. Springer Verlag, 2002.

[4] T. Hildebrandt, J. C. Godskesen, and M. Bundgaard. Bisimulation Congruences for Homer - a Calculus of Higher Order Mobile Embedded Resources. Technical Report TR-2004-52, IT University of Copenhagen, 2004.

[5] A. Jeffrey, J. Rathke. A theory of bisimulation for a fragment of concurrent ML with local names. Theoretical Computer Science. 323:1-48, 2004.

[6] A. Jeffrey, J. Rathke. Contextual equivalence for higher-order π-calculus revisited. Logical Methods in Computer Science, 1(1:4):1-22, 2005.

[7] S. Lenglet, A. Schmitt, and J. Stefani. Howe's method in calculi with passivation. In CONCUR'09, volume 5710 of LNCS, pages 448-462, 2009.

[8] S. Lenglet, A. Schmitt, and J. Stefani. Normal bisimulations in process calculi with passivation. In FoSSaCS'09, volume 5504 of LNCS, pages 257-271, 2009.

[9] S. Lenglet, A. Schmitt, J. Stefani. Characterizing Contextual Equivalence in Calculi with Passivation. Information and Computation, 209(11):1390-1433, 2011.

[10] R. Milner. A calculus of communication systems. Lecture Notes in Computer Science 92. Springer-Verlag, 1980.

[11] R. Milner, J. Parrow, and D. Walker. A calculus of mobile processes, (Part I and II). Information and Computation, 100:1-77, 1992.

[12] J.Parrow. An introduction to the π-calculus. In J. Bergstra, A. Ponse and S. Smolka editors, Handbook of Process Algebra, North-Holland, Amsterdam, 2001.

[13] D. Sangiorgi. Expressing mobility in process algebras: first-order and higher-order paradigms, Ph.D thesis, University of Einburgh, 1992.

[14] D. Sangiorgi. Bisimulation in higher-order calculi, Information and Computation, 131(2):141-178, 1996.

[15] A. Schmitt and J. Stefani. The Kell calculus: A family of higher order distributed process calculi. In Proceedings of GC2004, LNCS, Springer-Verlag, 2004.

Bit Level Encryption Standard (BLES): Version-III

[1]Gaurav Bhadra, [2] Tanya Bala, [3] Samik Banik, [4] Joyshree Nath, [5]Asoke Nath
[1,2,3,5]Department of Computer Science, St. Xavier's College(Autonomous),Kolkata, India
[4]Machine Intelligence Unit, Indian Statistical Institute, Kolkata, India
E-mail: [1]gaurav.bhadra@gmail.com,[2]bala.tanya@gmail.com,
[3]sam.xavo@gmail.com,[4]joyshreenath@gmail.com, [5]asokejoy1@gmail.com

Abstract: *In the present paper the authors have introduced a new symmetric key cryptographic method called Bit Level Encryption Standard (BLES) Version-III which is based on bit level columnar transposition method, bit-wise generalized vernam cipher method with feedback and bit-wise XOR operation. Recently Nath et al has developed BLES Version-I where they have used bit exchange method but with some fixed block size which were multiple of 2. Due to even power of two sometimes there were some repeats of characters in the encrypted file if the input plain text has also duplicate characters. To eliminate that problem Nath et al developed BLES Version–II where the authors have taken block size of square of odd numbers starting from three onwards. For scanning from right to left the authors used square of even numbers starting from four onwards. After finishing bit exchange the authors have performed bit-wise XOR to make the cryptosystem almost unbreakable. In the present work the authors changed the bit level encryption method by using bit level columnar transposition method in random order followed by bit level generalized vernam cipher method and bit level XOR operation. To make the encryption process strong the authors have reverse the entire content of the file and applied the he same encryption method. BLES version III is done pure bit level also the authors have used the feedback which gives extra strength to this method. The present method will be most suitable for encrypting short message, password, confidential key etc. The spectral analysis in the result sections shows that the BLES version-III method is free from known plain text attack, differential attack or any type brute force attack.*

Keywords: BLES, modified generalized vernam cipher method, bit level XOR operation, differential attack

1. Introduction

Due to rapid growth in data communication and network in last few years now it is a real challenge to everyone to send any confidential or important information from one computer to another computer. Due to open internet network it is now not at all difficult task to intercept any confidential data from internet. If the confidential data is not properly encrypted then any intruder can intercept data and can manipulate it. The confidentiality and genuineness of data has now become a very important issue in computer network. To send any important information from one user to another user normally the people are using e-mail as their transmission media. But the message of the e-mail can be trapped by the hacker between sender and receiver provided it is in raw form. So sending any kind of confidential message through e-mail is not proper solution. The confidential message may be trapped by any hacker between sender and receiver and then divert it to someone else. The time has come when the administration of any academic institute have to implement the security policies while sending any kind of data from one machine to other. The confidential data must be protected from any unwanted intruder to avoid any kind of disaster. It may be a big disaster when some senior personnel of a business company is sending some important business strategies to the Managing Director of his company and the entire information is hacked by some intruder or a hacker. After getting all information from internet the hacker can pass it to some rival company and this may create a real disaster in a company. This type of disaster may happen any time when the important data is moving from one machine to another machine in an unprotected manner. To get rid of this problem one has to send the encrypted text or cipher text from client to server or to another client. To protect any kind of hacking problems nowadays network security and cryptography is an emerging research area where the programmers are trying to develop some strong encryption algorithm so that no intruder can intercept the encrypted message. The authors here proposed method is symmetric key cryptography

The main advantage of symmetric key cryptography is that the key management is very simple as one key is used for both encryption as well as for decryption purpose. In symmetric key algorithm the key is called secret key and it should be known to sender and receiver both and no one else. In public key cryptosystem there are both merits and demerits. The merit is that there are two keys to be maintained. One key is called public key that is known to anybody and which can be used only to encrypt any plain text. There is another key called secret key or the private key that is known to receiver who is supposed to decrypt the encrypted message. The pair of keys are such that the private key can not be constructed from the public key so the hacker can not decrypt the encrypted text as they don't know the private key. The problem of Public key cryptosystem is that one has to do massive computation for encrypting any plain text. Moreover in some public key cryptography the size of encrypted message may increase. Due to massive computation the public key crypto system may not be suitable in some system like sensors network or mobile network. In the present work the authors are proposing a symmetric key method called BLES version-III method which can be applied in sensor network, mobile network, ATM network.

The present method uses bit level transposition method followed by bit level modified generalized vernam cipher method and then bit-wise XOR operations. Firstly, the entire file is converted into bits. After that the keygen()

function is called to generate encryption number and the randomization number. These two numbers are calculated from user entered secret key. The entire bits of the file is then placed in a 2-dimensional matrix of size nx8. The columns are extracted randomly according to the number found in the randomized matrix . After finishing bit-wise columnar transposition method the entire bit streams are taken block-wise and applied generalized cipher method with feedback. In first column the feedback bit is taken as '0' and then in subsequent column the carry bit is taken as the feedback. Finally the bit-wise XOR is performed where first bit is XROED with the last bit and substituted in first bit similarly the bit-2 is XORED with last but one bit and substituted in bit-2 and this way the entire bits were XORED. The above three methods were performed repeatedly according to encryption number.

The multiple encryptions make the system very secure.

2. BLES Version-III Algorithm:

<u>Encryption Algorithm:</u>

Step-0: Start
Step-1: Enter input file name (plaintext file) and store it in inputFile
Step-2: Enter output file name (ciphertext file) and store it in outputFile
Step-3: Enter the password.
Step-4: Copy the input file to a temporary file
Step-5: Use module-1 to compute the number of times to randomize and the encryption number
Step-6: i=1
Step-7: if i<=encryption number then goto step-8 else goto step-13
Step-8: Use module-2 to perform columnar transposition method
Step-9: Use module-3 to perform bitwise generalized vernam cipher method
Step-10: Use module-4 to perform bitwise XOR.
Step-11: Convert the file back to bytes and write it in the outputFile. This is the encrypted file
Step-12: i=i+1, goto step-7.
Step-13: End

<u>Module 1: Calculation of Encryption Number and Randomization Number (Keygen)</u>

Step-0: Start.
Step-1: len=length of the password
Step-2: If len<8 then, base=9-len
else base=1
Step-3:Initialize s1=0,i=0
Step-4: Calculate the following:
a)pow=base^(i+1)
b)n=ascii value of ith character of password
c)s1=s1+pow*n
Step-5: if i<len goto Step-4.
Step-6: s2=sum of digits of s1
Step-7: Randomization Number: r_times=s1%s2
Step-8: if r_times==0 or r_times>64, then r_times=64
Step-9:Initialize s3=0,i=0
Step-10: Calculate the following:
a)pow=base^(i+1)
b)n=ascii value of (len-1-i)[th] character of password
c)s3=s3+pow*n
Step-11: if i<len goto Step-4.
Step-12: s4=sum of digits of s3
Step-13: Encryption Number: en_num=s3%s4
Step-14: if en_num==0 or en_num>64, then
en_num=64
Step-15: End

Example:
Suppose the user entered a key= "ABCD"
Therefore the length of the key=4
i) To calculate randomization number we proceed as follows:
a. Calculate a sum from the given text key as follows:
Sum=Σ base^{postion} * ASCII value of character
Here for ASCII code of A=65, B=66, C=67, D=68
Base=5
Therefore s1=5^1 * 65 + 5^2 * 66 + 5^3 * 67 + 5^4 * 68=325+1650+8375+42500=51365

b. Calculate again sum of the digits in s1 as s2=5+1+3+6+5=20
c. Find the modulo with s1 to obtain randomization number:
R_times=s1 % s2=51365 % 20= 5
(ii) To calculate encryption number we proceed as follows:
a. Calculate a sum as follows:
S3=51*68+52*67+53*66+54*65=340+1675+8250+ 40625=50890
b. Sum of digits in s3 is s4=5+0+8+9+0=22
c. Therefore encryption number is:
en_num=s3 % s4=50890 % 22 =4

<u>Module 2: COLUMNAR TRANSPOSITION METHOD ALGORITHM</u>

Step-0: Start
Step-1: length=length of the file
Step-2: Convert the byte file to bits in reverse order.
Step-3: Extract 8 bits at a time.
Step-4: Complement the bits
Step-5: Xor bit-i with bit-(7-i) and store it in bit-(7-i), where i= {0,1,2,3}
Step-6: Store the bits in a file.
Step-7: Generate the key using Module Keygen
Step-8: Run=0, len=length*2
Step-9: while run<en_num repeat steps 10 to 16
Step-10: Extract all the bits from the file and store it column wise in a matrix col_matrix1 [4][len]
Step-11: Randomize the columns using MSA algorithm.
Step-12: Store randomized values in col_matrix2 [4][len]
Step-13: Divide the bits into four sections and store it in four files.
Step-14: Repeat the steps 10 to 12 for these for files.
Step-15: Store the randomized bits in the file.
Step-16: run=run+1
Step-17: End

Module 3:Bit-wise generalized Vernam Cipher method using feedback

Here key should be same length as the input file. The key is essentially a stream of bits. You have to decide how many bits should be '1' and how many bits should be '0'. Then randomize the bit pattern of the key pad. Apply vernam cipher method with the bit patterns of module1. This method you have to apply multiple times in both ways from left to right and then from right to left.

Step-0: Start.
Step-1: len=8*length of the password
Step-2: Initialize size=(square root of len) + 1, f=0, ky[] of size len, key[][] of size [size][size], arr[] with 8 zeros.
Step-3: If f<len/8 goto step 4 else goto step 10
Step-4: Extract a character from pass and store it in val
Step-5: if number of elemens in ky[]<len goto Step-6 else goto step 9.
Step-6: Extract 8 bits of val at a time and store them in var[]
Step-7: val=val/2 after extraction of each bit
Step-8: Reverse the elements of arr and store them in ky[]
Step-9: f=f+1
Step-10: Initialize x=0
Step-11: Store the elements of ky[] in the 2D array key[][].
Step-12: Randomize the elements of key[][] and store them in a key file till the length of the key file becomes equal to the number of bits in the input file.
Step 13: Initialize run=0
Step 14: if run<en_num goto step 15 else goto step 24.
Step-15: Initialize feedback=0.
Step-16:val=bit extracted from input file.
Step-17: k=bit extracted from key file
Step 18: s=binary sum of val, k and feedback.
Step 19: if $s=(0)_2$ or $s=(10)_2$ then cipher text bit=$(0)_2$, else if $s=(1)_2$ or $s=(11)_2$ then cipher text bit=$(1)_2$, feedback=carry of the sum in both the cases.
Step 20: Store the cipher text in a temporary file file2.
Step 21: Reverse the contents of file 2 and store it in another temporary file file1.
Step 22: run=run+1.
Step 23: Goto step 14.
Step 24: Reverse the contents of file1.
Step 25: End.

Module 4: Bit-wise XOR

We perform bit-wise XOR with bit-1 with bit-n(last bit) and substitute in position-n and bit-2 with bit-n-2 and substitute in position-n-2. This way the complete file you have to perform xor operation.

Step-0: Start.
Step-1: Store the end location (n-1) in End
Step-2: Store starting location (0) in Start
Step-3: If value at end== value at end, store 0 in end else store 1 in end.
Step-4: Start=Start+1
Step-5: End = End -1
Step-6: if End >= n/2, then goto step 3.
Step-7: End.

Decryption Algorithm:

Step-0: Start
Step-1: Enter input file name (Encrypted File) and store it in inputFile
Step-2: Enter output file name (Decrypted File) and store it in outputFile
Step-3: Enter the password
Step-4: Copy the input file to a temporary file
Step-5: Use module-1 to compute the number of times to randomize and the decryption number
Step-6: i=1
Step-7: if i<=decryption number then goto step-8 else goto step-13
Step-8: Use module-4 to perform bitwise XOR operation
Step-9: Use module-3 to perform bit generalized bitwise vernam cipher method.
Step-10: Use module-2 to perform columnar transposition method.
Step-11: Convert the file back to bytes and write it in the outputFile. This is the encrypted file.
Step-12: i=i+1, goto step-7.
Step-13: End

The modules have been described in our encryption algorithm. The only difference is that decryption methods will work in reverse order of the encryption process.

3. Results and Discussion

The present method i.e. BLES-III applied on various repeated patterns such as ASCII '0', ASCII '1' and so on. Normally none of the standard method will give good results on these patterns but the present method shows the results are quite satisfactory. We found it gives a random set of characters for any input stream of characters. Some of the results is shown in frequency graph and some encrypted patterns are shown as it is. The most interesting part is that out of 'n' characters if one character is different then also the encrypted patterns are coming different which is not possible in standard cryptographic methods. The following are the frequency graphs of the cipher text files obtained from files containing a sequence of 1000 single ASCII characters.

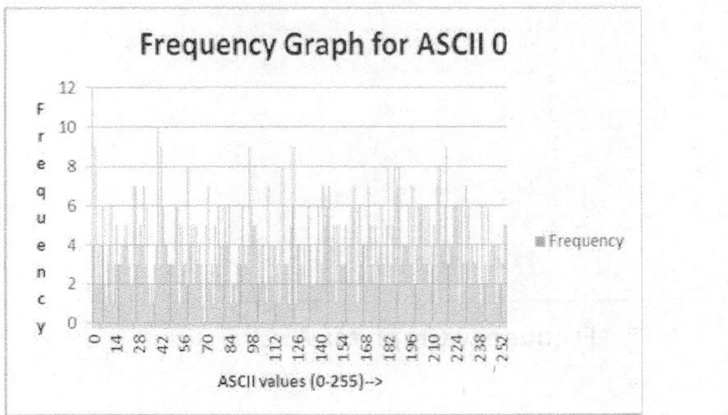

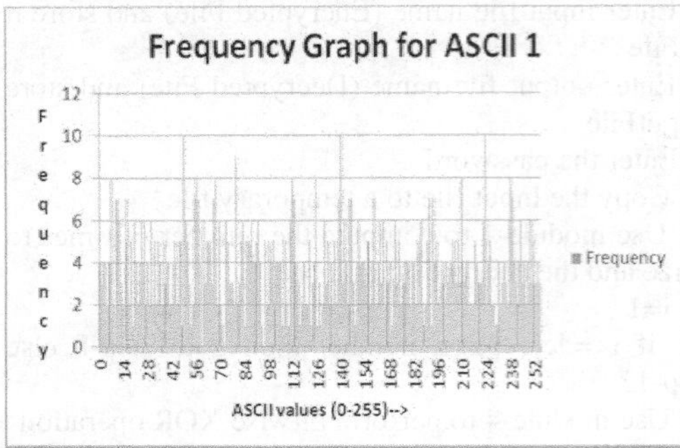
Frequency Graph for ASCII 1
Frequency
ASCII values (0-255)-->

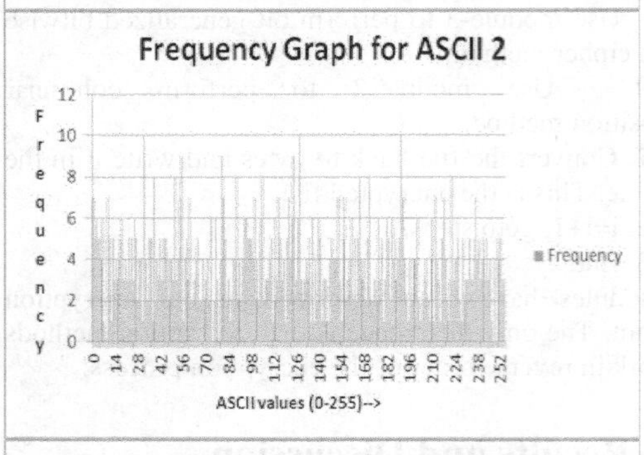
Frequency Graph for ASCII 2
Frequency
ASCII values (0-255)-->

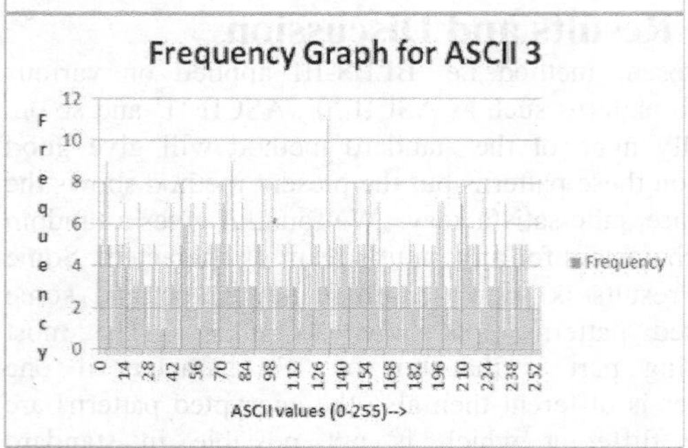
Frequency Graph for ASCII 3
Frequency
ASCII values (0-255)-->

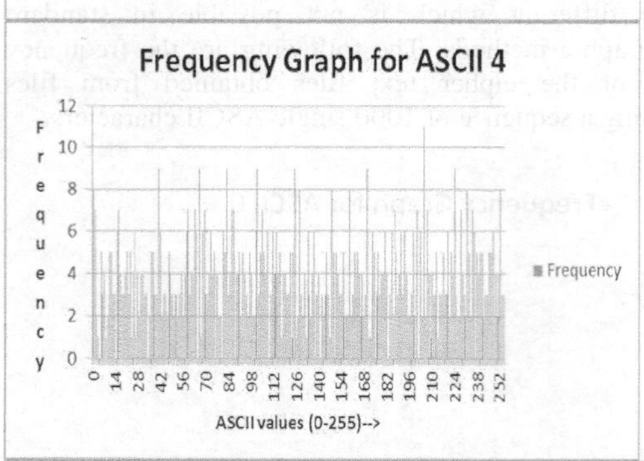
Frequency Graph for ASCII 4
Frequency
ASCII values (0-255)-->

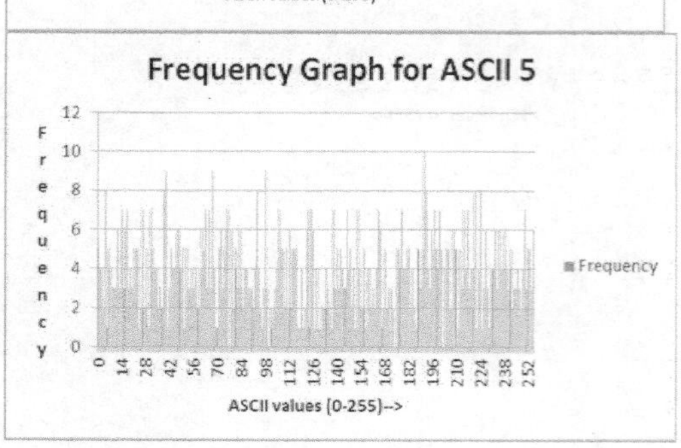
Frequency Graph for ASCII 5
Frequency
ASCII values (0-255)-->

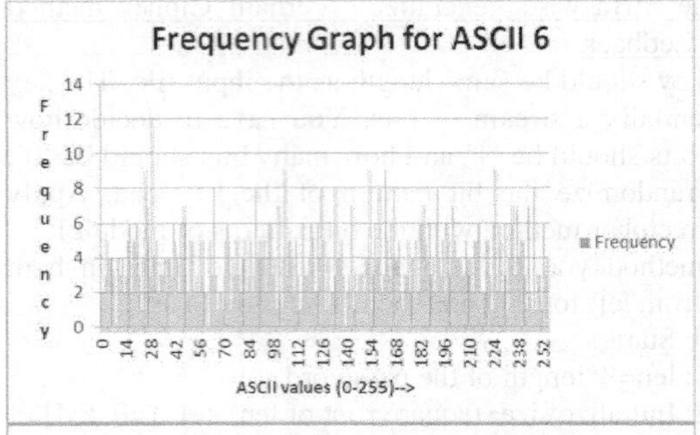
Frequency Graph for ASCII 6
Frequency
ASCII values (0-255)-->

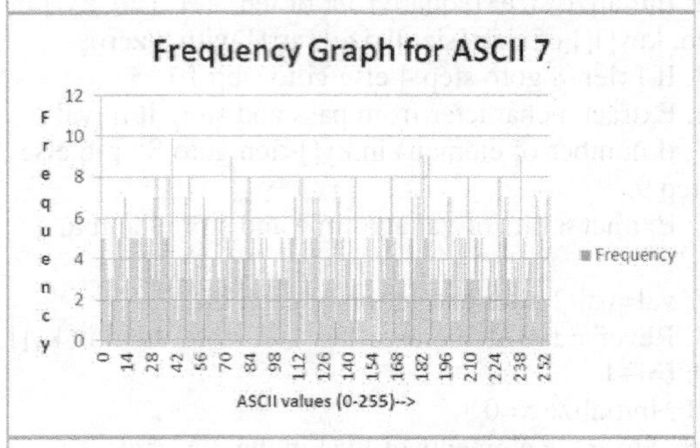
Frequency Graph for ASCII 7
Frequency
ASCII values (0-255)-->

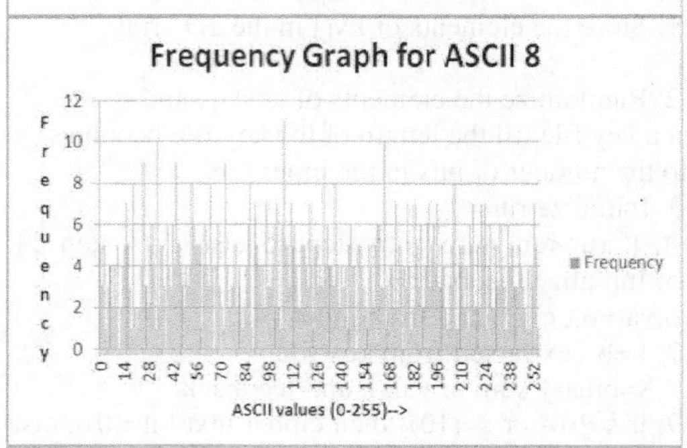
Frequency Graph for ASCII 8
Frequency
ASCII values (0-255)-->

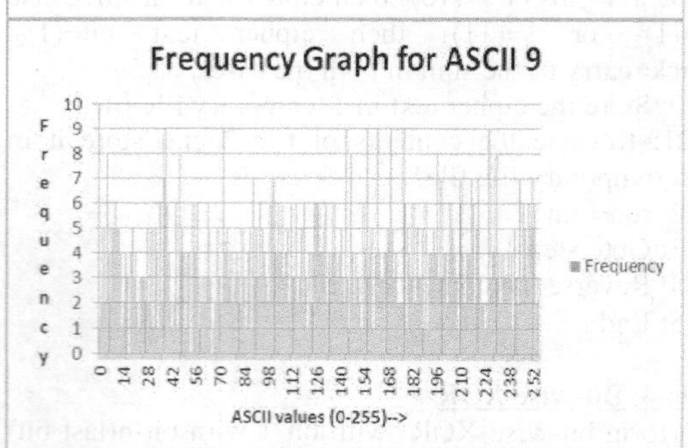
Frequency Graph for ASCII 9
Frequency
ASCII values (0-255)-->

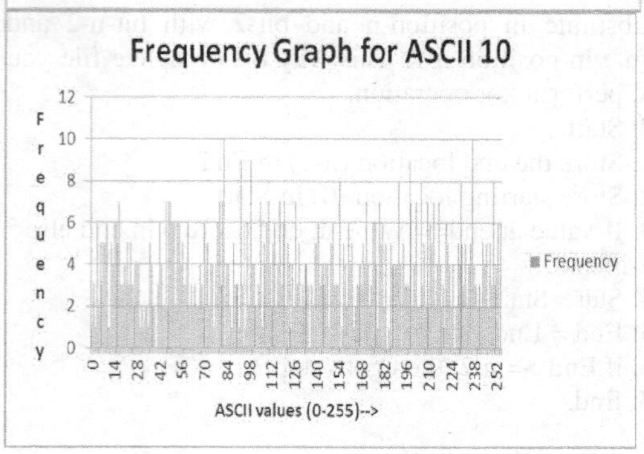
Frequency Graph for ASCII 10
Frequency
ASCII values (0-255)-->

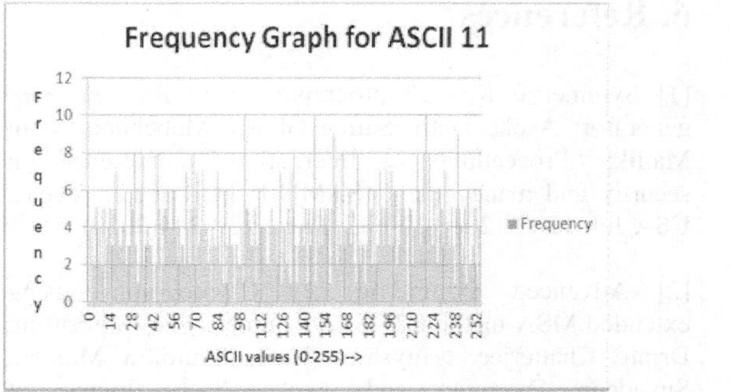

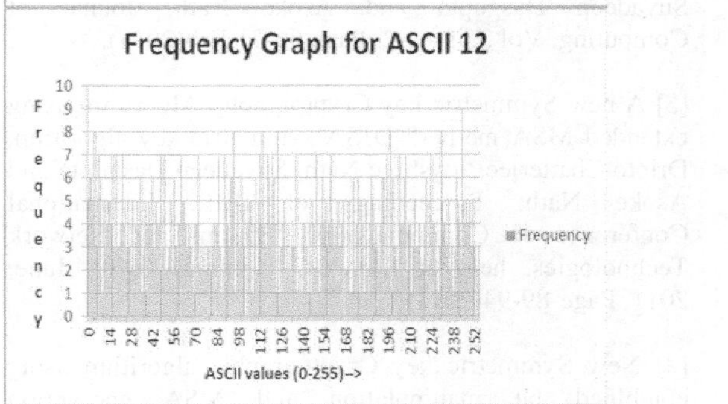

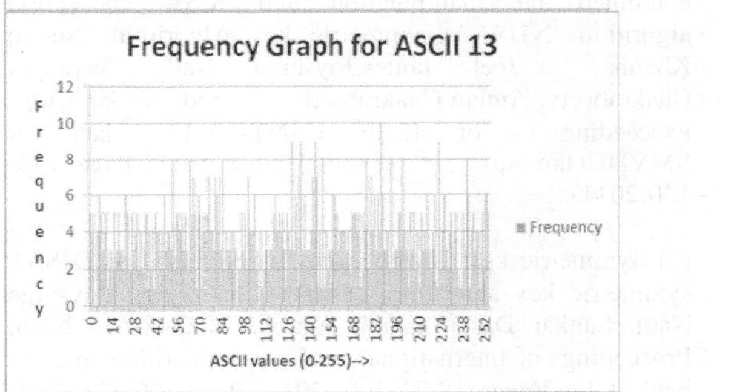

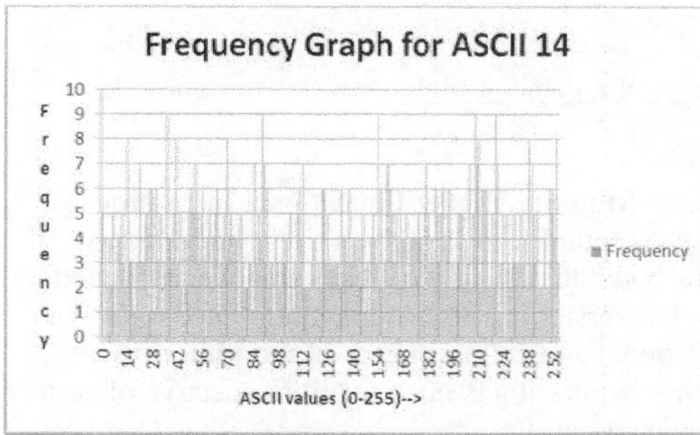

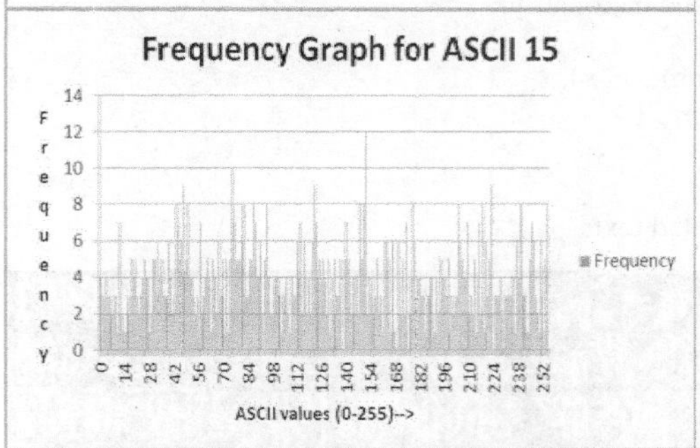

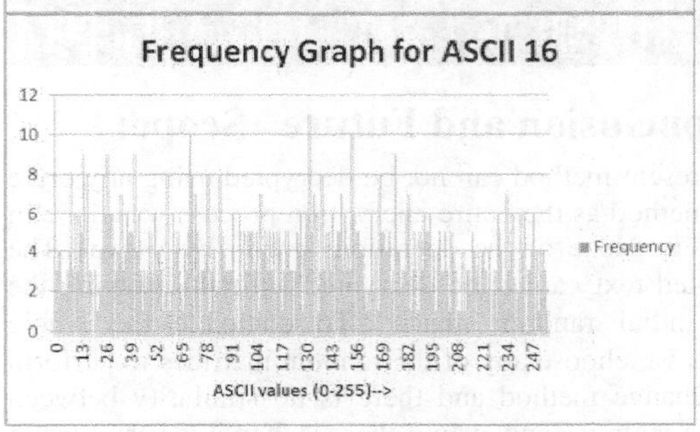

Some pairs cf similar text patterns and their corresponding cipher texts are as follows:

Pattern-1: aaaabaaaa
Password: 1234 Encryption No.:10 RandomizationNo: 8
Cipher text: _ſn♀iöBi╙▲←
Pattern-2: aaaacaaaa
Password: 1234 Encryption No.:10 RandomizationNo: 8
Cipher text: Ü~╟Ç╝'≡°≤═¥

Pattern-3: ababababa
Password: abcde: Encryption No.:9 RandomizationNo: 9
Cipher text: ╘ƒù╬Z<┴fΩ▒>
Pattern-4: abababab b
Password: abcde: Encryption No.: 9 RandomizationNo: 9
Cipher text: ◘²↕Cyç½D┘╞

Pattern-5: 15ASCII '0' + ASCII '1'
Password: qwerty Encryption No.:18 RandomizationNo: 12
Cipher text: ₧oçε»1╒kCd:)q+»≥
Pattern-6: 15ASCII '0' + 2ASCII '1'
Password: qwerty Encryption No.:18 RandomizationNo: 12
Cipher text : ╧åJ♀Cα╚↓∆ƒx β╥☼u┘

Pattern-7: 15ASCII '0' + ASCII '1' + 15ASCII '0'
Password: pass Encryption No.:15 RandomizationNo: 64
Cipher text : ≤▲N]╓╔ ▒dú_Ç╛≈┤Ä8B¥æC~▼┘♀úÜ╙ ♣»
Pattern-8: 15ASCII '0' + ASCII '2' + 15ASCII '0'
Password: pass Encryption No.:15 RandomizationNo: 64
Cipher text:
ùi≥b♣r²K:∆ÇÉóâⁿ/²mà$╛îMp]C₧☻☼(í

Pattern-9: babababab
Password: wxyz Encryption No.:8 RandomizationNo: 24
Cipher text:)C≡K║ƒz¼y←♀
Pattern-10: aababab ab
Password: wxyz Encryption No.:8 RandomizationNo: 24
Cipher text: ¼c╘↨╓£$îcúú

Encryption of a piece of plain text:

Plain text:
A Christian Minority Higher Educational Institution, St. Xavier's was founded in 1860 by a Catholic Minority Religious body, the Society of Jesus, and was affiliated to Calcutta University in 1862. While preference is shown to the educational and cultural needs of the Minority community, admission is open to all irrespective of caste, creed and nationality!

Password : 1234
En_num : 10
R_num : 8

Encrypted text:

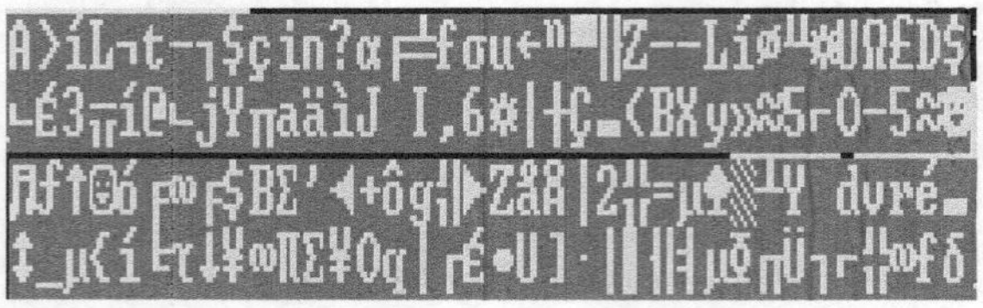

4. Conclusion and Future Scope:

The present method can not be decrypted using any brute force method as the entire encryption process was done in bit level. None of the operations are in byte level. The encrypted text cannot be decrypted without knowing the exact initial random matrix. To complete the whole process we choose any of the random matrices to perform bit exchange method and there is no similarity between any two matrices and even if there is then it is very hard to find out the similar ones. The spectral analysis shows that our present method is free from standard cryptography attacks namely brute force attack, known plain text attack and differential attack. BLES-III may be most effective to encrypt short message service (SMS) in mobile phone or to encrypt password. BLES-III was tested on various types of files such as audio file, video file, any database file etc and in every case the result found was quite satisfactory. The present bit level encryption method may be made further complex by adding random bit-wise permutation method, bit wise left shift and right shift method and bit-wise complement operations in random order. The authors are now working on that to make the ultimate bit level standard unbreakable.

5. Acknowledgments

We are very much grateful to the Department of Computer Science to give us this opportunity to work on symmetric key Cryptography. One of the authors (AN) sincerely expresses his gratitude to Fr. Dr. J. Felix Raj, Principal of St. Xavier's College (Autonomous), Kolkata for giving constant encouragement in doing research in cryptography.

6. References

[1] Symmetric Key Cryptography using Random Key generator: Asoke Nath, Saima Ghosh, Meheboob Alam Mallik: "Proceedings of International conference on security and management (SAM'10" held at Las Vegas, USA Jull 12-15, 2010), Vol-2, Page: 239-244(2010).

[2] Advanced Symmetric key Cryptography using extended MSA method: DJSSA symmetric key algorithm: Dripto Chatterjee, Joyshree Nath, Soumitra Mondal, Suvadeep Dasgupta and Asoke Nath, Jounal of Computing, Vol 3, issue-2, Page 66-71,Feb(2011).

[3] A new Symmetric key Cryptography Algorithm using extended MSA method: DJSA symmetric key algorithm, Dripto Chatterjee, Joyshree Nath, Suvadeep Dasgupta and Asoke Nath: Proceedings of IEEE International Conference on Communication Systems and Network Technologies, held at SMVDU (Jammu) 03-06 June, 2011, Page-89-94(2011).

[4] New Symmetric key Cryptographic algorithm using combined bit manipulation and MSA encryption algorithm: NJJSAA symmetric key Algorithm: Neeraj Khanna, Joel James,Joyshree Nath, Sayantan Chakraborty, Amlan Chakrabarti and Asoke Nath : Proceedings of IEEE CSNT-2011 held at SMVDU(Jammu) 03-06 June 2011, Page 125-130(2011).

[5] Symmetric key Cryptography using modified DJSSA symmetric key algorithm, Dripto Chatterjee, Joyshree Nath, Sankar Das, Shalabh Agarwal and Asoke Nath, Proceedings of International conference Worldcomp 2011 held at LasVegas 18-21 July 2011, Page-306-311, Vol-1(2011).

[6] An Integrated symmetric key cryptography algorithm using generalized vernam cipher method and DJSA method: DJMNA symmetric key algorithm : Debanjan Das, Joyshree Nath, Megholova Mukherjee, Neha Chaudhury and Asoke Nath: Proceedings of IEEE International conference : World Congress WICT-2011 to be held at Mumbai University 11-14 Dec, 2011, Page No.1203-1208(2011).

[7] Symmetric key cryptosystem using combined cryptographic algorithms- generalized modified vernam cipher method, MSA method and NJJSAA method: TTJSA algorithm – Trisha Chatterjee, Tamodeep Das, Joyshree Nath, Shayan Dey and Asoke Nath, Proceedings of IEEE International conference: World Congress WICT-2011 t held at Mumbai University 11-14 Dec, 2011, Page No. 1179-1184(2011).

[8] Symmetric key Cryptography using two-way updated – Generalized Vernam Cipher method: TTSJA algorithm, International Journal of Computer Applications(IJCA, USA), Vol 42, No.1, March, Pg: 34 -39(2012).

[9] Ultra Encryption Standard(UES) Version-I: Symmetric Key Cryptosystem using generalized modified Vernam Cipher method, Permutation method and Columnar Transposition method, Satyaki Roy, Navajit Maitra, Joyshree Nath,Shalabh Agarwal and Asoke Nath, Proceedings of IEEE sponsored National Conference on Recent Advances in Communication, Control and Computing Technology-RACCCT 2012, 29-30 March held at Surat, Page 81-88(2012).

[10] An Integrated Symmetric Key Cryptographic Method – Amalgamation of TTJSA Algorithm, Adbvanced Caeser Cipher Algorithm, Bit Rotation and reversal Method : SJA Algorithm., International Journal of Modern Education and Computer Science, Somdip Dey, Joyshree Nath, Asoke Nath,(IJMECS), ISSN: 2075-0161 (Print), ISSN: 2075-017X (Online), Vol-4, No-5, Page 1-9,2012.

[11] An Advanced Combined Symmetric Key Cryptographic Method using Bit manipulation, Bit Reversal, Modified Caeser Cipher(SD-REE), DJSA method, TTJSA method: SJA-I Algorithm, Somdip dey, Joyshree Nath, Asoke Nath, International Journal of Computer Applications(IJCA 0975-8887, USA), Vol. 46, No.20, Page- 46-53,May, 2012.

[12] Ultra Encryption Standard(UES) Version-IV: New Symmetric Key Cryptosystem with bit-level columnar Transposition and Reshuffling of Bits, Satyaki Roy, Navajit Maitra, Joyshree Nath, Shalabh Agarwal, Asoke Nath, International Journal of Computer Applications, USA, Vol 51-No 1, Page 28-35(2012).

[13] Bit Level Encryption Standard(BLES): Version-I, Neeraj Khanna, Dripto Chatterjee, Joyshree Nath, Asoke Nath, International Journal of Computer Applications, USA, Vol 52-No 2, Page 41-46(2012).

[14] Bit Level Encryption Standard (BLES): Versiob-II, Gaurav Bhadra, Tanya Bala, Samik Banik, Joyshree Nath and Asoke Nath, Proceedings of IEEE International Conference WICT-2012 held at IIITM-K, Trivandrum Oct 30 to Nov 1, 2012, Page No. 121-127(2012).

[15] Bit Level Generalized Modified Vernam Cipher Method with Feedback, Prabal Banerjee, Asoke Nath, International Journal of Advanced Computer Research(ISSN(print):2249- 7277 ISSN(online): 2277-7970), Volume-2, Number-4 Issue-6, Page-24-30, Dec(2012).

[16] Cryptography and Network Security, William Stallings, Prectice Hall of India.

Energy Efficient Multi Level Authentication in Sensor Network

A. Shish Ahmad, B. Dr. Mohd. Rizwan Beg
CSE Department, Integral University, Lucknow, India

Abstract- *Sensor networks are deployed for various monitoring applications. The sensed data is reported to base station in multi hop fashion. The reporting should be in secure manner so that the adversary can't forge the data and can be prevented from any masquerade attack. Public key schemes are best suited for one-way authentication as compare to symmetric one, but consume more energy at sensor on applying them.*

We has proposed three level of authentication(MLA) using symmetric and asymmetric approaches. We have applied the algorithm in such a way that the total energy consumption in the process is minimized. We have identified those calculations which are not necessary to be performed on sensor node, shifted to base stations to save the energy at nodes. In this fashion, we are able to provide a complete security service including confidentiality, authentication, data integrity in the network and also extend the life time of sensor network. Our proposed approach is oriented for to those application areas where authentication is the primary concern.

Key Words-RC4, Stream Cipher, Block Cipher, Encryption and Decryption, Sensor network, Security, Authentication, DSS, Deffie-Hellman.

1. Introduction

Wireless sensor networks have become a promising future to many applications, such as smart houses, smart farms, smart parking, smart hospitals, habitat monitoring, building and structure monitoring, distributed robotics, industrial and manufacturing, and national security. In addition to common network threats, sensor networks are more vulnerable to security breaches because they are physically accessible by adversaries. Imagine the damage caused by compromised sensor network in sensitive military and hospital applications. These are often deployed in unattended environments, thus leaving these networks vulnerable to passive and active attacks by the adversary. The conversation between sensor nodes Can be eavesdropped by the adversary .The adversary can be aware of the conversation between the sensors and can forge the data. Sensor nodes should be resilient to these attacks. Since Sensor nodes are resource constrained and run on battery, energy consumption should be low to make it operate for many days.

Authentication & confidentiality is very much concern in battle-field scenarios, where fraudulent node impersonate as a legitimate sensor .Public key methods consist of power hungry function, so symmetric key approaches are preferred for applying confidentiality on sensors as compare to asymmetric one. But symmetric approaches do not give complete security services like authentication etc. Here we have applied public key approaches in such a way that total energy consumption decreases as compare to traditional one, as well as we are able to gain full security services.

Due to the small battery backup of Sensor Node, security algorithm must consume low power. Symmetric key are efficient for providing security services like confidentiality, but its is more Vulnerable and does not provide all the security services like authentication as provided by public key methods. Public key algorithm is less efficient than symmetric key algorithm because it consume more energy than symmetric key due to power function calculation to generate encoded data.

1.1 Our Contribution

In form of a security framework we make three level energy efficient authentication in securing sensor networks:

Energy efficient Digital signature standard (EEDSS) in such a way to mitigate the authentication related attacks.

Energy efficient Deffie-Hellman (EEDHA)/ Energy efficient Elleptic Curve cryptography (EEECC) in such a way to ensure the authentication and key distribution related issues.

Open feedback mode (OFB) using RC4 instead of DES for providing confidentiality and authentication both efficiently.

So here we are providing a complete security mechanism (authentication, confidentiality & Key distribution) with three level authentication. Here we are also saving the energy of sensor nodes by identifying & shifting those steps which are not necessary to be performed on sensor node to base station.

1.2 Implementation assumption

- Each Sensor Node has unique id assigned before deployement.
- Sensor nodes are homogeneous and Static.
- Constant power supply, i.e no change in capacitance, resistance and inductance in hardware
- It should be ensured that adversary cannot compromise Sensor Nodes immediately after nodes are deployed. He takes a few minutes of time to compromise them after they are deployed.
- Each Sensor node has a comparator also.
- 8051 microcontroller in sensor of XLAT=11.0592 MHz and 12 clock per machine cycle.
- Radio frequency module is constant. Transmission and receiving power is constant.

2. Energy Efficient Digital Signature standard- First Level Authentication

This is the first phase of authentication in sensor network. Here we are applying DSS approach in energy efficient way. We applied DSS in such a way that the total energy consumption at sensor node is decreases for producing the signature. Here we have identified and shifted those steps of Digital signature algorithm to the base station.

A digital signature is an authentication mechanism that enables the creator of a message to attach a code that acts as a signature. Typically the signature is formed by taking the hash of the message and encrypting the message with the creator's private key. The signature guarantees the source and integrity of the message.

The National Institute of Standards and Technology (NIST) has published Federal Information Processing Standard FIPS 186, known as the Digital Signature Standard (DSS). The DSS makes use of the Secure Hash Algorithm (SHA)

2.1 The DSS Approach

The DSS uses an algorithm that is designed to provide only the digital signature function. Unlike RSA, it cannot be used for encryption or key exchange. Nevertheless, it is a public-key technique.

In the RSA approach, the message to be signed is input to a hash function that produces a secure hash code of fixed length. This hash code is then encrypted using the sender's private key to form the signature. Both the message and the signature are then transmitted. The recipient takes the message and produces a hash code. The recipient also decrypts the signature using the sender's public key. If the calculated hash code matches the decrypted signature, the signature is accepted as valid. Because only the sender knows the private key, only the sender could have produced a valid signature.

The DSS approach also makes use of a hash function. The hash code is provided as input to a signature function along with a random number generated for this particular signature. The signature function also depends on the sender's private key (PRa) and a set of parameters known to a group of communicating principals. We can consider this set to constitute a global public key (PUG)The result is a signature consisting of two components, labeled s and r.

Following figure illustrate the DSS approach

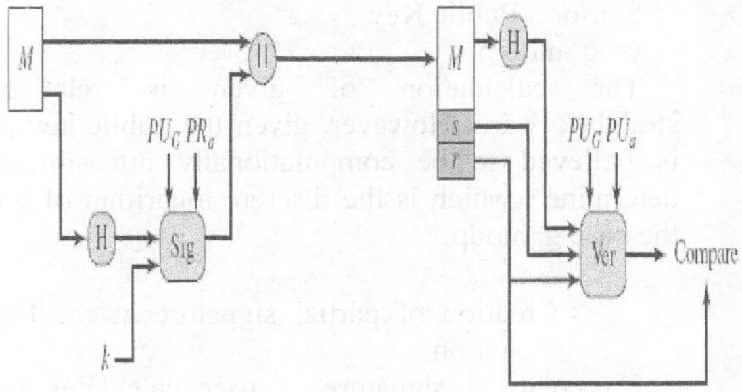

Figure 1: DSS Approach

At the receiving end, the hash code of the incoming message is generated. This plus the signature is input to a verification function. The verification function also depends on the global public key as well as the sender's public key (PUa) , which is paired with the sender's private key. The output of the verification function is a value that is equal to the signature component if the signature is valid. The signature function is such that only the sender, with knowledge of the private key, could have produced the valid signature.

2.2 Proposed method-

To provide the authentication in sensor network, we will use DSA as follows.

This is the first level authentication. Our method is elaborated in three phases. Following phases summarizes the proposed method

1) *Phase-1-* Before deployment of the sensors

Selection of Global Public-Key Components-

We choose three parameters at base station that are public and can be common to a group of sensor.

To choose these parameter a 160-bit prime number is chosen. Next, a prime number p is selected with a length between 512 and 1024 bits such that q divides (p - 1). Finally, g is chosen to be of the form h(p-1)/q mod p, where h is an integer between 1 and (p-1) and with the restriction that must be greater than 1 as follows.

p prime number where 2L _ 1 <p < 2L for 512 <= L <=1024 and L a multiple of 64; i.e., bit length of between 512 and 1024 bits in increments of 64 bits.

q prime divisor of (p _ 1), where 2159 <q< 2160; i.e., bit length of 160 bits.

g h(p _ 1)/q mod p, where h is any nteger with 1< h< (p _ 1) such that h(p _ 1)/q od p>1

- .Selection of private keys & generation of public keys

Next we choose different private keys for each sensor and calculate its corresponding public key and deploy pair of private & public to each sensor as follows.

- Sensor's Private Key

x random or pseudorandom integer with 0< x< q.

Sensor's Public Key

$y= g^x \bmod p$

The calculation of given is relatively straightforward. However, given the public key , it is believed to be computationally infeasible to determine , which is the discrete logarithm of y to the base g, modp.

- Creation of partial signature at the base station

To create a signature, a user calculates two quantities, r and s , that are functions of the public key components (p,q,g) , the user's private key (x), , and an additional integer k that should be generated randomly or pseudorandomly and be unique for each signing as follows.

Because in signing r is not depended on message, so we pre calculate the value of r and value of K-1and deploy it to the sensors before the deployment of the sensors with their public key.

. r= (gk mod p) mod q

Signature= (r, s)

Where k is random or pseudorandom integer with 0< k< q.

Deploy the signature value at the corresponding with their public key.

2) Phase-I1- Deployment of the sensors

After loading the signing function and public key, we deploy the sensors in random fashion.

3) Phase-II1- After deployment of the sensors

After deployment each sensor shares its public key to its neighbours.

After sensing the message and calculating the message hash H (M), the sensor calculate rest of signature part s as follows.

s = [K-1 (H(M) _ xr)] mod q

The sensor forward this message to its next hop with its signature.

The receiving senor verify the coming message by its signature as follows, and if its find legitimate then it forward this message with its own signature to next hop.

w= (s')-1 mod q

u1= [H(M')w] mod q

u2 =(r')w mod q

v = [(gu1 yu2) mod p] mod q

where v is the is a function of the public key components, the sender's public key, and the hash code of the incoming message

if v==r, message is accepted and forward it to next hop else reject the coming message.

2.3 Analysis and Result

Calculation of r &K-1at base station before deployement

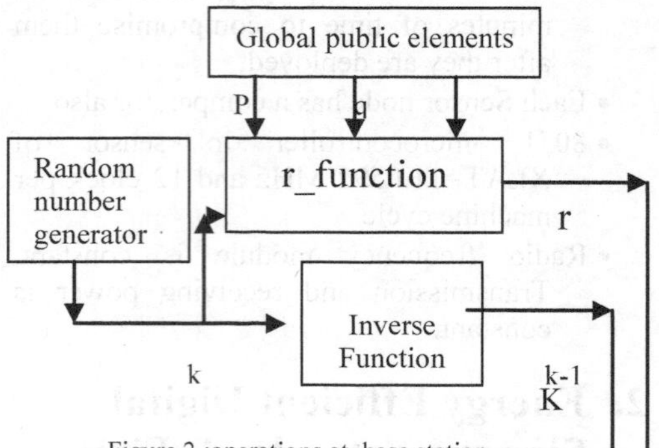

Figure 2 :operations at base station

r= r_function(k, p, q, g) = (gk mod p) mod q

Preparation of sign at sending senor after deployment

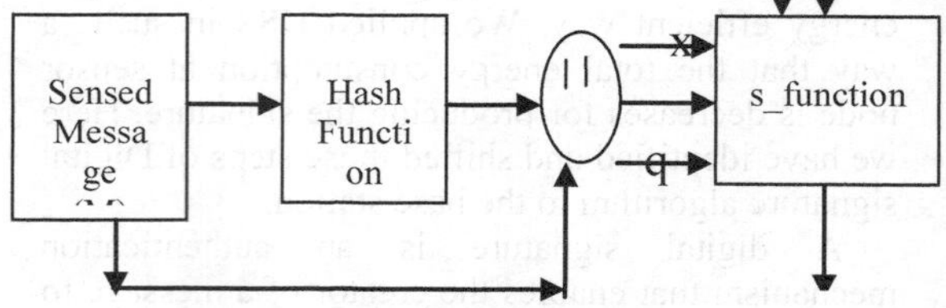

Figure 3:operations at sender end (sensor) S

s= s_functiom(H(M), k, x, r, q) = (k_1 (H(M) + xr))mod q

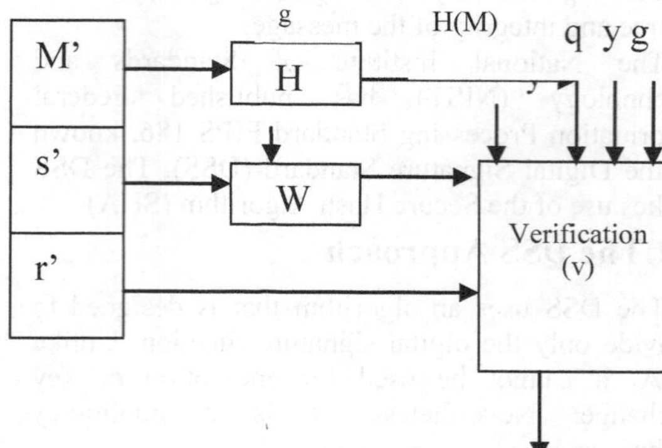

Figure 4:operations at receiver end (sensor/Base)

w=W(s', q) =s'_1 mod q

v=Verification(y, q, g, H(M'), w, r')

= ((g(H(M')w) mod q yr'w mod q) mod p) mod q

From the above figure 2, we can see that we save those energy of sensors by which are involved for the calculation of r & k-1by shifting these steps at the base station.

- Time taken for calculation of r =(12/11.0592) * number of machine cycle (13)* private keys of sensor
- Time taken for calculation of k-1= (12/11.0592) * number of machine cycle (16)*((k/10)+1)
- Total time saved (Tcpu)= Time taken for calculation of r + Time taken for calculation of k-1
- Total Energy saved (E) ≈ K1* Trfm + K2 * Tcpu_new

where Tcpu_new = time taken by the CPU at increased bit rate , Trfm = time taken by the transmission of data. K1 and K2 are the constant that depend on the current consumption of the RFM and CPU respectively at chosen frequency and transmission power.

Let private key is 255. Let value of k is also 255.

Total time Total time saved (Tcpu)= 3.597 +460.0694

So E ≈ Tcpu≈ 463.66614 μs/ per sensor=0.4636661ms/sensor.

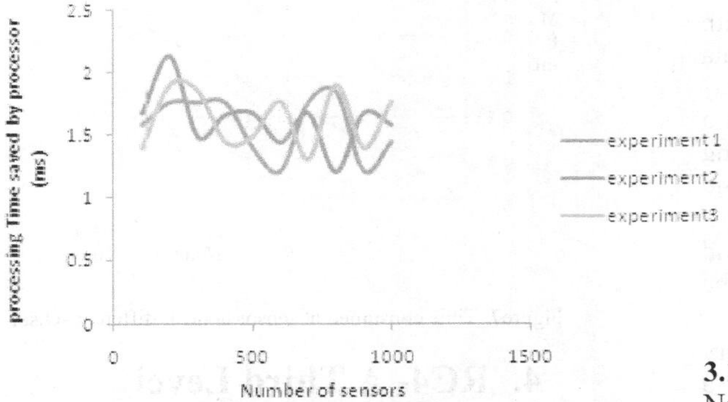

Figure 5: Time consumed at sensor node at different sensor

3. EEECC/EEDHA- Second Level Authentication

This is the second phase of authentication. We used Energy efficient ECC & Energy efficient DHA, to distribute the private & public key between sensor nodes. This technique is energy efficient because, we are identifying the steps which are not necessary to be performed at sensor node shifted to base station used for generation of symmetric keys between the node. We use that private & public key and generate symmetric key.

3.1 EEDHA Phases

3.1.1 Phase1: Before deployment of the Sensor Nodes using Deffie Hellman algorithm

- The Base Station select global elements q and α such that q should be a prime number not more than 1024 bits and α should be less than q and also be the primitive root of q or generator(base) of q.
- The base station select any private value X that should be less than q for every node differently and for itself also.
- The base station calculate public value for every station (including itself as node) Y by using following equation

Y=α^X mod .

Now we deployed every node with private and public values I,e, X and Y respectively with only public value q.

3.1.2 Phase 2*:* After deployment of each Sensor Nodes using Deffie Hellman algorithm

- Now every node of our static network broadcast their public value Y to its neighboring nodes with its id.
- Now every node calculate its secret key (that will be different for each pair) by using following equation.
  K=Y^X mod q
- Now every node has a secret key to exchange the message to each other with its id. This show confidentiality, data integrity and authentication to each other.
- Then as first message every node sends a HELLO packet to its neighbors containing its id and a nonce starting with 1 and encrypted with respective Key.
- Now the receiving node receives and decrypts the HELLO packet and store the Nonce with id.
- For any next message between them every packet contains the Nonce with a increment of one with the data so that the receiver can verify that the current data is not a duplicate one using comparator. So it can prevent the replay attack.

3.1.3 Phase 3*:* Addition of a new node in exiting Network using Deffie Hellman algorithm

- Now if a new Sensor Node is deploys to the exiting one with the same public values that is X, Y & q. It exchanges the public value Y and q to its neighbors.
- By using above method the neighbors generate the corresponding keys by selecting any random value X that should be less than q.

3.2 EEECC Phases

3.2.1 Phase1 Before deployment of the Sensor Nodes using ECC

- The Base Station select a large integer q, which is either prime number p or an integer of the form 2m and elliptic curve parameter a and b for following equation.

Y2 + xy = x3 + ax2 + b.

This defines the elliptic group of points Eq(a,b). The base station also picks a base point G from the above points whose order is a very large value n.

- The base station select private value n1,n2…..nN for sensor nodes 1,2….n respectively, which is less than n for every station and for itself also. These are the private keys for each of the sensor nodes and base station.

- The base station generates public keys for each of the sensor nodes and for itself by following equation.
  P = n * G
  Where n and P are the private and public values of the nods.

3.2.2 Phase After deployment of each Sensor Nodes using ECC

- Now every node of our static network broadcast their public value P to its neighboring nodes with its id.
- Now every node calculate its secret key (that will be different for each pair) by using following equation, let second node is the neighbor of the first node, so by using following equation 1 and 2 generate same key K(symmetric Key) at both the end.
  K=n1 * p2 (at node 1) and K= n2 * p1 (at node 2)
- Now every node has a secret key to exchange the message to each other with its id. This show confidentiality, data integrity and authentication to each other.
- Then as first message every node sends a HELLO packet to its neighbors containing its id and a nonce starting with 1 and encrypted with respective Key.
- Now the receiving node receives and decrypts the HELLO packet and store the Nonce with id.
- For any next message between them every packet contains the Nonce with a increment of one with the data so that the receiver can verify that the current data is not a duplicate one using comparator. So it can prevent the replay attack.

3.2.3 Phase 3: Addition of a new node in exiting Network using ECC

- Now if a new Sensor Node is deploys to the exiting one with the same values that is nR, PR and G It exchanges the public value PR and G to its neighbors.
- By using above method the neighbors generate the corresponding keys by using its previous value that is encrypted with its symmetric key.

3.3 Analysis & Result

So in the above phases, we found and shifted those steps of key/Cipher text generation to the base station, which is not necessarily required at sensor node, because public key method involve power function calculation, which is more power hungry, we minimizes this consumption by shifting it.

Following low level assembly code shows one of the power function calculation for Deffie-Hellman algorithm.After shifting one power function calculation to the base station.

Total energy saved _ (clock per machine cycle/ frequency of processor) * Total mac\hine cycle to calculate the power_function.

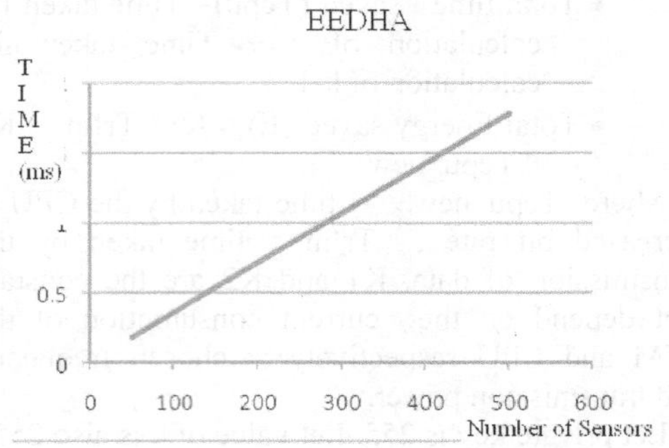

Figure6: Time consumed at sensor node at different sensor

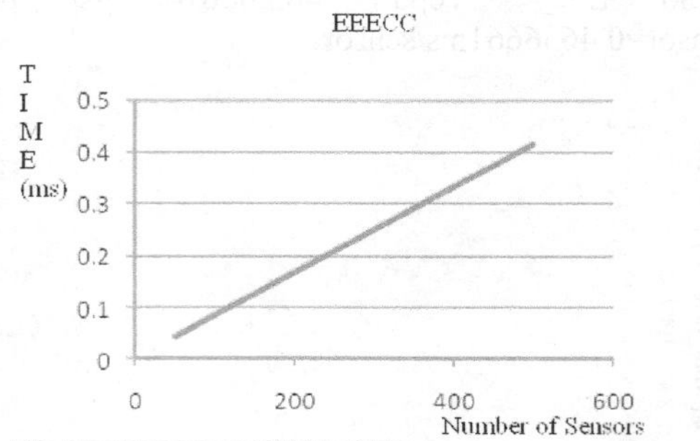

Figure7: Time consumed at sensor node at different sensor

4. RC4- A Third Level authentication

This is the third level of authentication, here the initialization vector act as authenticator. The key found from the second phase used as key for applying the confidentiality using RC4.

Its implementation is also very easy in Output feed back mode because output feedback mode is only supported stream cipher technique and consists of several simple machine operations, which makes the processing very fast. According to the journals , RC4 is 5 times faster than DES and 15 times faster than Triple-DES. Key size for the algorithm is very flexible, which ranges from 1 to 255 bytes (8 to 1024 bits). The bytes of the static memory used as an underlying key base changes after every byte processes. Secure Socket Layer / Transport Layer Security (SSL/ TLS) and Wired Equivalent Privacy (WEP) protocol use RC4. SSL/ TLS uses some other algorithms too. This cipher is mainly used to encrypt/ decrypt files and data in transit.

4.1 RC4 Security and Efficiency

RC4 should be considered secure if keys of length higher than 128 bits are used. In WEP, RC4 in combination with a particular method for generating its keys, was broken. The weakness is not of RC4 itself, but how it is used in WEP. RC4 is extremely efficient in software implementations, since only byte operations are used.

RC4 should be considered secure if keys of length higher than 128 bits are used. In WEP, RC4 in combination with a particular method for generating its keys, was broken. The weakness is not of RC4 itself, but how it is used in WEP. RC4 is extremely efficient in software implementations, since only byte operations are used.

RC4 falls short of the standards set by cryptographers for a secure cipher in several ways, and thus is not recommended for use in new applications.

Unlike a modern stream cipher (such as those in eSTREAM), RC4 does not take a separate nonce alongside the key. This means that if a single long-term key is to be used to securely encrypt multiple streams, the cryptosystem must specify how to combine the nonce and the long-term key to generate the stream key for RC4. One approach to addressing this is to generate a "fresh" RC4 key by hashing a long-term key with a nonce. However, many applications that use RC4 simply concatenate key and nonce; RC4's weak key schedule then gives rise to a variety of serious problems.

Many stream ciphers are based on linear feedback shift registers (LFSRs), which while efficient in hardware are less so in software. The design of RC4 avoids the use of LFSRs, and is ideal for software implementation, as it requires only byte manipulations. It uses 256 bytes of memory for the state array, S[0] through S[255], k bytes of memory for the key, key[0] through key[k-1], and integer variables, i, j, and k. Performing a modulus 256 can be done with a bitwise AND with 255 (or on most platforms, simple addition of bytes ignoring overflow)

4.2 Stream Cipher V/S Block Cipher

Stream ciphers are often used in applications where plaintext comes in quantities of unknowable length where as in Block ciphers the length of the plaintext is known .

In Stream Ciphers the encryption and decryption process is done bit by bit where as in Block Ciphers the encryption and decryption process is done on the block of data .

Stream Ciphers are more faster than Block Ciphers because in Stream Ciphers the encryption/decryption is performed bit by bit while in Block Ciphers the encryption/decryption is performed on the block of data .

Block ciphers must be used in ciphertext stealing or residual block termination mode to avoid padding, while stream ciphers eliminate this issue by naturally operating on the smallest unit that can be transmitted (usually bytes).

Stream ciphers are often used in applications where plaintext comes in quantities of unknowable length—for example, a secure wireless connection. If a block cipher were to be used in this type of application, the designer would need to choose either transmission efficiency or implementation complexity, since block ciphers cannot directly work on blocks shorter than their block size.

In cryptography, a stream cipher is a symmetric key cipher where plaintext bits are combined with a pseudorandom cipher bit stream (keystream), typically by an exclusive-or (XOR) operation . In cryptography, a block cipher is a symmetric key cipher which operates on fixed-length groups of bits, termed blocks, with an unvarying transformation .

4.2 Encryption And Decryption Of Rc4

4.2.1 Encryption

The encryption in RC4 is done with the help of two algorithms shown below-

The key-scheduling algorithm (KSA): The key-scheduling algorithm is used to initialize the permutation in the array "S". "keylength" is defined as the number of bytes in the key and can be in the range $1 \leq$ keylength ≤ 256, typically between 5 and 16, corresponding to a key length of 40 – 128 bits. First, the array "S" is initialized to the identity permutation. S is then processed for 256 iterations in a similar way to the main PRGA algorithm, but also mixes in bytes of the key at the same time.

The pseudo-random generation algorithm (PRGA): The lookup level of RC4. The output byte is selected by looking up the values of S(i) and S(j), adding them together modulo 256, and then looking up the sum in S; S(S(i) + S(j)) is used as a byte of the key stream, K. For many iterations as are needed, the PRGA modifies the state and outputs a byte of the key stream. In each iteration, the PRGA increments i, adds the value of S pointed to by i to j, exchanges the values of S[i] and S[j], and then outputs the value of S at the location S[i] + S[j] (modulo 256). Each value of S is swapped at least once in every 256 iterations

4.2.2 Decryption

It is reverse of encryption process i.e., in this the k which we get in the key generation process is XOR with the cipher text which we get from encryption process. So the equation is as follows-

P.T = (k XOR C.T)

Where P.T = Plain Text
C.T = Cipher Text
k = Key

4.3 Output Feedback Mode

The output feedback(OFB) mode has advantages over cipher feed-back mode, because in encryption process it encrypt the data in stream mode.

The output feedback (OFB) mode makes a block cipher into a synchronous stream cipher: it generates keystream blocks, which are then XORed with the plaintext blocks to get the ciphertext. Just as with other stream ciphers, flipping a bit in the ciphertext produces a flipped bit in the plaintext at the same location. This property allows many error correcting codes to function normally even when applied before encryption.

Following is the systematic diagram of output feedback mode operation. Because of the symmetry of the XOR operation, encryption and decryption are exactly the same:

Following is the proposed diagram of OFB mode using RC4 as stream cipher encryption. In this technique we encrypt data bit by bit or character by character to increase the encryption speed. Here the initialization vector can be used as a key for providing the authentication.

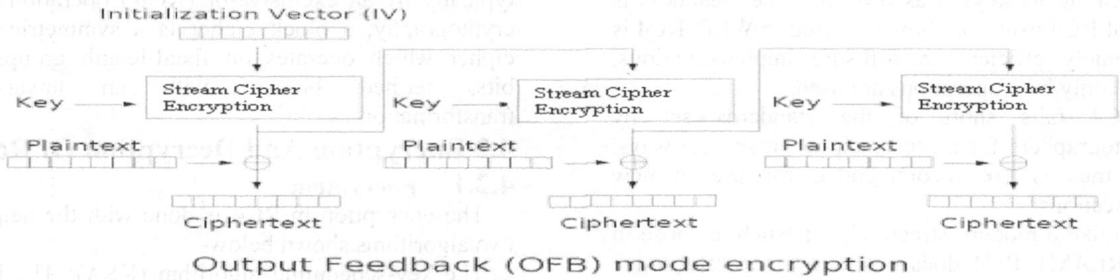

Figure 8: OFB

Each output feedback block cipher operation depends on all previous ones, and so cannot be performed in parallel. However, because the plaintext or cipher text is only used for the final XOR, the block cipher operations may be performed in advance, allowing the final step to be performed in parallel once the plaintext or cipher text is available. It is possible to obtain an OFB mode key stream by using CBC mode with a constant string of zeroes as input. This can be useful, because it allows the usage of fast hardware implementations of CBC mode for OFB mode encryption.

Using OFB mode with limited feedback like CFB mode reduces the average cycle length by a factor of 232 or more. A mathematical model proposed by Davies and Parkin and substantiated by experimental results showed that only with full feedback an average cycle length near to the obtainable maximum can be achieved. For this reason, support for limited feedback was removed from the specification of OFB.

4.4 Analysis of OFB

The first advantage of using OFB method is tha5 bit errors in transmission do not propagate. For example, if a bit error occurs in C1 , only the recovered value of P1 is affected; subsequent plaintext units are not corrupted. With CFB, C1 also serves as input to the shift register and therefore causes additional corruption downstream.

The second advantage of using OFB method is the use of Initialization vector (IV) as authentication key using MAC as authenticator .We can also use IV to prevent replay attack, because at each iteration we shift the IV left, so cable to behave as a nonce each time to denote that this current message is a fresh message.

The third advantage of using OFB is that we can encrypt the message using stream Cipher technique and that will increase the encryption and decryption time, so the energy consumption will decrease.

The fourth advantage is that no padding is required at the end of data to complete the block, so overhead decreases.

4.5 Result And Analysis

We have proposed that if we use RC4 (a stream cipher technique) instead of DES (i.e; block cipher technique) in output feed back mode the total time for encryption and decryption will reduce at sensor node.

To prove the above method, following graph shows the time taken for encryption/Decryption using RC4 as stream cipher and Hill Cipher as a block.

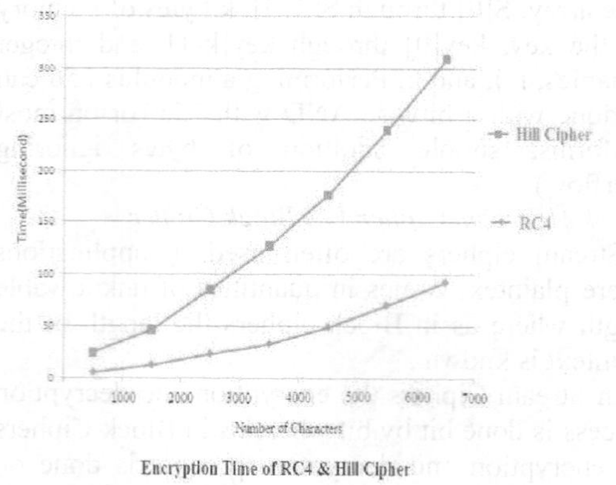

Figure 9: Comparision between stream & Block cipher

Here we observed that the time taken for stream cipher is much less than block cipher.

As per above discussion it seems that encryption as well as decryption speed in stream cipher is more than block cipher. Also in CFB and OFB block cipher modes of operation is much faster than CBC mode.

As well as no bit padding is require in stream cipher for encryption, but in block cipher we add extra bit to complete the block for encryption.

Using CFB or OFB using we get more security services at sensor node i.e. Confidentiality, authentication, data integrity and freshness of the message.

So in future we can use block cipher encryption techniques in such a way that it can consume less time and less power as stream cipher.

5. Conclusion And Future Work

Multi level authentication(MLA) assures there is no impersonation in the network and secure our network from intruder nodes strongly. This application is preferred in those areas where the higher level of authentication is required like battlefield scenarios and in defence application where authentication matters.

Appling multilevel authentication total energy consumption is increased slightly as the result shows(in terms of processor time).

Using above techniques we are getting, a number of security services like authentication, confidentiality, data integrity, non-repudiation, etc. With complete security solutions, we are also minimizing routing overhead, because the intermediate node will reject the messages to move forward generated from a false node.

So by using MLA we are getting complete security services at a cost of sightly increased energy.

6. REFERENCES:

[1] P. Ekdahl, T. Johansson. "A new version ot the stream cipher SNOW", available from http://www.it.lth.se/cryptology/snow/, 2002.

[2] Stinson, D. Cryptography: Theory and Practice. Boca Raton,FL: Press,2002

[3] Rescorla, E. SSL and TLS: Designing and Building Secure system, Reading , MA : addition-Welsey, 2001.

[4] Knudsen. L., et al. "Analysis method for alledged RC4." Proceedings, ASIACRYPT '98, 1998.

[5] Mister, S.; and Tavares, S. "Cryptography of RC4 like Cipher." Proceeding, workshop in selected areas of cryptography, SAC 1998.

[6] Fluhrer, S. and McGrew, D. "Statistical analysis of the alleged RC4 key stream Generator. " Proceeding, Fast software encryption 2000.

[7] Whitfield Diffie, Paul C. van Oorschot, Michael J. Wiener "Authentication and Authenticated Key Exchanges" Designs, Codes and Cryptography, 2, 107-125 (1992),

[8] Akl, S. "Digital signature: A Tutorial Survey", Computer, 1983.

[9] W. Du, R. Wang, and P. Ning "An Efficient Scheme for Authenticating Public Keys in Sensor Networks," In Proc. MobiHoc'05, pp.58-67, May 25-28, 2005.

[10] National Institure of Standards and Technology: Proposed Federal Information Processing Standard for Digital Signature Standard (DSS). Federal Register, vol.56, no. 169, pp. 42980C42982 (1991)

[11] Mantin, I., Shamir, A. "A practical attack on broadcast RC4." Proceeding, Fast software encryption 2001.

[12] M. D. Galanis, P. Kitsos, G. Kostopoulos, O. Koufopavlou, Comparison of the Performanceof Stream Ciphers for Wireless Communications, proceedings of CCCT'04, Austin, Texas, USA,August 14-17, 2004.

[13] Blake, I.; Seroussi, G.; and smart, N. Elliptic Curves in Cryptography. Cambridge; Cambridge University Press, 1999.

[14] L. Batina, J. Lano, N. Mentens, B. Preneel, I. Verbauwhede, S. B. Ä Ors, Energy, Performance,Area versus Security Trade-o®s for Stream Ciphers, in ECRYPT Workshop, SASC - The State of the Art of Stream Ciphers, pp. 302-310, 2004.

[15] A. Perrig, et al., "SPINS: Security protocols for sensor network," Wireless Networks, vol. 8, no. 5, Sept. 2002, pp. 521-534.

[16] D. W. Davies and G. I. P. Parkin. The average cycle size of the key stream in output feedback encipherment. In Advances in Cryptology, Proceedings of CRYPTO 82, pages 263–282, 1982.

[17] Virgil D. Gligor, Pompiliu Donescu, "Fast Encryption and Authentication: XCBC Encryption and XECB Authentication Modes". Proc. Fast Software Encryption, 2001: 92-108

[18] Charanjit S. Jutla, "Encryption Modes with Almost Free Message Integrity", Proc. Eurocrypt 2001, LNCS 2045, May 2001.

[19] Chungen, Yanhong Ge, "The Public Key Encryption to Improve the Security on Wireless Sensor Networks" 2009 Second International Conference on Information and Computing Science,978-0-7695-3634-7/09 $25.00 © 2009 IEEE,DOI 10.1109/ICIC.2009.

[20] Willliam Stallings " Cryptography and Network Security" Principles and Practice" fifth Edition.

[21] SHISH AHMAD, RIZWAN .BEG, S.Q. ABBASS. 2010.Energy Efficient Sensor Network Security Using Stream Cipher Mode of Operation. IEEE ICCCT -2010.

[22] SHISH AHMAD, RIZWAN BEG, S.Q. ABBASS. 2010. Energy Saving Secure framework for Sensor Network using Elliptic Curve Cryptography. IJCA Special issue on MANTES.

Energy Efficient Encryption using Counter mode of operation in Wireless Sensor Network

A. Shish Ahmad, B. Dr. Mohd. Rizwan Beg
CSE Department, Integral University, Lucknow, India

Abstract- *Sensor networks are deployed for various monitoring applications. The reporting should be in secure manner so that the adversary can't forge the data and can be prevented from any disclosure. In this paper we have identified those calculations which are not necessary to be performed on sensor node for securing the network, shifted to base stations to save the energy at nodes. Using pre-processing approach saves energy consumption at nodes for producing Secured/ Encrypted data. So here we are proposing EEECMO method Energy Efficient Encryption using Counter mode of operation in such a way that before the deployment, the base station process the part of the security algorithm that involve the key in the setup phase. In this fashion, we are getting secure communication network without the distribution of the key among the sensor nodes and also minimizes energy consumption at sensor node.*

Key Words- Sensor network, Security, confidentiality, Block Cipher, Encryption and Decryption, , Counter mode, pre-processing, Stream Cipher.

1. Introduction

Wireless sensor networks have become a promising future to many applications, such as smart houses, smart farms, smart parking, smart hospitals, habitat monitoring, building and structure monitoring, distributed robotics, industrial and manufacturing, and national security. In addition to common network threats, sensor networks are more vulnerable to security breaches because they are physically accessible by adversaries. Imagine the damage caused by compromised sensor network in sensitive military and hospital applications. These are often deployed in unattended environments, thus leaving these networks vulnerable to passive and active attacks by the adversary. The conversation between sensor nodes Can be eavesdropped by the adversary .The adversary can be aware of the conversation between the sensors and can forge the data. Sensor nodes should be resilient to these attacks. Since Sensor nodes are resource constrained and run on battery, energy consumption should be low to make it operate for many days.

Confidentiality is very much concern in battle-field scenarios, where fraudulent node impersonate as a legitimate sensor.

Security in ad hoc networks is an essential component for basic network functions like packet forwarding and routing and network operation can be easily jeopardized if countermeasures are not embedded into the basic network functions at the early stages of their design. The disclosure threat involves the leakage of Security information from the system to a party that should not have seen the information and is a threat against the confidentiality of the information.

Data confidentiality is a core security primitive for ad hoc networks. It ensures that the message cannot be understood by anyone other than the authorized personnel. With wireless communication, anyone can sniff the messages going through the air, and without proper encryption all the information is easily available. Due to the small battery backup of Sensor Node, security algorithm must consume low power. Symmetric key are efficient for providing security services like confidentiality.

Security Solutions should minimize the amount of computation and communication required to ensure the security services to accommodate the limited energy and computational resources of mobile, ad hoc-enabled devices.

Generally DES algorithm is a basic building block for providing data security. To apply DES in a variety of applications, four ``"modes of operations have been defined. These four modes are intended to cover virtually all the possible applications of encryptions of encryption for which DES could be used.

Here we are proposing Energy Efficient Encryption using Counter mode of operation (EEECMO) using DES algorithm for providing confidentiality in such a way that total energy consumption decreases at Sensor node. Using the property of property of pre-processing in CTR, we pre-process those steps which is not necessary to be performed at sensor node to base station.

The Proposed method uses the key at the base station only to produce the credential that play role to encrypt the sensed data at Sensor nodes/sensor aggregator, so there is no need to distribute the key in sensor network. It saves a lot of problem arises to distribute the key as well as saves energy to distribute the key.

2. Counter MODE (CTR)

Although interest in the counter (CTR) mode has increased recently with applications to ATM (asynchronous transfer mode) network security and IP sec (IP security) .A counter equal to the plaintext block size is used. The only requirement stated in SP 800-38A is that the counter value must be different for each plaintext block that is encrypted. Typically, the counter is initialized to some value and then incremented by 1 for each subsequent block (modulo 2^b, where b is the block size). For encryption, the counter is encrypted and then XORed with the plaintext block to produce the cipher text block; there is no chaining. For decryption, the same sequence of counter values is used, with each encrypted counter XORed with a ciphertext block to recover the corresponding plaintext block. Thus, the initial counter value must be made available for decryption. Given a sequence of counters T1, T2, Á , TN, we can define CTR mode as follows.

- Encryption

$$C_j=P_j \oplus E(K,T_j) \quad j=1,2......N-1.$$
$$C_N=P_N \oplus MSB_u\,[E(K,T_N)]$$

- Decryption

$$P_j=C_j \oplus E(K,T_j) \quad j=1,2......N-1.$$
$$P_N=C_N \oplus MSB_u\,[E(K,T_N)]$$

For the last plaintext block, which may be a partial block of bits, the most significant bits of the last output block are used for the XOR operation; the remaining b-u bits are discarded. Unlike the ECB, CBC, and CFB modes, we do not need to use padding because of the structure of the CTR mode.

As with the OFB mode, the initial counter value must be a nonce; that is T_1, must be different for all of the messages encrypted using the same key. Further, all Ti values across all messages must be unique. If, contrary to this requirement, a counter value is used multiple times, then the confidentiality of all of the plaintext blocks corresponding to that counter value may be compromised. In particular, if any plaintext block that is encrypted using a given counter value is known, then the output of the encryption function can be determined easily from the associated ciphertext block. This output allows any other plaintext blocks that are encrypted using the same counter value to be easily recovered from their associated ciphertext blocks.

One way to ensure the uniqueness of counter values is to continue to increment the counter value by 1 across messages. That is, the first counter value of the each message is one more than the last counter value of the preceding message.

Following are advantages of CTR mode.

A. **Hardware efficiency**: Unlike the three chaining modes, encryption (or decryption) in CTR mode can be done in parallel on multiple blocks of plaintext or cipher text. For the chaining modes, the algorithm must complete the computation on one block before beginning on the next block. This limits the maximum throughput of the algorithm to the reciprocal of the time for one execution of block encryption or decryption. In CTR mode, the throughput is only limited by the amount of parallelism that is achieved.

B. **Software efficiency:** Similarly, because of the opportunities for parallel execution in CTR mode, processors that support parallel features, such as aggressive pipelining, multiple instruction dispatch per clock cycle, a large number of registers, and SIMD instructions, can be effectively utilized.

C. **Pre-processing**: The execution of the underlying encryption algorithm does not depend on input of the plaintext or cipher text. Therefore, if sufficient memory is available and security is maintained, preprocessing can be used to prepare the output of the encryption boxes that feed into the XOR functions. When the plaintext or ciphertext input is presented, then the only computation is a series of XORs. Such a strategy greatly enhances throughput.

D. **Random access:** The ith block of plaintext or ciphertext can be processed in random-access fashion. With the chaining modes, block cannot be computed until the i-1 prior block are computed. There may be applications in which a ciphertext is stored and it is desired to decrypt just one block; for such applications, the random access feature is attractive.

E. **Provable security**: It can be shown that CTR is at least as secure as the other modes.

F. **Simplicity**: Unlike ECB and CBC modes, CTR mode requires only the implementation of the encryption algorithm and not the decryption algorithm. This matters most when the decryption algorithm differs substantially from the encryption algorithm, as it does for AES. In addition, the decryption key scheduling need not be implemented.

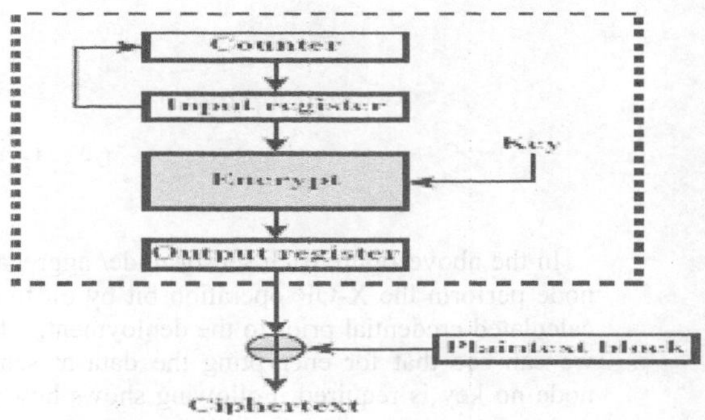

FIGURE 1: OPERATION OF CTR

3. PROPOSED METHOD

Our proposed method is Energy Efficient Encryption using Counter mode of operation

(EEECMO) for securing Sensor network is divided into 3-Phases.

3.1 Phase 1-:

This is the setup phase performed at base station before the deployment of the sensor node.
We choose the incremental Counter of 64-bit and keys k1,k2......Kn, Where n is the number of sensor nodes. Apply the DES encryption as follows, as shift register and select s-bits depend on the size of sensed data to be encrypted.

Here we are using different keys to produce the credential at different respective nodes, that play role to produce the cipher text at nodes after deployment.
The shift register value (after selecting s- bits) store at each node and deploy it randomly.

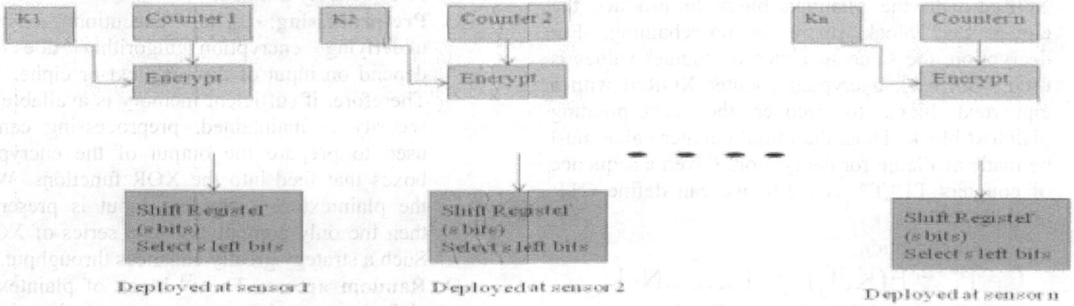

Fig 2: Operation Performed at base station

3.2 Phase 2-:

This starts after the deployment of the senor nodes. Using End to End encryption the sensor encrypt the sensed data with the help of the

Credential loaded previously in setup phase as follows.

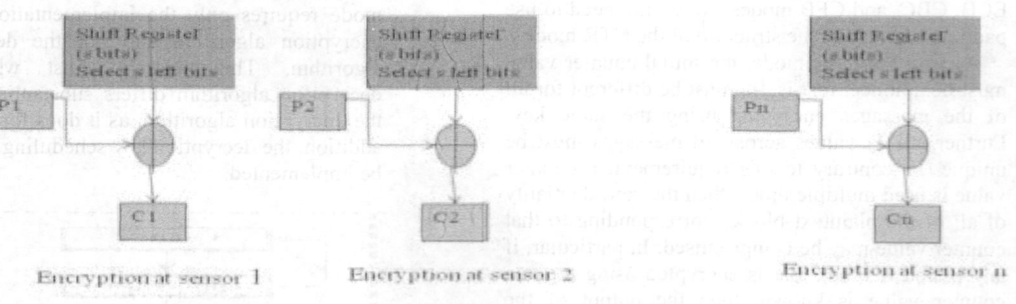

Figure 3: Operation Performed at sensor nodes

In the above figure each sensor node/ aggregator node perform the X-OR operation bit by bit to the calculated credential prior to the deployment. Here we can see that for encrypting the data at sensor node no key is required. Following shows how the cipher text calculated.

$C_j = P_j \oplus MSB_s(E_{Ki}(\text{Counter (address)}_j))$ where j = 1….. N

After calculating the cipher text each node send that encrypted data to base station. After receiving the encrypted data from each node/ aggregator the base station perform the third phase of EEECMO.

3.3 Phase 3- After receiving the encrypted data from the network, the base station starts the decryption as follows. The Decrypted data is found as follows

Pj = Cj MSBs(E Ki (Counter (address)j) where j = 1….. N

The plaintext is calculated by X-ORing the coming Cipher text with the shifted s-bits found by apply DES encryption with the same key on incremental counter.

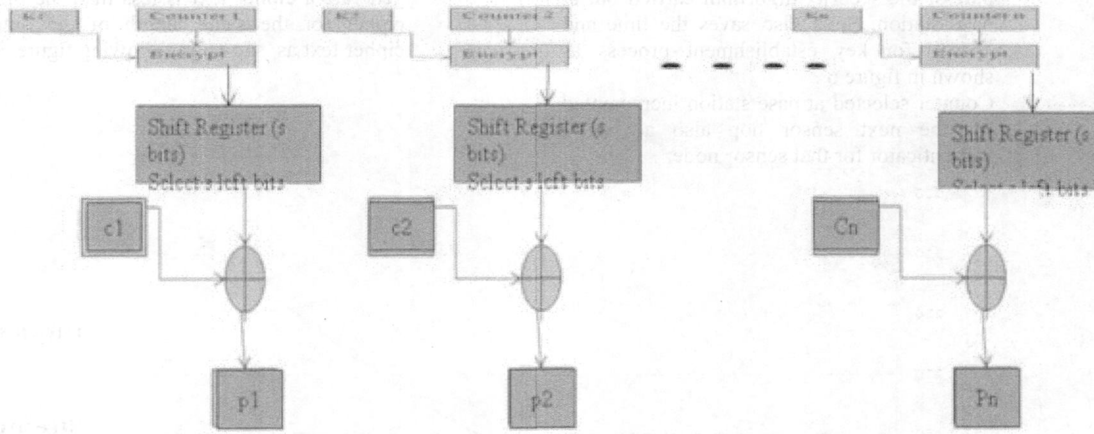

Figure 4: Operation Performed at base Station

4. RESULT AND ANALYSIS

Keys Plays its role in the first phase i.e. is the setup phase in which we apply the DES encryption using different keys at base station only. After encryption we are choosing only s-bits from 64-bit credential. The s-bit block size depends on the size of data send by the sensor aggregator/ sensor node to the base station after deployment. The key does not participate in second phase of encryption process, so there is no need of key establishment in network.

Secondly because the encryption in first phase does not depend on the message, so we can pre-process that part on base station only.

Another advantage of using only s-bits is to perform stream encryption (may be a character of 8-bit) instead of block cipher technique. So instead of using block cipher technique like DES, we can choose any stream cipher technique like RC4. Following are the advantages of using stream cipher over block cipher.

1. Stream ciphers are often used in applications where plaintext comes in quantities of unknowable length where as in Block ciphers the length of the plaintext is known.
2. In Stream Ciphers the encryption and decryption process is done bit by bit where as in Block Ciphers the encryption and decryption process is done on the block of data .
3. Stream Ciphers are more faster than Block Ciphers because in Stream Ciphers the encryption/decryption is performed bit by bit while in Block Ciphers the encryption/decryption is performed on the block of data .
4. Block ciphers must be used in ciphertext stealing or residual block termination mode to avoid padding, while stream ciphers eliminate this issue by naturally operating on the smallest unit that can be transmitted (usually bytes).
5. Stream ciphers are often used in applications where plaintext comes in quantities of unknowable length—for example, a secure wireless connection.
6. If a block cipher were to be used in this type of application, the designer would need to choose either transmission efficiency or implementation complexity, since block ciphers cannot directly work on blocks shorter than their block size.
7. In cryptography, a stream cipher is a symmetric key cipher where plaintext bits are combined with a pseudorandom cipher bit stream (key stream), typically by an exclusive-or (XOR) operation. In cryptography, a block cipher is a symmetric key cipher which operates on fixed-length groups of bits, termed blocks, with an unvarying transformation.

So instead of apply DES for encryption, we can go for stream cipher algorithm for encryption like RC4,.

So following are advantages of using EEECMO.

1. The Throughput, hardware & software efficiency of overall network system will increase due to the pre-processing of security algorithm.

2. Energy consumption at sensor node decreases, because of pre-processing of the part of the security algorithm carried out at base station. So it also saves the time and energy for key establishment process as shown in figure 6 .
3. Counter selected at base station incremented for the next sensor hop also act as a authenticator for that sensor node.
4. Stream cipher is faster than block cipher. Also the computation time it takes to generate a cipher text is less than the block cipher for the same length of the output cipher text as shown in following figure 5.

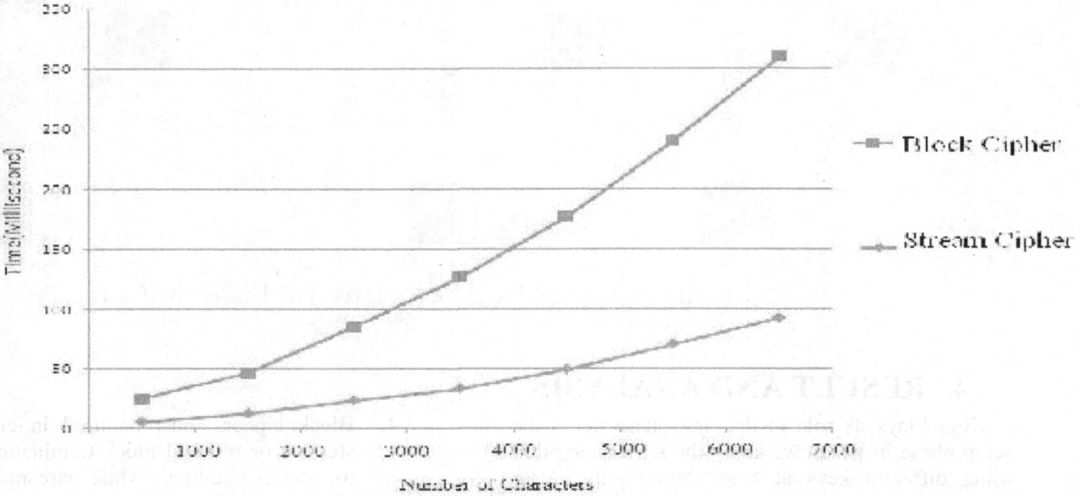

Figure 5: Encryption time of stream & Block cipher

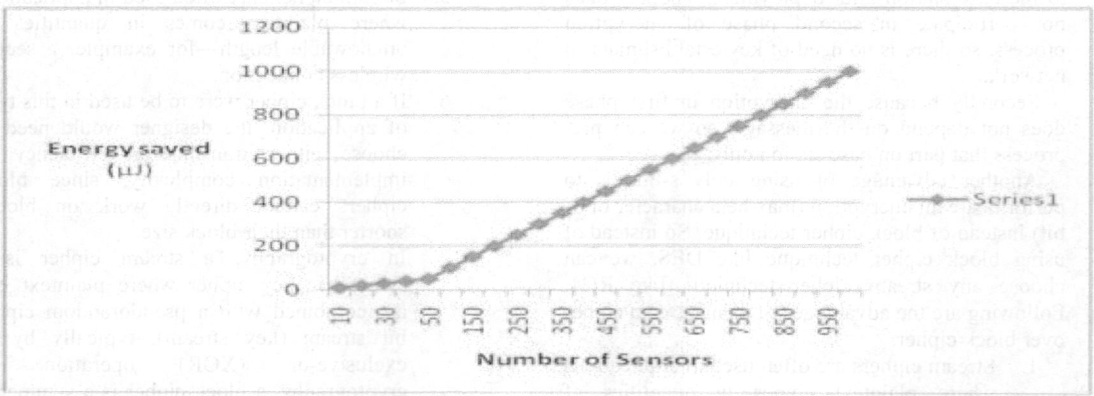

Figure 6: Energy saved in µJ with varied number of nodes

Figure 5 shows that the computation time for stream cipher is less than the block cipher, so selecting s-bits in shift register motivate us to use stream cipher encryption instead of block cipher. Figure 6 shows that the pre-processing approach used in counter mode of operation saves energy at sensor nodes. Figure indicates that as the network energy will be saved more by network if we increase number of nodes.

5. Conclusion

Using counter mode increases the hardware and software efficiency. Also due to the pre-processing we can save the energy by saving the computation cost of security algorithm at node.

The Throughput of overall network system increases due to the pre-processing of security algorithm. As the key does not participate to produce the cipher text at sensor node, because the requirement of the key does not depend on the]message, so here we are saving the effort, time and computation cost for distributing the key.

Also using counter mode we can go for the stream cipher approach instead of block cipher which also minimizes the computation cost.

So due to limited computational capabilities and limited battery power we can go for those approaches where part of the security algorithm can be computed at base instead of sensor node to minimize the energy consumption.

Also if the part of security algorithm does not depended on key at sensor node i.e. not depended on message, no distribution of key is required in network.

Stream cipher algorithms can more preferred because of compatibility to the sensors.

6. REFERENCES

[1] David Carman, Daniel Coffin, Bruno Dutertre, Vipin Swarup, Ronald Watro" **Forum Session: Security for Wireless Sensor Networks",** Proceedings of the 19th Annual Computer Security Applications Conference (ACSAC 2003), 1063-9527/03 $17.00 © 2003 IEEE .

[2] P. Ekdahl, T. Johansson. A new version ot the stream cipher SNOW, available from http://www.it.lth.se/cryptology/snow/, 2002.

[3] Shish Ahmad, Rizwan beg, Qamar Abbas, Jameel Ahmad " Comparative study between stream cipher and block cipher using RC4 and Hill cipher". IJFCA 2010.

[4] Shish Ahmad, Dr. Mohd. Rizwan Beg"Comparative Study between Stream Cipher and Block Cipher using RC4 and Hill Cipher", **International Journal of Computer Applications**.URI:http://www.ijcaonline.org/archives/number25/465 -770,2010

[5] Dr. Mohd. Rizwan Beg, Shish Ahmad"Energy Efficient Sensor Network Security Using Stream Cipher Mode of Operation" in proceedings of **IEEE International Conference on Computer** and Communication Technology 2010 Available online ieeeexplore.org

[6] Niels Ferguson, Bruce Schneier, Tadayoshi Kohno, Cryptography Engineering, page 71, 2010.

[7] Alfred J. Menezes, Paul C. van Oorschot and Scott A. Vanstone (1996). Handbook of Applied Cryptography. CRC Press. ISBN 0-8493-8523-7.

[8] "Block Cipher Modes". NIST Computer Security Resource Center.

[9] A. Biryukov, A. Shamir, D. Wagner , Real Time Cryptanalysis of A5/1 on a PC, Proceedings of the Fast Software Encryption Workshop 2000, Springer-Verlag, Lecture Notes in Computer Science, 2000.

[10] H. Lipmaa, P. Rogaway, D. Wagner, Counter Mode Encryption, Proposal for the NIST Modes of Operation Workshop, http://csrc.nist.gov/encryption/modes/proposedmodes/ctr/ctr-spec.pdf.

[11] A. Biryukov and A. Shamir, Cryptanalytic Time/Memory/Data Tradeoffs for Stream Ciphers, The Proceedings of ASIACRYPT 2000, Springer-Verlag, 2000, pp. 1-13. Available online at http://www.wisdom.weizmann.ac.il/~albi/publications.html.

[12] P. Rogaway and D. Coppersmith, A software-optimized encryption algorithm, Journal of Cryptology, vol. 11, num. 4, pp. 273-287, 1998. Earlier version in Proceedings of the Fast Software Encryption Workshop, Lecture Notes in Computer Science, Vol. 809, R. Anderson, ed., SpringerVerlag, 1993.

[13]] M. Blaze, W. Diffie, R. Rivest, B. Schneier, T. Shimomura, E. Thompson, and M. Weiner, Minimal Key Lengths for Symmetric Ciphers to Provide Adequate Commercial Security, January 1996. Online athttp://www.counterpane.com/keylength. html.

[14] David A. McGrew, Cisco Systems, Inc." Counter Mode Security: Analysis and Recommendations" available at http://cr.yp.to/bib/2002/mcgrew.pdf.

[15] Willliam Stallings " Cryptography and Network Security" Principles and Practice" fifth Edition.

[16] Diffie,W., and Hellman, M. "Privacy and Authentication: An Introduction to Cryptography." Proceedings of the IEEE,March 1979.

Advanced Symmetric Key Cryptosystem using Bit and Byte Level Encryption Methods with Feedback

A. Prabal Banerjee[1] and B. Asoke Nath[2]
[1,2] Department of Computer Science, St. Xavier's College (Autonomous), Kolkata, India
[1]mail.prabal@gmail.com, [2]asokejoy1@gmail.com

Abstract - *In the present paper the authors have introduced a new symmetric key cryptographic method where the authors have applied bit level and byte level generalized modified vernam cipher method followed by bit-wise transposition method. Nath et al already developed method which was a combination of generalized bit level and byte level encryption methods. In the present method the authors have added one more encryption method that is bit-wise columnar transposition method. Nath et al also developed bit level encryption standard(BLES) Ver-I and Ver-II where they have used extensive bit level permutation, bit exchange, bit xor and bit shift encryption method. In the present study the authors have used both bit level generalized vernam cipher method and after that byte level vernam cipher method using feedback and finally the output is passed through bit-wise columnar transposition method to make the whole system more secured. The introduction of feedback in both bit level as well as byte level vernam cipher method prevents from standard attacks such as differential attack or known plain text attack. In the present paper the authors have used random key generator to construct the keypad for vernam cipher method. The present method will be most effective for encrypting short message, password, any confidential key etc.*

Keywords: BLES, bit-wise columnar transposition, differential attack, vernam cipher method

1 Introduction

In Internet when a person sends some confidential data from one computer to another computer then there is no guarantee that the confidential message can not be intercepted by any unwanted intruder. This is because the internet is now so open that any body can access any information and sometimes he/she can divert/forward to anyone also. So the security of data is now has a big question mark. Any kind of private data should not be sent in raw form from one computer to another. The private/confidential data must be encrypted first and then it should be sent over the internet. In the modern days e-mail is one most important method to send data from one machine to another or from one person to another person. But the question is how secured is this method. The hackers have made many packages and they have uploaded in various websites to break any password. So it is not at all a difficult task to break any password of any e-mail especially if it is very weak password. Once the password is hacked then anything can be done from that e-mail. So the e-mail must not contain any confidential information in raw form. The hackers are always try hack the password of e-mail. Anytime the disaster may come. So if the data is confidential/private then it must be encrypted first with some good encryption method and then it can be sent to someone. The security or the originality of data has now become a very important issue in data communication network. It is now a common practice in any academic institution to send marks, attendance or question papers, bank statement over e-mail. But this method is not fully secured as anybody can intercept the data from internet and misuse it. It is not at all difficult task for a hacker to intercept an e-mail and retrieve the confidential data especially if it is not encrypted. It must be ensured that in any kind of e-business, air or railway reservation system or in credit card or debit card system the data should not be tampered or intercepted by an unauthorized person. The disaster may happen in any corporate sector, business house when the data is sent from one computer to other computer in an unprotected manner. To overcome this problem one has to send the encrypted text or cipher text from client to server or to another client instead of sending in unencrypted form. To protect data from intruder or hacker now network security and cryptography is an emerging research area where the programmers are trying to develop some strong encryption algorithm so that no intruder can intercept the encrypted message. The cryptography methods can be divided into two categories : (i) symmetric key cryptography where one key is used for both encryption and decryption purpose. (ii) Public key cryptography where two different keys are used one for encryption and the other for decryption purpose. In symmetric key we have to maintain only one key and hence the key management is simple . In public key cryptography we maintain two keys one is public key which is known to everybody and that can be used for encryption purpose and there is another key called private key which is a secret key and that is used for decryption purpose only. In the present work the authors are proposing a symmetric key method where they have used bit level and byte level modified generalized vernam cipher method using feedback method followed by randomized bit level columnar transposition method The present method can be applied in corporate sectors, business house, academic institutions, Defense network etc. The present method performs the following:

The user has to enter some secret key and which is used to generate MSA matrix.
The program then generates all the required anagrams sufficient to encrypt all of the plaintext.
Then Bit level vernam cipher with feedback is applied , reverse file, apply again.
After that Byte level vernam cipher is applied with feedback. Reverse the file and again applied the same method.
Finally randomized Bit level transposition method applied.

The final bits were converted to bytes and write on to some output file.

The multiple key generation from a set of random characters and both bitwise and bytewise encoding make the system very secure.

2 Encryption Algorithm

The present method is dependent both on the text-key and the plaintext file size. From the text-key a randomization matrix is generated using the method developed by Nath et al(1). The algorithm of bit-level and byte level generalized vernam cipher method and bitwise columnar transposition is given as follows:

Step 1: Call Bitwise_Encrypt()

Step 2: Call Bytewise_Encrypt()

Step 3: Call Transpose_Encrypt()

Step 4: Exit

2.1 Function Bitwise_Encrypt ()

Step 1: Input a key string K

Step 2: Generate a 16x16 matrix (mat[][]) using the MSA algorithm for the key string K

Step 3: Input Filename P which is the plaintext on which the encryption is to be applied

Step 4: size=no. of bytes in file P, rand_no=1

Step 5: If size>=factorial of rand_no, rand_no=rand_no+1, repeat step 5

Step 6: Take 'rand_no' amount of characters from mat[][] and put in string buf

Step 7: Find all anagrams of buf and put in file F

Step 8: Call Encrypt_byte(P,F,mat)

Step 9: Reverse the contents of A into which function Encrypt_byte has written

Step 10: Call Encrypt_bit(A,mat)

Step 11: limit=number of bytes in file B

Step 12: i=0

Step 13: if i>=limit/8, goto step 23

Step 14: add=j=0

Step 15: if j>=8, goto step 20

Step 16: Read a character from B and store into ch

Step 17: add=add+(ch-48)*power(7-j)

Step 18: j=j+1

Step 19: Goto step 15

Step 20: Convert add to character and print into file C

Step 21: i=i+1

Step 22: Goto step 13

Step 23: Return control to calling function

2.2 Function Bytewise_Encrypt (File C)

Step 1: limit=number of bytes in File C, k=carry=0

Step 2: if k>limit , goto step 11

Step 3: Read a character from file C and store to ch

Step 4: ch=ch+mat[i][j]+carry

Step 5: Write ch to file D

Step 6: carry= ch % 256

Step 7: j=j+1, k=k+1

Step 8: if j=16, i=i+1 and j=0

Step 9: if i=16, i=0

Step 10: Goto step 2

Step 11: Exit

2.3 Function Encrypt_byte (File P, File F, mat[16][16])

Step 1: Find the number of bytes in the plaintext file P on which the encryption is to be applied. Let it contain no_of_bytes.

Step 2: carry=0

Step 3: Read a character from file F and store to ch

Step 4: Call char_to_bit(ch,key_bit)

Step 5: Read a byte ch from P

Step 6: Call char_to_bit(ch,text_pattern)

Step 7: k=0

Step 8: if k>=8, goto step 16

Step 9: add=text_pattern[k]+key_bit[k]+carry

Step 10: if add=1 or add=3, cipher_bit=1
else cipher_bit=0

Step 11: if add>=2, carry=1

else carry=0

Step 12: If carry=0, carry=cipher_bit

Step 13: Print cipher_bit into file A

Step 14: k=k+1

Step 15: Goto Step 8

Step 16: no_of_bytes=no_of_bytes-1

Step 17: If no_of bytes>0, goto step 3

Step 18: Return control to calling function

2.4 Function Encrypt_bit (File A, mat[16][16])

Step 1: Find the number of bytes in A on which the encryption is to be applied. Let it contain no_of_bytes.

Step 2: carry=0

Step 3: Read a character from file F and store to ch

Step 4: Call char_to_bit(ch,key_bit)

Step 5: n=0

Step 6: if n>=8, goto step 11

Step 7: Read a char from A

Step 8: text_pattern[n]=ch-48

Step 9: n=n+1

Step 10: Goto step 6

Step 11: k=0

Step 12: if k>=8, goto step 16

Step 13: add=text_pattern[k]+key_bit[k]+carry

Step 14: if add=1 or add=3, cipher_bit=1

else cipher_bit=0

Step 15: if add>=2, carry=1

else carry=0

Step 16: If carry=0, carry=cipher_bit

Step 17: Print cipher_bit into file B

Step 18: k=k+1

Step 19: Goto Step 8

Step 20: no_of_bytes=no_of_bytes-8

Step 21: If no_of bytes>0, goto step 3

Step 22: Return control to calling function

2.5 Function power (integer p) -- Function returns 2 to the power p

Step 1: ans=2

Step 2: if p!=0, return 1

Step 3: p=p-1

Step 4: if p=0, goto step 7

Step 5: ans=ans*2

Step 6: Goto step 4

Step 7: return ans

Step 8: Return control to calling function

2.6 Function char_to_bit (integer c, integer a[]) --Function changes a character to its corresponding bit pattern

Step 1: i=0

Step 2: if i>=8, goto step 4

Step 3: if ((ch)AND(1<<i))>0, a[7-i]=1

else a[7-i]=0

Step 4: Return control to calling function

2.7 Function Transpose_Encrypt()

Step 1: Take a file A. Say it has n characters.

Step 2: Define a n x 8 table. i=0.

Step 3: Read a character ch from file A.

Step 4: Convert ch into its corresponding bit pattern and save it in i^{th} row of the table.

Step 5: Take 8 numbers from MSA table such that each number modulo 8 is unique and covers whole of range 0 to 7. Let the numbers be $M_1, M_2, \ldots M_8$

Step 6 : For each of i from 1 to 8, choose M_i^{th} column of the table and save the contents into a temporary file T.

Step 7: Read 8 integers from file T. Compute its equivalent binary. Save into final file F.

Step 8: Repeat step 7 until whole of file T is read.

Step 9: Return control to calling function.

3 DECRYPTION ALGORITHM

Step 1: Call Transpose_Decrypt()

Step 2: Call Bytewise_Decrypt()

Step 3: Call Bitwise_Decrypt()

Step 4: Exit

3.1 Function Bitwise_Decrypt (File P)

Step 1: Input a key string K

Step 2: Generate a 16x16 matrix (mat[][]) using the MSA algorithm for the key string K

Step 3: size=no. of bytes in file P, rand_no=1

Step 4: If size>=factorial of rand_no, rand_no=rand_no+1, repeat step 4

Step 5: Take 'rand_no' amount of characters from mat[][] and put in string buf

Step 6: Find all anagrams of buf and put in file F

Step 7: Call Encrypt_byte(P,F,mat)

Step 8: Reverse the contents of B into which function Encrypt_byte has written

Step 9: Call Encrypt_bit(B,mat)

Step 10: limit=number of bytes in file B

Step 11: i=0

Step 12: if i>=limit/8, goto step 22

Step 13: add=j=0

Step 14: if j>=8, goto step 19

Step 15: Read a character from B and store into ch

Step 16: add=add+(ch-48)*power(7-j)

Step 17: j=j+1

Step 18: Goto step 14

Step 19: Convert add to character and print into file C

Step 20: i=i+1

Step 21: Goto step 12

Step 22: Exit

3.2 Function Bytewise_Decrypt (File P)

Step 1: Input Filename P which is the plaintext on which the encryption is to be applied

Step 2: limit=number of bytes in File P, k=carry=0

Step 3: if k>limit , goto step 12

Step 4: Read a character from file P and store to ch

Step 5: ch=ch - mat[i][j] - carry

Step 6:if ch<0, ch=ch+255

Step 7: carry= ch , Store ch in File A

Step 8: j=j+1, k=k+1

Step 9: if j=16, i=i+1 and j=0

Step 10: if i=16, i=0

Step 11: Goto step 3

Step 12: Exit

3.3 Function Transpose_Decrypt()

Step 1: Take file A on which transposition is to be applied and decrypted. Let it contain n characters

Step 2: Take tables T1 and T2 of size n x 8.

Step 3: Read a character from file A. Take its corresponding bit pattern and save in T1 by filling it column wise. Repeat the process until all the characters are read of file A.

Step 4: Take 8 numbers from MSA table such that each number modulo 8 is unique and covers whole of range 0 to 7. Let the numbers be $M_1, M_2, \dots M_8$

Step 5: For each of i from 1 to 8, choose M_i^{th} column of the table and copy the contents of the column into $(i-1)^{th}$ column of T2.

Step 6: Starting from row 0, take all rows, one at a time. Compute the corresponding byte for the bit pattern (each row is a bit pattern) and save in file F.

Step 7: Return control to calling function.

4 Randomixzation Of Matrix Using Meheboob, Saima & Asoke(Msa) Randomization Method

We first create a square matrix of size n x n where n can be 4, 8, 16 and 32. First we store numbers 0 to (n*n-1). We apply the following randomization techniques to create a random key matrix. The detail description of randomization methods is given by Nath et.al[1].

The following Randomization methods were applied on initial key matrix to obtain a randomized key matrix:
Step-1: call Function cycling()
Step-2: call Function upshift()
Step-3: call Function downshift()
Step-4: call Function leftshift()
Step-5: call Function rightshift()

5 Results And Discussion

The present method applied on various text files such as all characters ASCII '0', all characters ASCII '1' and the frequency distribution of the encrypted text is shown the below spectral graph.

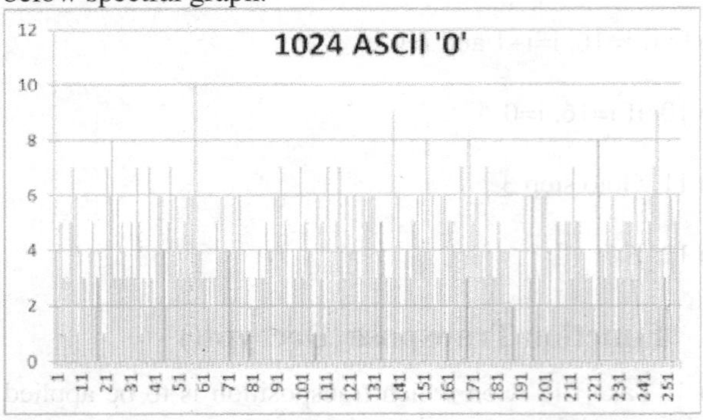

Fig-1: Frequency Spectral analyses of Plain Text file containing 1024 ASCII '0' and Key='a'.

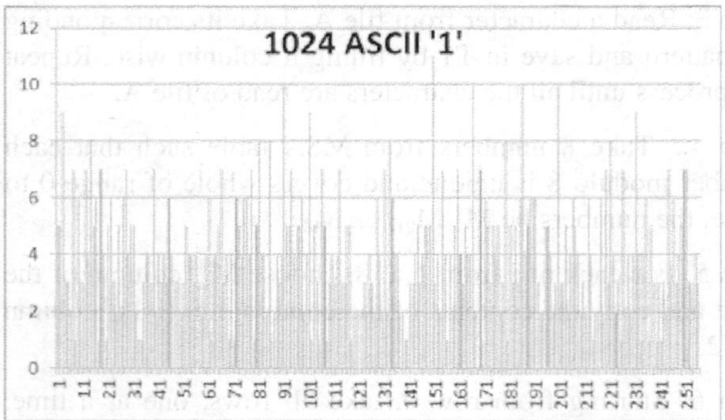

Fig-2: Frequency Spectral analyses of Plain Text file containing 1024 ASCII '1' and Key='a'.

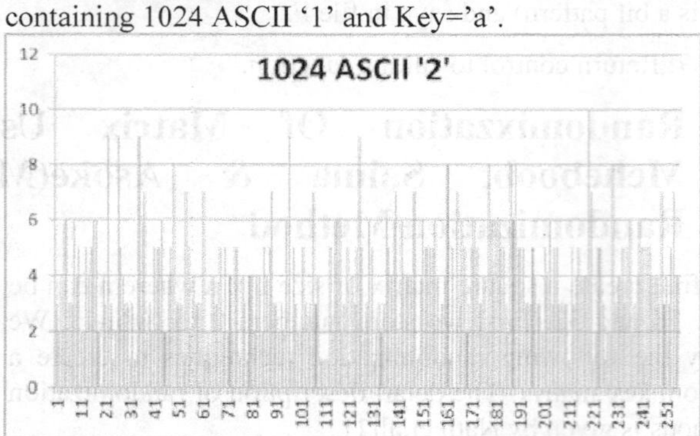

Fig-3: Frequency Spectral analyses of Plain Text file containing 1024 ASCII '2' and Key='a'.

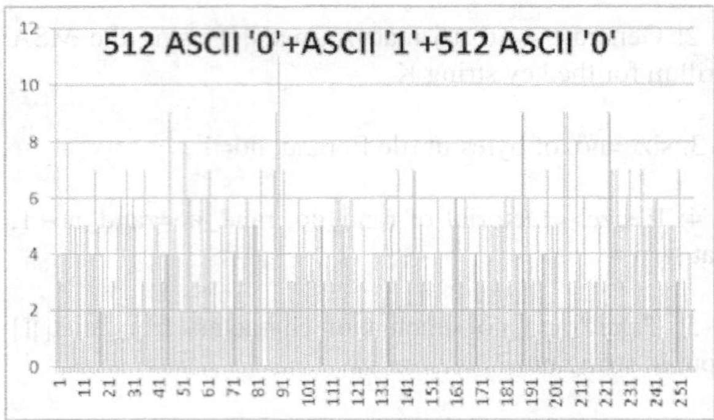

Fig-4: Frequency Spectral analyses of Plain Text file containing 512 ASCII '0',then 1 ASCII '1' and then 512 ASCII '0', encrypted using Key='a'.

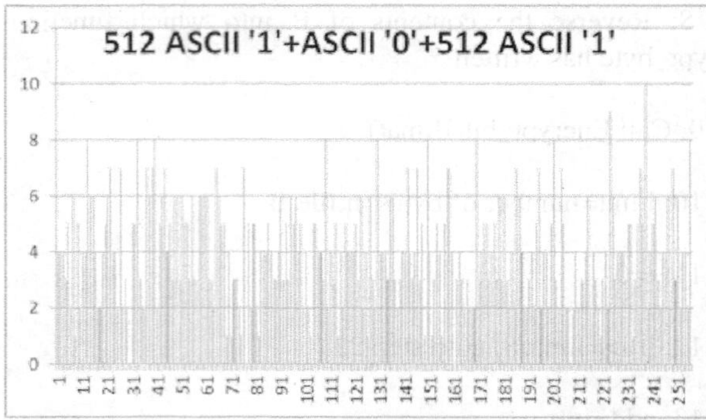

Fig-5: Frequency Spectral analyses of Plain Text file containing 512 ASCII '1',then 1 ASCII '0' and then 512 ASCII '1', encrypted using Key='a'.

Table 1: A Plain Text file containing a paragraph and its encrypted file after bit and bytewise encryption.

Plain text	Encrypted text
St. Francis Xavier is the Patron of St. Xavier's College. There is not an educated Indian who has not heard the name of Francis Xavier. It is to India that Ignatius of Loyola, the Founder of the Society of Jesus, sent his greatest son, Francis Xavier in 1542. Xavier was a zealous "missionary on the move". He sailed to Malacca and Japan in 1549 where he spent two and a half years. In April 1552 he set sail to China via Malacca from Goa, never to return alive. He died at Sancian, a small island facing china, on 2	淋□六䝘朕 읣뽄□⌘ 省柾磤 슮 鵸 蹮 [illegible]

December 1552. Wherever he went, he plunged himself into charitable and pastoral work preaching the message of God's love to people. He worked in India for 10 years from 1542 to 1552, called the Xaverian decade.	藝㵕□캜涀法뒩矘홱□蜆멦 煁楧齶 复σ嗡黣ሉ喇礔ञ □– 됆둦敎□□裸汽埗□ 藊□犷╋ □ 粒 揔⁛弓姃□뱲嬀 밞훶 쐧□□¡□꾗浊1때を □皦慬絍ㅂ □ด볼⁝粠헰◣ 巕찹깶삭ټ銬ثم 瓁榯□몬ʆ□韼쵧칋巙 獝끠歞 끡柴 □öz麭□□륛覍 췔礼ß 兀ि얹泑

6 Conclusion And Future Scope

The encrypted text cannot be decrypted without knowing the exact initial random matrix. The size of random matrix taken is 16x16. The numbers in 16x16 may be arranged in 256! Ways. To complete the whole process the authors have chosen any of the random matrix to perform bit exchange method and there is no similarity between any two matrices and even if there is then it is very hard to find out the similar ones. The order of encryption applied in this paper is bit-level first and then byte level. Multilevel applications of these techniques in different order will yield considerably different results. The spectral analysis shows that the present method is free from standard cryptography attacks namely brute force attack, known plain text attack and differential attack. The present method will be most effective to encrypt short message such as SMS in mobile phone, password encryption and any type of confidential message. If the file size is large then the present method will take more time to encrypt. So therefore our proposed method may be used in defense systems, Banking systems, Sensor networks, Mobile computing etc. The present method may be further upgraded by introducing bit level bit exchange method which is used in BLES Version-I.

7 Acknowledgement

The authors are very much grateful to the Department of Computer Science for giving the opportunity to work on symmetric key Cryptography. One of the authors (AN) sincerely expresses his gratitude to Fr. Dr. Felix Raj, Principal of St. Xavier's College (Autonomous) for giving constant encouragement in doing research in cryptography.

8 References

[1] Symmetric Key Cryptography using Random Key generator: Asoke Nath, Saima Ghosh, Meheboob Alam Mallik: "Proceedings of International conference on security and management(SAM '10)" held at Las Vegas, USA July 12-15, 2010), Vol-2, Page: 239-244(2010).

[2] Advanced Symmetric key Cryptography using extended MSA method: DJSSA symmetric key algorithm: Dripto Chatterjee, Joyshree Nath, Soumitra Mondal, Suvadeep Dasgupta and Asoke Nath, Journal of Computing, Vol 3, Issue-2, Page 66-71,Feb(2011).

[3] A new Symmetric key Cryptography Algorithm using extended MSA method: DJSA symmetric key algorithm, Dripto Chatterjee, Joyshree Nath, Suvadeep Dasgupta and Asoke Nath : Proceedings of IEEE International Conference on Communication Systems and Network Technologies, held at SMVDU(Jammu) 03-06 June,2011, Page-89-94(2011).

[4] New Symmetric key Cryptographic algorithm using combined bit manipulation and MSA encryption algorithm: NJJSAA symmetric key algorithm: Neeraj Khanna, Joel James,Joyshree Nath, Sayantan Chakraborty, Amlan Chakrabarti and Asoke Nath : Proceedings of IEEE CSNT-2011 held at SMVDU(Jammu) 03-06 June 2011, Page 125-130(2011).

[5] Symmetric key Cryptography using modified DJSSA symmetric key algorithm, Dripto Chatterjee, Joyshree Nath, Sankar Das, Shalabh Agarwal and Asoke Nath, Proceedings of International conference Worldcomp 2011 held at Las Vegas 18-21 July 2011, Page-306-311, Vol-1(2011).

[6] An Integrated symmetric key cryptography algorithm using generalized vernam cipher method and DJSA method: DJMNA symmetric key algorithm: Debanjan Das, Joyshree Nath, Megholova Mukherjee, Neha Chaudhury and Asoke Nath: Proceedings of IEEE International conference: World Congress WICT-2011 held at Mumbai University 11-14 Dec, 2011, Page No.1203-1208(2011).

[7] Symmetric key cryptosystem using combined cryptographic algorithms- generalized modified vernam cipher method, MSA method and NJJSAA method: TTJSA algorithm – Trisha Chatterjee, Tamodeep Das, Joyshree Nath, Shayan Dey and Asoke Nath, Proceedings of IEEE International conference: World Congress WICT-2011 t held at Mumbai University 11-14 Dec, 2011, Page No. 1179-1184(2011).

[8] Symmetric key Cryptography using two-way updated Generalized Vernam Cipher method: TTSJA algorithm, International Journal of Computer Applications (IJCA, USA), Vol 42, No.1, March, Pg: 34 -39(2012).

[9] Ultra Encryption Standard(UES) Version-I: Symmetric Key Cryptosystem using generalized modified Vernam Cipher method, Permutation method and Columnar Transposition method, Satyaki Roy, Navajit Maitra, Joyshree Nath, Shalabh Agarwal and Asoke Nath, Proceedings of IEEE sponsored National Conference on Recent Advances in Communication, Control and Computing Technology -RACCCT 2012, 29-30 March held at Surat, Page 81-88(2012).

[10] An Integrated Symmetric Key Cryptographic Method – Amalgamation of TTJSA Algorithm, Advanced Caeser Cipher Algorithm, Bit Rotation and reversal Method: SJA Algorithm., International Journal of Modern Education and Computer Science, Somdip Dey, Joyshree Nath, Asoke Nath,(IJMECS), ISSN: 2075-0161 (Print), ISSN: 2075-017X (Online), Vol-4, No-5, Page 1-9,2012.

[11] An Advanced Combined Symmetric Key Cryptographic Method using Bit manipulation, Bit Reversal, Modified Caeser Cipher(SD-REE), DJSA method, TTJSA method: SJA-I Algorithm, Somdip dey, Joyshree Nath, Asoke Nath, International Journal of Computer Applications(IJCA 0975-8887, USA), Vol. 46, No.20, Page- 46-53,May, 2012.
[12] Ultra Encryption Standard(UES) Version-IV: New Symmetric Key Cryptosystem with bit-level columnar Transposition and Reshuffling of Bits, Satyaki Roy, Navajit Maitra, Joyshree Nath, Shalabh Agarwal and Asoke Nath, International Journal of Computer Applications(IJCA)(0975-8887) USA Volume 51-No.1.,Aug, Page. 28-35(2012)
[13] Bit Level Encryption Standard(BLES) : Version-I, Neeraj Khanna, Dripto Chatterjee, Joyshree Nath and Asoke Nath, International Journal of Computer Applications(IJCA)(0975-8887) USA Volume 52-No.2.,Aug, Page.41-46(2012).
[14] Bit Level Generalized Modified Vernam Cipher Method with Feedback, Prabal Banerjee, Asoke Nath, Proceedings of International Conference on Emerging Trends and Technologies held at Indore, Dec 15-16,2012.
[15] Cryptography and Network Security, William Stallings, Prentice Hall of India

Modern Encryption Standard (MES) : Version-III

[1]Rahul Deep Sircar, [2]Gunjan Sekhon, [3]Asoke Nath
[1,2,3] Department of Computer Science, St. Xavier's College (Autonomous), Kolkata, India
e-mail: [1]rahul.deep.sircar@gmail.com,[2]gunjansekhon1991@gmail.com,[3]asokejoy1@.gmail.com

Abstract : *In the present paper the authors have introduced a new symmetric key cryptographic method called Modern encryption Standard (MES) Version-III. Sircar et. al already published Modern Encryption Standard version-II(MES-II) where the authors have used used Modified generalized vernam cipher method with feedback with different block size from left to right and after that entire content is divided into two files and then combine them by taking 2nd half first and the 1st block. The generalised modified Vernam Cipher method again applied from left to right with different block sizes. In the present method i.e in MES-III the authors have combined three encryption methods one after another. Firstly in method-1 the authors have used blockwise generalized vernam cipher method. Secondly in method-2 the input file is the encrypted file obtained after method-1. In method-2 the authors have applied the permutation method to reshuffle the entire file. Thirdly in method-3 the authors have applied bit-wise vernam cipher method. In method-3 the input file will be the second encrypted file obtained after method-2.In result section the authors have shown the results obtained after method-1,method-2,method-3. The result shows the encryption method is free from common attacks such as any kind of brute force method or known plain text method. The entire software is developed in Matlab. The authors have applied MES-III on various types of files and found that it works successfully. It is almost impossible to break the present method without knowing the exact key and all three methods. MES-III will be applicable to encrypt password, any confidential key, bank data, defense data etc.*

Keywords - MES, vernam cipher, blockwise, encryption, Matlab

1. Introduction

Cryptography and cryptanalysis is now a very important research area in modern digital communication network. Internet access is now free to anyone. The Hackers have created in various websites where they constantly upload crack software. Using that software anyone can break any password and can log into any confidential site. There are no proper rules from any Government to stop for doing this. Due to hacking problem now it always advised to user to change their all important password in a regular interval. It is also advised that the password should be hard. E-mail is one important area where the hacker tries to get illegal access to it. The data in e-mail should be always well protected. While sending any kind of confidential message or information from one user to another user one must send it in encrypted form otherwise anyone can hack the message during data communication. When a user is working in a network environment then the user must be very careful about his/her confidential data. It must be in encrypted form otherwise anyone can intercept it provided he/she knows the IP address of that machine. This may be further extended when two users are sending message to each other from two distant places. A hacker may listen in between and can divert the message to someone else or can modify and send it to the receiver. This is actually middleman attack. If the data is in original form or in raw form then at any moment this may be attacked by a middleman and it may create some disaster also. The authenticity of data is now a big challenge. To tackle this problem the people were trying to develop good encryption method to encrypt confidential data. At the same time the hackers are also not remain idle. They also develop some brute force method to decrypt the encrypted text without knowing actual encryption or the decryption algorithm. So it some sort of game between the cryptographer and the hackers. Cryptographer always tries to win the game. Two types of cryptography algorithms are used one is called symmetric key where one key is used for encryption and as well as decryption purpose and other method is called public key cryptography. In public key two keys are used one key is used only for encryption purpose which is called public key and the other key is used to decrypt the encrypted text and it called as private key or the secret key. In public key cryptography the extensive computation is required in comparison to symmetric key cryptography. Nath et al [1,2,3,4,5,6] developed different symmetric key cryptosystem. The advantage of symmetric key method is that the key management is very simple. Recently Nath et al developed cryptography method called Modern Encryption Standard ver-I and Ver-II. In the present method Nath et al have developed upgraded version of MES-II called as MES-III. In the present method the authors have used three independent cryptography methods namely generalized modified vernam cipher method in variable block size and with feedback, randomized permutation method and bit-wise generalized vernam cipher method. Modified generalized vernam cipher method, bit-wise vernam cipher method already been developed by Nath et al in BLES-I, II. But in the present method the authors have used variable block size in both bye wise and bit wise vernam cipher with feedback. In the result section the authors have shown the output of method-1, then method-1 and 2 and finally method-1, 2, 3 combined of some known plain text. The output shows that the encryption is very strong as the encrypted text is totally different if there is only one character different in two patterns. The standard encryption algorithm like RSA or DES if we apply on a pattern where all characters are same then after encryption the encrypted text will also show same repeated pattern. But the present method applied on repeated pattern but the output contains totally different pattern. The entire software developed in Matlab. In the present work the authors are proposing a symmetric key method called Modern Encryption Standard Version III (MES-III) which can be used to encrypt data in sensor network, mobile network, and ATM network, defense or even in corporate sector also. MES-III may be very useful to encrypt password, short message, encryption key etc.

2. Algorithm For Modern Encryption Standard Ver-III :

2.1 Vernam Cipher with Feedback (blockwise):

Function of Method 1 in MES-III:

In Method 1 of MES-III we read the input file and divide it into blocks of 2,4,6…,n where n=length of the input plain text file. We encrypt each block using Vernam Cipher Encryption with Feedback using a keypad generated from a user input key. We then reverse the contents of the encrypted file. Then we divide the file into 2 files, say 'file1' and 'file2'. We then concatenate the contents of 'file2' to the end of 'file1'. This whole process is carried out the same number of times as the as the length of the user input key. This is the end of method 1

2.1.1. Encryption Algorithm : main() module:

This function takes names of the plain text file and cipher text file as input from the user. It also takes the key used for encryption as input and executes the complete blockwise encryption algorithm by calling the various functions involved in this encryption method.

Step 1: Start main
Step 2: e_flag=1
Step 3: Input fi1e1 to plain text file
Step 3a: Input file2 to store cipher text file
Step 4: Open file1 in read mode
Step 4a: Open file2 in write mode
Step 5: file_len=sizeof(file1)//to calculate size of the input text rounded down to the nearest even number
Step 6: if modulus(file_len,2)=0 then max_len=file_len
Step 6a: else max_len=file_len-1
Step 7: Initialize all elements of array key_indx(row)=0 where row=max_len
Step 8: Input file_key // User has to enter file_key of any length
Step 9: key_len=length(file_key)
Step 10: Open a file 'temp1.txt'in write mode //'temp1.txt' will temporarily hold input text during encryption process
Step 11: Copy 'file1' to 'temp1.txt'
Step 12: times=key_len //'times' is the number of times the total encryption process will take place
Step 13: i=1 //steps 13-36 carry out the entire encryption process, that is calling the encrypt function, reversing, splitting and merging the files
Step 14: block_size=0
Step 15: while block_size<=max_len
Step 16: goto beginning of the file 'temp1.txt'
Step 17: block_size=block_size+2 //taking initial block size as 2, block size is increased by 2 for every encryption step
Step 18: n_block=(max_len/block_size) //for a particular block size, number of blocks is calculated
Step 19: key_indx=ps_keygen(file_key,block_size) // key_index holds index values for generated keypad
Step 20: j=1 //steps 20-27 carry out encryption process by calling the 'encrypt' function 1 block at a time
Step 21: Open a file 'temp2.txt' in write mode //'temp2.txt' holds the text in a particular block for encryption
Step 22: Copy 'temp1.txt' to 'temp2.txt'
Step 23: Call encrypt(filet2,file2,key_indx) //this will encrypt the contents of 'filet2' and write it in 'file2'
Step 24: j=j+1
Step 24a: if j<=n_block,goto step 21
Step 25: copy residual characters from 'temp1.txt' to file2
Step 29: close 'temp1.txt'
Step 27: Call filecopy(file2,filet) //after encryption, encrypted text is stored in 'filet' for reversing, splitting and merging
Step 28: Open 'temp1.txt' in read mode
Step 29: close file2
Step 30: Open file2 in write mode
Step 31: End while loop from step 15
Step 32: Call filereverse(filet)// To reverse the contents of filet
Step 33: Call filesplitting(filet,e_flag)// It splits filet into 2 files say file_1 and file_2.
Step 34: Call mergefile(filet) // this concatenates contents of file_1 to the end of file_2 and stores it in filet
Step 35: i=i+1
Step 35a: if i<=times, goto step 14
Step 37: Call filecopy(filet,file2)//this copes the contents of filet into file2
Step 38: Close all files
Step 39: Delete temporary files
Step 40: End

2.1.2. Decryption Algorithm : Main() module:

This function takes names of the cipher text file and deciphered text file as input from the user. It executes the complete blockwise decryption algorithm by calling the various functions involved in this decryption method.

Step 1: Start main
Step 2: e_flag=0
Step 3: Input fi1e1 to plain text file
Step 3a: Input file2 to store cipher text file
Step 4: Open file1 in read mode
Step 4a: Open file2 in write mode
Step 5: file_len=sizeof(file1)
Step 6: Initialize all elements of array key_indx(row)=0 where row=max_len
Step 7: Open a file 'temp1.txt'in write mode //'temp1.txt' is a temporary file where encrypted text will be stored during decryption
Step 8: Copy 'file1' to 'temp1.txt'
Step 9: i=1 //steps 9-30 carry out the entire decryption process, that is splitting, merging and reversing the files and calling the decrypt function

Step 10: block_size=max_len //the 'block_size' is set to the largest possible block size to reverse the encryption process
Step 11: Call filesplitting(filet,e_flag)// It splits filet into 2 files say file_1 and file_2.
Step 12: Call mergefile(filet) // this concatenates contents of file_1 to the end of file_2 and stores it in filet
Step 13: Call filereverse(filet)// To reverse the contents of filet
Step 14: while block_size>=0
Step 15: n_block=floor(max_len/block_size) //For a particular block size, the number of blocks is calculated
Step 16: key_indx=ps_keygen(file_key,block_size))// key_index holds index values for generated key
Step 17: j=1 //steps 17-24 carry out decryption process by calling 'decrypt' function 1 block at a time
Step 18: Open a file 'temp2.txt' in write mode //'temp2.txt' holds the text in a particular block for decryption
Step 19: Copy 'temp1.txt' to 'temp2.txt'
Step 20: k=k+1
Step 20a: if k<=block_size,goto step 20
Step 21: Call decrypt(filet2,file2,key_indx))//this will decrypt the contents of 'filet2' and write it in 'file2'
Step 22: j=j+1
Step 22a: if j<=n_block,goto step 18
Step 23: copy residual characters from 'temp1.txt' to file2
Step 24: close 'temp1.txt'
Step 25: Call filecopy(file2,filet) //This function will copy contents of file2 into filet
Step 26: Open 'temp1.txt' in read mode
Step 27: Open file2 in write mode
Step 28: block_size=block_size-2 //'block_size' is decreased by 2 and the decryption process is repeated if the condition of the while loop is satisfied
Step 29: End while loop from step 14
Step 30: i=i+1
Step 30a: if i<=times,goto step 10
Step 31: Call filecopy(filet,file2)//this copes the contents of filet into file2
Step 32: Close all files
Step 33: Delete temporary files
Step 34: End

2.1.3. function encrypt(file1,file2,key_indx):

Function to encrypt file1 using key_index and then store in file2. The function uses generalized modified Vernamcipher method proposed by Nath et al.
This function carries out vernam cipher method with feedback to encrypt the input file

Step 1: Start
Step 2: Open file1 in read mode
Step 2a: Open file2 in append mode
Step 3: Initialize all elements of arrays ch_indx(rows)=0,sum(rows)=0,fdbk(rows) =0 where rows=max_len
Step 4: feedback=0
Step 5: i=1
Step 6: ch=read a character from file1,ch_indx(i)=int(ch)
Step 7: i=i+1
Step 7a: if i<=file_len,goto Step-6
Step 8: i=1 //Steps 8-15 carry out Vernam Cipher Encryption with Feedback encryption
Step 9: tsum=ch_indx(i)+key_indx(i)+feedback
Step 10: fdbk(i)=tsum
Step 11: if tsum>=256, tsum(i)=mod(tsum,256)
Step 12: sum(i)=tsum
Step 13: feedback=sum(i)
Step 14: ch=char(sum(i)),write to file2
Step 15: i=i+1
Step 15a: if i<=block_size,goto step 9
Step 16: End

2.1.4. function decrypt(file1,file2,key_indx):

This function takes names of the cipher text file and deciphered text file as input from the user. It executes the complete decryption algorithm by calling the various functions involved in this decryption method.

Step 1: Start
Step 2: Open file1 in read mode
Step 2a: Open file2 in append mode
Step 3: Initialize all elements of arrays ch_indx(rows)=0,sum(rows)=0,pt_indx(rows) =0 where rows=max_len
Step 4: feedback=0
Step 5: i=1 //Steps 5-16 carry out decryption of the Vernam Cipher method with Feedback
Step 6: ch=read a character from file1,ch_indx(i)=int(ch)
Step 7: i=i+1
Step 7a: if i<=file_len,goto Step-6
Step 8: i=1
Step 9: tsum=ch_indx(i)+key_indx(i)+feedback
Step 10: if tsum<0, tsum=tsum+256
Step 10a:else if tsum>=256, , tsum(i)=mod(tsum,256)
Step 11: sum(i)=tsum
Step 13: feedback=ch_indx(i)
Step 14:fdbk(i)=feedback
Step 15: ch=char(pt_indx(i)),write to file2
Step 16: i=i+1
Step 16a: if i<=block_size,goto step 9
Step 17: End

2.1.5. function filereverse(file_name) :

Function is to reverse the content of file_name and to store in the same file.

Step 1: Store file_name in file1 and 'temp_rev.txt' in file2
Step 2: Open file1 in 'r' mode using file ID fp1 and open file2 in 'w' mode using file ID fp2
Step 3: Store the length of fp1 in n
Step 4: Initialize i to (n-1)
Step 5: Go to i'th position from the beginning of the file.
Step 6: Read the character in that position and store in it ch.
Step 7: Write ch to fp2
Step 8: If i=0, continue, else decrement the value of i by 1 and go to step 6
Step 9: Call function filecopy() passing file2 and file1 as parameters
Step 10: Close fp2
Step 11: End

2.1.6. function filesplitting(file_name,e_flag):

Function to split a file file_name into two files file1.txt and file2.txt

Step 1: Store file_name in file1, 'split_file1.txt' in file2 and 'split_file2.txt' in file3
Step 2: Open file1 in 'r' mode using file ID fp1,open file2 in 'w' mode using file ID fp2 and open file3 in 'w' mode using file ID fp3
Step 3: Store the length of fp1 in n
Step 4: If e_flag=1, store ceiling value of n/2 in n1, else store floor value of n/2 in n1
Step 5: Store n-n1 in n2
Step 6: Initialize i=1
Step 7: Read a character from fp1 and store it in ch. Write ch to fp2
Step 8: If i=n1, continue, else go to step 7
Step 9: Initialize i=1
Step 10: Read a character from fp1 and store it in ch. Write ch to fp3
Step 11: If i=n2, continue, else go to step 10
Step 12: End

2.1.7. function mergefile(file_name) :

Function to combine two split files file1.txt and file2.txt to get one file, by putting file2.txt first then file1.txt

Step 1: Store file_name in file3, 'split_fil1.txt' in file1 and 'split_file2.txt' in file2
Step 2: Open file1 in 'r' mode using file ID fp1,open file2 in 'r' mode using file ID fp2 and open file3 in 'w' mode using file ID fp3
Step 3: Store the length of fp1 in n1 and length of fp2 in n2
Step 4: Initialize i to 1
Step 5: Read a character from fp2 and store it in ch. Write ch to fp3
Step 6: If i=n2, continue, else go to step 5
Step 7: Read a character from fp1 and store it in ch. Write ch to fp3
Step 8: If i=n2, continue, else go to step 7
Step 9: Close fp1 and fp2
Step 10: End

2.1.8. function filecopy(file_1,file_2) :

Function to copy file_1 to file_2

Step 1: Store file_1 in file1 and file_2 in file2
Step 2: Open file1 in 'r+' mode using file ID fp1 and open file2 in 'w+' mode using file ID fp2
Step 3: Store the length of fp1 in n
Step 4: Initialize i to 1
Step 5: Read a character from fp1 and store it in ch. Write ch to fp2
Step 6: If i=n,continue,else go to step 5
Step 7: End

2.2 Randomization method:

Function of Method 2 in MES-III:
In Method 1 of MES-III we read the input file and divide it into blocks of 2,4,6…,n where n=length of the input plain text file. We apply randomization function on each of the blocks successively Inside the randomize function different operations like leftshift, rightshift, upshift, downshift, diagshift are performed on the matrix blocks. .The output of one block becomes the input for the other block. Same way decryption is done using the functions in a reverse way, since the functions are complementary to each other.

2.2.1 Encryption Algorithm : main() module:

This method randomizes the content of a plain text file with help of matrix element operations like leftshift, rightshift, upshift, downshift, diagshift are performed on the matrix blocks till the largest block size that can be formed in a square matrix. The residual bytes are copied as it is. In simple English language it jumbles up the contents of the text file.
Step 0:Start main
Step 1:Input file1 name of encrypted file name
Step 2:Input file name of output file
Step 3:Open file1 in read mode and seek the file pointer to the starting of the file
Step 4: Length of file1 file_len is calculated and it is closed again
Step 5:In a nested for loop,matsize is equal size of n in nxn largest matrix is found out
Step 6:i=1 to 1024;j=1 to 1024
Step 7:a(i,j)=' '
Step 8:times=matsize-1
Step 9:Array initialized a=zeros(i,j)//initializing each cell of array a to zeros
Step 10:Open temp1 in write mode
Step 11:Copy the contents of file1 to temp1
Step 12:fclose('all')
Step 13:i=2
Ste p14:calculate isq=i*i
Step 15:calculate noofblocks=floor(file_len/isq)
Step 16:calculate bytescopied=noofblocks*isq
Step 17:calculate residual bytes of the file as res_bytes=file_len-bytescopied
Step 18:open file temp1 in read mode
Step 19:open file2 in write mode
Step 20:k=1
Step 21:read each input character from file temp1 and make array(u1,u2)
Step 22:call shufarr= msaencryptfinal(a,i) ;// randomization of array elements
Step 23:Each character from the shuffarr(u1,u2) is written in file2
Step 24:If k<noofblocks then goto Step 21
Step 25:Position of residual bytes is found in file2
Step 26:inneri=pos
Step 27:Each character read from temp1 file
Step 28:Written into file2 //copying residual bytes into the file 2
Step 29:If inneri<=file_len then goto Step 27
Step 30:Contents of file 2 copied into temp1

Step 31:If i<=matsize,goto Step 14
Step 32:Display count value //for no of iterations
Step 33:Copy contents of temp1 to file2
Step 34:fclose('all')
Step 35:Delete temp1 file
Step 36:End

2.2.2. Decryption Algorithm : Main() module:

This method is to get back the original file contents as it was before the randomization. This main function gets the original contents of the file before randomization was performed by starting the matrix block size from the largest size and proceeding in decreasing order till largest block size of 2.Remaining process is similar to encryption.

Step 0:Start main
Step 1:Input file1 name of encrypted file name
Step 2:Input file name of output file
Step 3:Open file1 in read mode and seek the file pointer to the starting of the file
Step 4: Length of file1 file_len is calculated and it is closed again
Step 5:In a nested for loop,matsize is equal size of n in nxn largest matrix is found out
Step 6:i=1 to 1024;j=1 to 1024
Step 7:a(i,j)=' '
Step 8:times=matsize-1
Step 9:Array initialized a=zeros(i,j) //initializing each cell of array a to zeros
Step 10:Open temp1 in write mode
Step 11:Copy the contents of file1 to temp1
Step 12:fclose('all')
Step 13:i=matsize //starting from the largest block size
Step 14:calculate isq=i*i
Step 15:calculate noofblocks=floor(file_len/isq)
Step 16:calculate bytescopied=noofblocks*isq
Step 17:calculate residual bytes of the file as res_bytes=file_len-bytescopied
Step 18:open file temp1 in read mode
Step 19:open file2 in write mode
Step 20:k=1
Step 21:read each input character from file temp1 and make array(u1,u2)
Step 22:call shufarr= msaderyptfinal(a,i) ;// to randomization of array elements
Step 23:Each character from the shuffarr(u1,u2) is written in file2
Step 24:If k<noofblocks then goto Step 21
Step 25:Position of residual bytes is found in file2 //residual bytes are copied as it is.0
Step 26:inneri=pos
Step 27:Each character read from temp1 file
Step 28:Written into file2 //copying residual bytes into the file 2
Step 29:If inneri<=file_len then goto Step 27
Step 30:Contents of file 2 copied into temp1
Step 31:If i<=matsize,goto Step 14
Step 32:Display count value //for no of iterations
Step 33:Copy contents of temp1 to file2
Step 34:fclose('all')
Step 35:Delete temp1 file
Step 36:End

2.2.3 function[shufarr]=msaencryptfinal(a,i):

This method performs matrix operations on the square array in a given order.

Step 0:Start
Step 1:function[shufarr]=msaencryptfinal(a,i) // to randomize elements of the array
Step 2:a1=diagshift(a,i) // apply diagonal shift
Step 3:a2=leftshift(a1,i) // apply left shift
Step 4:a3=diagshift(a2,i) // apply diagonal shift
Step 5:a4=upshift(a3,i) // apply up shift
Step 6:a5=diagshift(a4,i) // apply diagonal shift
Step 7:a6=rightshift(a5,i) //apply right shift
Step 8:a7=diagshift(a6,i) // apply diagonal shift
Step 9:a8=downshift(a7,i) // apply down shift
Step 10:a9=diagshift(a8,i) // apply diagonal shift
Step 11:shufarr=diagshift(a9,i) // apply diagonal shift
Step 12:End

2.2.4. function[shufarr]=msadecryptfinal(a,i):

This method performs matrix operations on the square array in the reverse order as is in the encryption function.

Step 0:Start
Step 1:function [orig]=msadecryptfinal(b,i) //to get the original array before randomization
Step 2:b1=revdiagshift(b,i) // apply reverse diagonal shift
Step 3:b2=revdiagshift(b1,i) // apply reverse diagonal shift
Step 4:b3=upshift(b2,i) // apply up shift
Step 5:b4=revdiagshift(b3,i) // apply reverse diagonal shift
Step 6:b5=leftshift(b4,i) // apply left shift
Step 7;b6=revdiagshift(b5,i) // apply reverse diagonal shift
Step 8:b7=downshift(b6,i) // apply down shift
Step 9:b8=revdiagshift(b7,) // apply reverse diagonal shift
Step 10:b9=rightshift(b8,i) // apply right shift
Step 11:orig=revdiagshift(b9,i) //apply reverse diagonal shift
Step 12:End

2.2.5. function[a]=diagshift(a,n):

This function performs diagonal shift on the array elements.

Step 0:Start
Step 1:function[a]=diagshift(a,n)
Step 2:tmp=a(n,n); //tmp is a temporary variable
Step 3:i=n
Step 4 a(i,i)=a(i-1,i-1);
Step 5 If i>=2 ,then goto Step 4
Step 6 Calculate a(1,1)=tmp
Step 7 End

2.2.6. function [a]=revdiagshift(a,n):

This function performs reverse diagonal shift on the array elements.

Step 0:Start
Step 1:function [a]=revdiagshift(a,n)
Step 2:tmp=a(1,1) //tmp is a temporary variable
Step 3:i=1
Step 4:a(i,i)=a(i+1,i+1);

Step 5:If i>n-1,then goto Step 4
Step 6 Calculate a(n,n)=tmp
Step 7 End

2.2.7. function[a]=upshift(a,n):
This function performs reverse diagonal shift on the array elements.

Step 0:Start
Step 1:function[a]=upshift(a,n)
Step 2:i=1
Step 3:tmp=a(1,i) //tmp is a temporary variable
Step 4:j=2
Step 5: a(j-1,i)=a(j,i);
Step 6:If j<n then goto Step 5
Step 7:If i<n then goto Step 3
Step 8: Calculate a(n,i)=tmp
Step 9:End

2.2.8 function[a]=downshift(a,n):
This function performs downshift on the array elements.

Step 0:Start
Step 1:function[a]=downshift(a,n)
Step 2:i=1
Step 3:tmp=a(n,i) //tmp is a temporary variable
Step 4:j=n
Step 5:calculate a(j,i)=a(j-1,i)
Step 6:if j>2 then goto Step 5
Step 7:calculate a(1,i)=tmp
Step 8:If i<n then goto Step 3
Step 9:End

2.2.9. function[a]=leftshift(a,n):
This function performs leftshift on the array elements.

Step 0:Start
Step 1:function[a]=leftshift(a,n)
Step 2:i=1
Step 3:temp=a(i,1) //tmp is a temporary variable
Step 4:j=2
Step 5: calculate a(i,j-1)=a(i,j)
Step 6:If j<n then goto Step 5
Step 7:Calculate a(i,n)=temp
Step 8:If i<n then goto Step 3
Step 9:End

2.2.10. function[a]=rightshift(a,n):
This function performs rightshift on the array elements.

Step 0:Start
Step 1:function[a]=rightshift(a,n)
Step 2:i=1
Step 3:temp=a(i,1) //tmp is a temporary variable
Step 4:j=n
Step 5:Calculate a(i,j)=a(i,j-1)
Step 6:If j>2then goto Step 5
Step 7:Calculate a(i,1)=tmp
Step 8:If i<n then goto Step 3
Step 9:End

2.3. Bitwise method:

Function of Method 3 in MES-III:
In Method 3 of MES-III we take the output text from Method 2 and convert the entire output into bits. Then using the algorithm of Method 2 we shuffle the bits a certain number of times to obtain a different output text for every particular input text. The number of time the shuffle operation occurs on the text file depends is a number which differs depending on the text in the input file. We then convert the bits to bytes and out the final cipher text of MES-III method.

2.3.1 Encryption Algorithm : main() module:

This encryption method reduces the plain text to bits and carries out the method 2 process on it

Step 1: Start main
Step 2: Input file1 to plain text file
Step 2a: Input file2 to store cipher text file
Step3: Open file1 in read mode
Step 3a: Open file2 in write mode
Step 4: file_len=sizeof(file1)
Step 5: size=8*file_len //size holds the size of the plain text when converted to bits
Step 6: Initialize all elements of ar(row)=0,ar1(row)=0,bin_arr(8)=0 where row=size //arrays used for blockwise encryption
Step 7: ii=1
Step 8: isq=ii*ii
Step 9: if isq<=size, matsize=ii//size of the n on largest nxn matrix that can be generated from this
Step 10: ii=ii+1
Step 10a: if ii<=(size/2), goto step 8
Step 11: initialize all elements of a(1024,1024)= ' '
Step 12: Initialize all elements of a(i,j)=0
Step 13:pos=0,s=0,dig=0,s1=0,count=0 //variables used to calculate how many times encryption will take place
Step 14: ch=read character from file1
Step 15: bin_arr=dec_to_bin(ch) //dec_to_bin will return a binary array which will be stored in bin_arr
Step 16: store sum of ASCII value of all characters in plain text in s // this will also be used to calculate the number of times encryption will be done
Step 17: store binary values of each character in 'ar'
Step 18: increment value of s1 by 1 for every '1' present in 'ar' //this will also be used to calculate the number of times encryption will be done
Step 19: times1=floor((s/s1)), times2=mod(s,s1), times=times1+times2 //times=the number of times encryption will occur. This varies for any slight variation in plain text
Step 20: while times>40 // this is to make sure the loop is not too large so that it will cause a lengthy encryption process
Step 21: s2=sumofdigits(times)
Step 22: times=s2*s1
Step 23: end while loop started in step 20
Step 24: ext_i=1 //Steps 24-35 carry out the encryption process by calling 'msaencryptfinal()' for each block

Step 25: i=2
Step 26: count=count+1,pos1=0,pos2=0,isq=i*i
Step 27: noofblocks=floor(size/isq), bytescopied=noofblocks*isq, res_bytes=size-bytescopied
Step 28: k=1
Step 29: read each input character from file temp1 and make array(u1,u2),pos1=pos1+1
Step 30: call shufarr= msaencryptfinal(a,i) //function for randomization of array elements
Step 31: Each character from the shuffarr(u1,u2) is written in file2,pos2=po2+1
Step 32: k=k+1
Step 32a: If k<=nocfblocks then goto Step 29
Step 33: transfer residual bytes from 'ar' to 'ar1'
Step 34: transfer bits from ar1 to ar for further shuffling
Step 35: i=i+1
Step 35a: if i<=matsize,goto step 26
Step 36: ext_i=ext_i+1
Step 36a: if ext_i<=times,goto step 25
Step 37: i=1
Step 38: pos=0
Step 39: bin_arr(pos+1)=ar(i+pos) //creating 8 bits array
Step 40: pos=pos+1
Step 40a: if pos<=7 then goto step 39
Step 41: num=bin_to_dec(bin_arr) // binary to integer
Step 42:ch=char(num),write ch to file2 //creating Cipher text file
Step 43: i=i+8
Step 43a: if i<=size then goto step 38
Step 44: End

2.3.2. Decryption Algorithm : Main() module:

Step 1: Start main
Step 2: Input file1 to plain text file
Step 2a: Input file2 to store cipher text file
Step 3: Open file1 in read mode
Step 3a: Open file2 in write mode
Step 4: file_len=sizeof(file1)
Step 5: size=8*file_len
Step 6: Initialize all elements of ar(row)=0,ar1(row)=0,bin_arr(8)=0 where row=size //arrays used for blockwise decryption
Step 7: ii=1
Step 8: isq=ii*ii
Step 9: if isq<=size, matsize=ii//size of the n on largest nxn matrix that can be generated from this
Step 10: ii=ii+1
Step 10a: if ii<=(size/2), goto step 8
Step 11: initialize all elements of a(1024,1024)= ' '
Step 12: Initialize all elements of a(i,j)=0
Step 13: pos=0,count=0, i=1
Step 14: ch=read character from file1
Step 15: bin_arr=dec_to_bin(ch) //character to binary
Step 16: store sum of ASCII value of all characters in input text in 's' //this will also be used to calculate the number of times encryption will be done
Step 17: ext_i=1 //Steps 17-28 carry out the decryption process by calling 'msadecryptfinal()' for each block
Step 18: i=matsize
Step 19: count=count+1,pos1=0,pos2=0,isq=i*i
Step 20: noofblocks=floor(size/isq), bytescopied=noofblocks*isq, res_bytes=size-bytescopied
Step 21: k=1
Step 22: read each input character from file temp1 and make array(u1,u2),pos1=pos1+1
Step 23: call shufarr= msadecryptfinal(a,i) //function for randomization of array elements
Step 24: Each character from the shuffarr(u1,u2) is written in file2,pos2=po2+1
Step 25: k=k+1
Step 25a: If k<=noofblocks then goto step 22
Step 26: transfer the residual bits from 'ar' to 'ar1'
Step 27: transfer bits from ar1 to ar for further shuffling
Step 28: i=i-1
Step 28a: if i>=2,goto step 19
Step 29: ext_i=ext_i+1
Step 29a: if ext_i<=times,goto step 18
Step 30: i=1 //Steps 44-50 carry out conversion from bits to bytes and writing into output file
Step 31: pos=0
Step 32: bin_arr(pos+1)=ar(i+pos)//creating an array of 8 bits
Step 33: pos=pos+1
Step 33a: if pos<=7,goto step 32
Step 34: num=bin_to_dec(bin_arr)// binary to integer
Step 35:ch=char(num),write ch to file2// integer to character
Step 36: i=i+8
Step 36a: if i<=size,goto step 31
Step 37: End

2.3.3. function [arr]=dec_to_bin(ch):

This function takes a character as input and returns the binary of it's ASCII as an array

Step 1: Start
Step 2: Initialize all elements of arr(8)=0
Step 3: c1=int(ch)
Step 4: Convert ch to bits and store in arr
Step 5: End

2.3.4. function [num]=bin_to_dec(arr):

This function takes a binary array as input and returns an integer which is the decimal of the binary array entered

Step 1: Start
Step 2: num=0
Step 3: Convert arr to decimal and store in num
Step 4: End

2.3.5. function [sum]=sumofdigits(n):

This function calculates the sum of the digits of the number n. It is called by the main encryption function to calculate how many times encryption will occur

Step 1: Start
Step 2: copy=n,sum=0
Step 3: while copy>0
Step 4: d=mod(copy,10)
Step 5: copy=copy/10
Step 6: sum=sum+d
Step 7: end while loop started in step 3

Step-8: End

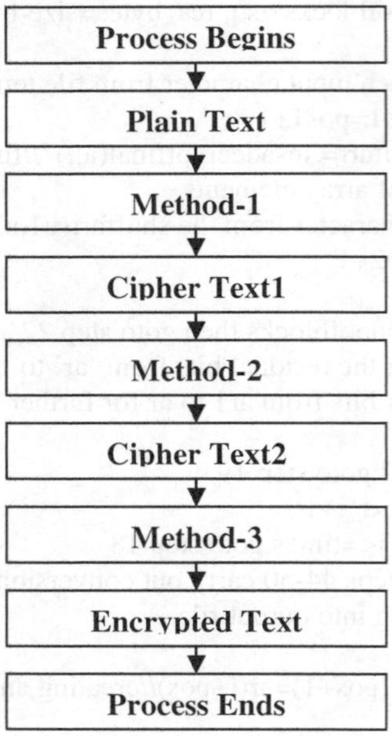

Transition diagram for the proposed algorithm MES Version-III

3. Results and Discussion:

MES-III applied on all possible type of files and the results found satisfactory. In table-1 we have shown different standard plain text and the corresponding encrypted text after method-1, method-1 and method-2 and then method-1,2 and 3 together. The results show that it almost impossible to get back the original text without knowing the exact key and exact decryption algorithm. MES-III applied on a small paragraph and output is also shown in a separate table.

Table-1: Some standard input plain text and the corresponding Cipher Text

Input Text	Method 1	Method-1 + Method 2	Method_1 + Method_2 + Method 3
he_is_goon	□@»'tž¾Þ m'	m¾Þ»□@ÿ ÿtÿ	þ†ÞŸ□|{ï± ß
he_is_good	□@»'tVf-·	-Vf»□@ÿt·	YP¨¬ôµIå• Ý
caaaaaaa	aâ…□□ùù □	aâÿ□□ùù□	›^‰‡ðóÏ
baaaaaaa	□ê¸ß'□×™	□ê¸ßÿ□×ÿ	Šg›M}ößv
aaaacaaaa	¿òë!°»b¶	¶»bë¿ò°!	º"]ýìÌ¹(É
aaaabaaaa	¿òë!□,‹†¶	¶ÿÿë¿òÿ!□	æöÁ×ýôþý .
aaaaaaac	¿òë!rÉ-Ú	¿òë!rÉ-Ú	Y— O°ÿm32
aaaaaaab	¿òë!@éq{	¿òë!@éq{	9êŽèS□û□
111111111	Ï"ûqü□kú&	&kúûÏ"□qü	ûü_%˜Ù '
111101111	Ï"ûqûÖ;-&	&;-ûÏ"Öqû	SåH_Žh÷ëî

Test Case :

Plain Text - To promote a society of liberty, justice, equality, fraternity and freedom.

Encrypted Text –

4. Conclusion and Future Scope:

The encrypted text cannot be decrypted without knowing the exact initial random matrix. MES-III is a combination of 3 independent methods and hence to decrypt the encrypted text one has to apply the decryption algorithm in proper way and the key should be also correct. The encrypted text of some standard text shows that the present method is free from known plain text attack, brute force attack or differential attack. MES-III will be most effective to encrypt short message such as SMS in mobile phone, password encryption and any type of confidential message. The method was tested the present method on any type file such as text, audio, video or any other file and we find that it is working perfectly ok. The present method may be further upgraded by using some complex bit-wise operations such as XOR, left shift, complement etc. The feedback mechanism can be further made nonlinear to make the whole system more complex. The authors are now working on those complex operations.

5. Acknowledgement

We are very much grateful to the Department of Computer Science to give us this opportunity to work on symmetric key Cryptography. One of the authors (AN) sincerely expresses his gratitude to Fr. Dr. Felix Raj, Principal of St. Xavier's College(Autonomous) for giving constant encouragement in doing research in cryptography.

6. References

[1] Symmetric Key Cryptography using Random Key generator : Asoke Nath, Saima Ghosh, Meheboob Alam Mallik: "Proceedings of International conference on security and management(SAM'10" held at Las Vegas, USA Jull 12-15, 2010), Vol-2, Page: 239-244(2010).

[2] Advanced Symmetric key Cryptography using extended MSA method: DJSSA symmetric key algorithm: Dripto Chatterjee, Joyshree Nath, Soumitra Mondal, Suvadeep Dasgupta and Asoke Nath, Jounal of Computing, Vol 3, issue-2, Page 66-71,Feb(2011).

[3] A new Symmetric key Cryptography Algorithm using extended MSA method :DJSA symmetric key algorithm, Dripto Chatterjee, Joyshree Nath, Suvadeep Dasgupta and Asoke Nath : Proceedings of IEEE International Conference on Communication Systems and Network Technologies, held at SMVDU(Jammu) 03-06 June,2011, Page-89-94(2011).

[4] New Symmetric key Cryptographic algorithm using combined bit manipulation and MSA encryption algorithm: NJJSAA symmetric key algorithm :Neeraj Khanna, Joel James,Joyshree Nath, Sayantan Chakraborty, Amlan Chakrabarti and Asoke Nath : Proceedings of IEEE CSNT-2011 held at SMVDU(Jammu) 03-06 June 2011, Page 125-130(2011).

[5] Symmetric key Cryptography using modified DJSSA symmetric key algorithm, Dripto Chatterjee, Joyshree Nath, Sankar Das, Shalabh Agarwal and Asoke Nath, Proceedings of International conference Worldcomp 2011 held at LasVegas 18-21 July 2011, Page-306-311, Vol-1(2011).

[6] An Integrated symmetric key cryptography algorithm using generalized vernam cipher method and DJSA method: DJMNA symmetric key algorithm : Debanjan Das, Joyshree Nath, Megholova Mukherjee, Neha Chaudhury and Asoke Nath: Proceedings of IEEE International conference : World Congress WICT-2011 to be held at Mumbai University 11-14 Dec, 2011, Page No.1203-1208(2011).

[7] Symmetric key cryptosystem using combined cryptographic algorithms- generalized modified vernam cipher method, MSA method and NJJSAA method: TTJSA algorithm – Trisha Chatterjee, Tamodeep Das, Joyshree Nath, Shayan Dey and Asoke Nath, Proceedings of IEEE International conference : World Congress WICT-2011 t held at Mumbai University 11-14 Dec, 2011, Page No. 1179-1184(2011).

[8] Symmetric key Cryptography using two-way updated – Generalized Vernam Cipher method: TTSJA algorithm, International Journal of Computer Applications(IJCA, USA), Vol 42, No.1, March, Pg: 34 -39(2012).

[9] Ultra Encryption Standard(UES) Version-I: Symmetric Key Cryptosystem using generalized modified Vernam Cipher method, Permutation method and Columnar Transposition method, Satyaki Roy, Navajit Maitra, Joyshree Nath,Shalabh Agarwal and Asoke Nath, Proceedings of IEEE sponsored National Conference on Recent Advances in Communication, Control and Computing Technology-RACCCT 2012, 29-30 March held at Surat, Page 81-88(2012).

[10] An Integrated Symmetric Key Cryptographic Method – Amalgamation of TTJSA Algorithm, Adbvanced Caeser Cipher Algorithm, Bit Rotation and reversal Method : SJA Algorithm., International Journal of Modern Education and Computer Science, Somdip Dey, Joyshree Nath, Asoke Nath,(IJMECS), ISSN: 2075-0161 (Print), ISSN: 2075-017X (Online), Vol-4, No-5, Page 1-9,2012.

[11] An Advanced Combined Symmetric Key Cryptographic Method using Bit manipulation, Bit Reversal, Modified Caeser Cipher(SD-REE), DJSA method, TTJSA method: SJA-I Algorithm, Somdip dey, Joyshree Nath, Asoke Nath, International Journal of Computer Applications(IJCA 0975-8887, USA), Vol. 46, No.20, Page- 46-53,May, 2012.

[12] Ultra Encryption Standard(UES) Version-IV: New Symmetric Key Cryptosystem with bit-level columnar Transposition and Reshuffling of Bits, Satyaki Roy, Navajit Maitra, Joyshree Nath, Shalabh Agarwal, Asoke Nath, International Journal of Computer Applications, USA, Vol 51-No 1, Page 28-35(2012).

[13] Bit Level Encryption Standard(BLES): Version-I, Neeraj Khanna, Dripto Chatterjee, Joyshree Nath, Asoke Nath, International Journal of Computer Applications, USA, Vol 52-No 2, Page 41-46(2012).

[14] Cryptography and Network Security, William Stallings, Prectice Hall of India.

SESSION

QUANTUM COMPUTING

Chair(s)

TBA

Equivalence of the Foulis-Holland Theorems and the Orthomodular Law in Quantum Logic: Part 1

Jack K. Horner
P. O. Box 266
Los Alamos, New Mexico 87544 USA

FCS 2013

Abstract

The optimization of quantum computing circuitry and compilers at some level must be expressed in terms of quantum-mechanical behaviors and operations. In much the same way that the structure of conventional propositional (Boolean) logic (BL) is the logic of the description of the behavior of classical physical systems and is isomorphic to a Boolean algebra (BA), so also the algebra, C(H), of closed linear subspaces of (equivalently, the system of linear operators on (observables in)) a Hilbert space is a logic of the descriptions of the behavior of quantum mechanical systems and is a model of an ortholattice (OL). An OL can thus be thought of as a kind of "quantum logic" (QL). C(H) is also a model of an orthomodular lattice (OML), which is an ortholattice to which the orthomodular law has been conjoined. Now a QL can be thought of as a BL in which the distributive law does not hold. Under certain commutativity conditions, a QL does satisfy the distributive law; among the most well known of these relationships are the Foulis-Holland theorems (FHTs). Here I provide an automated deduction of one of the four FHTs from OML.

Keywords: automated deduction, quantum computing, orthomodular lattice, Foulis-Holland theorems, Hilbert space

1.0 Introduction

The optimization of quantum computing circuitry and compilers at some level must be expressed in terms of the description of quantum-mechanical behaviors ([1], [17], [18], [20]). In much the same way that conventional propositional (Boolean) logic (BL,[12]) is the logical structure of description of the behavior of classical physical systems (e.g. "the measurements of the position and momentum of particle P are commutative", i.e., can be measured in either order, yielding the same results) and is isomorphic to a Boolean lattice ([10], [11], [19]), so also the algebra, *C(H)*, of the closed linear subspaces of (equivalently, the system of linear operators on (observables in)) a Hilbert space *H* ([1], [4], [6], [9], [13]) is *a* logic of the descriptions of the behavior of quantum mechanical systems (e.g., "the measurements of the position and momentum of particle P are *not* commutative") and is a model ([10]) of an ortholattice (OL; [4]). An OL can thus be thought of as a kind of "quantum logic" (QL; [19]). Figure 1 shows a set of axioms for an orthlolattice.

Lattice axioms

```
x = c(c(x))                          (AxLat1)
x v y = y v x                        (AxLat2)
(x v y) v z = x v (y v z)            (AxLat3)
(x ^ y) ^ z = x ^ (y ^ z)            (AxLat4)
x v (x ^ y) = x                      (AxLat5)
x ^ (x v y) = x                      (AxLat6)
```

Ortholattice axioms

```
c(x) ^ x = 0                         (AxOL1)
c(x) v x = 1                         (AxOL2)
x ^ y = c(c(x) v c(y))               (AxOL3)
```

A useful definition

```
1_2 = y v ((x ^ c(y)) v (c(x) ^ c(y)))
```

```
where
x, y are variables ranging over lattice nodes
^ is lattice meet
v is lattice join
c(x) is the orthocomplement of x
<-> means if and only if
= is equivalence ([12])
1 is the maximum lattice element (= x v c(x))
0 is the minimum lattice element (= c(1))
```

Figure 1. Lattice, ortholattice, ortholattice axioms, and a useful definition.

C(H) is also a model of an orthomodular lattice (OML; [4], [7]), which is an OL conjoined with the orthomodularity axiom (OMLaw):

```
y v (c(y) ^ (x v y)) =
    x v y          (OMLaw)
```

The rationalization of the OMA as a claim proper to physics has proven problematic ([13], Section 5-6), motivating the question of whether the OMA is required in an adequate characterization of QL. Thus formulated, the question suggests that the OMA and its equivalents are specific to an OML, and that as a consequence, banning the OMA from QL yields a "truer" quantum logic.

Now a QL can be thought of as a BL in which the distributive law

```
(D)  (x v (y ^ z) =
       (x v y) ^ (x v z))
```

does not hold. Under certain commutativity conditions, a QL does satisfy the distributive law; among the most well known of these relationships are the Foulis-Holland theorems (FHTs ([7])):

```
% Foulis-Holland theorem FH1
(C(x,y) & C(x,z)) -> ( (x ^ (y v z)) = ((x ^ y) v (x ^ z)) )

% Foulis-Holland theorem FH2
(C(x,y) & C(x,z)) -> ( (y ^ (x v z)) = ((y ^ x) v (y ^ z)) )


% Foulis-Holland theorem FH3
(C(x,y) & C(x,z)) -> ( (x v (y ^ z)) = ((x v y) ^ (x v z)) )
% Foulis-Holland theorem FH4
(C(x,y) & C(x,z)) -> ( (y v (x ^ z)) = ((y v x) ^ (y v z)) )

where C(x,y), "x commutes with y" is defined as

      C(x,y) <-> (x = ((x ^ y) v (x ^ c(y))))
```

Figure 2. The Foulis-Holland theorems.

2.0 Method

The OML axiomatizations of Megill, Pavičić, and Horner ([5], [14], [15], [16], [21]) were implemented in a *prover9* ([2]) script ([3]) configured to derive FH1, then executed in that framework on a Dell Inspiron 545 with an Intel Core2 Quad CPU Q8200 (clocked @ 2.33 GHz) and 8.00 GB RAM, running under the *Windows Vista Home Premium /Cygwin* operating environment.

3.0 Results

Figure 3 shows the proof, generated by [3] on the platform described in Section 2.0, that FH1 is implied by an OML:

```
============================== PROOF =================================

% Proof 1 at 3.67 (+ 0.06) seconds: "Foulis-Holland Theorem 1".
% Length of proof is 90.

4 C(x,y) & C(x,z) -> x ^ (y v z) = (x ^ y) v (x ^ z) # label("Foulis-Holland Theorem 1")
# label(non_clause) # label(goal).  [goal].
13 x = c(c(x)) # label("AxL1").  [assumption].
14 c(c(x)) = x.  [copy(13),flip(a)].
15 x v y = y v x # label("AxL2").  [assumption].
16 (x v y) v z = x v (y v z) # label("AxL3").  [assumption].
18 x v (x ^ y) = x # label("AxL5").  [assumption].
19 x ^ (x v y) = x # label("AxL6").  [assumption].
20 c(x) ^ x = 0 # label("AxOL1").  [assumption].
21 c(x) v x = 1 # label("AxOL2").  [assumption].
22 x v c(x) = 1.  [copy(21),rewrite([15(2)])].
23 x ^ y = c(c(x) v c(y)) # label("AxOL3").  [assumption].
67 1_2 = x v ((y ^ c(x)) v (c(y) ^ c(x))) # label("Df. 2.20").  [assumption].
68 x v (c(y v x) v c(c(y) v x)) = 1_2.
[copy(67),rewrite([23(3),14(4),23(7),14(6),14(6),15(7)]),flip(a)].
75 x v (c(x) ^ (y v x)) = y v x # label("OMLaw").  [assumption].
```

```
76 x v c(x v c(y v x)) = y v x.  [copy(75),rewrite([23(3),14(2)])].
77 (c1 ^ c2) v (c1 ^ c3) != c1 ^ (c2 v c3) # label("Foulis-Holland Theorem 1") #
answer("Foulis-Holland Theorem 1").  [deny(4)].
78 c(c(c1) v c(c2 v c3)) != c(c(c1) v c(c2)) v c(c(c1) v c(c3)) # answer("Foulis-Holland
Theorem 1").  [copy(77),rewrite([23(3),23(9),23(18)]),flip(a)].
83 c(1) = 0.  [back_rewrite(20),rewrite([23(2),14(2),22(2)])].
84 c(c(x) v c(x v y)) = x.  [back_rewrite(19),rewrite([23(2)])].
85 x v c(c(x) v c(y)) = x.  [back_rewrite(18),rewrite([23(1)])].
89 x v (y v z) = y v (x v z).  [para(15(a,1),16(a,1,1)),rewrite([16(2)])].
97 x v (c(x) v y) = 1 v y.  [para(22(a,1),16(a,1,1)),flip(a)].
98 x v (y v c(x v y)) = 1.  [para(22(a,1),16(a,1)),flip(a)].
99 x v (c(x v y) v c(c(y) v x)) = 1_2.  [para(15(a,1),68(a,1,2,1,1))].
108 x v c(x v c(x v y)) = y v x.  [para(15(a,1),76(a,1,2,1,2,1))].
110 x v (y v c(x v (y v c(z v (x v y))))) = z v (x v y).
[para(76(a,1),16(a,1)),rewrite([16(7)]),flip(a)].
113 1_2 = 1.  [para(76(a,1),68(a,1,2,1,1)),rewrite([84(13),15(7),15(8),22(8)]),flip(a)].
124 x v (c(x v y) v c(c(y) v x)) = 1.  [back_rewrite(99),rewrite([113(8)])].
133 c(x) v c(x v y) = c(x).  [para(84(a,1),14(a,1,1)),flip(a)].
137 c(0 v c(x)) = x.  [para(22(a,1),84(a,1,1,2,1)),rewrite([83(3),15(3)])].
141 1 v x = 1.  [para(83(a,1),84(a,1,1,1)),rewrite([137(6)])].
144 x v (c(x) v y) = 1.  [back_rewrite(97),rewrite([141(5)])].
146 x v c(c(x) v y) = x.  [para(14(a,1),85(a,1,2,1,2))].
150 x v 0 = x.  [para(22(a,1),85(a,1,2,1)),rewrite([83(2)])].
151 x v c(y v c(x)) = x.  [para(76(a,1),85(a,1,2,1))].
163 x v (y v c(x)) = y v 1.  [para(22(a,1),89(a,1,2)),flip(a)].
165 x v (y v c(x v c(z v x))) = y v (z v x).  [para(76(a,1),89(a,1,2)),flip(a)].
193 x v 1 = 1.  [para(141(a,1),15(a,1)),flip(a)].
195 x v (y v c(x)) = 1.  [back_rewrite(163),rewrite([193(5)])].
196 0 v x = x.  [para(150(a,1),15(a,1)),flip(a)].
207 x v (y v (c(x v y) v z)) = 1.  [para(144(a,1),16(a,1)),flip(a)].
210 x v (y v (z v c(x v y))) = 1.  [para(195(a,1),16(a,1)),flip(a)].
215 x v (c(c(x) v y) v z) = x v z.  [para(146(a,1),16(a,1,1)),flip(a)].
217 x v (y v c(c(x) v z)) = y v x.  [para(146(a,1),89(a,1,2)),flip(a)].
220 c(x) v c(y v x) = c(x).  [para(14(a,1),151(a,1,2,1,2))].
221 x v (c(y v c(x)) v z) = x v z.  [para(151(a,1),16(a,1,1)),flip(a)].
225 x v (y v c(z v c(x))) = y v x.  [para(151(a,1),89(a,1,2)),flip(a)].
230 x v (y v c(y v x)) = 1.  [para(15(a,1),98(a,1,2,2,1))].
234 c(x) v (c(x v y) v z) = c(x) v z.  [para(133(a,1),16(a,1,1)),flip(a)].
236 c(x) v (y v c(x v z)) = y v c(x).  [para(133(a,1),89(a,1,2)),flip(a)].
257 c(x) v (c(y v x) v z) = c(x) v z.  [para(220(a,1),16(a,1,1)),flip(a)].
259 c(x v y) v c(y v c(x v y)) = c(y).
[para(220(a,1),76(a,1,2,1,2,1)),rewrite([14(6),15(5),220(11)])].
260 c(x) v (y v c(z v x)) = y v c(x).  [para(220(a,1),89(a,1,2)),flip(a)].
262 x v (y v (c(y v x) v z)) = 1.
[para(230(a,1),16(a,1,1)),rewrite([141(2),16(5)]),flip(a)].
313 x v (y v (z v c(y v x))) = 1.  [para(15(a,1),210(a,1,2,2,2,1))].
326 c(c(x) v y) v (z v x) = z v x.
[para(146(a,1),110(a,1,2,2,1,2,2,1,2)),rewrite([215(10),165(9),146(9)])].
665 x v (y v (c(z v c(x)) v u)) = y v (x v u).  [para(221(a,1),89(a,1,2)),flip(a)].
741 x v c(x v c(y v c(x v y))) = 1.
[para(98(a,1),124(a,1,2,1,1)),rewrite([83(2),15(6),196(8)])].
855 c(x) v (y v (c(z v x) v u)) = c(x) v (y v u).
[para(326(a,1),215(a,1,2,1,1)),rewrite([16(6),16(9)])].
935 c(x) v (y v (c(x v z) v u)) = y v (c(x) v u).  [para(234(a,1),89(a,1,2)),flip(a)].
1166 c(x) v (y v (z v c(x v u))) = y v (z v c(x)).
[para(16(a,1),236(a,1,2)),rewrite([16(9)])].
1409 c(x) v (y v (z v c(u v x))) = y v (z v c(x)).
[para(16(a,1),260(a,1,2)),rewrite([16(9)])].
3700 x v c(y v c(x v y)) = x.
[para(741(a,1),108(a,1,2,1)),rewrite([83(2),150(2),15(5)]),flip(a)].
3710 x v c(y v c(y v x)) = x.  [para(15(a,1),3700(a,1,2,1,2,1))].
3719 x v c(y v x) = x v c(y).
[para(3700(a,1),151(a,1,2,1)),rewrite([15(5),236(5)]),flip(a)].
3992 c(x v y) v c(y v c(x)) = c(y).  [back_rewrite(259),rewrite([3719(5)])].
4092 x v c(x v y) = x v c(y).
[para(3710(a,1),151(a,1,2,1)),rewrite([15(5),260(5)]),flip(a)].
4093 x v (c(y v x) v z) = x v (c(y) v z).
[para(207(a,1),3710(a,1,2,1,2,1)),rewrite([83(6),150(6),15(6),935(6)]),flip(a)].
4094 x v (y v c(z v x)) = x v (y v c(z)).
[para(210(a,1),3710(a,1,2,1,2,1)),rewrite([83(6),150(6),15(6),1166(6)]),flip(a)].
```

```
4098 x v (c(x v y) v z) = c(y) v (x v z).
[para(262(a,1),3710(a,1,2,1,2,1)),rewrite([83(6),150(6),15(6),855(6)]),flip(a)].
4099 x v (y v c(x v z)) = x v (y v c(z)).
[para(313(a,1),3710(a,1,2,1,2,1)),rewrite([83(6),150(6),15(6),1409(6)]),flip(a)].
4102 c(x v y) v c(c(y) v x) = c(x).
[para(124(a,1),3710(a,1,2,1,2,1)),rewrite([83(8),150(8),15(8),260(8),15(4),133(4)]),flip(
a)].
4338 x v c(y v (z v x)) = x v c(y v z).  [para(16(a,1),3719(a,1,2,1))].
4342 c(x) v c(y v c(z v x)) = c(x) v c(y).
[para(3719(a,1),257(a,1,2)),rewrite([257(6)]),flip(a)].
4374 x v c(y v (x v z)) = x v c(y v z).  [para(89(a,1),4092(a,1,2,1))].
4419 c(x v c(c(y) v z)) = c(x v y) v c(c(y) v (x v c(z))).
[para(217(a,1),3992(a,1,1,1)),rewrite([15(8),4099(8)]),flip(a)].
4565 c(x v c(y v z)) = c(z v (x v c(y))) v c(x v c(z)).
[para(225(a,1),4102(a,1,2,1)),rewrite([14(2),15(4),4094(4),14(10)]),flip(a)].
4868 x v (y v (c(z v x) v u)) = y v (x v (c(z) v u)).
[para(4093(a,1),89(a,1,2)),flip(a)].
5175 c(x v y) v c(c(y) v (x v z)) = c(x v y) v c(x v z).
[para(4098(a,1),4374(a,1,2,1))].
5188 c(x v c(c(y) v z)) = c(x v y) v c(x v c(z)).
[back_rewrite(4419),rewrite([5175(13)])].
5751 c(x v y) v c(y v c(z v x)) = c(y).
[para(4338(a,1),4342(a,1,2,1)),rewrite([15(11),220(11)])].
5776 c(x v c(y v z)) v c(z v x) = c(x).  [para(5751(a,1),15(a,1)),flip(a)].
5896 c(x v c(y v z)) v c(y v x) = c(x).  [para(15(a,1),5776(a,1,1,1,2,1))].
6089 c(x v (y v c(z v u))) v c(z v (x v y)) = c(x v y).  [para(16(a,1),5896(a,1,1,1))].
6099 c(x v (c(y v z) v c(y v u))) v c(y v (x v c(z))) = c(x v c(y v z)).
[para(4099(a,1),5896(a,1,2,1)),rewrite([16(6)])].
6193 c(x v (c(y v z) v u)) = c(x v (z v (c(y) v u))) v c(x v (c(z) v u)).
[para(665(a,1),4102(a,1,2,1)),rewrite([14(2),15(5),4868(5),14(12)]),flip(a)].
6227 c(x v c(y v z)) = c(x v (z v c(y))) v c(x v c(z)).
[back_rewrite(6099),rewrite([6193(7),133(4),16(16),6089(15)]),flip(a)].
6529 c(x v (y v z)) v c(x v c(y)) = c(x v z) v c(x v c(y)).
[back_rewrite(5188),rewrite([6227(5),14(2)])].
6557 c(x v (y v c(z))) v c(y v c(x)) = c(y v c(z)) v c(y v c(x)).
[back_rewrite(4565),rewrite([6227(4),6529(8)]),flip(a)].
6566 $F # answer("Foulis-Holland Theorem 1").
[back_rewrite(78),rewrite([6227(8),89(7),6557(15)]),xx(a)].

============================== end of proof ==========================
```

Figure 3. Summary of a *prover9* ([2]) proof of FHT1 from OML. The proofs assume the default inference rules of *prover9*. The general form of a line in this proof is "*line_number conclusion [derivation]*", where *line_number* is a unique identifier of a line in the proof, and *conclusion* is the result of applying the *prover9* inference rules (such as *para*modulation, *copy*ing, and *rewrit*ing), noted in square brackets (denoting the *derivation*), to the lines cited in those brackets. Note that some of "logical" proof lines in the above have been transformed to two text lines, with the *derivation* appearing on a text line following a text line containing the first part of that logical line. The detailed syntax and semantics of these notations can be found in [2]. All *prover9* proofs are by default proofs by contradiction.

The total time to produce the proofs in Figure 3 on the platform described in Section 2.0 was approximately 3.7 seconds.

4.0 Discussion

The results of Section 3.0 motivate several observations:

1. FH1 is derivable from OML.

2. The proof in Section 3.0 is, as far as I know, novel.

3. Companion papers provide derivations of the remaining FHTs from OML, and a derivation of the OMLaw from an OML without the OMLaw, conjoined with the FHTs. The union of these proofs constitutes a proof of the equivalence of the OMLaw and the FHTs within OML theory.

5.0 Acknowledgements

This work benefited from discussions with Tom Oberdan, Frank Pecchioni, Tony Pawlicki, and the late John K. Prentice, whose passion for foundations of physics inspired those of us privileged to have known him. For any infelicities that remain, I am solely responsible.

6.0 References

[1] von Neumann J. *Mathematical Foundations of Quantum Mechanics*. 1936. Translated by R. T. Beyer. Princeton. 1983.

[2] McCune WW. *prover9 and mace4*. URL http://www.cs.unm.edu/~mccune/prover9/. 2009.

[3] Horner JK. *prover9* scripts for FH1. 2011. Available from the author on request.

[4] Dalla Chiara ML and Giuntini R. *Quantum Logics*. URL http://xxx.lanl.gov/abs/quant-ph/0101028. 2004.

[5] Megill ND and Pavičić M. Orthomodular lattices and quantum algebra. *International Journal of Theoretical Physics* 40 (2001), pp. 1387-1410.

[6] Akhiezer NI and Glazman IM. *Theory of Linear Operators in Hilbert Space. Volume I.* Translated by M. Nestell. Frederick Ungar. 1961.

[7] Holland, Jr. SS Orthomodularity in infinite dimensions: a theorem of M. Solèr. *Bulletin of the American Mathematical Society* 32 (1995), pp. 205-234.

[8] Marsden EL and Herman LM. *A condition for distribution in orthomodular lattices.* Kansas State University Technical Report #40. 1974.

[9] Knuth DE and Bendix PB. Simple word problems in universal algebras. In J. Leech, ed. *Computational Problems in Abstract Algebra.* Pergamon Press. 1970. pp. 263-297.

[10] Chang CC and Keisler HJ. *Model Theory.* North-Holland. 1990. pp. 38-39.

[11] Birkhoff G. *Lattice Theory.* Third Edition. American Mathematical Society. 1967.

[12] Church A. *Introduction to Mathematical Logic. Volume I.* Princeton. 1956.

[13] Jauch J. *Foundations of Quantum Mechanics.* Addison-Wesley. 1968.

[14] Megill ND. *Metamath.* URL http://us.metamath.org/qlegif/mmql.html#unify. 2004.

[15] Horner JK. An automated deduction system for orthomodular lattice theory. *Proceedings of the 2005 International Conference on Artificial Intelligence.* CSREA Press. 2005. pp. 260-265.

[16] Horner JK. An automated equational logic deduction of join elimination in orthomodular lattice theory. *Proceedings of the 2007 International Conference on Artificial Intelligence.* CSREA Press. 2007. pp. 481-488.

[17] Messiah A. *Quantum Mechanics*. Dover. 1958.

[18] Horner JK. Using automated theorem-provers to aid the design of efficient compilers for quantum computing. *Los Alamos National Laboratory Quantum Institute Workshop.* December 9–10, 2002. URL http://www.lanl.gov/science/centers/quantum/qls_pdfs/horner.pdf.

[19] Birkhoff G and von Neumann J. The logic of quantum mechanics. *Annals of Mathematics* 37 (1936), 823-243.

[20] Nielsen MA and Chuang L . *Quantum Computation and Quantum Information*. Cambridge. 2000.

[21] Pavičić M and Megill N. Quantum and classical implicational algebras with primitive implication. *International Journal of Theoretical Physics* 37 (1998), 2091-2098. ftp://m3k.grad.hr/pavicic/quantum-logic/1998-int-j-theor-phys-2.ps.gz.

Equivalence of the Foulis-Holland Theorems and the Orthomodular Law in Quantum Logic: Part 2

Jack K. Horner
P. O. Box 266
Los Alamos, New Mexico 87544 USA

FCS 2013

Abstract

The optimization of quantum computing circuitry and compilers at some level must be expressed in terms of quantum-mechanical behaviors and operations. In much the same way that the structure of conventional propositional (Boolean) logic (BL) is the logic of the description of the behavior of classical physical systems and is isomorphic to a Boolean algebra (BA), so also the algebra, C(H), of closed linear subspaces of (equivalently, the system of linear operators on (observables in)) a Hilbert space is a logic of the descriptions of the behavior of quantum mechanical systems and is a model of an ortholattice (OL). An OL can thus be thought of as a kind of "quantum logic" (QL). C(H) is also a model of an orthomodular lattice (OML), which is an ortholattice to which the orthomodular law has been conjoined. Now a QL can be thought of as a BL in which the distributive law does not hold. Under certain commutativity conditions, a QL does satisfy the distributive law; among the most well known of these relationships are the Foulis-Holland theorems (FHTs). Here I provide an automated deduction of one of the four FHTs from OML.

Keywords: automated deduction, quantum computing, orthomodular lattice, Foulis-Holland theorems, Hilbert space

1.0 Introduction

The optimization of quantum computing circuitry and compilers at some level must be expressed in terms of the description of quantum-mechanical behaviors ([1], [17], [18], [20]). In much the same way that conventional propositional (Boolean) logic (BL,[12]) is the logical structure of description of the behavior of classical physical systems (e.g. "the measurements of the position and momentum of particle P are commutative", i.e., can be measured in either order, yielding the same results) and is isomorphic to a Boolean lattice ([10], [11], [19]), so also the algebra, *C(H)*, of the closed linear subspaces of (equivalently, the system of linear operators on (observables in)) a Hilbert space *H* ([1], [4], [6], [9], [13]) is *a* logic of the descriptions of the behavior of quantum mechanical systems (e.g., "the measurements of the position and momentum of particle P are *not* commutative") and is a model ([10]) of an ortholattice (OL; [4]). An OL can thus be thought of as a kind of "quantum logic" (QL; [19]). Figure 1 shows a set of axioms for an orthlolattice.

```
Lattice axioms

        x = c(c(x))                        (AxLat1)
        x v y = y v x                      (AxLat2)
        (x v y) v z = x v (y v z)          (AxLat3)
        (x ^ y) ^ z = x ^ (y ^ z)          (AxLat4)
        x v (x ^ y) = x                    (AxLat5)
        x ^ (x v y) = x                    (AxLat6)

Ortholattice axioms
        c(x) ^ x = 0                       (AxOL1)
        c(x) v x = 1                       (AxOL2)
        x ^ y = c(c(x) v c(y))             (AxOL3)

A useful definition
        1_2 = y v ((x ^ c(y)) v (c(x) ^ c(y)))


where
    x, y are variables ranging over lattice nodes
    ^ is lattice meet
    v is lattice join
    c(x) is the orthocomplement of x
    <-> means if and only if
    =  is equivalence ([12])
    1 is the maximum lattice element (= x v c(x))
    0 is the minimum lattice element (= c(1))
```

Figure 1. Lattice, ortholattice, ortholattice axioms, and a useful definition.

C(H) is also a model of an orthomodular lattice (OML; [4], [7]), which is an OL conjoined with the orthomodularity axiom (OMLaw):

```
y v (c(y) ^ (x v y)) =
    x v y        (OMLaw)
```

The rationalization of the OMA as a claim proper to physics has proven problematic ([13], Section 5-6), motivating the question of whether the OMA is required in an adequate characterization of QL. Thus formulated, the question suggests that the OMA and its equivalents are specific to an OML, and that as a consequence, banning the OMA from QL yields a "truer" quantum logic.

Now a QL can be thought of as a BL in which the distributive law

```
(D)   (x v (y ^ z) =
      (x v y) ^ (x v z))
```

does not hold. Under certain commutativity conditions, a QL does satisfy the distributive law; among the most well known of these relationships are the Foulis-Holland theorems (FHTs ([7])):

```
% Foulis-Holland theorem FH1
(C(x,y) & C(x,z)) ->  ( (x ^ (y v z)) = ((x ^ y) v (x ^ z))  )

% Foulis-Holland theorem FH2
(C(x,y) & C(x,z)) ->  ( (y ^ (x v z)) = ((y ^ x) v (y ^ z))  )


% Foulis-Holland theorem FH3
(C(x,y) & C(x,z)) ->  ( (x v (y ^ z)) = ((x v y) ^ (x v z))  )

% Foulis-Holland theorem FH4
(C(x,y) & C(x,z)) ->  ( (y v (x ^ z)) = ((y v x) ^ (y v z))  )


where C(x,y), "x commutes with y" is defined as

      C(x,y) <-> (x = ((x ^ y) v (x ^ c(y))))
```

Figure 2. The Foulis-Holland theorems.

2.0 Method

The OML axiomatizations of Megill, Pavičić, and Horner ([5], [14], [15], [16], [21]) were implemented in a *prover9* ([2]) script ([3]) configured to derive FH2, then executed in that framework on a Dell Inspiron 545 with an Intel Core2 Quad CPU Q8200 (clocked @ 2.33 GHz) and 8.00 GB RAM, running under the *Windows Vista Home Premium /Cygwin* operating environment.

3.0 Results

Figure 3 shows the proof, generated by [3] on the platform described in Section 2.0, that FH2 is implied by an OML:

```
============================== PROOF =================================

% Proof 1 at 4.24 (+ 0.17) seconds: "Foulis-Holland Theorem 2".
% Length of proof is 82.
% Level of proof is 15.
% Maximum clause weight is 29.
% Given clauses 311.

4 C(x,y) & C(x,z) -> y ^ (x v z) = (y ^ x) v (y ^ z) # label("Foulis-Holland Theorem 2")
# label(non_clause) # label(goal).  [goal].
13 x = c(c(x)) # label("AxL1").  [assumption].
14 c(c(x)) = x.  [copy(13),flip(a)].
15 x v y = y v x # label("AxL2").  [assumption].
16 (x v y) v z = x v (y v z) # label("AxL3").  [assumption].
18 x v (x ^ y) = x # label("AxL5").  [assumption].
19 x ^ (x v y) = x # label("AxL6").  [assumption].
20 c(x) ^ x = 0 # label("AxOL1").  [assumption].
21 c(x) v x = 1 # label("AxOL2").  [assumption].
22 x v c(x) = 1.  [copy(21),rewrite([15(2)])].
23 x ^ y = c(c(x) v c(y)) # label("AxOL3").  [assumption].
67 1_2 = x v ((y ^ c(x)) v (c(y) ^ c(x))) # label("Df. 2.20").  [assumption].
68 x v (c(y v x) v c(c(y) v x)) = 1_2.
[copy(67),rewrite([23(3),14(4),23(7),14(6),14(6),15(7)]),flip(a)].
75 x v (c(x) ^ (y v x)) = y v x # label("OMLaw").  [assumption].
```

```
76 x v c(x v c(y v x)) = y v x.  [copy(75),rewrite([23(3),14(2)])].
77 (c2 ^ c1) v (c2 ^ c3) != c2 ^ (c1 v c3) # label("Foulis-Holland Theorem 2") #
answer("Foulis-Holland Theorem 2").  [deny(4)].
78 c(c(c2) v c(c1 v c3)) != c(c(c1) v c(c2)) v c(c(c2) v c(c3)) # answer("Foulis-Holland
Theorem 2").  [copy(77),rewrite([23(3),15(5),23(9),23(18)]),flip(a)].
83 c(1) = 0.  [back_rewrite(20),rewrite([23(2),14(2),22(2)])].
84 c(c(x) v c(x v y)) = x.  [back_rewrite(19),rewrite([23(2)])].
85 x v c(c(x) v c(y)) = x.  [back_rewrite(18),rewrite([23(1)])].
89 x v (y v z) = y v (x v z).  [para(15(a,1),16(a,1,1)),rewrite([16(2)])].
97 x v (c(x) v y) = 1 v y.  [para(22(a,1),16(a,1,1)),flip(a)].
98 x v (y v c(x v y)) = 1.  [para(22(a,1),16(a,1)),flip(a)].
99 x v (c(x v y) v c(c(y) v x)) = 1_2.  [para(15(a,1),68(a,1,2,1,1))].
101 x v (c(y v x) v (c(c(y) v x) v z)) = 1_2 v z.
[para(68(a,1),16(a,1,1)),rewrite([16(9)]),flip(a)].
108 x v c(x v c(x v y)) = y v x.  [para(15(a,1),76(a,1,2,1,2,1))].
110 x v (y v c(x v (y v c(z v (x v y))))) = z v (x v y).
[para(76(a,1),16(a,1)),rewrite([16(7)]),flip(a)].
113 1_2 = 1.  [para(76(a,1),68(a,1,2,1,1)),rewrite([84(13),15(7),15(8),22(8)]),flip(a)].
122 x v (c(y v x) v (c(c(y) v x) v z)) = 1 v z.  [back_rewrite(101),rewrite([113(9)])].
124 x v (c(x v y) v c(c(y) v x)) = 1.  [back_rewrite(99),rewrite([113(8)])].
133 c(x) v c(x v y) = c(x).  [para(84(a,1),14(a,1,1)),flip(a)].
137 c(0 v c(x)) = x.  [para(22(a,1),84(a,1,1,2,1)),rewrite([83(3),15(3)])].
141 1 v x = 1.  [para(83(a,1),84(a,1,1,1)),rewrite([137(6)])].
143 x v (c(y v x) v (c(c(y) v x) v z)) = 1.  [back_rewrite(122),rewrite([141(10)])].
144 x v (c(x) v y) = 1.  [back_rewrite(97),rewrite([141(5)])].
146 x v c(c(x) v y) = x.  [para(14(a,1),85(a,1,2,1,2))].
150 x v 0 = x.  [para(22(a,1),85(a,1,2,1)),rewrite([83(2)])].
151 x v c(y v c(x)) = x.  [para(76(a,1),85(a,1,2,1))].
163 x v (y v c(x)) = y v 1.  [para(22(a,1),89(a,1,2)),flip(a)].
165 x v (y v c(x v c(z v x))) = y v (z v x).  [para(76(a,1),89(a,1,2)),flip(a)].
193 x v 1 = 1.  [para(141(a,1),15(a,1)),flip(a)].
195 x v (y v c(x)) = 1.  [back_rewrite(163),rewrite([193(5)])].
196 0 v x = x.  [para(150(a,1),15(a,1)),flip(a)].
207 x v (y v (c(x v y) v z)) = 1.  [para(144(a,1),16(a,1)),flip(a)].
210 x v (y v (z v c(x v y))) = 1.  [para(195(a,1),16(a,1)),flip(a)].
215 x v (c(c(x) v y) v z) = x v z.  [para(146(a,1),16(a,1,1)),flip(a)].
220 c(x) v c(y v x) = c(x).  [para(14(a,1),151(a,1,2,1,2))].
221 x v (c(y v c(x)) v z) = x v z.  [para(151(a,1),16(a,1,1)),flip(a)].
234 c(x) v (c(x v y) v z) = c(x) v z.  [para(133(a,1),16(a,1,1)),flip(a)].
235 c(x v y) v c(x v (y v z)) = c(x v y).  [para(16(a,1),133(a,1,2,1))].
236 c(x) v (y v c(x v z)) = y v c(x).  [para(133(a,1),89(a,1,2)),flip(a)].
257 c(x) v (c(y v x) v z) = c(x) v z.  [para(220(a,1),16(a,1,1)),flip(a)].
260 c(x) v (y v c(z v x)) = y v c(x).  [para(220(a,1),89(a,1,2)),flip(a)].
313 x v (y v (z v c(y v x))) = 1.  [para(15(a,1),210(a,1,2,2,2,1))].
326 c(c(x) v y) v (z v x) = z v x.
[para(146(a,1),110(a,1,2,2,1,2,2,1,2)),rewrite([215(10),165(9),146(9)])].
665 x v (y v (c(z v c(x)) v u)) = y v (x v u).  [para(221(a,1),89(a,1,2)),flip(a)].
741 x v c(x v c(y v c(x v y))) = 1.
[para(98(a,1),124(a,1,2,1,1)),rewrite([83(2),15(6),196(8)])].
855 c(x) v (y v (c(z v x) v u)) = c(x) v (y v u).
[para(326(a,1),215(a,1,2,1,1)),rewrite([16(6),16(9)])].
935 c(x) v (y v (c(x v z) v u)) = y v (c(x) v u).  [para(234(a,1),89(a,1,2)),flip(a)].
1409 c(x) v (y v (z v c(u v x))) = y v (z v c(x)).
[para(16(a,1),260(a,1,2)),rewrite([16(9)])].
3700 x v c(y v c(x v y)) = x.
[para(741(a,1),108(a,1,2,1)),rewrite([83(2),150(2),15(5)]),flip(a)].
3710 x v c(y v c(y v x)) = x.  [para(15(a,1),3700(a,1,2,1,2,1))].
3719 x v c(y v x) = x v c(y).
[para(3700(a,1),151(a,1,2,1)),rewrite([15(5),236(5)]),flip(a)].
4093 x v (c(y v x) v z) = x v (c(y) v z).
[para(207(a,1),3710(a,1,2,1,2,1)),rewrite([83(6),150(6),15(6),935(6)]),flip(a)].
4099 x v (y v c(x v z)) = x v (y v c(z)).
[para(313(a,1),3710(a,1,2,1,2,1)),rewrite([83(6),150(6),15(6),1409(6)]),flip(a)].
4102 c(x v y) v c(c(y) v x) = c(x).
[para(124(a,1),3710(a,1,2,1,2,1)),rewrite([83(8),150(8),15(8),260(8),15(4),133(4)]),flip(
a)].
4105 c(x v y) v (c(c(x) v y) v z) = c(y) v z.
[para(143(a,1),3710(a,1,2,1,2,1)),rewrite([83(9),150(9),15(9),855(9),257(5)]),flip(a)].
4338 x v c(y v (z v x)) = x v c(y v z).  [para(16(a,1),3719(a,1,2,1))].
4342 c(x) v c(y v c(z v x)) = c(x) v c(y).
[para(3719(a,1),257(a,1,2)),rewrite([257(6)]),flip(a)].
```

```
4360 c(x v y) v c(y v (z v x)) = c(x v y).
[para(15(a,1),235(a,1,2,1)),rewrite([16(4)])].
4868 x v (y v (c(z v x) v u)) = y v (x v (c(z) v u)).
[para(4093(a,1),89(a,1,2)),flip(a)].
5751 c(x v y) v c(y v c(z v x)) = c(y).
[para(4338(a,1),4342(a,1,2,1)),rewrite([15(11),220(11)])].
5776 c(x v c(y v z)) v c(z v x) = c(x).  [para(5751(a,1),15(a,1)),flip(a)].
5896 c(x v c(y v z)) v c(y v x) = c(x).  [para(15(a,1),5776(a,1,1,1,2,1))].
6089 c(x v (y v c(z v u))) v c(z v (x v y)) = c(x v y).  [para(16(a,1),5896(a,1,1,1))].
6099 c(x v (c(y v z) v c(y v u))) v c(y v (x v c(z))) = c(x v c(y v z)).
[para(4099(a,1),5896(a,1,2,1)),rewrite([16(6)])].
6108 c(x v (y v z)) v c(z v x) = c(z v x).  [para(4360(a,1),15(a,1)),flip(a)].
6193 c(x v (c(y v z) v u)) = c(x v (z v (c(y) v u))) v c(x v (c(z) v u)).
[para(665(a,1),4102(a,1,2,1)),rewrite([14(2),15(5),4868(5),14(12)]),flip(a)].
6227 c(x v c(y v z)) = c(x v (z v c(y))) v c(x v c(z)).
[back_rewrite(6099),rewrite([6193(7),133(4),16(16),6089(15)]),flip(a)].
6566 c(c3 v (c(c1) v c(c2))) v c(c(c2) v c(c3)) != c(c(c1) v c(c2)) v c(c(c2) v c(c3)) #
answer("Foulis-Holland Theorem 2").  [back_rewrite(78),rewrite([6227(8),15(7),16(7)])].
7290 c(x v (y v z)) v c(z v c(x)) = c(y v z) v c(z v c(x)).
[para(6108(a,1),4105(a,1,2))].
7291 $F # answer("Foulis-Holland Theorem 2").  [resolve(7290,a,6566,a)].

============================== end of proof ==========================
```

Figure 3. Summary of a *prover9* ([2]) proof of FH2 from OML. The proofs assume the default inference rules of *prover9*. The general form of a line in this proof is "*line_number conclusion [derivation]*", where *line_number* is a unique identifier of a line in the proof, and *conclusion* is the result of applying the *prover9* inference rules (such as *para*modulation, *copy*ing, and *rewrit*ing), noted in square brackets (denoting the *derivation*), to the lines cited in those brackets. Note that some of "logical" proof lines in the above have been transformed to two text lines, with the *derivation* appearing on a text line following a text line containing the first part of that logical line. The detailed syntax and semantics of these notations can be found in [2]. All *prover9* proofs are by default proofs by contradiction.

The total time to produce the proofs in Figure 3 on the platform described in Section 2.0 was approximately 4.4 seconds.

4.0 Discussion

The results of Section 3.0 motivate several observations:

1. FH2 is derivable from OML.

2. The proof in Section 3.0 is, as far as I know, novel.

3. Companion papers provide derivations of the remaining FHTs from OML, and a derivation of the OMLaw from an OML without the OMLaw, conjoined with the FHTs. The union of these proofs constitutes a proof of the equivalence of the OMLaw and the FHTs within OML theory.

5.0 Acknowledgements

This work benefited from discussions with Tom Oberdan, Frank Pecchioni, Tony Pawlicki, and the late John K. Prentice, whose passion for foundations of physics inspired those of us privileged to have known him. For any infelicities that remain, I am solely responsible.

6.0 References

[1] von Neumann J. *Mathematical Foundations of Quantum Mechanics*. 1936. Translated by R. T. Beyer. Princeton. 1983.

[2] McCune WW. *prover9 and mace4*. URL http://www.cs.unm.edu/~mccune/prover9/. 2009.

[3] Horner JK. *prover9* scripts for FH2. 2011. Available from the author on request.

[4] Dalla Chiara ML and Giuntini R. *Quantum Logics*. URL http://xxx.lanl.gov/abs/quant-ph/0101028. 2004.

[5] Megill ND and Pavičić M. Orthomodular lattices and quantum algebra. *International Journal of Theoretical Physics* 40 (2001), pp. 1387-1410.

[6] Akhiezer NI and Glazman IM. *Theory of Linear Operators in Hilbert Space. Volume I.* Translated by M. Nestell. Frederick Ungar. 1961.

[7] Holland, Jr. SS Orthomodularity in infinite dimensions: a theorem of M. Solèr. *Bulletin of the American Mathematical Society* 32 (1995), pp. 205-234.

[8] Marsden EL and Herman LM. *A condition for distribution in orthomodular lattices.* Kansas State University Technical Report #40. 1974.

[9] Knuth DE and Bendix PB. Simple word problems in universal algebras. In J. Leech, ed. *Computational Problems in Abstract Algebra.* Pergamon Press. 1970. pp. 263-297.

[10] Chang CC and Keisler HJ. *Model Theory.* North-Holland. 1990. pp. 38-39.

[11] Birkhoff G. *Lattice Theory.* Third Edition. American Mathematical Society. 1967.

[12] Church A. *Introduction to Mathematical Logic. Volume I.* Princeton. 1956.

[13] Jauch J. *Foundations of Quantum Mechanics.* Addison-Wesley. 1968.

[14] Megill ND. *Metamath.* URL http://us.metamath.org/qlegif/mmql.html#unify. 2004.

[15] Horner JK. An automated deduction system for orthomodular lattice theory. *Proceedings of the 2005 International Conference on Artificial Intelligence.* CSREA Press. 2005. pp. 260-265.

[16] Horner JK. An automated equational logic deduction of join elimination in orthomodular lattice theory. *Proceedings of the 2007 International Conference on Artificial Intelligence.* CSREA Press. 2007. pp. 481-488.

[17] Messiah A. *Quantum Mechanics.* Dover. 1958.

[18] Horner JK. Using automated theorem-provers to aid the design of efficient compilers for quantum computing. *Los Alamos National Laboratory Quantum Institute Workshop.* December 9–10, 2002. URL http://www.lanl.gov/science/centers/quantum/qls_pdfs/horner.pdf.

[19] Birkhoff G and von Neumann J. The logic of quantum mechanics. *Annals of Mathematics* 37 (1936), 823-243.

[20] Nielsen MA and Chuang L . *Quantum Computation and Quantum Information.* Cambridge. 2000.

[21] Pavičić M and Megill N. Quantum and classical implicational algebras with primitive implication. *International Journal of Theoretical Physics* 37 (1998), 2091-2098. ftp://m3k.grad.hr/pavicic/quantum-logic/1998-int-j-theor-phys-2.ps.gz.

Equivalence of the Foulis-Holland Theorems and the Orthomodular Law in Quantum Logic: Part 3

Jack K. Horner
P. O. Box 266
Los Alamos, New Mexico 87544 USA

FCS 2013

Abstract

The optimization of quantum computing circuitry and compilers at some level must be expressed in terms of quantum-mechanical behaviors and operations. In much the same way that the structure of conventional propositional (Boolean) logic (BL) is the logic of the description of the behavior of classical physical systems and is isomorphic to a Boolean algebra (BA), so also the algebra, C(H), of closed linear subspaces of (equivalently, the system of linear operators on (observables in)) a Hilbert space is a logic of the descriptions of the behavior of quantum mechanical systems and is a model of an ortholattice (OL). An OL can thus be thought of as a kind of "quantum logic" (QL). C(H) is also a model of an orthomodular lattice (OML), which is an ortholattice to which the orthomodular law has been conjoined. Now a QL can be thought of as a BL in which the distributive law does not hold. Under certain commutativity conditions, a QL does satisfy the distributive law; among the most well known of these relationships are the Foulis-Holland theorems (FHTs). Here I provide an automated deduction of one of the four FHTs from OML.

Keywords: automated deduction, quantum computing, orthomodular lattice, Foulis-Holland theorems, Hilbert space

1.0 Introduction

The optimization of quantum computing circuitry and compilers at some level must be expressed in terms of the description of quantum-mechanical behaviors ([1], [17], [18], [20]). In much the same way that conventional propositional (Boolean) logic (BL,[12]) is the logical structure of description of the behavior of classical physical systems (e.g. "the measurements of the position and momentum of particle P are commutative", i.e., can be measured in either order, yielding the same results) and is isomorphic to a Boolean lattice ([10], [11], [19]), so also the algebra, *C(H)*, of the closed linear subspaces of (equivalently, the system of linear operators on (observables in)) a Hilbert space *H* ([1], [4], [6], [9], [13]) is *a* logic of the descriptions of the behavior of quantum mechanical systems (e.g., "the measurements of the position and momentum of particle P are *not* commutative") and is a model ([10]) of an ortholattice (OL; [4]). An OL can thus be thought of as a kind of "quantum logic" (QL; [19]). Figure 1 shows a set of axioms for an orthlolattice

```
Lattice axioms

        x = c(c(x))                         (AxLat1)
        x v y = y v x                       (AxLat2)
        (x v y) v z = x v (y v z)           (AxLat3)
        (x ^ y) ^ z = x ^ (y ^ z)           (AxLat4)
        x v (x ^ y) = x                     (AxLat5)
        x ^ (x v y) = x                     (AxLat6)

Ortholattice axioms
        c(x) ^ x = 0                        (AxOL1)
        c(x) v x = 1                        (AxOL2)
        x ^ y = c(c(x) v c(y))              (AxOL3)

A useful definition
         1_2 = y v ((x ^ c(y)) v (c(x) ^ c(y)))


where
    x, y are variables ranging over lattice nodes
    ^ is lattice meet
    v is lattice join
    c(x) is the orthocomplement of x
    <-> means if and only if
    =  is equivalence ([12])
    1 is the maximum lattice element (= x v c(x))
    0 is the minimum lattice element (= c(1))
```

Figure 1. Lattice, ortholattice, ortholattice axioms, and a useful definition.

C(H) is also a model of an orthomodular lattice (OML; [4], [7]), which is an OL conjoined with the orthomodularity axiom (OMLaw):

```
y v (c(y) ^ (x v y)) =
      x v y        (OMLaw)
```

The rationalization of the OMA as a claim proper to physics has proven problematic ([13], Section 5-6), motivating the question of whether the OMA is required in an adequate characterization of QL. Thus formulated, the question suggests that the OMA and its equivalents are specific to an OML, and that as a consequence, banning the OMA from QL yields a "truer" quantum logic.

Now a QL can be thought of as a BL in which the distributive law

```
(D)    (x v (y ^ z) =
            (x v y) ^ (x v z))
```

does not hold. Under certain commutativity conditions, a QL does satisfy the distributive law; among the most well known of these relationships are the Foulis-Holland theorems (FHTs ([7])):

```
% Foulis-Holland theorem FH1
(C(x,y) & C(x,z)) ->  ( (x ^ (y v z)) = ((x ^ y) v (x ^ z))  )

% Foulis-Holland theorem FH2
(C(x,y) & C(x,z)) ->  ( (y ^ (x v z)) = ((y ^ x) v (y ^ z))  )


% Foulis-Holland theorem FH3
(C(x,y) & C(x,z)) ->  ( (x v (y ^ z)) = ((x v y) ^ (x v z))  )

% Foulis-Holland theorem FH4
(C(x,y) & C(x,z)) ->  ( (y v (x ^ z)) = ((y v x) ^ (y v z))  )

where C(x,y), "x commutes with y" is defined as

      C(x,y) <-> (x = ((x ^ y) v (x ^ c(y))))
```

Figure 2. The Foulis-Holland theorems.

2.0 Method

The OML axiomatizations of Megill, Pavičić, and Horner ([5], [14], [15], [16], [21]) were implemented in a *prover9* ([2]) script ([3]) configured to derive FH3, then executed in that framework on a Dell Inspiron 545 with an Intel Core2 Quad CPU Q8200 (clocked @ 2.33 GHz) and 8.00 GB RAM, running under the *Windows Vista Home Premium /Cygwin* operating environment.

3.0 Results

Figure 3 shows the proof, generated by [3] on the platform described in Section 2.0, that FH3 is implied by an OML:

```
============================== PROOF =================================

% Proof 1 at 2.32 (+ 0.11) seconds: "Foulis-Holland Theorem 3".
% Length of proof is 54.

4 C(x,y) & C(x,z) -> x v (y ^ z) = (x v y) ^ (x v z) # label("Foulis-Holland Theorem 3")
# label(non_clause) # label(goal).  [goal].
13 x = c(c(x)) # label("AxL1").  [assumption].
14 c(c(x)) = x.  [copy(13),flip(a)].
15 x v y= y v x# label("AxL2").  [assumption].
16 (x v y) v z = x v (y v z) # label("AxL3").  [assumption].
18 x v (x ^ y) = x # label("AxL5").  [assumption].
19 x ^ (x v y) = x # label("AxL6").  [assumption].
20 c(x) ^ x = 0 # label("AxOL1").  [assumption].
21 c(x) v x = 1 # label("AxOL2").  [assumption].
22 x v c(x) = 1.  [copy(21),rewrite([15(2)])].
23 x ^ y = c(c(x) v c(y)) # label("AxOL3").  [assumption].
67 1_2 = x v ((y ^ c(x)) v (c(y) ^ c(x))) # label("Df. 2.20").  [assumption].
68 x v (c(y v x) v c(c(y) v x)) = 1_2.
[copy(67),rewrite([23(3),14(4),23(7),14(6),14(6),15(7)]),flip(a)].
75 x v (c(x) ^ (y v x)) = y v x # label("OMLaw").  [assumption].
```

```
76 x v c(x v c(y v x)) = y v x.  [copy(75),rewrite([23(3),14(2)])].
77 c1 v (c2 ^ c3) != (c1 v c2) ^ (c1 v c3) # label("Foulis-Holland Theorem 3") #
answer("Foulis-Holland Theorem 3").  [deny(4)].
78 c(c(c1 v c2) v c(c1 v c3)) != c1 v c(c(c2) v c(c3)) # answer("Foulis-Holland Theorem
3").  [copy(77),rewrite([23(4),23(15)]),flip(a)].
83 c(1) = 0.  [back_rewrite(20),rewrite([23(2),14(2),22(2)])].
84 c(c(x) v c(x v y)) = x.  [back_rewrite(19),rewrite([23(2)])].
85 x v c(c(x) v c(y)) = x.  [back_rewrite(18),rewrite([23(1)])].
89 x v (y v z) = y v (x v z).  [para(15(a,1),16(a,1,1)),rewrite([16(2)])].
98 x v (y v c(x v y)) = 1.  [para(22(a,1),16(a,1)),flip(a)].
99 x v (c(x v y) v c(c(y) v x)) = 1_2.  [para(15(a,1),68(a,1,2,1,1))].
108 x v c(x v c(x v y)) = y v x.  [para(15(a,1),76(a,1,2,1,2,1))].
110 x v (y v c(x v (y v c(z v (x v y))))) = z v (x v y).
[para(76(a,1),16(a,1)),rewrite([16(7)]),flip(a)].
113 1_2 = 1.  [para(76(a,1),68(a,1,2,1,1)),rewrite([84(13),15(7),15(8),22(8)]),flip(a)].
124 x v (c(x v y) v c(c(y) v x)) = 1.  [back_rewrite(99),rewrite([113(8)])].
133 c(x) v c(x v y) = c(x).  [para(84(a,1),14(a,1,1)),flip(a)].
137 c(0 v c(x)) = x.  [para(22(a,1),84(a,1,1,2,1)),rewrite([83(3),15(3)])].
141 1 v x = 1.  [para(83(a,1),84(a,1,1,1)),rewrite([137(6)])].
146 x v c(c(x) v y) = x.  [para(14(a,1),85(a,1,2,1,2))].
150 x v 0 = x.  [para(22(a,1),85(a,1,2,1)),rewrite([83(2)])].
151 x v c(y v c(x)) = x.  [para(76(a,1),85(a,1,2,1))].
165 x v (y v c(x v c(z v x))) = y v (z v x).  [para(76(a,1),89(a,1,2)),flip(a)].
196 0 v x = x.  [para(150(a,1),15(a,1)),flip(a)].
215 x v (c(c(x) v y) v z) = x v z.  [para(146(a,1),16(a,1,1)),flip(a)].
220 c(x) v c(y v x) = c(x).  [para(14(a,1),151(a,1,2,1,2))].
230 x v (y v c(y v x)) = 1.  [para(15(a,1),98(a,1,2,2,1))].
234 c(x) v (c(x v y) v z) = c(x) v z.  [para(133(a,1),16(a,1,1)),flip(a)].
236 c(x) v (y v c(x v z)) = y v c(x).  [para(133(a,1),89(a,1,2)),flip(a)].
259 c(x v y) v c(y v c(x v y)) = c(y).
[para(220(a,1),76(a,1,2,1,2,1)),rewrite([14(6),15(5),220(11)])].
260 c(x) v (y v c(z v x)) = y v c(x).  [para(220(a,1),89(a,1,2)),flip(a)].
262 x v (y v (c(y v x) v z)) = 1.
[para(230(a,1),16(a,1,1)),rewrite([141(2),16(5)]),flip(a)].
326 c(c(x) v y) v (z v x) = z v x.
[para(146(a,1),110(a,1,2,2,1,2,2,1,2)),rewrite([215(10),165(9),146(9)])].
741 x v c(x v c(y v c(x v y))) = 1.
[para(98(a,1),124(a,1,2,1,1)),rewrite([83(2),15(6),196(8)])].
855 c(x) v (y v (c(z v x) v u)) = c(x) v (y v u).
[para(326(a,1),215(a,1,2,1,1)),rewrite([16(6),16(9)])].
3700 x v c(y v c(x v y)) = x.
[para(741(a,1),108(a,1,2,1)),rewrite([83(2),150(2),15(5)]),flip(a)].
3710 x v c(y v c(y v x)) = x.  [para(15(a,1),3700(a,1,2,1,2,1))].
3719 x v c(y v x) = x v c(y).
[para(3700(a,1),151(a,1,2,1)),rewrite([15(5),236(5)]),flip(a)].
3992 c(x v y) v c(y v c(x)) = c(y).  [back_rewrite(259),rewrite([3719(5)])].
4092 x v c(x v y) = x v c(y).
[para(3710(a,1),151(a,1,2,1)),rewrite([15(5),260(5)]),flip(a)].
4098 x v (c(x v y) v z) = c(y) v (x v z).
[para(262(a,1),3710(a,1,2,1,2,1)),rewrite([83(6),150(6),15(6),855(6)]),flip(a)].
4422 c(c(x v y) v z) = c(c(x) v z) v c(c(y) v (x v z)).
[para(234(a,1),3992(a,1,1,1)),rewrite([14(8),15(7),4098(7)]),flip(a)].
4544 $F # answer("Foulis-Holland Theorem 3").
[back_rewrite(78),rewrite([4422(10),133(7),14(3),4092(9),89(8),4092(10)]),xx(a)].

============================== end of proof ==============================
```

Figure 3. Summary of a *prover9* ([2]) proof of FH3 from OML. The proofs assume the default inference rules of *prover9*. The general form of a line in this proof is "*line_number conclusion [derivation]*", where *line_number* is a unique identifier of a line in the proof, and *conclusion* is the result of applying the *prover9* inference rules (such as *para*modulation, *copy*ing, and *rewrit*ing), noted in square brackets (denoting the *derivation*), to the lines cited in those brackets. Note that some of "logical" proof lines in the above have been transformed to two text lines, with the *derivation* appearing on a text line following a text line containing the first part of that logical line. The detailed syntax and semantics of these notations can be found in [2]. All *prover9* proofs are by default proofs by contradiction.

The total time to produce the proofs in Figure 3 on the platform described in Section 2.0 was approximately 2.4 seconds.

4.0 Discussion

The results of Section 3.0 motivate several observations:

1. FH3 is derivable from OML.

2. The proof in Section 3.0 is, as far as I know, novel.

3. Companion papers provide derivations of the remaining FHTs from OML, and a derivation of the OMLaw from an OML without the OMLaw, conjoined with the FHTs. The union of these proofs constitutes a proof of the equivalence of the OMLaw and the FHTs within OML theory.

5.0 Acknowledgements

This work benefited from discussions with Tom Oberdan, Frank Pecchioni, Tony Pawlicki, and the late John K. Prentice, whose passion for foundations of physics inspired those of us privileged to have known him. For any infelicities that remain, I am solely responsible.

6.0 References

[1] von Neumann J. *Mathematical Foundations of Quantum Mechanics*. 1936. Translated by R. T. Beyer. Princeton. 1983.

[2] McCune WW. *prover9 and mace4*. URL http://www.cs.unm.edu/~mccune/prover9/. 2009.

[3] Horner JK. *prover9* scripts for FH3. 2011. Available from the author on request.

[4] Dalla Chiara ML and Giuntini R. *Quantum Logics*. URL http://xxx.lanl.gov/abs/quant-ph/0101028. 2004.

[5] Megill ND and Pavičić M. Orthomodular lattices and quantum algebra. *International Journal of Theoretical Physics* 40 (2001), pp. 1387-1410.

[6] Akhiezer NI and Glazman IM. *Theory of Linear Operators in Hilbert Space. Volume I.* Translated by M. Nestell. Frederick Ungar. 1961.

[7] Holland, Jr. SS Orthomodularity in infinite dimensions: a theorem of M. Solèr. *Bulletin of the American Mathematical Society* 32 (1995), pp. 205-234.

[8] Marsden EL and Herman LM. *A condition for distribution in orthomodular lattices.* Kansas State University Technical Report #40. 1974.

[9] Knuth DE and Bendix PB. Simple word problems in universal algebras. In J. Leech, ed. *Computational Problems in Abstract Algebra.* Pergamon Press. 1970. pp. 263-297.

[10] Chang CC and Keisler HJ. *Model Theory.* North-Holland. 1990. pp. 38-39.

[11] Birkhoff G. *Lattice Theory.* Third Edition. American Mathematical Society. 1967.

[12] Church A. *Introduction to Mathematical Logic. Volume I.* Princeton. 1956.

[13] Jauch J. *Foundations of Quantum Mechanics.* Addison-Wesley. 1968.

[14] Megill ND. *Metamath.* URL http://us.metamath.org/qlegif/mmql.html#unify. 2004.

[15] Horner JK. An automated deduction system for orthomodular lattice theory.

Proceedings of the 2005 International Conference on Artificial Intelligence. CSREA Press. 2005. pp. 260-265.

[16] Horner JK. An automated equational logic deduction of join elimination in orthomodular lattice theory. *Proceedings of the 2007 International Conference on Artificial Intelligence.* CSREA Press. 2007. pp. 481-488.

[17] Messiah A. *Quantum Mechanics*. Dover. 1958.

[18] Horner JK. Using automated theorem-provers to aid the design of efficient compilers for quantum computing. *Los Alamos National Laboratory Quantum Institute Workshop.* December 9–10, 2002. URL http://www.lanl.gov/science/centers/quantum/qls_pdfs/horner.pdf.

[19] Birkhoff G and von Neumann J. The logic of quantum mechanics. *Annals of Mathematics* 37 (1936), 823-243.

[20] Nielsen MA and Chuang L . *Quantum Computation and Quantum Information*. Cambridge. 2000.

[21] Pavičić M and Megill N. Quantum and classical implicational algebras with primitive implication. *International Journal of Theoretical Physics* 37 (1998), 2091-2098. ftp://m3k.grad.hr/pavicic/quantum-logic/1998-int-j-theor-phys-2.ps.gz.

Equivalence of the Foulis-Holland Theorems and the Orthomodular Law in Quantum Logic: Part 4

Jack K. Horner
P. O. Box 266
Los Alamos, New Mexico 87544 USA

FCS 2013

Abstract

The optimization of quantum computing circuitry and compilers at some level must be expressed in terms of quantum-mechanical behaviors and operations. In much the same way that the structure of conventional propositional (Boolean) logic (BL) is the logic of the description of the behavior of classical physical systems and is isomorphic to a Boolean algebra (BA), so also the algebra, C(H), of closed linear subspaces of (equivalently, the system of linear operators on (observables in)) a Hilbert space is a logic of the descriptions of the behavior of quantum mechanical systems and is a model of an ortholattice (OL). An OL can thus be thought of as a kind of "quantum logic" (QL). C(H) is also a model of an orthomodular lattice (OML), which is an ortholattice to which the orthomodular law has been conjoined. Now a QL can be thought of as a BL in which the distributive law does not hold. Under certain commutativity conditions, a QL does satisfy the distributive law; among the most well known of these relationships are the Foulis-Holland theorems (FHTs). Here I provide an automated deduction of one of the four FHTs from OML.

Keywords: automated deduction, quantum computing, orthomodular lattice, Foulis-Holland theorems, Hilbert space

1.0 Introduction

The optimization of quantum computing circuitry and compilers at some level must be expressed in terms of the description of quantum-mechanical behaviors ([1], [17], [18], [20]). In much the same way that conventional propositional (Boolean) logic (BL,[12]) is the logical structure of description of the behavior of classical physical systems (e.g. "the measurements of the position and momentum of particle P are commutative", i.e., can be measured in either order, yielding the same results) and is isomorphic to a Boolean lattice ([10], [11], [19]), so also the algebra, *C(H)*, of the closed linear subspaces of (equivalently, the system of linear operators on (observables in)) a Hilbert space *H* ([1], [4], [6], [9], [13]) is *a* logic of the descriptions of the behavior of quantum mechanical systems (e.g., "the measurements of the position and momentum of particle P are *not* commutative") and is a model ([10]) of an ortholattice (OL; [4]). An OL can thus be thought of as a kind of "quantum logic" (QL; [19]). Figure 1 shows a set of axioms for an orthlolattice.

```
Lattice axioms

        x = c(c(x))                        (AxLat1)
        x v y = y v x                      (AxLat2)
        (x v y) v z = x v (y v z)          (AxLat3)
        (x ^ y) ^ z = x ^ (y ^ z)          (AxLat4)
        x v (x ^ y) = x                    (AxLat5)
        x ^ (x v y) = x                    (AxLat6)

Ortholattice axioms
        c(x) ^ x = 0                       (AxOL1)
        c(x) v x = 1                       (AxOL2)
        x ^ y = c(c(x) v c(y))             (AxOL3)


A useful definition
         1_2 = y v ((x ^ c(y)) v (c(x) ^ c(y)))


where
    x, y are variables ranging over lattice nodes
    ^ is lattice meet
    v is lattice join
    c(x) is the orthocomplement of x
    <-> means if and only if
    =  is equivalence ([12])
    1 is the maximum lattice element (= x v c(x))
    0 is the minimum lattice element (= c(1))
```

Figure 1. Lattice, ortholattice, ortholattice axioms, and a useful definition.

C(H) is also a model of an orthomodular lattice (OML; [4], [7]), which is an OL conjoined with the orthomodularity axiom (OMLaw):

```
y v (c(y) ^ (x v y)) =
      x v y          (OMLaw)
```

The rationalization of the OMA as a claim proper to physics has proven problematic ([13], Section 5-6), motivating the question of whether the OMA is required in an adequate characterization of QL. Thus formulated, the question suggests that the OMA and its equivalents are specific to an OML, and that as a consequence, banning the OMA from QL yields a "truer" quantum logic.

Now a QL can be thought of as a BL in which the distributive law

```
(D)   (x v (y ^ z) =
        (x v y) ^ (x v z))
```

does not hold. Under certain commutativity conditions, a QL does satisfy (D); among the most well known of these relationships are the Foulis-Holland theorems (FHTs ([7])):

```
% Foulis-Holland theorem FH1
(C(x,y) & C(x,z)) ->  ( (x ^ (y v z)) = ((x ^ y) v (x ^ z))  )

% Foulis-Holland theorem FH2
(C(x,y) & C(x,z)) ->  ( (y ^ (x v z)) = ((y ^ x) v (y ^ z))  )

% Foulis-Holland theorem FH3
(C(x,y) & C(x,z)) ->  ( (x v (y ^ z)) = ((x v y) ^ (x v z))  )

% Foulis-Holland theorem FH4
(C(x,y) & C(x,z)) ->  ( (y v (x ^ z)) = ((y v x) ^ (y v z))  )

where C(x,y), "x commutes with y" is defined as

      C(x,y) <-> (x = ((x ^ y) v (x ^ c(y))))
```

Figure 2. The Foulis-Holland theorems.

2.0 Method

The OML axiomatizations of Megill, Pavičić, and Horner ([5], [14], [15], [16], [21]) were implemented in a *prover9* ([2]) script ([3]) configured to derive FH4, then executed in that framework on a Dell Inspiron 545 with an Intel Core2 Quad CPU Q8200 (clocked @ 2.33 GHz) and 8.00 GB RAM, running under the *Windows Vista Home Premium /Cygwin* operating environment.

3.0 Results

Figure 3 shows the proof, generated by [3] on the platform described in Section 2.0, that FH4 is implied by an OML:

```
============================== PROOF =================================

% Proof 1 at 3.68 (+ 0.06) seconds: "Foulis-Holland Theorem 4".
% Length of proof is 96.

4 C(x,y) & C(x,z) -> y v (x ^ z) = (y v x) ^ (y v z) # label("Foulis-Holland Theorem 4")
# label(non_clause) # label(goal).  [goal].
13 x = c(c(x)) # label("AxL1").  [assumption].
14 c(c(x)) = x.  [copy(13),flip(a)].
15 x v y = y v x # label("AxL2").  [assumption].
16 (x v y) v z = x v (y v z) # label("AxL3").  [assumption].
18 x v (x ^ y) = x # label("AxL5").  [assumption].
19 x ^ (x v y) = x # label("AxL6").  [assumption].
20 c(x) ^ x = 0 # label("AxOL1").  [assumption].
21 c(x) v x = 1 # label("AxOL2").  [assumption].
22 x v c(x) = 1.  [copy(21),rewrite([15(2)])].
23 x ^ y = c(c(x) v c(y)) # label("AxOL3").  [assumption].
67 1_2 = x v ((y ^ c(x)) v (c(y) ^ c(x))) # label("Df. 2.20").  [assumption].
68 x v (c(y v x) v c(c(y) v x)) = 1_2.
[copy(67),rewrite([23(3),14(4),23(7),14(6),14(6),15(7)]),flip(a)].
75 x v (c(x) ^ (y v x)) = y v x # label("OMLaw").  [assumption].
76 x v c(x v c(y v x)) = y v x.  [copy(75),rewrite([23(3),14(2)])].
```

```
77 c2 v (c1 ^ c3) != (c2 v c1) ^ (c2 v c3) # label("Foulis-Holland Theorem 4") #
answer("Foulis-Holland Theorem 4").  [deny(4)].
78 c(c(c1 v c2) v c(c2 v c3)) != c2 v c(c(c1) v c(c3)) # answer("Foulis-Holland Theorem
4").  [copy(77),rewrite([23(4),15(11),23(15)]),flip(a)].
83 c(1) = 0.  [back_rewrite(20),rewrite([23(2),14(2),22(2)])].
84 c(c(x) v c(x v y)) = x.  [back_rewrite(19),rewrite([23(2)])].
85 x v c(c(x) v c(y)) = x.  [back_rewrite(18),rewrite([23(1)])].
89 x v (y v z) = y v (x v z).  [para(15(a,1),16(a,1,1)),rewrite([16(2)])].
97 x v (c(x) v y) = 1 v y.  [para(22(a,1),16(a,1,1)),flip(a)].
98 x v (y v c(x v y)) = 1.  [para(22(a,1),16(a,1)),flip(a)].
99 x v (c(x v y) v c(c(y) v x)) = 1_2.  [para(15(a,1),68(a,1,2,1,1))].
101 x v (c(y v x) v (c(c(y) v x) v z)) = 1_2 v z.
[para(68(a,1),16(a,1,1)),rewrite([16(9)]),flip(a)].
108 x v c(x v c(x v y)) = y v x.  [para(15(a,1),76(a,1,2,1,2,1))].
110 x v (y v c(x v (y v c(z v (x v y))))) = z v (x v y).
[para(76(a,1),16(a,1)),rewrite([16(7)]),flip(a)].
113 1_2 = 1.  [para(76(a,1),68(a,1,2,1,1)),rewrite([84(13),15(7),15(8),22(8)]),flip(a)].
122 x v (c(y v x) v (c(c(y) v x) v z)) = 1 v z.  [back_rewrite(101),rewrite([113(9)])].
124 x v (c(x v y) v c(c(y) v x)) = 1.  [back_rewrite(99),rewrite([113(8)])].
133 c(x) v c(x v y) = c(x).  [para(84(a,1),14(a,1,1)),flip(a)].
137 c(0 v c(x)) = x.  [para(22(a,1),84(a,1,1,2,1)),rewrite([83(3),15(3)])].
141 1 v x = 1.  [para(83(a,1),84(a,1,1,1)),rewrite([137(6)])].
143 x v (c(y v x) v (c(c(y) v x) v z)) = 1.  [back_rewrite(122),rewrite([141(10)])].
144 x v (c(x) v y) = 1.  [back_rewrite(97),rewrite([141(5)])].
146 x v c(c(x) v y) = x.  [para(14(a,1),85(a,1,2,1,2))].
150 x v 0 = x.  [para(22(a,1),85(a,1,2,1)),rewrite([83(2)])].
151 x v c(y v c(x)) = x.  [para(76(a,1),85(a,1,2,1))].
163 x v (y v c(x)) = y v 1.  [para(22(a,1),89(a,1,2)),flip(a)].
165 x v (y v c(x v c(z v x))) = y v (z v x).  [para(76(a,1),89(a,1,2)),flip(a)].
193 x v 1 = 1.  [para(141(a,1),15(a,1)),flip(a)].
195 x v (y v c(x)) = 1.  [back_rewrite(163),rewrite([193(5)])].
196 0 v x = x.  [para(150(a,1),15(a,1)),flip(a)].
207 x v (y v (c(x v y) v z)) = 1.  [para(144(a,1),16(a,1)),flip(a)].
210 x v (y v (z v c(x v y))) = 1.  [para(195(a,1),16(a,1)),flip(a)].
215 x v (c(c(x) v y) v z) = x v z.  [para(146(a,1),16(a,1,1)),flip(a)].
217 x v (y v c(c(x) v z)) = y v x.  [para(146(a,1),89(a,1,2)),flip(a)].
220 c(x) v c(y v x) = c(x).  [para(14(a,1),151(a,1,2,1,2))].
221 x v (c(y v c(x)) v z) = x v z.  [para(151(a,1),16(a,1,1)),flip(a)].
225 x v (y v c(z v c(x))) = y v x.  [para(151(a,1),89(a,1,2)),flip(a)].
230 x v (y v c(y v x)) = 1.  [para(15(a,1),98(a,1,2,2,1))].
234 c(x) v (c(x v y) v z) = c(x) v z.  [para(133(a,1),16(a,1,1)),flip(a)].
236 c(x) v (y v c(x v z)) = y v c(x).  [para(133(a,1),89(a,1,2)),flip(a)].
257 c(x) v (c(y v x) v z) = c(x) v z.  [para(220(a,1),16(a,1,1)),flip(a)].
259 c(x v y) v c(y v c(x v y)) = c(y).
[para(220(a,1),76(a,1,2,1,2,1)),rewrite([14(6),15(5),220(11)])].
260 c(x) v (y v c(z v x)) = y v c(x).  [para(220(a,1),89(a,1,2)),flip(a)].
262 x v (y v (c(y v x) v z)) = 1.
[para(230(a,1),16(a,1,1)),rewrite([141(2),16(5)]),flip(a)].
313 x v (y v (z v c(y v x))) = 1.  [para(15(a,1),210(a,1,2,2,2,1))].
326 c(c(x) v y) v (z v x) = z v x.
[para(146(a,1),110(a,1,2,2,1,2,2,1,2)),rewrite([215(10),165(9),146(9)])].
665 x v (y v (c(z v c(x)) v u)) = y v (x v u).  [para(221(a,1),89(a,1,2)),flip(a)].
741 x v c(x v c(y v c(x v y))) = 1.
[para(98(a,1),124(a,1,2,1,1)),rewrite([83(2),15(6),196(8)])].
855 c(x) v (y v (c(z v x) v u)) = c(x) v (y v u).
[para(326(a,1),215(a,1,2,1,1)),rewrite([16(6),16(9)])].
935 c(x) v (y v (c(x v z) v u)) = y v (c(x) v u).  [para(234(a,1),89(a,1,2)),flip(a)].
1166 c(x) v (y v (z v c(x v u))) = y v (z v c(x)).
[para(16(a,1),236(a,1,2)),rewrite([16(9)])].
1409 c(x) v (y v (z v c(u v x))) = y v (z v c(x)).
[para(16(a,1),260(a,1,2)),rewrite([16(9)])].
3700 x v c(y v c(x v y)) = x.
[para(741(a,1),108(a,1,2,1)),rewrite([83(2),150(2),15(5)]),flip(a)].
3710 x v c(y v c(y v x)) = x.  [para(15(a,1),3700(a,1,2,1,2,1))].
3719 x v c(y v x) = x v c(y).
[para(3700(a,1),151(a,1,2,1)),rewrite([15(5),236(5)]),flip(a)].
3992 c(x v y) v c(y v c(x)) = c(y).  [back_rewrite(259),rewrite([3719(5)])].
4092 x v c(x v y) = x v c(y).
[para(3710(a,1),151(a,1,2,1)),rewrite([15(5),260(5)]),flip(a)].
4093 x v (c(y v x) v z) = x v (c(y) v z).
[para(207(a,1),3710(a,1,2,1,2,1)),rewrite([83(6),150(6),15(6),935(6)]),flip(a)].
```

```
4094 x v (y v c(z v x)) = x v (y v c(z)).
[para(210(a,1),3710(a,1,2,1,2,1)),rewrite([83(6),150(6),15(6),1166(6)]),flip(a)].
4098 x v (c(x v y) v z) = c(y) v (x v z).
[para(262(a,1),3710(a,1,2,1,2,1)),rewrite([83(6),150(6),15(6),855(6)]),flip(a)].
4099 x v (y v c(x v z)) = x v (y v c(z)).
[para(313(a,1),3710(a,1,2,1,2,1)),rewrite([83(6),150(6),15(6),1409(6)]),flip(a)].
4102 c(x v y) v c(c(y) v x) = c(x).
[para(124(a,1),3710(a,1,2,1,2,1)),rewrite([83(8),150(8),15(8),260(8),15(4),133(4)]),flip(
a)].
4105 c(x v y) v (c(c(x) v y) v z) = c(y) v z.
[para(143(a,1),3710(a,1,2,1,2,1)),rewrite([83(9),150(9),15(9),855(9),257(5)]),flip(a)].
4338 x v c(y v (z v x)) = x v c(y v z).   [para(16(a,1),3719(a,1,2,1))].
4342 c(x) v c(y v c(z v x)) = c(x) v c(y).
[para(3719(a,1),257(a,1,2)),rewrite([257(6)]),flip(a)].
4374 x v c(y v (x v z)) = x v c(y v z).   [para(89(a,1),4092(a,1,2,1))].
4419 c(x v c(c(y) v z)) = c(x v y) v c(c(y) v (x v c(z))).
[para(217(a,1),3992(a,1,1,1)),rewrite([15(8),4099(8)]),flip(a)].
4422 c(c(x v y) v z) = c(c(x) v z) v c(c(y) v (x v z)).
[para(234(a,1),3992(a,1,1,1)),rewrite([14(8),15(7),4098(7)]),flip(a)].
4544 c(c1 v c(c2)) v c(c(c1) v c(c2 v c3)) != c2 v c(c(c1) v c(c3)) # answer("Foulis-
Holland Theorem 4").   [back_rewrite(78),rewrite([4422(10),89(17),133(16),15(14)])].
4566 c(x v c(y v z)) = c(z v (x v c(y))) v c(x v c(z)).
[para(225(a,1),4102(a,1,2,1)),rewrite([14(2),15(4),4094(4),14(10)]),flip(a)].
4869 x v (y v (c(z v x) v u)) = y v (x v (c(z) v u)).
[para(4093(a,1),89(a,1,2)),flip(a)].
5176 c(x v y) v c(c(y) v (x v z)) = c(x v y) v c(x v z).
[para(4098(a,1),4374(a,1,2,1))].
5189 c(x v c(c(y) v z)) = c(x v y) v c(x v c(z)).
[back_rewrite(4419),rewrite([5176(13)])].
5752 c(x v y) v c(y v c(z v x)) = c(y).
[para(4338(a,1),4342(a,1,2,1)),rewrite([15(11),220(11)])].
5777 c(x v c(y v z)) v c(z v x) = c(x).   [para(5752(a,1),15(a,1)),flip(a)].
5897 c(x v c(y v z)) v c(y v x) = c(x).   [para(15(a,1),5777(a,1,1,1,2,1))].
6090 c(x v (y v c(z v u))) v c(z v (x v y)) = c(x v y).   [para(16(a,1),5897(a,1,1,1))].
6100 c(x v (c(y v z) v c(y v u))) v c(y v (x v c(z))) = c(x v c(y v z)).
[para(4099(a,1),5897(a,1,2,1)),rewrite([16(6)])].
6194 c(x v (c(y v z) v u)) = c(x v (z v (c(y) v u))) v c(x v (c(z) v u)).
[para(665(a,1),4102(a,1,2,1)),rewrite([14(2),15(5),4869(5),14(12)]),flip(a)].
6228 c(x v c(y v z)) = c(x v (z v c(y))) v c(x v c(z)).
[back_rewrite(6100),rewrite([6194(7),133(4),16(16),6090(15)]),flip(a)].
6530 c(x v (y v z)) v c(x v c(y)) = c(x v z) v c(x v c(y)).
[back_rewrite(5189),rewrite([6228(5),14(2)])].
6558 c(x v (y v c(z))) v c(y v c(x)) = c(y v c(z)) v c(y v c(x)).
[back_rewrite(4566),rewrite([6228(4),6530(8)]),flip(a)].
6559 $F # answer("Foulis-Holland Theorem 4").
[back_rewrite(4544),rewrite([6228(13),89(12),6558(20),4105(19),14(3)]),xx(a)].

============================== end of proof ==========================
```

Figure 3. Summary of a *prover9* ([2]) proof of FH4 from OML. The proofs assume the default inference rules of *prover9*. The general form of a line in this proof is "*line_number conclusion [derivation]*", where *line_number* is a unique identifier of a line in the proof, and *conclusion* is the result of applying the *prover9* inference rules (such as *para*modulation, *copy*ing, and *rewrit*ing), noted in square brackets (denoting the *derivation*), to the lines cited in those brackets. Note that some of "logical" proof lines in the above have been transformed to two text lines, with the *derivation* appearing on a text line following a text line containing the first part of that logical line. The detailed syntax and semantics of these notations can be found in [2]. All *prover9* proofs are by default proofs by contradiction.

The total time to produce the proofs in Figure 3 on the platform described in Section 2.0 was approximately 4 seconds.

4.0 Discussion

The results of Section 3.0 motivate several observations:

1. FH4 is derivable from OML.

2. The proof in Section 3.0 is, as far as I know, novel.

3. Companion papers provide derivations of the remaining FHTs from OML, and a derivation of the OMLaw from an OML without the OMLaw, conjoined with the FHTs. The union of these proofs constitutes a proof of the equivalence of the OMLaw and the FHTs within OML theory.

5.0 Acknowledgements

This work benefited from discussions with Tom Oberdan, Frank Pecchioni, Tony Pawlicki, and the late John K. Prentice, whose passion for foundations of physics inspired those of us privileged to have known him. For any infelicities that remain, I am solely responsible.

6.0 References

[1] von Neumann J. *Mathematical Foundations of Quantum Mechanics*. 1936. Translated by R. T. Beyer. Princeton. 1983.

[2] McCune WW. *prover9 and mace4*. URL http://www.cs.unm.edu/~mccune/prover9/. 2009.

[3] Horner JK. *prover9* scripts for FH4. 2011. Available from the author on request.

[4] Dalla Chiara ML and Giuntini R. *Quantum Logics*. URL http://xxx.lanl.gov/abs/quant-ph/0101028. 2004.

[5] Megill ND and Pavičić M. Orthomodular lattices and quantum algebra. *International Journal of Theoretical Physics* 40 (2001), pp. 1387-1410.

[6] Akhiezer NI and Glazman IM. *Theory of Linear Operators in Hilbert Space. Volume I.* Translated by M. Nestell. Frederick Ungar. 1961.

[7] Holland, Jr. SS Orthomodularity in infinite dimensions: a theorem of M. Solèr. *Bulletin of the American Mathematical Society* 32 (1995), pp. 205-234.

[8] Marsden EL and Herman LM. *A condition for distribution in orthomodular lattices.* Kansas State University Technical Report #40. 1974.

[9] Knuth DE and Bendix PB. Simple word problems in universal algebras. In J. Leech, ed. *Computational Problems in Abstract Algebra.* Pergamon Press. 1970. pp. 263-297.

[10] Chang CC and Keisler HJ. *Model Theory.* North-Holland. 1990. pp. 38-39.

[11] Birkhoff G. *Lattice Theory.* Third Edition. American Mathematical Society. 1967.

[12] Church A. *Introduction to Mathematical Logic. Volume I.* Princeton. 1956.

[13] Jauch J. *Foundations of Quantum Mechanics.* Addison-Wesley. 1968.

[14] Megill ND. *Metamath.* URL http://us.metamath.org/qlegif/mmql.html#unify. 2004.

[15] Horner JK. An automated deduction system for orthomodular lattice theory. *Proceedings of the 2005 International*

Conference on Artificial Intelligence. CSREA Press. 2005. pp. 260-265.

[16] Horner JK. An automated equational logic deduction of join elimination in orthomodular lattice theory. *Proceedings of the 2007 International Conference on Artificial Intelligence.* CSREA Press. 2007. pp. 481-488.

[17] Messiah A. *Quantum Mechanics*. Dover. 1958.

[18] Horner JK. Using automated theorem-provers to aid the design of efficient compilers for quantum computing. *Los Alamos National Laboratory Quantum Institute Workshop.* December 9–10, 2002. URL http://www.lanl.gov/science/centers/quantum/qls_pdfs/horner.pdf.

[19] Birkhoff G and von Neumann J. The logic of quantum mechanics. *Annals of Mathematics* 37 (1936), 823-243.

[20] Nielsen MA and Chuang L . *Quantum Computation and Quantum Information*. Cambridge. 2000.

[21] Pavičić M and Megill N. Quantum and classical implicational algebras with primitive implication. *International Journal of Theoretical Physics* 37 (1998), 2091-2098. ftp://m3k.grad.hr/pavicic/quantum-logic/1998-int-j-theor-phys-2.ps.gz.

Equivalence of the Foulis-Holland Theorems and the Orthomodular Law in Quantum Logic: Part 5

Jack K. Horner
P. O. Box 266
Los Alamos, New Mexico 87544 USA

FCS 2013

Abstract

The optimization of quantum computing circuitry and compilers at some level must be expressed in terms of quantum-mechanical behaviors and operations. In much the same way that the structure of conventional propositional (Boolean) logic (BL) is the logic of the description of the behavior of classical physical systems and is isomorphic to a Boolean algebra (BA), so also the algebra, C(H), of closed linear subspaces of (equivalently, the system of linear operators on (observables in)) a Hilbert space is a logic of the descriptions of the behavior of quantum mechanical systems and is a model of an ortholattice (OL). An OL can thus be thought of as a kind of "quantum logic" (QL). C(H) is also a model of an orthomodular lattice (OML), which is an ortholattice to which the orthomodular law has been conjoined. Now a QL can be thought of as a BL in which the distributive law does not hold. Under certain commutativity conditions, a QL does satisfy the distributive law; among the most well known of these relationships are the Foulis-Holland theorems (FHTs). Here I provide an automated deduction of the OMLaw, from OML without the OMLaw, conjoined with one of the FHTs.

Keywords: automated deduction, quantum computing, orthomodular lattice, Foulis-Holland theorems, Hilbert space

1.0 Introduction

The optimization of quantum computing circuitry and compilers at some level must be expressed in terms of the description of quantum-mechanical behaviors ([1], [17], [18], [20]). In much the same way that conventional propositional (Boolean) logic (BL,[12]) is the logical structure of description of the behavior of classical physical systems (e.g. "the measurements of the position and momentum of particle P are commutative", i.e., can be measured in either order, yielding the same results) and is isomorphic to a Boolean lattice ([10], [11], [19]), so also the algebra, *C(H)*, of the closed linear subspaces of (equivalently, the system of linear operators on (observables in)) a Hilbert space *H* ([1], [4], [6], [9], [13]) is *a* logic of the descriptions of the behavior of quantum mechanical systems (e.g., "the measurements of the position and momentum of particle P are *not* commutative") and is a model ([10]) of an ortholattice (OL; [4]). An OL can thus be thought of as a kind of "quantum logic" (QL; [19]).

```
Lattice axioms

      x = c(c(x))                                (AxLat1)
      x v y = y v x                              (AxLat2)
      (x v y) v z = x v (y v z)                  (AxLat3)
      (x ^ y) ^ z = x ^ (y ^ z)                  (AxLat4)
      x v (x ^ y) = x                            (AxLat5)
      x ^ (x v y) = x                            (AxLat6)

Ortholattice axioms
      c(x) ^ x = 0                               (AxOL1)
      c(x) v x = 1                               (AxOL2)
      x ^ y = c(c(x) v c(y))                     (AxOL3)


A useful definition
       1_2 = y v ((x ^ c(y)) v (c(x) ^ c(y)))


where
   x, y are variables ranging over lattice nodes
   ^ is lattice meet
   v is lattice join
   c(x) is the orthocomplement of x
   <-> means if and only if
   =  is equivalence ([12])
   1 is the maximum lattice element (= x v c(x))
   0 is the minimum lattice element (= c(1))
```

Figure 1. Lattice, ortholattice, ortholattice axioms, and a useful definition.

C(H) is also a model of an orthomodular lattice (OML; [4], [7]), which is an OL conjoined with the orthomodularity axiom (OMLaw):

```
y v (c(y) ^ (x v y)) =
   x v y        (OMLaw)
```

The rationalization of the OMA as a claim proper to physics has proven problematic ([13], Section 5-6), motivating the question of whether the OMA is required in an adequate characterization of QL. Thus formulated, the question suggests that the OMA and its equivalents are specific to an OML, and that as a consequence, banning the OMA from QL yields a "truer" quantum logic.

Now a QL can be thought of as a BL in which the distributive law

```
(D)    (x v (y ^ z) =
          (x v y) ^ (x v z))
```

does not hold. Under certain commutativity conditions, a QL does satisfy (D); among the most well known of these relationships are the Foulis-Holland theorems (FHTs ([7])):

```
% Foulis-Holland theorem FH1
(C(x,y) & C(x,z)) ->  ( (x ^ (y v z)) = ((x ^ y) v (x ^ z))  )

% Foulis-Holland theorem FH2
(C(x,y) & C(x,z)) ->  ( (y ^ (x v z)) = ((y ^ x) v (y ^ z))  )


% Foulis-Holland theorem FH3
(C(x,y) & C(x,z)) ->  ( (x v (y ^ z)) = ((x v y) ^ (x v z))  )

% Foulis-Holland theorem FH4
(C(x,y) & C(x,z)) ->  ( (y v (x ^ z)) = ((y v x) ^ (y v z))  )


where C(x,y), "x commutes with y" is defined as

        C(x,y) <-> (x = ((x ^ y) v (x ^ c(y))))
```

Figure 2. The Foulis-Holland theorems.

2.0 Method

The OML axiomatizations of Megill, Pavičić, and Horner ([5], [14], [15], [16], [21]), without the OMLaw, but conjoined with the FH2, were implemented in a *prover9* ([2]) script ([3]) configured to derive the OMLaw, then executed in that framework on a Dell Inspiron 545 with an Intel Core2 Quad CPU Q8200 (clocked @ 2.33 GHz) and 8.00 GB RAM, running under the *Windows Vista Home Premium /Cygwin* operating environment.

3.0 Results

Figure 3 shows the proof, generated by [3] on the platform described in Section 2.0, that the OMLaw is implied by an OML with the OMLaw, conjoined with the FH2:

```
============================== PROOF =================================

% Proof 1 at 0.09 (+ 0.01) seconds: "OMLaw".
% Length of proof is 43.

3 C(x,y) <-> x = (x ^ y) v (x ^ c(y)) # label("Df: commutes") #
label(non_clause).  [assumption].
5 C(x,y) & C(x,z) -> y ^ (x v z) = (y ^ x) v (y ^ z) #
label("Foulis-Holland Theorem 2") # label(non_clause).
[assumption].
8 y v (c(y) ^ (x v y)) = x v y # label("OMLaw") #
label(non_clause) # label(goal).  [goal].
13 x = c(c(x)) # label("AxL1").  [assumption].
14 c(c(x)) = x.  [copy(13),flip(a)].
15 x v y = y v x # label("AxL2").  [assumption].
16 (x v y) v z = x v (y v z) # label("AxL3").  [assumption].
```

```
18 x v (x ^ y) = x # label("AxL5").  [assumption].
19 x ^ (x v y) = x # label("AxL6").  [assumption].
20 c(x) ^ x = 0 # label("AxOL1").  [assumption].
21 c(x) v x = 1 # label("AxOL2").  [assumption].
22 x v c(x) = 1.  [copy(21),rewrite([15(2)])].
23 x ^ y = c(c(x) v c(y)) # label("AxOL3").  [assumption].
65 -C(x,y) | (x ^ y) v (x ^ c(y)) = x # label("Df: commutes").
[clausify(3)].
66 -C(x,y) | c(c(x) v y) v c(c(x) v c(y)) = x.
[copy(65),rewrite([23(2),23(7),14(8),15(9)])].
67 C(x,y) | (x ^ y) v (x ^ c(y)) != x # label("Df: commutes").
[clausify(3)].
68 C(x,y) | c(c(x) v y) v c(c(x) v c(y)) != x.
[copy(67),rewrite([23(2),23(7),14(8),15(9)])].
81 -C(x,y) | -C(x,z) | (y ^ x) v (y ^ z) = y ^ (x v z) #
label("Foulis-Holland Theorem 2").  [clausify(5)].
82 -C(x,y) | -C(x,z) | c(c(y) v c(x v z)) = c(c(y) v c(x)) v
c(c(y) v c(z)).
[copy(81),rewrite([23(3),23(7),23(13)]),flip(c)].
86 c1 v (c(c1) ^ (c2 v c1)) != c2 v c1 # label("OMLaw") #
answer("OMLaw").  [deny(8)].
87 c1 v c(c1 v c(c1 v c2)) != c1 v c2 # answer("OMLaw").
[copy(86),rewrite([15(6),23(7),14(4),15(12)])].
88 c(1) = 0.  [back_rewrite(20),rewrite([23(2),14(2),22(2)])].
89 c(c(x) v c(x v y)) = x.  [back_rewrite(19),rewrite([23(2)])].
90 x v c(c(x) v c(y)) = x.  [back_rewrite(18),rewrite([23(1)])].
94 x v (y v z) = y v (x v z).
[para(15(a,1),16(a,1,1)),rewrite([16(2)])].
102 x v (c(x) v y) = 1 v y.  [para(22(a,1),16(a,1,1)),flip(a)].
109 C(x,c(x)) | 0 v c(c(x) v c(x)) != x.
[para(22(a,1),68(b,1,2,1)),rewrite([88(8),15(8)])].
123 C(x,1) | c(0 v c(x)) v c(1 v c(x)) != x.
[para(88(a,1),68(b,1,2,1,2)),rewrite([15(5),15(9),15(11)])].
125 c(x) v c(x v y) = c(x).  [para(89(a,1),14(a,1,1)),flip(a)].
129 c(0 v c(x)) = x.
[para(22(a,1),89(a,1,1,2,1)),rewrite([88(3),15(3)])].
131 C(x,x v y) | c(1 v y) v x != x.
[para(89(a,1),68(b,1,2)),rewrite([94(5),102(5)])].
133 1 v x = 1.  [para(88(a,1),89(a,1,1,1)),rewrite([129(6)])].
134 c(x v x) = c(x).
[para(89(a,1),89(a,1,1,2)),rewrite([14(2)])].
135 C(x,1) | x v 0 != x.
[back_rewrite(123),rewrite([129(6),133(5),88(4)])].
149 C(x,x v y) | 0 v x != x.
[back_rewrite(131),rewrite([133(4),88(4)])].
152 C(x,c(x)) | 0 v x != x.
[back_rewrite(109),rewrite([134(7),14(5)])].
158 x v 0 = x.  [para(22(a,1),90(a,1,2,1)),rewrite([88(2)])].
162 C(x,1).  [back_rewrite(135),rewrite([158(4)]),xx(b)].
172 0 v x = x.
[hyper(66,a,162,a),rewrite([15(3),133(3),88(2),88(4),15(4),129(5)
])].
```

```
176 C(x,c(x)).  [back_rewrite(152),rewrite([172(4)]),xx(b)].
177 C(x,x v y).  [back_rewrite(149),rewrite([172(4)]),xx(b)].
216 x v c(x v c(x v y)) = x v y.
[hyper(82,a,177,a,b,176,a),rewrite([22(4),88(4),15(4),172(4),14(3
),15(5),125(5),14(3),14(5),15(4)]),flip(a)].
217 $F # answer("OMLaw").  [resolve(216,a,87,a)].
============================== end of proof ==========================
```

Figure 3. Summary of a *prover9* ([2]) proof of the OMLaw from OML without the OMLaw, conjoined with the FH2. The proofs assume the default inference rules of *prover9*. The general form of a line in this proof is "*line_number conclusion [derivation]*", where *line_number* is a unique identifier of a line in the proof, and *conclusion* is the result of applying the *prover9* inference rules (such as *para*modulation, *copy*ing, and *rewrit*ing), noted in square brackets (denoting the *derivation*), to the lines cited in those brackets. Note that some of "logical" proof lines in the above have been transformed to two text lines, with the *derivation* appearing on a text line following a text line containing the first part of that logical line. The detailed syntax and semantics of these notations can be found in [2]. All *prover9* proofs are by default proofs by contradiction.

The total time to produce the proofs in Figure 3 on the platform described in Section 2.0 was approximately 0.1 seconds.

4.0 Discussion

The results of Section 3.0 motivate several observations:

1. The OMLaw is derivable from the OML without the OMLaw, conjoined with the FHTs.

2. The proof in Section 3.0 uses only FH2, not FH1, FH3, or FH4.

4. The proof in Section 3.0 is, as far as I know, novel.

5. The right-hand side (RHS) of FH1, together with AxOL3, implies, via modus tollens, the RHS of FH2, so FH1 -> FH2. (The full proof is at most six steps long.)

6. Companion papers provide derivations of the FHTs from OML. The union of these proofs (and observation (5) in this section) constitutes a proof of the equivalence of the OMLaw and the FHTs within OML theory.

5.0 Acknowledgements

This work benefited from discussions with Tom Oberdan, Frank Pecchioni, Tony Pawlicki, and the late John K. Prentice, whose passion for foundations of physics inspired those of us privileged to have known him. For any infelicities that remain, I am solely responsible.

6.0 References

[1] von Neumann J. *Mathematical Foundations of Quantum Mechanics*. 1936. Translated by R. T. Beyer. Princeton. 1983.

[2] McCune WW. *prover9 and mace4*. URL http://www.cs.unm.edu/~mccune/prover9/. 2009.

[3] Horner JK. *prover9* scripts for OMLaw from FH2. 2011. Available from the author on request.

[4] Dalla Chiara ML and Giuntini R. *Quantum Logics*. URL http://xxx.lanl.gov/abs/quant-ph/0101028. 2004.

[5] Megill ND and Pavičić M. Orthomodular lattices and quantum algebra. *International Journal of Theoretical Physics* 40 (2001), pp. 1387-1410.

[6] Akhiezer NI and Glazman IM. *Theory of Linear Operators in Hilbert Space. Volume I*. Translated by M. Nestell. Frederick Ungar. 1961.

[7] Holland, Jr. SS Orthomodularity in infinite dimensions: a theorem of M. Solèr. *Bulletin of the American Mathematical Society* 32 (1995), pp. 205-234.

[8] Marsden EL and Herman LM. *A condition for distribution in orthomodular lattices*. Kansas State University Technical Report #40. 1974.

[9] Knuth DE and Bendix PB. Simple word problems in universal algebras. In J. Leech, ed. *Computational Problems in Abstract Algebra*. Pergamon Press. 1970. pp. 263-297.

[10] Chang CC and Keisler HJ. *Model Theory*. North-Holland. 1990. pp. 38-39.

[11] Birkhoff G. *Lattice Theory*. Third Edition. American Mathematical Society. 1967.

[12] Church A. *Introduction to Mathematical Logic. Volume I*. Princeton. 1956.

[13] Jauch J. *Foundations of Quantum Mechanics*. Addison-Wesley. 1968.

[14] Megill ND. *Metamath*. URL http://us.metamath.org/qlegif/mmql.html#unify. 2004.

[15] Horner JK. An automated deduction system for orthomodular lattice theory. *Proceedings of the 2005 International Conference on Artificial Intelligence*. CSREA Press. 2005. pp. 260-265.

[16] Horner JK. An automated equational logic deduction of join elimination in orthomodular lattice theory. *Proceedings of the 2007 International Conference on Artificial Intelligence*. CSREA Press. 2007. pp. 481-488.

[17] Messiah A. *Quantum Mechanics*. Dover. 1958.

[18] Horner JK. Using automated theorem-provers to aid the design of efficient compilers for quantum computing. *Los Alamos National Laboratory Quantum Institute Workshop*. December 9–10, 2002. URL http://www.lanl.gov/science/centers/quantum/qls_pdfs/horner.pdf.

[19] Birkhoff G and von Neumann J. The logic of quantum mechanics. *Annals of Mathematics* 37 (1936), 823-243.

[20] Nielsen MA and Chuang L . *Quantum Computation and Quantum Information*. Cambridge. 2000.

[21] Pavičić M and Megill N. Quantum and classical implicational algebras with primitive implication. *International Journal of Theoretical Physics* 37 (1998), 2091-2098. ftp://m3k.grad.hr/pavicic/quantum-logic/1998-int-j-theor-phys-2.ps.gz.

Equivalence of the Foulis-Holland Theorems and the Orthomodular Law in Quantum Logic: Part 6

Jack K. Horner
P. O. Box 266
Los Alamos, New Mexico 87544 USA

FCS 2013

Abstract

The optimization of quantum computing circuitry and compilers at some level must be expressed in terms of quantum-mechanical behaviors and operations. In much the same way that the structure of conventional propositional (Boolean) logic (BL) is the logic of the description of the behavior of classical physical systems and is isomorphic to a Boolean algebra (BA), so also the algebra, C(H), of closed linear subspaces of (equivalently, the system of linear operators on (observables in)) a Hilbert space is a logic of the descriptions of the behavior of quantum mechanical systems and is a model of an ortholattice (OL). An OL can thus be thought of as a kind of "quantum logic" (QL). C(H) is also a model of an orthomodular lattice (OML), which is an ortholattice to which the orthomodular law has been conjoined. Now a QL can be thought of as a BL in which the distributive law does not hold. Under certain commutativity conditions, a QL does satisfy the distributive law; among the most well known of these relationships are the Foulis-Holland theorems (FHTs). Here I provide an automated deduction of the OMLaw, from OML without the OMLaw, conjoined with one of the FHTs.

Keywords: automated deduction, quantum computing, orthomodular lattice, Foulis-Holland theorems, Hilbert space

1.0 Introduction

The optimization of quantum computing circuitry and compilers at some level must be expressed in terms of the description of quantum-mechanical behaviors ([1], [17], [18], [20]). In much the same way that conventional propositional (Boolean) logic (BL,[12]) is the logical structure of description of the behavior of classical physical systems (e.g. "the measurements of the position and momentum of particle P are commutative", i.e., can be measured in either order, yielding the same results) and is isomorphic to a Boolean lattice ([10], [11], [19]), so also the algebra, *C(H)*, of the closed linear subspaces of (equivalently, the system of linear operators on (observables in)) a Hilbert space *H* ([1], [4], [6], [9], [13]) is *a* logic of the descriptions of the behavior of quantum mechanical systems (e.g., "the measurements of the position and momentum of particle P are *not* commutative") and is a model ([10]) of an ortholattice (OL; [4]). An OL can thus be thought of as a kind of "quantum logic" (QL; [19]). Figure 1 shows a set of axioms for an orthlolattice.

```
Lattice axioms

     x = c(c(x))                           (AxLat1)
     x v y = y v x                         (AxLat2)
     (x v y) v z = x v (y v z)             (AxLat3)
     (x ^ y) ^ z = x ^ (y ^ z)             (AxLat4)
     x v (x ^ y) = x                       (AxLat5)
     x ^ (x v y) = x                       (AxLat6)

Ortholattice axioms
     c(x) ^ x = 0                          (AxOL1)
     c(x) v x = 1                          (AxOL2)
     x ^ y = c(c(x) v c(y))                (AxOL3)

A useful definition
     1_2 = y v ((x ^ c(y)) v (c(x) ^ c(y)))


where
   x, y are variables ranging over lattice nodes
   ^ is lattice meet
   v is lattice join
   c(x) is the orthocomplement of x
   <-> means if and only if
   = is equivalence ([12])
   1 is the maximum lattice element (= x v c(x))
   0 is the minimum lattice element (= c(1))
```

Figure 1. Lattice, ortholattice, ortholattice axioms, and a useful definition.

C(H) is also a model of an orthomodular lattice (OML; [4], [7]), which is an OL conjoined with the orthomodularity axiom (OMLaw):

```
y v (c(y) ^ (x v y)) =
         x v y          (OMLaw)
```

The rationalization of the OMA as a claim proper to physics has proven problematic ([13], Section 5-6), motivating the question of whether the OMA is required in an adequate characterization of QL. Thus formulated, the question suggests that the OMA and its equivalents are specific to an OML, and that as a consequence, banning the OMA from QL yields a "truer" quantum logic.

Now a QL can be thought of as a BL in which the distributive law

```
(D)    (x v (y ^ z) =
        (x v y) ^ (x v z))
```

does not hold. Under certain commutativity conditions, a QL does satisfy (D); among the most well known of these relationships are the Foulis-Holland theorems (FHTs ([7])):

```
% Foulis-Holland theorem FH1
(C(x,y) & C(x,z)) -> ( (x ^ (y v z)) = ((x ^ y) v (x ^ z)) )

% Foulis-Holland theorem FH2
(C(x,y) & C(x,z)) -> ( (y ^ (x v z)) = ((y ^ x) v (y ^ z)) )

% Foulis-Holland theorem FH3
(C(x,y) & C(x,z)) -> ( (x v (y ^ z)) = ((x v y) ^ (x v z)) )

% Foulis-Holland theorem FH4
(C(x,y) & C(x,z)) -> ( (y v (x ^ z)) = ((y v x) ^ (y v z)) )


where C(x,y), "x commutes with y" is defined as

      C(x,y) <-> (x = ((x ^ y) v (x ^ c(y))))
```

Figure 2. The Foulis-Holland theorems.

2.0 Method

The OML axiomatizations of Megill, Pavičić, and Horner ([5], [14], [15], [16], [21]), without the OMLaw, but conjoined with the FH4, were implemented in a *prover9* ([2]) script ([3]) configured to derive the OMLaw, then executed in that framework on a Dell Inspiron 545 with an Intel Core2 Quad CPU Q8200 (clocked @ 2.33 GHz) and 8.00 GB RAM, running under the *Windows Vista Home Premium /Cygwin* operating environment.

3.0 Results

Figure 3 shows the proof, generated by [3] on the platform described in Section 2.0, that the OMLaw is implied by an OML with the OMLaw, conjoined with FH4:

```
=============================== PROOF =================================

% Proof 1 at 2.29 (+ 0.08) seconds: "OMLaw".
% Length of proof is 44.

3 C(x,y) <-> x = (x ^ y) v (x ^ c(y)) # label("Df: commutes") #
label(non_clause).  [assumption].
4 C(x,y) & C(x,z) -> y v (x ^ z) = (y v x) ^ (y v z) #
label("Foulis-Holland Theorem 4") # label(non_clause).
[assumption].
5 y v (c(y) ^ (x v y)) = x v y # label("OMLaw") #
label(non_clause) # label(goal).  [goal].
10 x = c(c(x)) # label("AxL1").  [assumption].
11 c(c(x)) = x.  [copy(10),flip(a)].
12 x v y = y v x # label("AxL2").  [assumption].
13 (x v y) v z = x v (y v z) # label("AxL3").  [assumption].
```

```
15 x v (x ^ y) = x # label("AxL5").  [assumption].
16 x ^ (x v y) = x # label("AxL6").  [assumption].
17 c(x) ^ x = 0 # label("AxOL1").  [assumption].
18 c(x) v x = 1 # label("AxOL2").  [assumption].
19 x v c(x) = 1.  [copy(18),rewrite([12(2)])].
20 x ^ y = c(c(x) v c(y)) # label("AxOL3").  [assumption].
62 -C(x,y) | (x ^ y) v (x ^ c(y)) = x # label("Df: commutes").
[clausify(3)].
63 -C(x,y) | c(c(x) v y) v c(c(x) v c(y)) = x.
[copy(62),rewrite([20(2),20(7),11(8),12(9)])].
64 C(x,y) | (x ^ y) v (x ^ c(y)) != x # label("Df: commutes").
[clausify(3)].
65 C(x,y) | c(c(x) v y) v c(c(x) v c(y)) != x.
[copy(64),rewrite([20(2),20(7),11(8),12(9)])].
76 -C(x,y) | -C(x,z) | y v (x ^ z) = (y v x) ^ (y v z) #
label("Foulis-Holland Theorem 4").  [clausify(4)].
77 -C(x,y) | -C(x,z) | c(c(y v x) v c(y v z)) = y v c(c(x) v
c(z)).  [copy(76),rewrite([20(3),20(10)]),flip(c)].
78 c1 v (c(c1) ^ (c2 v c1)) != c2 v c1 # label("OMLaw") #
answer("OMLaw").  [deny(5)].
79 c1 v c(c1 v c(c1 v c2)) != c1 v c2 # answer("OMLaw").
[copy(78),rewrite([12(6),20(7),11(4),12(12)])].
80 c(1) = 0.  [back_rewrite(17),rewrite([20(2),11(2),19(2)])].
81 c(c(x) v c(x v y)) = x.  [back_rewrite(16),rewrite([20(2)])].
82 x v c(c(x) v c(y)) = x.  [back_rewrite(15),rewrite([20(1)])].
86 x v (y v z) = y v (x v z).
[para(12(a,1),13(a,1,1)),rewrite([13(2)])].
94 x v (c(x) v y) = 1 v y.  [para(19(a,1),13(a,1,1)),flip(a)].
101 C(x,c(x)) | 0 v c(c(x) v c(x)) != x.
[para(19(a,1),65(b,1,2,1)),rewrite([80(8),12(8)])].
115 C(x,1) | c(0 v c(x)) v c(1 v c(x)) != x.
[para(80(a,1),65(b,1,2,1,2)),rewrite([12(5),12(9),12(11)])].
117 c(x) v c(x v y) = c(x).  [para(81(a,1),11(a,1,1)),flip(a)].
121 c(0 v c(x)) = x.
[para(19(a,1),81(a,1,1,2,1)),rewrite([80(3),12(3)])].
122 C(x,c(x v y)) | x v c(1 v y) != x.
[para(81(a,1),65(b,1,1)),rewrite([11(7),86(6),94(6)])].
125 1 v x = 1.  [para(80(a,1),81(a,1,1,1)),rewrite([121(6)])].
126 c(x v x) = c(x).
[para(81(a,1),81(a,1,1,2)),rewrite([11(2)])].
127 C(x,1) | x v 0 != x.
[back_rewrite(115),rewrite([121(6),125(5),80(4)])].
142 C(x,c(x v y)) | x v 0 != x.
[back_rewrite(122),rewrite([125(5),80(5)])].
144 C(x,c(x)) | 0 v x != x.
[back_rewrite(101),rewrite([126(7),11(5)])].
150 x v 0 = x.  [para(19(a,1),82(a,1,2,1)),rewrite([80(2)])].
153 C(x,c(x v y)).  [back_rewrite(142),rewrite([150(5)]),xx(b)].
154 C(x,1).  [back_rewrite(127),rewrite([150(4)]),xx(b)].
164 0 v x = x.
[hyper(63,a,154,a),rewrite([12(3),125(3),80(2),80(4),12(4),121(5)
])].
```

```
168 C(x,c(x)).  [back_rewrite(144),rewrite([164(4)]),xx(b)].
219 c(x v c(x v c(x v y))) = c(x v y).
[hyper(77,a,153,a,b,168,a),rewrite([12(3),12(8),117(8),11(6),12(5
),11(11),12(10),19(10),80(10),12(10),164(10)])].
5239 x v c(x v c(x v y)) = x v y.
[para(219(a,1),11(a,1,1)),rewrite([11(3)]),flip(a)].
5240 $F # answer("OMLaw").  [resolve(5239,a,79,a)].
============================== end of proof ==========================
```

Figure 3. Summary of a *prover9* ([2]) proof of the OMLaw from OML without the OMLaw, conjoined with the FH4. The proofs assume the default inference rules of *prover9*. The general form of a line in this proof is "*line_number conclusion [derivation]*", where *line_number* is a unique identifier of a line in the proof, and *conclusion* is the result of applying the *prover9* inference rules (such as *para*modulation, *copy*ing, and *rewrit*ing), noted in square brackets (denoting the *derivation*), to the lines cited in those brackets. Note that some of "logical" proof lines in the above have been transformed to two text lines, with the *derivation* appearing on a text line following a text line containing the first part of that logical line. The detailed syntax and semantics of these notations can be found in [2]. All *prover9* proofs are by default proofs by contradiction.

The total time to produce the proofs in Figure 3 on the platform described in Section 2.0 was approximately 2.4 seconds.

4.0 Discussion

The results of Section 3.0 motivate several observations:

1. The OMLaw is derivable from the OML without the OMLaw, conjoined with the FHTs.

2. The proof in Section 3.0 uses only FH4, not FH1, FH2, or FH3.

4. The proof in Section 3.0 is, as far as I know, novel.

5. Companion papers provide derivations of the FHTs from OML. The union of these proofs constitutes a proof of the equivalence of the OMLaw and the FHTs within OML theory.

5.0 Acknowledgements

This work benefited from discussions with Tom Oberdan, Frank Pecchioni, Tony Pawlicki, and the late John K. Prentice, whose passion for foundations of physics inspired those of us privileged to have known him. For any infelicities that remain, I am solely responsible.

6.0 References

[1] von Neumann J. *Mathematical Foundations of Quantum Mechanics*. 1936. Translated by R. T. Beyer. Princeton. 1983.

[2] McCune WW. *prover9 and mace4*. URL http://www.cs.unm.edu/~mccune/prover9/. 2009.

[3] Horner JK. *prover9* scripts for OMLaw from FH2. 2011. Available from the author on request.

[4] Dalla Chiara ML and Giuntini R. *Quantum Logics*. URL http://xxx.lanl.gov/abs/quant-ph/0101028. 2004.

[5] Megill ND and Pavičić M. Orthomodular lattices and quantum algebra. *International Journal of Theoretical Physics* 40 (2001), pp. 1387-1410.

[6] Akhiezer NI and Glazman IM. *Theory of Linear Operators in Hilbert Space. Volume I*. Translated by M. Nestell. Frederick Ungar. 1961.

[7] Holland, Jr. SS Orthomodularity in infinite dimensions: a theorem of M. Solèr. *Bulletin of the American Mathematical Society* 32 (1995), pp. 205-234.

[8] Marsden EL and Herman LM. *A condition for distribution in orthomodular lattices*. Kansas State University Technical Report #40. 1974.

[9] Knuth DE and Bendix PB. Simple word problems in universal algebras. In J. Leech, ed. *Computational Problems in Abstract Algebra*. Pergamon Press. 1970. pp. 263-297.

[10] Chang CC and Keisler HJ. *Model Theory*. North-Holland. 1990. pp. 38-39.

[11] Birkhoff G. *Lattice Theory*. Third Edition. American Mathematical Society. 1967.

[12] Church A. *Introduction to Mathematical Logic. Volume I*. Princeton. 1956.

[13] Jauch J. *Foundations of Quantum Mechanics*. Addison-Wesley. 1968.

[14] Megill ND. *Metamath*. URL http://us.metamath.org/qlegif/mmql.html#unify. 2004.

[15] Horner JK. An automated deduction system for orthomodular lattice theory. *Proceedings of the 2005 International Conference on Artificial Intelligence*. CSREA Press. 2005. pp. 260-265.

[16] Horner JK. An automated equational logic deduction of join elimination in orthomodular lattice theory. *Proceedings of the 2007 International Conference on Artificial Intelligence*. CSREA Press. 2007. pp. 481-488.

[17] Messiah A. *Quantum Mechanics*. Dover. 1958.

[18] Horner JK. Using automated theorem-provers to aid the design of efficient compilers for quantum computing. *Los Alamos National Laboratory Quantum Institute Workshop*. December 9–10, 2002. URL http://www.lanl.gov/science/centers/quantum/qls_pdfs/horner.pdf.

[19] Birkhoff G and von Neumann J. The logic of quantum mechanics. *Annals of Mathematics* 37 (1936), 823-243.

[20] Nielsen MA and Chuang L . *Quantum Computation and Quantum Information*. Cambridge. 2000.

[21] Pavičić M and Megill N. Quantum and classical implicational algebras with primitive implication. *International Journal of Theoretical Physics* 37 (1998), 2091-2098. ftp://m3k.grad.hr/pavicic/quantum-logic/1998-int-j-theor-phys-2.ps.gz.

Equivalence of the Foulis-Holland Theorems and the Orthomodular Law in Quantum Logic: Part 7

Jack K. Horner
P. O. Box 266
Los Alamos, New Mexico 87544 USA

FCS 2013

Abstract

The optimization of quantum computing circuitry and compilers at some level must be expressed in terms of quantum-mechanical behaviors and operations. In much the same way that the structure of conventional propositional (Boolean) logic (BL) is the logic of the description of the behavior of classical physical systems and is isomorphic to a Boolean algebra (BA), so also the algebra, C(H), of closed linear subspaces of (equivalently, the system of linear operators on (observables in)) a Hilbert space is a logic of the descriptions of the behavior of quantum mechanical systems and is a model of an ortholattice (OL). An OL can thus be thought of as a kind of "quantum logic" (QL). C(H) is also a model of an orthomodular lattice (OML), which is an ortholattice to which the orthomodular law has been conjoined. Now a QL can be thought of as a BL in which the distributive law does not hold. Under certain commutativity conditions, a QL does satisfy the distributive law; among the most well known of these relationships are the Foulis-Holland theorems (FHTs). Here I provide an automated deduction of the OMLaw, from OML without the OMLaw, conjoined with one of the FHTs.

Keywords: automated deduction, quantum computing, orthomodular lattice, Foulis-Holland theorems, Hilbert space

1.0 Introduction

The optimization of quantum computing circuitry and compilers at some level must be expressed in terms of the description of quantum-mechanical behaviors ([1], [17], [18], [20]). In much the same way that conventional propositional (Boolean) logic (BL,[12]) is the logical structure of description of the behavior of classical physical systems (e.g. "the measurements of the position and momentum of particle P are commutative", i.e., can be measured in either order, yielding the same results) and is isomorphic to a Boolean lattice ([10], [11], [19]), so also the algebra, *C(H)*, of the closed linear subspaces of (equivalently, the system of linear operators on (observables in)) a Hilbert space *H* ([1], [4], [6], [9], [13]) is *a* logic of the descriptions of the behavior of quantum mechanical systems (e.g., "the measurements of the position and momentum of particle P are *not* commutative") and is a model ([10]) of an ortholattice (OL; [4]). An OL can thus be thought of as a kind of "quantum logic" (QL; [19]). Figure 1 shows a set of axioms for an orthlolattice.

```
Lattice axioms

      x = c(c(x))                              (AxLat1)
      x v y = y v x                            (AxLat2)
      (x v y) v z = x v (y v z)                (AxLat3)
      (x ^ y) ^ z = x ^ (y ^ z)                (AxLat4)
      x v (x ^ y) = x                          (AxLat5)
      x ^ (x v y) = x                          (AxLat6)

Ortholattice axioms
      c(x) ^ x = 0                             (AxOL1)
      c(x) v x = 1                             (AxOL2)
      x ^ y = c(c(x) v c(y))                   (AxOL3)


A useful definition
       1_2 = y v ((x ^ c(y)) v (c(x) ^ c(y)))


where
   x, y are variables ranging over lattice nodes
   ^ is lattice meet
   v is lattice join
   c(x) is the orthocomplement of x
   <-> means if and only if
   = is equivalence ([12])
   1 is the maximum lattice element (= x v c(x))
   0 is the minimum lattice element (= c(1))
```

Figure 1. Lattice, ortholattice, ortholattice axioms, and a useful definition.

C(H) is also a model of an orthomodular lattice (OML; [4], [7]), which is an OL conjoined with the orthomodularity axiom (OMLaw):

```
    y v (c(y) ^ (x v y)) =
        x v y          (OMLaw)
```

The rationalization of the OMA as a claim proper to physics has proven problematic ([13], Section 5-6), motivating the question of whether the OMA is required in an adequate characterization of QL. Thus formulated, the question suggests that the OMA and its equivalents are specific to an OML, and that as a consequence, banning the OMA from QL yields a "truer" quantum logic.

Now a QL can be thought of as a BL in which the distributive law

```
(D)    (x v (y ^ z) =
     (x v y) ^ (x v z))
```

does not hold. Under certain commutativity conditions, a QL does satisfy (D); among the most well known of these relationships are the Foulis-Holland theorems (FHTs ([7])):

```
% Foulis-Holland theorem FH1
(C(x,y) & C(x,z)) ->  ( (x ^ (y v z)) = ((x ^ y) v (x ^ z))  )

% Foulis-Holland theorem FH2
(C(x,y) & C(x,z)) ->  ( (y ^ (x v z)) = ((y ^ x) v (y ^ z))  )

% Foulis-Holland theorem FH3
(C(x,y) & C(x,z)) ->  ( (x v (y ^ z)) = ((x v y) ^ (x v z))  )

% Foulis-Holland theorem FH4
(C(x,y) & C(x,z)) ->  ( (y v (x ^ z)) = ((y v x) ^ (y v z))  )

where C(x,y), "x commutes with y" is defined as

      C(x,y) <-> (x = ((x ^ y) v (x ^ c(y))))
```

Figure 2. The Foulis-Holland theorems.

2.0 Method

The OML axiomatizations of Megill, Pavičić, and Horner ([5], [14], [15], [16], [21]), without the OMLaw, but conjoined with the FH3, were implemented in a *prover9* ([2]) script ([3]) configured to derive the OMLaw, then executed in that framework on a Dell Inspiron 545 with an Intel Core2 Quad CPU Q8200 (clocked @ 2.33 GHz) and 8.00 GB RAM, running under the *Windows Vista Home Premium /Cygwin* operating environment.

3.0 Results

Figure 3 shows the proof, generated by [3] on the platform described in Section 2.0, that the OMLaw is implied by an OML with the OMLaw, conjoined with FH3:

```
============================== PROOF =================================

% Proof 1 at 0.06 (+ 0.05) seconds: "OMLaw".
% Length of proof is 44.


3 C(x,y) <-> x = (x ^ y) v (x ^ c(y)) # label("Df: commutes") #
label(non_clause).  [assumption].
4 C(x,y) & C(x,z) -> x v (y ^ z) = (x v y) ^ (x v z) #
label("Foulis-Holland Theorem 3") # label(non_clause).
[assumption].
5 y v (c(y) ^ (x v y)) = x v y # label("OMLaw") #
label(non_clause) # label(goal).  [goal].
10 x = c(c(x)) # label("AxL1").  [assumption].
11 c(c(x)) = x.  [copy(10),flip(a)].
12 x v y = y v x # label("AxL2").  [assumption].
```

```
13 (x v y) v z = x v (y v z) # label("AxL3").  [assumption].
15 x v (x ^ y) = x # label("AxL5").  [assumption].
16 x ^ (x v y) = x # label("AxL6").  [assumption].
17 c(x) ^ x = 0 # label("AxOL1").  [assumption].
18 c(x) v x = 1 # label("AxOL2").  [assumption].
19 x v c(x) = 1.  [copy(18),rewrite([12(2)])].
20 x ^ y = c(c(x) v c(y)) # label("AxOL3").  [assumption].
62 -C(x,y) | (x ^ y) v (x ^ c(y)) = x # label("Df: commutes").
[clausify(3)].
63 -C(x,y) | c(c(x) v y) v c(c(x) v c(y)) = x.
[copy(62),rewrite([20(2),20(7),11(8),12(9)])].
64 C(x,y) | (x ^ y) v (x ^ c(y)) != x # label("Df: commutes").
[clausify(3)].
65 C(x,y) | c(c(x) v y) v c(c(x) v c(y)) != x.
[copy(64),rewrite([20(2),20(7),11(8),12(9)])].
76 -C(x,y) | -C(x,z) | x v (y ^ z) = (x v y) ^ (x v z) #
label("Foulis-Holland Theorem 3").  [clausify(4)].
77 -C(x,y) | -C(x,z) | c(c(x v y) v c(x v z)) = x v c(c(y) v
c(z)).  [copy(76),rewrite([20(3),20(10)]),flip(c)].
78 c1 v (c(c1) ^ (c2 v c1)) != c2 v c1 # label("OMLaw") #
answer("OMLaw").  [deny(5)].
79 c1 v c(c1 v c(c1 v c2)) != c1 v c2 # answer("OMLaw").
[copy(78),rewrite([12(6),20(7),11(4),12(12)])].
80 c(1) = 0.  [back_rewrite(17),rewrite([20(2),11(2),19(2)])].
81 c(c(x) v c(x v y)) = x.  [back_rewrite(16),rewrite([20(2)])].
82 x v c(c(x) v c(y)) = x.  [back_rewrite(15),rewrite([20(1)])].
86 x v (y v z) = y v (x v z).
[para(12(a,1),13(a,1,1)),rewrite([13(2)])].
94 x v (c(x) v y) = 1 v y.  [para(19(a,1),13(a,1,1)),flip(a)].
101 C(x,c(x)) | 0 v c(c(x) v c(x)) != x.
[para(19(a,1),65(b,1,2,1)),rewrite([80(8),12(8)])].
115 C(x,1) | c(0 v c(x)) v c(1 v c(x)) != x.
[para(80(a,1),65(b,1,2,1,2)),rewrite([12(5),12(9),12(11)])].
121 c(0 v c(x)) = x.
[para(19(a,1),81(a,1,1,2,1)),rewrite([80(3),12(3)])].
123 C(x,x v y) | c(1 v y) v x != x.
[para(81(a,1),65(b,1,2)),rewrite([86(5),94(5)])].
125 1 v x = 1.  [para(80(a,1),81(a,1,1,1)),rewrite([121(6)])].
126 c(x v x) = c(x).
[para(81(a,1),81(a,1,1,2)),rewrite([11(2)])].
127 C(x,1) | x v 0 != x.
[back_rewrite(115),rewrite([121(6),125(5),80(4)])].
141 C(x,x v y) | 0 v x != x.
[back_rewrite(123),rewrite([125(4),80(4)])].
144 C(x,c(x)) | 0 v x != x.
[back_rewrite(101),rewrite([126(7),11(5)])].
150 x v 0 = x.  [para(19(a,1),82(a,1,2,1)),rewrite([80(2)])].
152 x v x = x.
[para(80(a,1),82(a,1,2,1,2)),rewrite([12(3),121(4)])].
154 C(x,1).  [back_rewrite(127),rewrite([150(4)]),xx(b)].
```

```
164 0 v x = x.
[hyper(63,a,154,a),rewrite([12(3),125(3),80(2),80(4),12(4),121(5)
])].
168 C(x,c(x)).  [back_rewrite(144),rewrite([164(4)]),xx(b)].
169 C(x,x v y).  [back_rewrite(141),rewrite([164(4)]),xx(b)].
201 x v (x v y) = x v y.  [para(152(a,1),13(a,1,1)),flip(a)].
206 x v c(x v c(x v y)) = x v y.
[hyper(77,a,168,a,b,169,a),rewrite([19(2),80(2),201(3),164(4),11(
3),11(3)]),flip(a)].
207 $F # answer("OMLaw").  [resolve(206,a,79,a)].

============================== end of proof ==========================
```

Figure 3. Summary of a *prover9* ([2]) proof of the OMLaw from OML without the OMLaw, conjoined with the FH3. The proofs assume the default inference rules of *prover9*. The general form of a line in this proof is "*line_number conclusion [derivation]*", where *line_number* is a unique identifier of a line in the proof, and *conclusion* is the result of applying the *prover9* inference rules (such as *para*modulation, *copy*ing, and *rewrit*ing), noted in square brackets (denoting the *derivation*), to the lines cited in those brackets. Note that some of "logical" proof lines in the above have been transformed to two text lines, with the *derivation* appearing on a text line following a text line containing the first part of that logical line. The detailed syntax and semantics of these notations can be found in [2]. All *prover9* proofs are by default proofs by contradiction.

The total time to produce the proofs in Figure 3 on the platform described in Section 2.0 was approximately 0.1 seconds.

4.0 Discussion

The results of Section 3.0 motivate several observations:

1. The OMLaw is derivable from the OML without the OMLaw, conjoined with the FHTs.

2. The proof in Section 3.0 uses only FH3, not FH2, FH3, or FH4.

3. The proof in Section 3.0 is, as far as I know, novel.

4. Companion papers provide derivations of the FHTs from OML. The union of these proofs constitutes a proof of the equivalence of the OMLaw and the FHTs within OML theory.

5.0 Acknowledgements

This work benefited from discussions with Tom Oberdan, Frank Pecchioni, Tony Pawlicki, and the late John K. Prentice, whose passion for foundations of physics inspired those of us privileged to have known him. For any infelicities that remain, I am solely responsible.

6.0 References

[1] von Neumann J. *Mathematical Foundations of Quantum Mechanics*. 1936. Translated by R. T. Beyer. Princeton. 1983.

[2] McCune WW. *prover9 and mace4*. URL http://www.cs.unm.edu/~mccune/prover9/. 2009.

[3] Horner JK. *prover9* scripts for OMLaw from FH3. 2011. Available from the author on request.

[4] Dalla Chiara ML and Giuntini R. *Quantum Logics*. URL http://xxx.lanl.gov/abs/quant-ph/0101028. 2004.

[5] Megill ND and Pavičić M. Orthomodular lattices and quantum algebra. *International Journal of Theoretical Physics* 40 (2001), pp. 1387-1410.

[6] Akhiezer NI and Glazman IM. *Theory of Linear Operators in Hilbert Space. Volume I.* Translated by M. Nestell. Frederick Ungar. 1961.

[7] Holland, Jr. SS Orthomodularity in infinite dimensions: a theorem of M. Solèr. *Bulletin of the American Mathematical Society* 32 (1995), pp. 205-234.

[8] Marsden EL and Herman LM. *A condition for distribution in orthomodular lattices.* Kansas State University Technical Report #40. 1974.

[9] Knuth DE and Bendix PB. Simple word problems in universal algebras. In J. Leech, ed. *Computational Problems in Abstract Algebra.* Pergamon Press. 1970. pp. 263-297.

[10] Chang CC and Keisler HJ. *Model Theory.* North-Holland. 1990. pp. 38-39.

[11] Birkhoff G. *Lattice Theory.* Third Edition. American Mathematical Society. 1967.

[12] Church A. *Introduction to Mathematical Logic. Volume I.* Princeton. 1956.

[13] Jauch J. *Foundations of Quantum Mechanics.* Addison-Wesley. 1968.

[14] Megill ND. *Metamath.* URL http://us.metamath.org/qlegif/mmql.html#unify. 2004.

[15] Horner JK. An automated deduction system for orthomodular lattice theory. *Proceedings of the 2005 International Conference on Artificial Intelligence.* CSREA Press. 2005. pp. 260-265.

[16] Horner JK. An automated equational logic deduction of join elimination in orthomodular lattice theory. *Proceedings of the 2007 International Conference on Artificial Intelligence.* CSREA Press. 2007. pp. 481-488.

[17] Messiah A. *Quantum Mechanics*. Dover. 1958.

[18] Horner JK. Using automated theorem-provers to aid the design of efficient compilers for quantum computing. *Los Alamos National Laboratory Quantum Institute Workshop.* December 9–10, 2002. URL http://www.lanl.gov/science/centers/quantum/qls_pdfs/horner.pdf.

[19] Birkhoff G and von Neumann J. The logic of quantum mechanics. *Annals of Mathematics* 37 (1936), 823-243.

[20] Nielsen MA and Chuang L . *Quantum Computation and Quantum Information.* Cambridge. 2000.

[21] Pavičić M and Megill N. Quantum and classical implicational algebras with primitive implication. *International Journal of Theoretical Physics* 37 (1998), 2091-2098. ftp://m3k.grad.hr/pavicic/quantum-logic/1998-int-j-theor-phys-2.ps.gz.

SESSION

GRAMMAR RULES AND TEXT COMPRESSION METHODS

Chair(s)

Prof. Hamid Arabnia
University of Georgia

Improving Compression Performance with a Star Encoding Front End: A Linguistic Comparison

Ebru Celikel Cankaya[1], **Omar Darwish**[2]

[1,2]Department of Computer Science, University of Texas at Dallas, Richardson, Texas, United States

Abstract – *We introduce a front end encryption scheme to a conventional compression algorithm to improve its compression performance. We apply our technique on text to achieve better lossless compression rates with no significant runtime overhead. We extend our work to include different source languages, namely English, French, German, and Spanish to see the effect of source language on the overall performance. Our approach yields promising results on standard corpora for each language as it offers improved compression rate (with28.9% at most on Arithmetic Coding algorithm when the source language is English). Our scheme also promises to provide security, when the dictionary of star encoding is not revealed to unintended third parties.*

Keywords: Text Compression, Pre-processing, Lossless Transformation, Star Encoding, Security

1 Introduction

In a world where technology prominently rules, research focuses on relaxing the boundaries introduced by theoretical restrictions. Data compression is one of these areas. Whether for storage and/or transmission, compression helps achieve significant gain in storage/channel efficiency. In the context of lossless text compression, we once were bound by Shannon's upper limit: the shortest possible encoding of text in a particular source alphabet is directly proportional to its entropy [1]. With the most naïve model, i.e. zero-order model, this boundary is as large as 4.75 BPC for English. As new models are introduced, such as models that base themselves on an order *n* context –hence named order-n model-, the compression rate is getting better (for example, 2.77 BPC for an order-3 model). Our aim in this paper is to improve even better the lossless compression rate of text. We propose employing star encoding as a front end to conventional compression schemes as Arithmetic Coding [2], Huffman Coding [3], Prediction by Partial Matching (PPM) [4], and Burrows Wheeler Transform (BWT) [5] to achieve this improvement. We also investigate the effect of star encoding preceding conventional compression on different source languages as English, French, German, and Spanish.

We hope this work can serve as a practical tool to store larger data on limited storage, and or transmit more data at a time on network applications such as social media, search engines, and general communication.

We further consider an extension for our idea that will involve an asymmetric encryption scheme that will conceal the star encoding dictionary from adversaries. This will augment a security feature to our proposed scheme, so that it can be used for mass data oriented platforms such as clouds.

2 Related Work

Recently, a greater number of researchers have shifted their focus from generating new compression algorithms to instead making it easier for existing compression technology to perform better through text pre-processing. In this paper, we explain some of the existing preprocessing techniques and propose an approach of our own.

Dictionary based pre-processing is a trivial idea that is referred to for improving compression performance on text. Rexline and Roberts [6], show that preprocessing can not only help the main compressor perform better, it can also contribute by performing pre-compression. Regarding the fact that roughly 1000 words are used daily in average English text, and almost 80 percent of English words are greater than 3 characters in length, it would be efficient to convert the most frequently used words to 3 character code. The authors suggest StarNT encoding: the first word is encoded as 'a', the next word as 'b',…,27th as 'A', 28th as 'B', 53rd as "aa", 54th as "ab". As this pattern continues, "ZZ" would be assigned to the 2757th word, "aaa" to the 2758th word and so on. This means that using only 3 characters, 143,364 words (52 + 52^2 + 52^3) can be encoded, which is much more than needed by the average language. From this, pre-compression is achieved.

Another scholar work by [7] improves the word replacement transformation by altering the characters used for encoding. It focuses on improving encoding and decoding time while simultaneously increasing compression rates. This idea is further studied by [8], where the most frequently occurring words are mapped with the shortest encoded counterparts. One variation proposed in [9], is that in addition to the dictionary that contains the most frequently occurring words (which is estimated to be an average 20-30 percent of any given English literature), a list of stop words be used. This list would be encoding in a slightly different way than the dictionary in order to produce a shorter encoding per word.

Another statistical approach to encoding is the proposed in [10]. Based on the fact that words show a more biased frequency than characters (this is also exploited by the Lempel-Ziv family of compressors), authors pursue word oriented pre-processing that has the potential of better compressibility. The authors first compress text with a word-based, byte-oriented compressor, then pass it to a character oriented compressor. This work employs Dense Coding (DC), which is faster to search than the plaintext due to its self-synchronizing code characteristic, in the expense of increased overall compression time.

Other methods of compression involve certain preprocessing techniques. The authors of [11] demonstrate this concept in their paper, which focuses on white space compression. They estimate that on average, around 15 percent of a text file is spacing, so eliminating this spacing would make a text file approximately 15 percent smaller. To accomplish this, they exploit the fact that most words are either lowercase, uppercase, or begin with an uppercase letter that is followed by lowercase letters. If a word is written in any of these ways, is followed by a space, and its last two characters are lowercase, then a space can be represented by simply capitalizing the last letter of this word.

Star (*) Encoding is a known technique, whose goal is to produce as many redundant characters as possible, which can be very useful when coupled with BWT [5], so that it will be easier for a traditional compressor (such as a Huffman or Arithmetic compressor) to achieve better compressibility. We expand the use of star encoding as a front end to conventional lossless compression algorithms: Arithmetic Coding, Huffman Coding, PPM, and BWT on different text on various source languages (English, French, German, and Spanish) and compare compression performances.

Yet another pre-processing approach is to replace parts of a word instead of the whole word. Static Text Compression Algorithm (STECA) [12] is a language dependent approach that tries document the most common bigrams and trigrams for a given language. Although the algorithm's static structure may be seen as a negative, it owes its speed to this design: it generates a dictionary of the most commonly occurring couplets and triplets, "ed" or "tio" in English, for example. This dictionary is then used to assign a numerical value to each bigram and trigram. With the help of this dictionary, these frequently occurring sequences are replaced by their numerical value in words that contain them.

As expected, there is not a need for an excessively long list of frequently occurring bigrams or trigrams since this method works better the more frequent the character sequence occurs naturally for the given language. Even though there is a relatively small amount of numerical codes, numbers are still needed to be represented in the encoded output. This can be solved simply by using an escape number such as 0.

The last encoding scheme we discuss is "Edge-Guided (EG)" which is described in [13]. This encoding scheme does not use a dictionary, but instead focuses on the way that words interact with each other. Words and word sequences are encoded as "vertices" and "edges" respectively. To start, each distinct word or letter grouping in a sentence or stream is mapped as a vertex. These vertices are then connected to each other by edges which represent the flow of the sentence.

An Edge-Guided encoder generates three streams Text, Word, and Edge which are then passed to an encoder such as PPM. The Word stream contains the distinct words found in the original sentences, separated by an escape sequence. The Text stream describes if the next word in the sentence is a new vertex, creating a new edge, or following an existing edge. Finally, the Edge stream is a numerical stream that is matched with the Text stream to specify where edges connect. As expected, this technique is very useful for text that features abundant word redundancy.

3 Our Scheme

In this section, we describe our design and present the details of our scheme. Figure 1 presents an overview of our scheme with its components: To realize a lossless compression scheme, the sender takes the plaintext and applies star encoding as a front end to preprocess the input text. We anticipate that this preprocess will introduce abundant redundancy (due to the injection of multiple '*' symbols), which in turn will help improve compressibility. For star encoding, the sender employs a shared dictionary. The same dictionary is later employed by the receiver to decode the star encoded text at the recipient site. We then apply conventional lossless text compression algorithms, namely Arithmetic Coding, Huffman Coding, Prediction by

Partial Matching, and Burrows Wheeler Transform to investigate the effect of using star encoding as a front end to the compression process. We further apply our compression scheme to different source languages to see the degree of sensitivity of source languages to star encoding based preprocessing. Once the conventional compression algorithm compresses the star encoded input, the ciphertext is transferred to the receiver.

The receiver applies the steps applied by sender in reverse order: He first decompresses the ciphertext, then star decodes the decompressed text using the same shared dictionary to retrieve the original text. The dictionary, when unavailable to third parties but just sender and receiver contributes as a means to provide security to the system. Therefore, our scheme becomes a method that provides improved compression with added security.

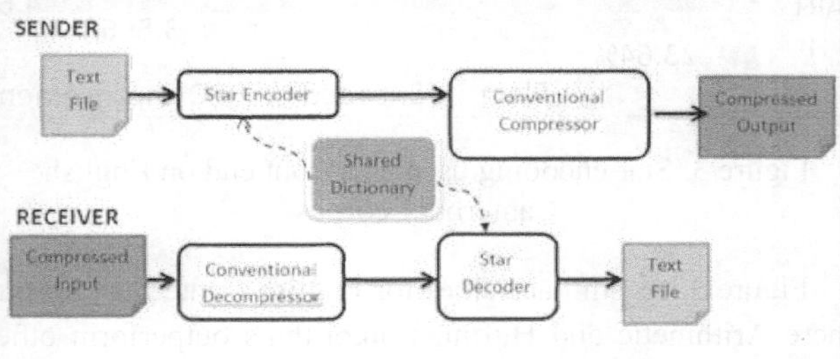

Figure 1. Overall system schema.

3.1 Corpora

We run our experiments on 4 different common source languages: English, French, German, and Spanish. For English, standard Calgary and Canterbury corpora are used. For the other source languages, text from available corpora is compiled. A standard pre-processing that filters punctuation marks, non-alphabet characters and multiple occurrences of spaces is applied to the individual language wordlists and each document before encoding and compression.

File Name	Size (kB)	Description
Calgary		
bib	111261	Bibliography
book1	768771	Fiction book
book2	610856	non-fiction book
news	377109	USENET batch file
paper1	53161	Technical paper
paper2	82199	Technical paper
trans	93695	Transcript of terminal session
Canterbury		
asyoulike	152089	Shakespeare
alice29	125179	English text
fields	11150	C source
Ice10	426754	Technical writing
Plrabn12	481861	Poetry

Table 1. English Corpora with selected text files from Calgary Corpus and Canterbury Corpus [14][15].

File Name	Size (Byte)	Description
doc1.txt	17720	Binnenhandel Der DDR
doc2.txt	17106	Pressemitteilung - 132/4/70- NRW
history.txt	16487	Bemerkungen Zur Modernen Darstellung Natinaler
horror.txt	15223	Der Schrecken Von Takera
scope.txt	15545	Brunte Horoskop

Table 2. Dereko German Corpus with selected text files from COSMAS II database [16].

File Name	Size (Byte)	Description
anthology	97059	Anthologie du Journalisme
darwinOrigins	1391304	L'origine des espèces
dominique	442548	Dominique
football	20466	Notes sur le foot-ball (1897)
meditations	176650	Les meditations

Table 3. French Corpus with selected text files from Corpus of Spoken French [17].

File Name	Size (Byte)	Description
pachecho.txt	78708	Pachecos y Palomeques
palabras.txt	43610	Palabras y plumas
palau.txt	69133	El palau de vidre
palomares.txt	15318	Palomares (Palomares)
ramilletes.txt	8307	Los ramilletes

Table 4. Spanish Corpus with selected text files from [18].

3.2 Star Encoding as a Front End

Star encoding was applied in a way that is similar to what is described in [19]. After the first stage of pre-processing, each individual corpus text file is then encoded using a variation of the Star Encoding. Using wordlists for each source language, a dictionary tree D is generated. This tree is then split into multiple, lexicographically sorted dictionaries D_x where x denotes the length of the words it contains, making it a Length Index Preserving Transformation (LIPT). For example, the English wordlist that we used had minimum and maximum word lengths of 2 and 22 characters respectively. From these sub-dictionaries, encoding and decoding maps were generated. For encoding, the plain words are mapped to their star encoding counterparts. Words in a given sub-dictionary are mapped to an encoded word that is the same length. The first word is simply a string consisting of the asterisk *. For example, the first four letter word in the sub dictionary would be encoded to "****". The next 52 words are encoded to "a***", "b***", ..., "z***", "A***", "B***", ..., "Z***". The 54 word would start the pattern in the second character, with the first character remaining an asterisk for the next 52 words: "*a**", "*b**",..."*z**". This pattern is continued till "Z" is reached at the last character for the given word length: "***Z". The next word restarts the pattern at the second character, but the first character remains 'a': "aa**", "ab**", ... "aZ**", "a*a*", ... ,"a**Z." The pattern continues till the encoding limit for the current word length is reached (i.e, the last encoded string is "ZZZZ").

3.3 Compression Algorithms

We employ the four widely used conventional compression algorithms to test the performance improvement of our star encoding front end on each. These algorithms are Arithmetic Coding, Huffman Coding, PPM, and BWT.

4 Results

Our experiments focus on employing star encoding as a front end, anticipating a better compression rate later on when we further apply conventional compression algorithms individually. Results show that with some exceptions, we obtain a significant improvement over conventional compression for text on each source language. Figures 2 and 3 present the result of star encoding used as a front end on English corpora Calgary and Canterbury, respectively. It should be noted that our scheme can be used to also provide security, in expense of time and extra data transfer, which will involve the encryption of star encoded dictionary with a symmetric encryption and sending the key to the receiver. This is due to the tradeoff between security and storage cost.

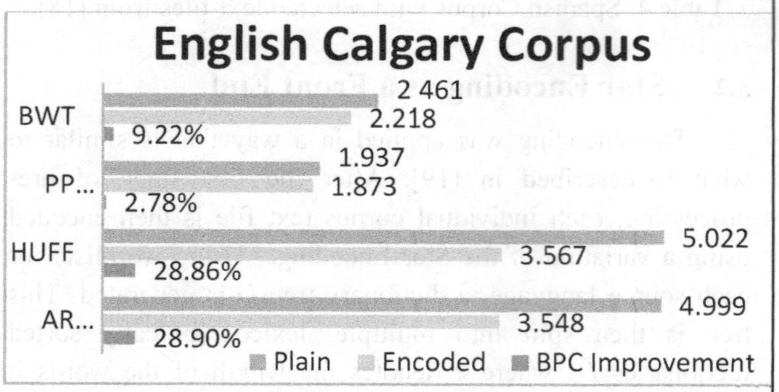

Figure 2. Star encoding used as a front end on English Calgary corpus

As seen in Figure 2, star encoding improves the Arithmetic Coding and Huffman Coding performances most with very similar percentage gains as 28.86% and 28.90%, respectively for English Calgary corpus. The poorest performance is in PPM with only 2.78% improvement, and the performance with BWT improves considerably at a rate of 9.22% on average for the selected five text files from Calgary corpus.

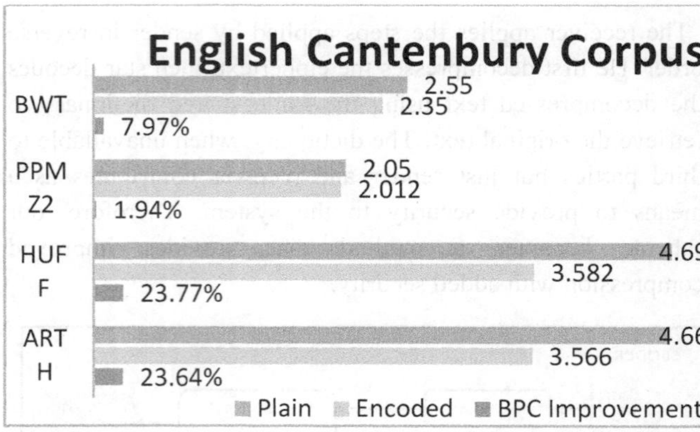

Figure 3. Star encoding used as a front end on English Canterbury corpus

Figure 3 has similar values for English Canterbury corpus, where Arithmetic and Huffman algorithms outperform other conventional compression algorithms, i.e. PPM and BWT, in the gain obtained with using star encoding as a front end. This time, Huffman Coding has a slightly better performance improvement with 23.77% than Arithmetic Coding, which has 23.64% performance improvement. Moreover, we see that in Canterbury corpus, the ordering in terms of improvement in the compression performance for the worst two algorithms comes out as similar as Calgary corpus: BWT poorer with 7.97% gain, and PPM with 1.94% gain only.

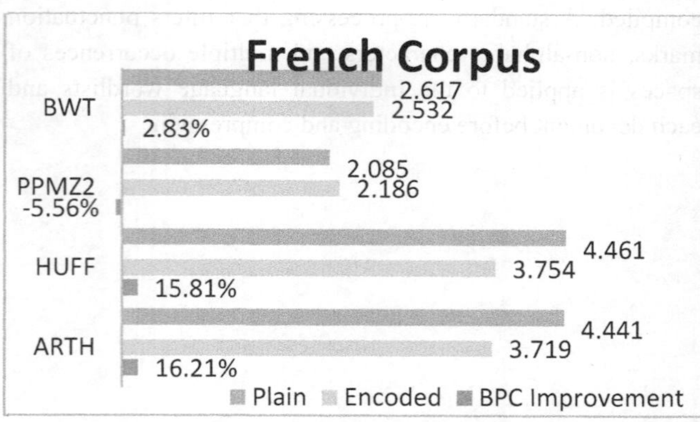

Figure 4. Star encoding used as a front end on French corpus

One of the aims of our work is to investigate the effect of implementing star encoding as a front end on different source languages. When we run our scheme on text in French corpus (Figure 4), we again get the best improvement rates for Arithmetic Coding (with 16.81%) and Huffman Coding (with 15.81%), though with lower rates this time. And interestingly, while BWT still performs next to worst (with 2.83%), PPM has an average performance loss in compression. This means that using star encoding as a front end in French text degrades the compression performance of PPM algorithm. These results obviously suggest that source language itself is a substantial parameter in lossless compression when star encoding is used as a front end.

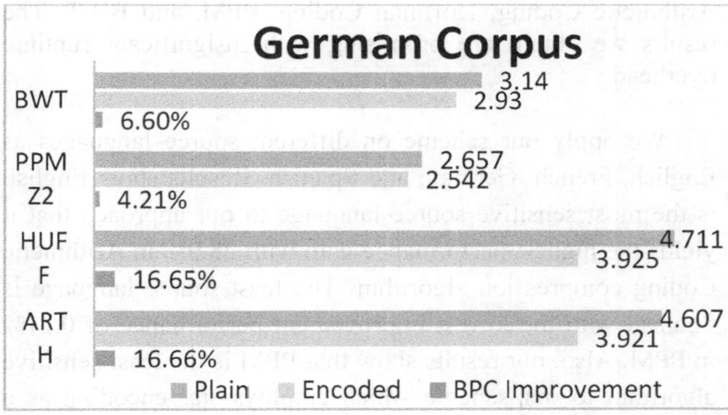

Figure 5. Star encoding used as a front end on German corpus

To inquire more about this effect, and find out the sensitivity of source languages to star encoding being applied as a front end, we repeated our experiments on two more source languages: German and Spanish. Figure 5 demonstrates the results we obtain on German corpus. Though Arithmetic Coding and Huffman Coding yield very close improvement rates as 16.66% and 16.65%, we see that PPM has the best improvement rate so far in German corpus. Then, we can conclude that German is more sensitive to star encoding when it is applied as a front end to PPM algorithm. For BWT, the improvement rate is similar to English and French corpora, with a percentage of 6.60%.

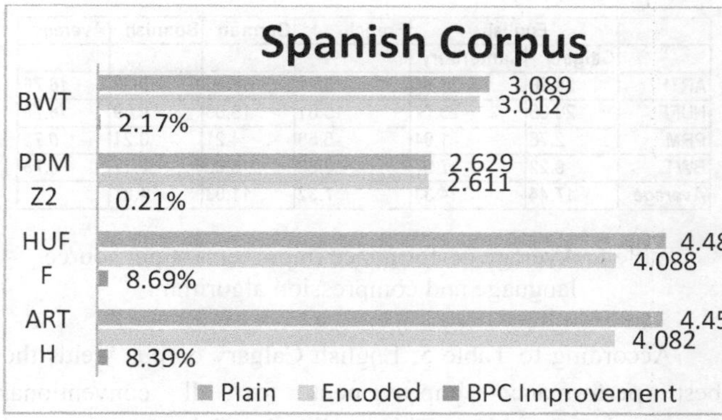

Figure 6. Star encoding used as a front end on Spanish corpus

When we employ Spanish as the source language, we get different results than previous source languages as seen in Figure 6: Arithmetic Coding and Huffman Coding only obtain around 8% improvement, BWT around 2%, and the improvement with PPM is almost negligible with an average rate of 0.21% only. These results prove that the least sensitive source language to employing star encoding as a front end to conventional compression algorithms among four source languages we consider is Spanish.

We also compare the rate of improvement for each conventional compression algorithm on each source language. Figure 7 displays the chart for average improvement rate when star encoding is employed as a front end to four conventional compression algorithms.

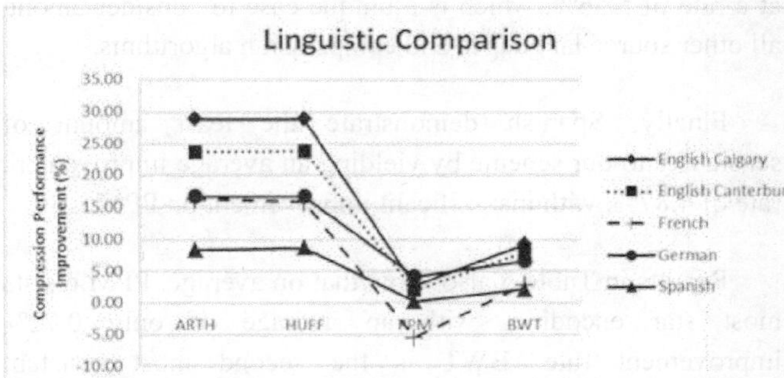

Figure 7. Linguistic Comparison for star encoding employed as a front end to conventional compression algorithms.

When we summarize the average compression rates obtained for each source language and for each conventional compression algorithm, we get Table 5.

	English		French	German	Spanish	*Average*
	Calgary	Canterbury				
ARTH	28.90	23.64	16.21	16.66	8.39	***18.76***
HUFF	28.86	23.77	15.81	16.65	8.69	***18.76***
PPM	2.78	1.94	-5.56	4.21	0.21	***0.72***
BWT	9.22	7.97	2.83	6.60	2.17	***5.76***
Average	**17.44**	**14.33**	**7.32**	**11.03**	**4.87**	

Table 5. Average performance improvement per source language and compression algorithm.

According to Table 5, English Calgary corpus yields the best performance improvement for all conventional compression algorithms. This implies that Calgary corpus, and hence English, is the most sensitive source language to employing star encoding as a front end to lossless compression with an average overall improvement rate of 17.44% (Calculated as the mean of improvement rates on four compression algorithms). This is followed by English Canterbury corpus with a mean improvement rate of 14.33%. This result supports the implication that English is the most sensitive source language to our proposed scheme, which employs star encoding as a front end before applying any compression.

Table 5 states that the second most sensitive source language seems to be German with an average improvement performance of 11.03%. The third most sensitive source language is French, where the average improvement percentage is measured as 7.32%. It should be noted that in German corpus, performance of PPM degraded significantly at a rate of 5.56%, which is a unique case to consider among all other source languages and compression algorithms.

Finally, Spanish demonstrate the least amount of sensitivity to our scheme by yielding an average improvement rate of 4.87%, with insignificant improvement on PPM.

Results in Table 5 also show that on average, PPM resists most star encoding, with an average of only 0.72% improvement rate. BWT is the second most resistant compression algorithm to our scheme. One should remember that these are already among the best performing compression algorithms and these results suggest that we reach the theoretical limits suggested by Shannon [1] after applying star encoding that no further improvement is possible. Arithmetic Coding and Huffman Coding respond to star encoding front end similarly with an average improvement rate of 18.76%.

For each source language, the rate of improvement is very similar for Arithmetic Coding and Huffman Coding extending in a stretch from almost 29% to around 8%. We should consider the fact that originally, both compression algorithms, i.e. Arithmetic Coding and Huffman perform already poorly on text, regardless of the source language. Whereas for BWT, and PPM the original compression rates on plaintext is already good at an average rate of 2BPC for each algorithm regardless of the source language. So, even the high improvement rate after using star encoding does not help make the compression performance of Arithmetic Coding and Huffman to reach the already good compression rates of BWT and PPM.

5 Conclusion and Future Work

We design and implement a front end to improve the performance of conventional compression algorithms as Arithmetic Coding, Huffman Coding, PPM, and BWT. The results we obtain are promising with insignificant runtime overhead.

We apply our scheme on different source languages as English, French, German, and Spanish. Results show English is the most sensitive source language to our approach that it yields the highest performance gain with 28.9% in Arithmetic Coding compression algorithm. The least source language is Spanish with the lowest improvement performance of 0.21% in PPM. Also, our results show that PPM is the least sensitive algorithm to our scheme which employs star encoding as a front end to improve compression performance. This is a supportive indicator that we reach theoretical bounds on especially already well performing compression algorithms such as PPM and BWT, while still obtaining considerable improvements in poorer performing compression algorithms as Arithmetic Coding and Huffman Coding.

Our scheme with its promising results can be used for non-punctuation sensitive text, such as a list of emails, where separate domains can be easily obtained from usernames later on. Also, we anticipate that our method can be used in name lists, books with predictive decoding. Furthermore, one can employ star encoding plus compression in a random process of encoding that only the sender, receiver know, though this can be prone to brute force attack. Word lists have to be the exact same to generate a perfect match, but a word list that isn't a perfect match, but close enough can still generate a relatively close decoding. We think this would work better for text files that are diverse in nature and would therefore require a large wordlist.

We plan on extending the implementation of our scheme to provide security. If the star encoding dictionary is encrypted with an asymmetric encryption algorithm, we can guarantee the secure transfer of the dictionary. This, in turn, provides an extra security to our scheme since any adversary who does not have the private key cannot recover the dictionary. Such a secure scheme that provides encryption as well as compression can well meet the most prominent requirement of today's data storage and transmission: handling cloud data securely.

6 References

[1] Shannon C. E., Waever W., "The Mathematical Theory of Communication, Volume 1", University of Illinois Press, 1949.

[2] Witten I., Neal R. M., Cleary J. G., "Arithmetic Coding for Data Compression", Communications of the ACM, 30(6), June 1987.

[3] Har-Peled S., "Huffman Coding", UIUC, Illinois, USA, December, 2007.

[4] Hossain I., "Prediction with Partial Match using two-dimensional approximate contexts", Picture Coding Symposium, pp. 181-184, Krakow, Poland, 2012.

[5] Kärkkäinen J., Mikkola P., Kempa D., "Grammar Precompression Speeds Up Burrows–Wheeler Compression", String Processing and Information Retrieval, Lecture Notes in Computer Science, Vol. 7608, pp. 330-335, 2012.

[6] Rexline S. J., Robert L., "Dictionary Based Preprocessing Methods in Text Compression - A Survey." *International Journal of Wisdom Based Computing.* 1(2), pp. 14-15. (Coimbatore, India 2011). Available: http://wisdombasedcomputing.com/vol1issue2august2011/paper8.pdf [Accessed Jan. 27, 2013].

[7] Rexline S. J., Robert L., "IWRT: Improved Word Replacement Transformation in Dictionary Based Lossless Text Compression." *European Journal of Scientific Research.* 86(2), pp. 194 – 196. . (Coimbatore, India 2011). Available: http://www.europeanjournalofscientificresearch.com/ISSUES/EJSR_86_2_06.pdf [Accessed Jan. 27,2013].

[8] Lourdusamy R., Shanmugasundaram S., "IIDBE: A Lossless Text Transform for Better Compression." *International Journal of Wisdom Based Computing.* 1(2), pp. 2-4. (Coimbatore, India 2011) Available: http://wisdombasedcomputing.com/vol1issue2august2011/paper6.pdf [Accessed Jan. 27, 2013].

[9] Boonjin V., Tadrat J., "An Experiment Study on Text Transformation for Compression Using Stoplists and Frequent Words." Information Technology: New Generations, 5th Int'l Conference, 2008, pp. 709-713. (Bangkok, Thailand 2008)

[10] Fariña A., Navarro G., Paramá J., "Boosting Text Compression with Word-Based Statistical Encoding." *Oxford University Press.* pp. 112, 115, 117-118. (Oxford, United Kingdom 2011) Available: http://comjnl.oxfordjournals.org/content/55/1/111.short [Accessed Jan. 29, 2013].

[11] Nadarajan R., Robert L., "Simple lossless preprocessing algorithms for text compression" *IET Software,* 3(1), pp. 37-45. (Coimbatore, India 2009).

[12] Carus A., Mesut A., "Fast Text Compression Using Multiple Static Dictionaries." *Information Technology Journal.* [On-line]. 2010, pp. 2-3. (Edirne, Turkey 2010). Available: http://docsdrive.com/pdfs/ansinet/itj/0000/17638-7638.pdf [Accessed Jan. 27, 2013]

[13] Martinez-Prieto M. A., Adiego J., Fuente P., "Natural Language Compression on Edge-Guided Text Processing", Journal of Information Sciences, Vol. 181(24). (Santiago, Chile 2011)

[14] English Calgary Corpus URL: http://corpus.canterbury.ac.nz/descriptions/#calgary, [Accessed on: 02/17/2013].

[15] English Canterbury Corpus URL: http://corpus.canterbury.ac.nz/descriptions/#cantrbry, [Accessed on: 02/17/2013].

[16] German Corpus URL: COSMAS II, Institute for Deutsche Sprache, http://www.ids-mannheim.de/cosmas2/projekt/registrierung/, [Accessed on: 02/17/2013]

[17] French Corpus URL: Corpus of Spoken French, Centre for Languages, Linguistics, & Area Studies, University of the West England, http://www.llas.ac.uk/resources/mb/80, [Accessed on: 02/17/2013]

[18] Spanish Corpus URL: http://www.cervantesvirtual.com/bib/seccion/literatura/psegundoniveld6b2.html?conten=catalogo [Accessed Jan. 21, 2013]

[19] Radescu R., "Transform Methods Used in Lossless Compression of Text Files." *Romanian Journal of Information Science and Technology.* pp. 102-105. (Bucharest, Romania 2009).

AUTOMATED SEMANTICS TREATMENT OF SEQUENCE DIAGRAM DEFINING GRAMMAR RULES

Fahad Alhumaidan and Nazir Ahmad Zafar
College of Computer Sciences and IT
King Faisal University, Hofuf, Saudi Arabia
Emails: {nazafar, falhumaidan}@kfu.edu.sa

ABSTRACT

UML diagrams being graphical in nature have informal semantics and it is difficult to develop automated tools for conversion and transformation of the diagrams. Formal methods are proved to be effective for semantics analysis of software systems. However, usage of formal methods is not very welcomed at early stages of software development. Hence, linking UML and formal techniques is needed to address the deficiencies existing in both approaches. In this paper, an approach is developed for transformation of simple sequence diagram by defining grammar rules. Formal specification of the procedure is described using Z notation by capturing hidden semantics under the diagrams. The model is analyzed and validated using Z/Eves tool. We believe that resultant approach will be useful for developing automated tools for modeling and verification of software systems.

KEY WORDS

Automation, UML Sequence diagram, semantics analysis, grammar rules, Z notation

1. Introduction

Although UML is accepted as a de-facto standard for development of object oriented systems but its diagrams are graphical in nature and are prone to causing errors [1]. The hidden semantics of the diagrams allows ambiguities at design level. For example, model in UML may have multiple interpretations and someone may not be able to understand what is put under the diagrams. Formal methods having well-defined semantics are at the early stage of development. A linkage of UML diagrams and formal methods will enhance the modeling power by defining semantic rules over the diagrams [2].

There exits few work in this area because the hidden semantics under UML diagrams cannot be transformed easily into formal notations. In the most relevant work, a mechanism for verifying sequence diagram is proposed by describing event-based deterministic finite automata from UML interaction diagram [3]. This is an interesting piece of work which is taken as starting point. In [4], a solution is proposed by translating UML sequence diagram combining description logic and computation tree logic. Statics analysis of UML interaction diagram is provided in [5] to check the well-formed-ness of the diagram. Jackson et al. [6], have developed Alloy Constraint Analyzer tool for description of systems whose state space involves relational structures. A study is presented based on web-service composition technique for cooperative composition modeling language [7]. An approach is demonstrated in [8] using XML to visualize TCOZ models into UML diagrams. An algorithmic approach is developed to check a consistency between sequence and state diagrams [9]. A procedure of creating tables and SQL code for Z specifications to UML diagrams is described in [10]. Intelligent approach of fusion recognition is described using petri-nets and fuzzy logic in [11]. An integrated approach is developed by combining B and UML in [12]. Kim et al., present a framework by integrating Object-Z and UML for requirements elicitation by a case study [13]. A tool is developed which takes class diagram and produces a list of comments on the diagrams in [14]. Few other relevant works can be found in [15-20]

In this paper, systematic procedure for formalizing and verifying sequence diagram is presented by defining grammar rules. The preliminary result of this research were presented in [21]. Advanced concepts, for example, loops, options, alternatives and reference are not considered. Cash withdraw from an ATM system is taken as a case study. First of all, a model of the system is presented using sequence diagram. Then state diagram is created by identifying states and transitions based on the objects and messages considering the time sequence same as in [21]. It is noted that many states of an object may exit in the life of an object. In the next, a mapping is defined to develop grammar for the diagram. Formal analysis of the transformation procedure is generalized based on the case study using Z notation. Z is used because it is a model oriented specification language used at an abstract level. The Z/Eves tool is used for model analysis because it is powerful one for analyzing the specification. Rest of the paper is organized as:

In section 2, transformation procedure from sequence to state diagram is presented. Formal specification of the procedure is described in section 3. Model analysis is given in section 4. The work is concluded in section 5.

2. Transformation of Sequence Diagram

In this section, critical analysis of sequence diagram is provided. Then formal procedure from sequence diagram to state diagram is presented by taking a case study of ATM cash withdraw system. Finally, grammar is developed to be used for further transformation.

2.1 ATM Cash Withdraw Case Study

The UML sequence diagram is used to realize details under the use cases and shows the interaction between objects by the roles. Sequence diagrams model messages for analysis and design for behavior interaction. The diagram represents messages and interactions in two dimensions. The interaction is in horizontal dimension whereas time is defined in the vertical line by resulting a two dimensional model as shown in Figure 1.

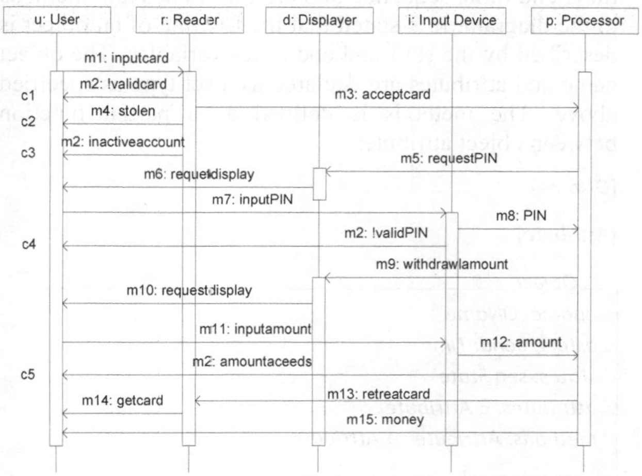

Figure 1. Sequence diagram for cash withdraw

UML sequence diagram is good modeling tool because it provides a dynamic view showing behavior which is not possible to extract from static system. Another important feature is its capability to represent parallelism between the complex components. The sequence diagram helps to discover architectural view and logical statements needed to define the system. Because of good modeling approach, sequence diagrams can be integrated easily because of the time dimension. In sequence diagram, object interaction, sequence order, responsibilities, functionalities and timings issues can be easily addressed. The diagram also facilitates the documentation at various levels of abstraction which is not easy when it is required to create from the static part of the system. Sequence diagram of ATM system as in the figure for cash withdraw is presented. At first the card is verified then PIN is entered for authentication. Finally, the cash is withdrawn if requested amount is less than the current balance of the customer.

2.2 Transformation Procedure

Sequence diagram in Figure 1 is transformed to state diagram as shown in Figure 2.

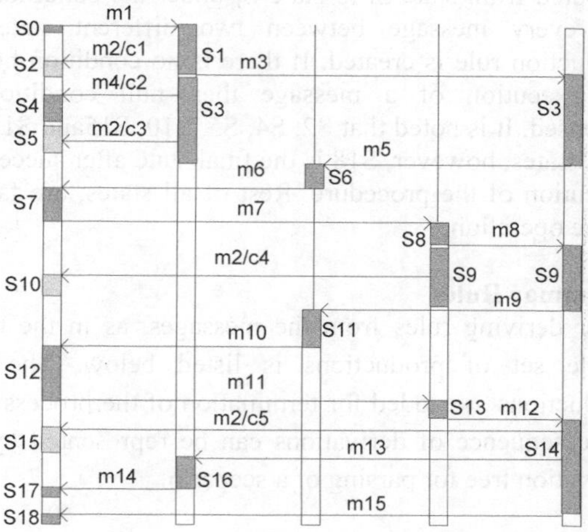

Figure 2. State diagram based on sequence diagram

In the transformation, each object may have many states. For example, the object user has ten states and the object reader has three states. It is noted that same message can be executed from two different pairs of states. For example, the message m2 is same for all the pairs of states (s1, s2), (s1, s4), (s3, s5), (s9, s10) and (s14, s15) which is repeated in case of failure of the transaction. A message may have execution condition. For example, c1, c2, c3, c4 and c5 are the message conditions.

Table 1
Mapping defining grammar for sequence diagram

#	Message	Production
1	(S0, m1, S1, null)	S0⇒m1S1, null
2	(S1, m2, S2, c1)	S1⇒m2S2, c1
3	(S1, m3, S3, null)	S1⇒m3S3, null
4	(S1, m4, S4, c2)	S1⇒m4S4, c2
5	(S3, m2, S5, c3)	S3⇒m2S5, c3
6	(S3, m5, S6, null)	S3⇒m5S6, null
7	(S6, m6, S7, null)	S6⇒m6S7, null
8	(S7, m7, S8, null)	S7⇒m7S8, null
9	(S8, m8, S9, null)	S8⇒m8S9, null
10	(S9, m2, S10, c4)	S9⇒m2S10, c4
11	(S9, m9, S11, null)	S9⇒m9S11, null
12	(S11, m10, S12, null)	S11⇒m10S12, null
13	(S12, m11, S13, null)	S12⇒m11S13, null
14	(S13, m12, S14, null)	S13⇒m12S14, null
15	(S14, m2, S15, c5)	S14⇒m2S15, c5
16	(S14, m13, S16, null)	S14⇒m13S16, null
17	(S16, m14, S17, null)	S16⇒m14S17, null
18	(S14, m15, S18, null)	S14⇒m15S18, null

The transformation procedure from state diagram to grammar development is listed in Table 1. In the table, the tuple (Si, mk, Sj, cp) represents that the message mk is executed from state Si to state Sj under the condition cp. For every message between two different states, a production rule is created. If there is no condition before the execution of a message then null condition is supposed. It is noted that S2, S4, S5, S10, S15and S18 are final states, however, S18 is the final state after successful execution of the procedure. Rest of all states, are failure of the operation.

Grammar Rules

After deriving rules from the messages, as in the table, whole set of productions is listed below. The null productions are added for termination of the process. The same sequence of derivations can be represented by the derivation tree for parsing of a scenario.

S0⇒m1S1, null; S1⇒m2S2, c1| m3S3, null| m4S4, c2; S2⇒∈; S3⇒m2S5, c3| m5S6, null; S4⇒∈; S5⇒∈; S6⇒m6S7, null; S7⇒m7S8, null; S8⇒m8S9, null; S9⇒m2S10, c4| m9S11, null; S10⇒∈; S11⇒m10S12, null; S12⇒m11S13, null; S13⇒m12S14, null; S14⇒m2S15, c5|m13S16, null| m15S18, null; S15⇒∈; S16⇒m14S17, null; S17⇒∈; S18⇒∈

Derivation

Any possible scenario of the diagram can be derived for validation by the above grammar. For example, the scenario m1m3m5m6m7m8m9m10m11m12m15 can be validated by the sequence of derivations as below:

S0 ⇒ m1S1
⇒ m1m3S3
⇒ m1m3m5S6
⇒ m1m3m5m6S7
⇒ m1m3m5m6m7S8
⇒ m1m3m5m6m7m8S9
⇒ m1m3m5m6m7m8m9m10S12
⇒ m1m3m5m6m7m8m9m10m11S13
⇒ m1m3m5m6m7m8m9m10m11m12S14
⇒ m1m3m5m6m7m8m9m10m11m12m15S18
⇒ m1m3m5m6m7m8m9m10m11m12m15.

3. Formal Analysis

In this section, formal analysis of transformation procedure is described using Z notation. At first, the sequence diagram consisting of objects and messages is specified. The time sequence is given primary importance in specification of the diagram. Then state diagram is created based on the sequence diagram. Finally, grammar is developed to be useful for derivation of all possible scenarios based on the diagram.

There can be many states of an object of sequence diagram. Hence state is defined before specification of an object. The state is defined by the schema, State, which consists of three variables that is state name, start time and end time. To declare types of name, start and end times SName and Time are used at an abstract level of specification in Z. A schema consists of two parts namely definition and predicate parts. In definition part of the schema, variables are defined whereas invariants are defined in the predicate part.

$[SName];\ Time == \mathbb{N}$

State

$sname: Sname;\ stime, etime: Time$

$stime \leq etime$

An object is represented by the schema Object which consists of six components namely object name, start time, end time, sequence of states, attributes and methods in the diagram. It is stated that the life line of an object is described by the start and end times variables. The object name and attributes are declared as a set type as specified above. The methods is defined as a partial function between object attributes.

$[OName]$

$[Attribute]$

Object

$oname: OName$
$ostart, oend: Time$
$states: \text{seq } State$
$attributes: \mathbb{F}\ Attribute$
$methods: Attribute \rightarrow\!\!\!\!\!+ Attribute$

$states \neq \langle\rangle$
$\# states \geq 1$
$\Rightarrow (\exists s1, s2: State \mid s1 \in \text{ran } states \wedge s2 \in \text{ran } states$
$\quad \bullet\ states\ 1 = s1 \wedge states\ (\# states) = s2$
$\quad \Rightarrow ostart \leq s1\ .\ stime \wedge s2\ .\ etime \leq oend)$
$\forall i: \mathbb{N} \mid \# states \geq 1 \wedge i \in 1\ ..\ \# states - 1$
$\quad \bullet\ \exists s1, s2: State$
$\quad\quad \bullet\ states\ i = s1 \wedge states\ (i + 1) = s2 \Rightarrow s1\ .\ etime \leq s2\ .\ stime$
$\forall input, output: Attribute \mid (input, output) \in methods$
$\quad \bullet\ input \in attributes \wedge output \in attributes$

The message in sequence diagram is defined by the schema Message, which consists of activation time, condition of execution, source and target objects. The activation time of a message is specified by the schema ActivationTime. It is stated that the start time is less than the finishing time of any message in the diagram. The next variable is condition that must be true before execution of a message. The condition has three values, i.e., true, false or null. The value null is used to represent that there is no triggering condition for the message. In predicate part of the schema, time ordering of the message is defined as an invariant.

Condition ::= NULL | TRUE | FALSE

```
__ActivationTime______________________
starttime, endtime: ℕ
______________________________________
starttime < endtime
______________________________________
```

```
__Message_____________________________
ActivationTime
condition: Condition
from, to: State
______________________________________
from . stime ≤ starttime ∧ endtime ≤ to . etime
______________________________________
```

Formal specification of the sequence diagram is provided by the schema SequenceModel as given below. The schema contains two components, communicating objects and messages used in the sequence diagram. In predicate part, it is stated that for every message there exist two objects in the sequence diagram and vice versa. In sequence diagram, it is less focused on messages itself and more on the order in which these are executed. The first message starts from the left-top and subsequent messages are then followed following order of execution. The message sent to the receiving object is implemented by the receiving object.

```
__SequenceModel_______________________
objects: 𝔽 Object
messages: 𝔽 Message
______________________________________
∀o1, o2: Object | o1 ∈ objects ∧ o2 ∈ objects
  • ∃s1, s2: State | s1 ∈ ran o1 . states ∧ s2 ∈ ran o2 . states
  • ∃m: Message | m ∈ messages • m . from = s1 ∧ m . to = s2
∀m: Message | m ∈ messages
  • ∃o1, o2: Object | o1 ∈ objects ∧ o2 ∈ objects
  • ∃s1, s2: State | s1 ∈ ran o1 . states ∧ s2 ∈ ran o2 . states
      • s1 = m . from ∧ s2 = m . to
______________________________________
```

The state diagram was created from the sequence diagram as in Figure 2. Formal specification of the state diagram is described below by using the schema StateDiagram which consists of five components, that is, start state, all possible states of the diagram, messages, transformation function and set of final states. The definitions are given in first part and constraints are defined in the second part of the schema.

In the predicate part of the schema, it is stated that start state is an element of the total states of the sequence diagram. For any message there exist two states reachable after execution of the message. The transition function takes a state, checks guard condition and triggers the message by moving to the next state of the object. The set of final states is represented by final which is subset of the set of total states.

```
__StateDiagram________________________
SequenceModel
start: State
states: 𝔽 State
messages: 𝔽 Message
delta: State × (Condition × Message) → State
final: 𝔽 State
______________________________________
start ∈ states
∀s1, s2: State | s1 ∈ states ∧ s2 ∈ states
  • ∃message: Message | message ∈ messages
    • message . from = s1 ∧ message . to = s2
∀message: Message | message ∈ messages
  • ∃s1, s2: State | s1 ∈ states ∧ s2 ∈ states
    • s1 = message . from ∧ s2 = message . to
∀s1: State | s1 ∈ states
  • ∃message: Message; cd: Condition; s2: State
    | message ∈ messages ∧ s2 ∈ states ∧ (s1, (cd, message))
∈ dom delta
    • delta (s1, (cd, message)) = s2
∀s: State | s ∈ final • s ∈ states
______________________________________
```

proof of *StateDiagram$domainCheck*
prove by reduce

4. Model Analysis

Even formal specification of a complex system is written in any of the formal language, it may cause potential errors. This is because, for a moment, we don't have any computer tool which may guarantee about complete correctness of model of a complex system. The Z/Eves is a powerful tool used for analyzing formal specification of the model. The tool is integrated with various model analysis facilities providing rigorous checking of the system to be developed and has an automated deduction capability.

The syntax checking, type checking and theorem proving facilities of the Z/Eves tool are used for analysis of the model. It is noted that syntax and type checking do not require any interaction with the theorem proving facility of the tool. The domain checking facility allowed us to write meaningful properties of the system. It is observed that domain checking of model is much harder than the syntax and type checking of the model. Further, the syntax and type checking are performed automatically whereas one has to interact with the theorem proving facility to perform the domain checking. Furthermore, we observed that proof 'by reduce' was sufficient for formal specification of this transformation procedure for domain checking.

The schema expansion facility was used to unravel the specification of the diagrams and procedures which simplified the model results that were not easy otherwise to understand the specification. Prove by reduce is used for analyzing the formal specification. Some of the results of the model analysis are shown in the Table 2. In the Table, the first column shows name of the schema to be analyzed and evaluated, the second column is for syntax and type check, third for domain checking, fourth for reduction facility and the last one for the proof by reduction. The symbol Y in the table shows that all schemas are well written by syntax and domain checking. However the * symbol, after Y, shows that proof is done by the reduction technique.

Table 2. Results of model analysis

Schema Name	Syntax Type Check	Domain Check	Reduction	Proof
State	Y	Y	Y	Y
Object	Y	Y	Y	Y
ActivationTime	Y	Y	Y	Y
Message	Y	Y	Y*	Y
SequenceModel	Y	Y	Y*	Y
StateDiagram	Y	Y	Y*	Y

5. Conclusion

An exhaustive survey of existing work was performed before starting this work. Some interesting work was found as discussed in section I but our work is different from others because of capturing hidden semantics under the graphical notations. A comparison to most relevant work is presented. For example, in [3] a transformation mechanism from sequence diagram to event deterministic finite automata is provided. There were two major drawbacks in that work. Firstly, the resultant automaton is not deterministic because there is no state for some transitions in the automata. Secondly, the verification mechanism does not provide full support for correctness.

This work is part of our project on formalization of UML diagrams to be useful for software development of complex systems [21-24]. In this paper, an approach is developed for transformation of UML sequence to state diagrams by removing flaws existing in the diagram. Then grammar is developed based on the state diagram for verifying messages and scenarios. The resultant approach will be useful in development of automated tools for construction and verification of software systems. Although we have taken a simple case study but the advantage of our approach is that a formal procedure of transformation from UML notations to mathematical model is described. Then algorithm is specified using Z notation and verification is provided using Z/Eves tool. The Z notation is used because of its abstract and expressive power [25]. The rich mathematical notations in Z made it possible to reason about behavior of graphical notations. The Z/Eves is a powerful tool used to analyze the specification [26].

In future work, the advanced concepts of sequence diagram will be considered and complete transformation algorithm from the diagram to formal models will be designed. It is noted that conversion of UML diagrams to mathematical models by synthesis of suitable notations is our major objective. Transition diagrams, graphs, grammar, etc. are the tools for developing the integrated approach.

Acknowledgement

We would like to thank Deanship of Scientific Research, King Faisal University, Saudi Arabia for their funding support to our project on formalization of UML diagrams for automating design and development processes in software systems.

References

[1] Yeung, W. L., Leung, K. R. P. H., Wang, J., Dong, W.: Improvements Towards Formalizing UML State Diagrams in CSP, Proceedings of 12th Asia Pacific Software Engineering Conference, Taiwan, 2005.

[2] Shroff, M., France, R. B.: Towards Formalization of UML Class Structures in Z, 21st International Conference on Computer Software and Applications, pp. 646-51, 1997.

[3] Chen, Z., Zhenhua, D.: Specification and Verification of UML2.0 Sequence Diagrams using Event Deterministic Finite Automata, 2011 Fifth International Conference on Secure Software Integration and Reliability Improvement – Companion, pp. 41-46, 2011.

[4] Li, M., Ruan, Y.: Approach to Formalizing UML Sequence Diagrams, 3rd International Workshop on Intelligent Systems and Applications (ISA), pp. 1-4, 2011.

[5] Li, X., Liu, Z., Jifeng H.: A Formal Semantics of UML Sequence Diagram, Proceedings of the 2004 Australian Software Engineering Conference, 2004.

[6] Jackson, D., Schechter, I., Shlyakhter, I.: Alcoa: The Alloy Constraint Analyzer, Proceedings of International Conference on Software Engineering, 2000.

[7] Xiuguo, Z., Liu, H.: Formal Verification for CCML Based Web Service Composition, Information Technology Journal, 2011.

[8] Sun, J., Dong, J. S., Liu, J., Wang, H.: A XML/XSL Approach to Visualize and Animate TCOZ, Proc. of 8th Asia-Pacific Software Engineering Conference, pp. 453-60, 2001.

[9] Litvak, B.: Behavioral Consistency Validation of UML Diagrams, First International Conference on Software Engineering and Formal Methods, 2003.

[10] Moeini, A., Mesbah, R. O.: Specification and Development of Database Applications based on Z and SQL, Proceedings of 2009 International Conference on Information Management and Engineering, pp. 399-405, 2009.

[11] Shi, Z.: Intelligent Target Fusion Recognition Based on Fuzzy Petri Nets, Information Technology Journal, 11, pp. 500-03, 2012.

[12] Leading, H., Souquieres, J.: Integration of UML and B Specification Techniques: Systematic Transformation from OCL Expressions into B, Proceedings of 9th Asia-Pacific Software Engineering Conference, 2002.

[13] Kim, S. K., Carrington, D. A.: An Integrated Framework with UML and Object-Z for Developing a Precise and Understandable Specification: The Light Control Case Study. Proceedings of Seventh Asia-Pacific Software Engineering Conference, pp. 240-48, 2000.

[14] Ali, N. H., Shukur, Z., Idris, S.: A Design of an Assessment System for UML Class Diagram, Int'l Conference on Computational Science and Applications, pp. 539–46, 2007.

[15] Miao, H., Liu, L., Li, L.: Formalizing UML Models with Object-Z, Proceedings of 4th International Conference on Formal Methods and Software Engineering, Springer, 2002.

[16] Mostafa, A. M., Manal, A. I., Hatem, E. B., Saad, E. M.: Toward a Formalization of UML2.0 Meta-model using Z Specifications, Proc. of 8th ACIS International Conference on Software Engineering, Artificial Intelligence, Networking and Parallel/ Distributed Computing, 3, pp. 694-701, 2007.

[17] Sengupta, S., Bhattacharya, S.: Formalization of UML Diagrams and Consistency Verification: A Z Notation Based Approach. Proceedings of India Software Engineering Conference, pp. 151-52, 2008.

[18] Zafar, N. A.: Modeling and Formal Specification of Automated Train Control System using Z Notation, IEEE Multi-topic Conference (INMIC'06), pp. 438-43, 2006.

[19] Zafar, N. A., Khan, S. A., Araki, A.: Towards Safety Properties of Moving Block Railway Interlocking System, Int'l Journal of Innovative Computing, Information & Control, 2012.

[20] Sohail, F., Zubairi, F., Sabir, N. Zafar, N. A.: Designing Verifiable and Reusable Data Access Layer Using Formal Methods and Design Patterns, International Conference on Computer Modeling and Simulation, 2009.

[21] Zafar, N. A., Alhumaidan, F.: Scenarios Verification in Sequence Diagram, International Conference on Computer and Engineering Technology, Canada, 2103.

[22] Zafar, N. A.: Event-Action Based Model for Identification and Formalization of Relations in UML State Diagrams, Archives Des Sciences Journal, 65(4), 2012.

[23] Zafar, N. A., Alhumaidan, F.: Transformation of Class Diagrams into Formal Specification, International Journal Computer Science and Network Security, 11, 289-95, 2011.

[24] Alhumaidan, F.:A Critical Analysis and Treatment of Important UML Diagrams Enhancing Modeling Power, Intelligent Information Management, 4(5), pp. 231-37, 2012.

[25] Spivey, J. M.: The Z Notation: A Reference Manual. Englewood Cliffs NJ, Prentice-Hall, 1989.

[26] Meisels, I., Saaltink, M.: The Z/Eves Reference Manual, Version 1.5, TR-97-5493-03d, ORA Canada, 1997.

Dr. Fahad M. Alhumaidan graduated from University of Newcastle Upon Tyne, UK. Currently, he is working as Assistant Professor in Information System Department at CCSIT. He is Vice Dean at College of Computer Sciences and Information Technology (CCSIT), at King Faisal University, Saudi Arabia. He is also Chairman of Computer Science Department. He is responsible for chairing various technical and administrative committees at the college. His research areas include Software Engineering, Object-oriented Paradigm, Integration of UML and Formal Methods, Business Process Management, Workflow Systems, Soft aspects of Information System, E-Business, Network & Communication. He has contributed for various funded research projects and completed successfully by publishing the results produced in international journals and conferences proceedings.

Nazir A. Zafar was born in 1969 in Pakistan. He received his M.Sc. (Math. in 1991), M. Phil (Math. in 1993), and M.Sc. (Nucl. Engg. in 1994) from Quaid-i-Azam University, Pakistan. He was awarded PhD degree in computer science from Kyushu University, Japan in 2004. Currently, he is working as Associate Professor at the College of Computer Sciences and Information Technology (CCSIT), King Faisal University (KF), Saudi Arabia. He is the founder of various research groups in the area of software engineering and formal methods. His current research interests are modelling of systems using formal approaches, integration of approaches, safety and security critical systems, etc. He is an active member of Pakistan Mathematical Society. Dr. Zafar has lectured at national and international level promoting use and applications of formal methods at academic as well as at industrial level. He has also administrative experience and qualities. For example, he has worked as Dean, Faculty of Information Technology, University of Central Punjab, Pakistan. He has leaded various scientific committees related to research and academic activities.

